MW00698912

CHILDREN AND CHILDHOOD
IN ROMAN ITALY

Children and Childhood
in Roman Italy

BERYL RAWSON

OXFORD
UNIVERSITY PRESS

OXFORD

UNIVERSITY PRESS

Great Clarendon Street, Oxford OX2 6DP

Oxford University Press is a department of the University of Oxford.
It furthers the University's objective of excellence in research, scholarship,
and education by publishing worldwide in

Oxford New York

Auckland Cape Town Dar es Salaam Hong Kong Karachi
Kuala Lumpur Madrid Melbourne Mexico City Nairobi
New Delhi Shanghai Taipei Toronto

With offices in

Argentina Austria Brazil Chile Czech Republic France Greece
Guatemala Hungary Italy Japan South Korea Poland Portugal
Singapore Switzerland Thailand Turkey Ukraine Vietnam

Oxford is a registered trade mark of Oxford University Press
in the UK and in certain other countries

Published in the United States
by Oxford University Press Inc., New York

© Beryl Rawson 2003

The moral rights of the author have been asserted
Database right Oxford University Press (maker)

First published 2003
First published in paperback 2005

British Library Cataloguing in Publication Data
Data available

Library of Congress Cataloging in Publication Data
Data available

Typeset by Hope Services (Abingdon) Ltd
Printed in Great Britain
on acid-free paper by
Biddles Ltd
King's Lynn, Norfolk

ISBN 0–19–924034–5   978–0–19–924034–0
ISBN 0–19–928517–9 (Pbk.)   978–0–19–928517–4 (Pbk.)

1 3 5 7 9 10 8 6 4 2

for Allan

ACKNOWLEDGEMENTS

IDEAS for this book began many years ago in a doctoral thesis (under the name of Wilkinson) supervised by Lily Ross Taylor. To her I owe my earliest academic debt in this field. Many debts have been accumulated since, as my work developed into various areas of 'the Roman family', other areas of Roman history, and into academic administration. I record only a few of such debts here, but other friends and colleagues will know of their help and my appreciation of it.

The Australian National University has supported me for many years, with space and resources, especially in Classics and in History, and—thanks largely to the efforts of my colleague Robert Barnes—excellent library holdings. The Australian Research Council has provided a series of research grants, which enabled me to benefit greatly from the assistance and friendship of Edyth Binkowski. From Art History, Michael Greenhalgh provided expertise and encouragement in compiling a digitized catalogue of monuments representing children in Roman Italy.

I thank the museums recorded in the List of Figures for their assistance with photographs and permissions. In addition, invaluable help in tracking down and viewing some of these items came from Maria Pia Malvezzi (Secretary of the British School at Rome) and Bill Edeson. Oxford University Press editors, especially Hilary O'Shea, have been generous and supportive in the protracted period of my bringing this project to completion, and I am grateful for their high level of professional expertise. The readers to whom OUP referred my project provided careful and helpful comments. One of these, Thomas Wiedemann, waived anonymity in order to provide advice to me in his own name. I regret that he is not with us to see the final result.

Christine Treadwell's support and expert word-processing skills were invaluable in getting the finished text ready for the publisher under difficult circumstances. Paul Johns rescued me often from computer trauma.

Over the years I have received valuable stimulation from a number of conferences. The three Roman Family conferences in Canberra between 1981 and 1994 brought together colleagues from many countries who debated a range of issues with energy and stimulating insights. I owe a debt to all who attended and especially those authors whose contributions appear as chapters in the three volumes which arose out of the conferences. A celebratory conference in my name in Sydney in 1999 enabled me to hear and then read many colleagues' perspectives on fields of research connected with my interests. I particularly thank the conveners of that conference, Suzanne Dixon and Kathryn Welch, and Suzanne as the editor of the subsequent volume, *Childhood, Class and Kin in the Roman World*. In the later stages of my writing, the 'Roman Crossings' conference in Sydney (1999) provided a forum for discussion of the material culture of Rome, the physical context in which children grew up: I was especially grateful for the presence of two of the most influential scholars in this field, Peter Wiseman and Andrew Wallace-Hadrill. In 2000 the conference in Fort Worth on 'the family' in the Roman and early Christian worlds, convened by David Balch and Carolyn Osiek, broadened my perspective and understanding. Since then, I have enjoyed a stimulating correspondence with Christian Laes.

Individual colleagues who have communicated with me over many years and whose scholarship and stimulation have been especially valuable include Richard Saller, Brent Shaw, Jane Gardner, Mark Golden, Susan Treggiari, and Mireille Corbier. Also in this group, and who particularly kept me going and encouraged me to complete the project, are Keith Bradley, John Crook, Tim Parkin, and Paul Weaver.

In sadness I acknowledge Magda and Allan, who did not live to see the book in printed form. Magda, a Hungarian migrant to Australia, identified with the material and encouraged my work over many years of friendship. There are no words to express my debt to Allan—my husband, my best friend, and my best critic, for whom *funus acerbum* was all too real an experience and who succumbed himself a few months before the text went off to the publisher.

I have taken advantage of this paperback edition to correct a few factual errors, omissions, and ambiguities in the original edition. I am grateful to colleagues who have pointed out some of these to me.

CONTENTS

LIST OF FIGURES

ABBREVIATIONS

AE	*L'Année épigraphique*, Paris.
ANU	Australian National University
ANU CDM	ANU Classics Museum
Att.	Cicero, *Epistulae ad Atticum*, ed. D. R. Shackleton Bailey (Cicero's *Letters to Atticus*). 7 vols. Cambridge, 1965–70.
BMCGC	*A Catalogue of the Greek Coins in the British Museum.* 28 vols. Bologna, 1963–4. Reprint of nineteenth-century edns.
BMCRE	*Coins of the Roman Empire in the British Museum*, ed. H. Mattingly. 6 vols. in 8. London, 1923–62, repr. 1966–76.
BMCRR	*Coins of the Roman Republic in the British Museum*, ed. H. A. Grueber. London, 1910, repr. 1970.
C.	*Codex Iustinianus*, ed. P. Krueger. Zurich, 1880.
CIL	*Corpus Inscriptionum Latinarum.* Berlin, 1876–1974.
Cohen	H. Cohen, *Description historique des monnaies frappées sous l'Empire romain.* Paris, 1880.
CTh.	*Codex Theodosianus*, ed. T. Mommsen and P. M. Meyer. Zurich, 1904–5, repr. 1970–1.
D.	*Digesta Iustiniani*, ed. T. Mommsen 1877, in *The Digest of Justinian*, ed. A. Watson. 4 vols. Philadelphia, 1985.
Fam.	Cicero, *Epistulae ad familiares*, ed. D. R. Shackleton Bailey. 2 vols. Cambridge, 1977.
Festus	Sex. Pompeius Festus, *De uerborum significatione*, ed. W. M. Lindsay. Leipzig, 1913, repr. 1965.

FIRA²	*Fontes Iuris Romani Anteiustiniani*, ed. S. Roccobono *et al.* 3 vols. Florence, 1968–9. Includes:
	   Gaius, *Institutes*
	   Paulus, *Sententiae*
	   Fragmenta Vaticani (*Frag. Vat.*)
	   Ulpian, *Regulae* (Ulpian, *Reg.*)

Fronto	M. Cornelius Fronto, *Correspondence*, ed. S. A. Naber (= N). Leipzig, 1867. Ed. and trans. C. R. Haines (= H). London, 1919–20.
Gramm.	Suetonius, *De grammaticis.*
Hunter Coll.	Hunter Collection. *Roman Imperial Coins in the Hunter Coin Cabinet*, ed. A. S. Robertson. 4 vols. London, 1962–77.
ICUR	*Inscriptiones Christianae Urbis Romae* (Rome, 1922–).
IG	*Inscriptiones Graecae* (Berlin, 1873–).
ILLRP	*Inscriptiones Latinae liberae reipublicae*, ed. A. Degrassi (Florence, 1958–63).
LIMC	*Lexicon Iconographicum Mythologiae Classicae.* 6 vols. in 12. Zurich and Munich, 1981–6.
LTUR	*Lexicon Topographicum Urbis Romae*, ed. E. M. Steinby. 6 vols. Rome, 1993–2000.
NH	Pliny the Elder, *Natural History.*
*OCD*³	*Oxford Classical Dictionary.* 3rd edn. Oxford, 1996.
ORF	*Oratorum Romanorum Fragmenta*, ed. H. Malcovati. 4th edn. Turin, 1976.
PIR	*Prosopographia Imperii Romani.* 3 vols. Berlin, 1897–8. 2nd edn. 1933–.
PL	*Patrologiae cursus completus . . .* , ed. J. P. Migne. Paris. *Patrologia Latina* (i.e. series [Latina] prima) 1844–.
RG	*Res Gestae Divi Augusti* (*The Achievements of the Deified Augustus*).
Rhet.	Suetonius, *De rhetoribus.*
RIC	*The Roman Imperial Coinage*, ed. H. Mattingly *et al.* 10 vols in 13. London, 1923–94.
RRC	*Roman Republican Coinage*, ed. M. Crawford. 2 vols. London, 1974.
RS	*Repertorium der christlich-antiken Sarkophage*, ed. F. Deichmann, G. Bovini, and H. Brandenburg. Wiesbaden, 1967.
SHA	Scriptores Historiae Augustae.
Sydenham	*The Coinage of the Roman Republic*, ed. E. A. Sydenham, rev. with indexes by G. C. Haines, ed. L. Ferrer and C. A. Hersh. London, 1952.

Introduction

> Open wide the doors of the gods, Parthenope; fill the
> garlanded shrines with clouds of Sheba's incense and with
> the breathing entrails of sacrificial animals. See, now, a third
> birth increases the line of the distinguished Menecrates.[1]

WHETHER a new child was always so welcome in Roman society depended on many factors, such as the parents' status and
financial situation, the sex of the child, how many siblings there
were. Diverse factors have always affected the welcome and fate
of newborn infants in any society. That children were, in principle and often in practice, welcome and valued and visible in
Roman society is the main argument of this book. Moreover,
there are distinctively Roman concepts and treatment of children
which can be identified.

In the almost half-century since Ariès' claim (1960) that there
had been no real concept of childhood before the sixteenth or
seventeenth century, there have been studies revealing real recognition of children in many phases of life in earlier societies.[2] The
society of Roman Italy, especially in the period covered in this
book (first century BCE to early third century CE),[3] was one of
those societies, sharing with them various features, for example
birth rituals, children's games and stories, distinctive dress, a role

---

[1] Statius, *Siluae* 4. 8. 1–4, celebrating the birth of a third son to Iulius
Menecrates and Polla at the end of the 1st c.

[2] e.g. Manson (1983); Pollock (1983); Wiedemann (1989); Corbier (1999*b*);
Avery and Reynolds (2000); Orme (2001).

[3] This choice of period is dictated largely by the sources available. I have
tried, however, to extend the picture beyond the all-too-frequent textbook
period of the late Republic and the Julio-Claudians, which derives from the
existence of major literary and historical sources for that period, especially
Cicero and Tacitus (although Tacitus is not a primary source for the Julio-
Claudians). Archaeological sources for that period have improved in recent
times, but not to the extent of those for the 2nd c. Epigraphic and legal sources
are also better and more copious for the Flavian period and the 2nd c. See
Chronological Guide and Glossary for periods and technical terms.

in public life, and even in circumstances of high mortality parents' grief and mourning at the early loss of their children.
Nevertheless, there are features which distinguish Roman society
from any before it and from many later ones. Those discussed in
later chapters include the importance attached to education and
sensitivity to the diversity of child development; the centrality of
the conjugal family (spouses, sons and daughters) in expressions
of sentiment and in many practical areas, e.g. law and housing; a
wider network of surrogate family in which carers, slaves, and
ex-slaves had an important place; a public life which stressed historical tradition and *exempla* (models) to guide a child's development and aspirations, and which provided entertainment and
ritual which stimulated and socialized a child's responses; an
unprecedentedly large and elaborate capital city full of visual and
aural messages; a body of legislation and legal commentary in
which children had an important place; and widespread, individualized funerary commemoration of children which emphasized
the 'father–mother–children triad'.[4]

Defining a culture more widely as Greek, Roman, Hellenized,
or Romanized has preoccupied many writers. I have come to the
conclusion that rigid definitions of these terms are not helpful or
even possible, as many of us know from attempts to define the
identity of our own national culture. What has been said recently
of Roman portraiture might be applied more generally to Roman
culture: 'indigenous heritage and international influences interacted over time to enrich both the form and function of the
Roman portrait gallery'.[5] The question of 'Greek or Roman' does,
however, pose a problem in the use of one well-known literary
source: Plutarch. Plutarch lived in Greece for most of his life and
wrote in Greek. Although he received Roman citizenship and
visited Rome and undoubtedly shared some of the same cultural

---

[4] A phrase used by Saller and Shaw (1984: 145). There is now lively debate as
to the representativeness of the commemorative material for everyday family life
and relationships, and this will be discussed below (e.g. in Ch. 6). The domination of the 'triad' in this material is incontrovertible; but it is clear that the
nuclear family relationships were not exclusive of other relationships, and indeed
that death and divorce often extended or replaced the family of origin.

[5] Gazda and Haeckl (1993: 295). One of the most recent books on cultural
identity, especially of Greeks in the Roman empire, is Whitmarsh (2001), where
there is excellent analysis of previous approaches (especially in 'Introduction').

outlook as other educated, upper-class men of the cosmopolitan Mediterranean world of his time, I am not convinced that he 'belonged' to Roman society in any deep sense and thus that he is a reliable source for values and concepts relevant to Roman children and childhood. I therefore make sparing use of him in this study.[6] He did have a considerable knowledge of Roman institutions and history, but perhaps too formalistic and legalistic a one. Saller (1999) has pointed out the misunderstanding of *paterfamilias* in Greek writers' commentaries on Rome—a failure to appreciate the specifically legal, inheritance context of this term and its absence from contexts of familial relationships. 'The Greeks appear to have originated the stereotype of the tyrannical Roman father' (1999: 191).

The evaluation of literature more generally for its representations of children and childhood would repay greater attention than I have been able to give it in this book. There has been much new work in Latin literary criticism in recent years, and although I have found it stimulating I do not have the expertise to take full advantage of it. For different reasons I do not give a full treatment of the position of children in Roman law. I draw extensively on the evidence of Roman law, but a full treatment would require a separate book, perhaps along the lines of Gardner (1986*b*) on women in Roman law and society.

Attitudes to children and childhood are attested in many kinds of evidence, including language and literature, the law, inscriptions, art, artefacts, and ritual. Some of this reflects only elite, upper-class attitudes (which might not even represent actual treatment of children), but the material evidence reflects a broader range of symbolism, ideology, perceptions, and practice. Even art and artefacts which are initiated by the upper classes can help structure a whole population's understanding of their world. This was particularly so in a society like that of ancient Rome, where there was no sharp distinction between public and private—where slaves, clients, and patrons mingled and often shared domestic and public space, where the senses and perceptions were

---

[6] Plutarch's biographies of Romans can be useful, especially as they draw on primary and other sources no longer available to us, although even here one needs to exercise caution, especially with Plutarch's interpretations. See below on biography in Ch. 1. K. R. Bradley (1999) provides a sensitive discussion of the 'images of childhood' in Plutarch's writing.

continually bombarded by the ubiquitous presence of sculpture, inscriptions, dedications, and many other varieties of monument and memorial. And the sub-elite classes appropriated many of these media for their own use, and perhaps initiated some forms and exerted their own influence on their 'betters'. The direction of social change is not always clear. But change in Roman society's dealings with children and representations of them is discernible in the first two or three centuries of the Principate. It provided fertile ground for implementation of Christian beliefs and practice.

One problem in identifying the time of accelerated change is that there is comparatively little contemporary evidence of any kind for Roman society before the first century BCE. In the second century BCE the Roman playwrights Plautus and Terence adapted Greek comedies and undoubtedly introduced Roman elements for their Roman audiences, but it is never easy to distinguish Greek from Roman, or imaginative from real life, in these plays. Other remains of Latin literature of the second century BCE yield little to throw light on social life. In the middle of the century Polybius, a Greek war-captive taken up by the Roman intelligentsia, wrote a history of Rome in Greek, and this yields some insights into Roman society, but the focus is war and politics. The *Digest* and other records of Roman law preserve very little of Roman thought and practice of this early period. Contemporary art and inscriptions survive in only a few scattered remains. Later literary sources (e.g. Livy, Plutarch, Appian, Cassius Dio) wrote of early Rome and Italy, sometimes using primary sources: each had his own special purpose, and was a construct of his own age and society, but there is little in these or earlier sources to suggest that children were in the foreground of public or private thought. No doubt families often welcomed new babies and cherished their children, but Roman society was still struggling to establish itself even in the second century and many military, political, and economic problems preoccupied the thoughts and activities of adult Romans. Increasing affluence and external security were contributing to Rome's development as less of a frontier society and more of a civilized and civilizing world capital, but it was in the first century BCE that this development accelerated, especially after the imposition of fairly general peace at home and abroad after 28 BCE.

The first half of the first century BCE, i.e. the late Republic, may be seen as a period of transition. Many Romans of that time were conscious of increased affluence and leisure and an enhanced intellectual and aesthetic life. Philosophers and authors were frequent house-guests and gave public readings and lectures, all of which encouraged a more thoughtful, reflective approach to life and morality. Rome was increasingly adorned, publicly and privately, with works of art, and those who could afford it were building bigger and grander homes in city and country (but many buildings were still firetraps and unhealthy, and the great leap forward in civic architecture and public facilities had to await Augustus and subsequent emperors). Slave numbers increased enormously, providing a great range of services for Romans and sometimes adding a valued dimension to Roman personal and family life. The first known tombs of private individuals, with reliefs and inscriptions attesting some *familia* links, belong to the first half of the first century BCE.[7] They include ex-slaves but no children.

Many experiences, however, must have preserved a harsh edge to emotional life and personal relationships: civil war (Italians against Romans in the 80s BCE and then Romans against Romans in the 40s and 30s), civic disorder (dictatorships, disfranchisement or reduced civic rights in successive generations of some families, violence, a slave rebellion, clashes between senate and popular assemblies, corruption and loss of credibility in the lawcourts, disruption to elections and public administration, economic problems, and food shortages), and difficulties abroad (repeated military and naval threats, large numbers of men on active service, problems in administration of provinces which created bad feeling not only between provincials and Romans but also between fellow-Romans of different classes and interests).

Augustus' 'revolution' removed much of this hard edge, and, after him, the first century (CE) might be characterized as a period of consolidation. One aspect of Augustus' work, his legislation on marriage, children, and freeing of slaves, had long-lasting effects. Whether or not it achieved its original aims,[8] it

---

[7] B. Rawson (1997*a*: 211); Ch. 1 below.
[8] Commentators still debate the aims of the marriage laws, with emphasis placed variously on morality, inheritance, and preservation of family lineages;

continued to be an important point of reference for several centuries, sometimes as a restriction from which individuals sought to obtain exemption. Even when Constantine removed the penalties on celibacy in 320, this was probably part of his wider strategy for easing the transmission of property, and the long Roman tradition of valuing and rewarding marriage and child-bearing remained intact. The changes were probably welcomed by those Christians (especially the clergy) who prized celibacy above marriage, but the significant change in values towards celibacy and asceticism belongs more to the late fourth and the fifth centuries (Evans Grubbs 1995: 120–39). As Augustus' legislation will be referred to often in following chapters, brief details are given here. The *lex Iulia de maritandis ordinibus* (18 BCE) and the *lex Papia Poppaea* (9 CE) provided rewards for marrying and having children and penalties for not doing so (the *ius liberorum*, the rights associated with having children). These affected inheritance (making it difficult for the celibate and childless to benefit from wills or to bequeath beyond the sixth degree of relationship), political office (giving married men with children accelerated access to magistracies and priority in choice of province to govern), and *tutela* (guardianship) (freeing women from financial supervision if they had three children—for freeborn women—or four—for ex-slave women). The *lex Aelia Sentia* (4 CE) allowed informally freed slaves to obtain full Roman citizenship by producing a child who reached the age of 1 year. It also established minimum age limits for an owner to free slaves and for a slave to be freed; but exceptions were allowed for younger slaves with particularly close relationships to their owners (see Chapter 6 below). It was in the Augustan period that the first representations of children appeared in Roman art—on private tomb reliefs and, soon after, on Augustus' Altar of Peace (the Ara Pacis). The private representations pre-dated Augustus' legislation and Altar, but they did become frequent thereafter. Thomas Wiedemann suggested to me that this growing frequency might have been connected with parents' claims to the *ius liberorum*, a

but the encouragement of marriage and procreation is clear. See Evans Grubbs (1995, esp. ch. 3) for further detail on Augustus' laws and their development into the 5th c.

visual way of showing that they qualified for these rights, even with deceased children.[9]

In 68–9, civil wars caused disruption, and Vespasian faced a new start. He had to put much of his effort into economic and political reconstruction, and he himself did not have the privileged cultural background of his predecessors. He did, however, see the value of education (reflected in his financing of Quintilian to teach and write on rhetoric), and his sons acquired the polish of an excellent education and inherited privilege. Titus reigned for too short a time to have much impact. Domitian left a reputation for political oppression, but he was also responsible for cultural and social initiatives which probably created a more civilized society for many, and might have been better appreciated by posterity if it had not been for the domination of senatorial writers in our literary tradition.

The renewed stability and increasing prosperity in the second century made possible a range of improvements in Roman society, many of which benefited children and families directly and indirectly. Circumstances offered scope for different preoccupations and greater expression of family sentiment at a social and personal level.[10] Some of my most respected colleagues reject the possibility of tracing change in Roman social relations.[11] Part of their scepticism is due to the lack of a set of comparable evidence over time. But surely the emergence of kinds of evidence better adapted to expressing family sentiment—funerary epitaphs, sculpture of sub-elite groups and individuals, and legal discussions of rights and responsibilities of children, guardians, wives, and mothers—is in itself a sign of different preoccupations.[12]

---

[9] On the question of whether children had to be living or ever-born to make their parents eligible for the *ius liberorum*, see Parkin (1992: 116–19).

[10] Family sentiment and bonds had always been important in Roman public life. During the Republic a small number of families dominated the senior political offices, and the criticism was sometimes made that the career of a quite ordinary man had advanced largely on the basis of his family name.

[11] See e.g. the 'Introduction' in Saller (1994); and K. R. Bradley (1999).

[12] Saller (1990/2000) points out that the jurists most cited in the *Digest* wrote in the late 2nd and early 3rd centuries, and that emperors of the 1st c. are underrepresented in the juristic texts. He therefore thinks that comparisons based on these texts can be misleading. The *Digest*, however, does tend to cite the original source for a new kind of legislation, e.g. Augustus' laws on marriage, adultery, and child-bearing, and on regulation of slavery and manumission. The

When sarcophagi were becoming the favoured receptacle for the dead in the second century CE (for those who could afford them), the new medium gave a prominent place to the representation of children. In the words of Huskinson (1996: 123), there was 'a creative burst of new subjects and types which are aimed specifically and visibly at the child'. The fact that there were few Roman sarcophagi before this does not undermine the recognition of this decoration as an important development. There is a series of funerary commemorations from the first century BCE in which there is an increasing role for the representation of children: the sarcophagi often use their greater scope for sculptural decoration to enhance this role. It is a development intrinsic not to the medium (sarcophagi) but to the time (the second century) in Roman Italy. Contemporary sarcophagi from the eastern Mediterranean do not have a similar emphasis on children. The sarcophagus and inscriptions of the Cornelii Scipiones family, dating from the third and second centuries BCE, have no record of non-adult children.[13] After the efflorescence of the second century CE, third-century sarcophagi carried more generalized types and themes, and sculpture on Christian sarcophagi carried biblical themes which were used with little differentiation for both children and adults. These developments are discussed in more detail in following chapters, especially Chapter 1.

I do not argue that spouses or parents and children developed greater love for one another, but that they found more occasions and ways of expressing family sentiment. This is not merely a function of the greater survival of more recent evidence: after the peak in the second century, this kind of evidence declines, and there is also a deterioration in political and economic circumstances and in external security. The second century (and the

Twelve Tables are also cited to illustrate the antiquity of some principles or enactments. The density of 2nd-c. discussion on the family matters cited above, and the emergence of active juristic commentary at this time, seems to me to indicate a new interest in such matters. Gardner (1996) explains much of the legal activity under Hadrian, which concerned the private interests of individuals, as being due to 'humane concern' for the unintended difficulties which had developed out of Augustus' legislation. It was only in the 2nd c. that these were seriously addressed.

[13] *CIL* 6. 1284–94 and *ILLRP* (*Imagines*) 132–9, discussed in B. Rawson (1997a: 209).

Flavian period preceding it) would reward much greater intensity of study than it has yet received for social developments. In the city of Rome, population and social life became more complex and diverse than ever before; a greater range of experience was available to all, even the poor and disadvantaged. In each generation, children's experiences were different from those of their parents; in general they witnessed more elaborate celebrations and ritual and they lived in a larger and more embellished city.[14] The changes in military recruitment and the abatement of active warfare meant that there were fewer absentee fathers away from Italy on military service. It is noteworthy that Evans' study (1991) of the effects of warfare on women and children in Italy does not go beyond the first century BCE. The stereotype of a militaristic Roman society, in which most people had personal experience of warfare, is inapplicable for the Principate. The different circumstances were bound to change relationships, especially those of spouses and those of fathers and children.

The values and activities of the urban capital permeated many other centres, in Italy and beyond. It is often claimed that Roman Italy remained predominantly a rural or peasant society. This cannot be quantified, but, irrespective of the proportions of the population in Rome, country towns, and on farms, the influence of Rome and of urban society should not be underestimated.[15] A recent book on early Christianity sees the importance of 'the city' as the seeding-ground for important social and spiritual developments, and it attributes the growth in Christian communities to what they offered (i.e. a surrogate family) to 'displaced and fragmented urbanites' (Hellerman 2001: 220). By the first century CE, Rome's cultural influence on the rest of Italy was widespread, allowing us to talk about 'Roman Italy'.[16] This influence spread beyond Italy, but stronger regional particularities would have to

[14] See Ch. 7 below. The spacing of triumphs and festivities e.g. the Secular Games sometimes gave parents experiences which their children did not share.

[15] MacMullen (1974) makes a valiant effort to identify and analyse aspects of rural society in the Roman world of 50 BCE to 284 CE, but he is hampered by the scarcity of primary evidence, and comparatively little of that is from Roman Italy. Woolf (1998: 138) discusses the 'profound influence' of urbanism on Narbonese Gaul, similar to that in most parts of Italy but different from the Gallic interior.

[16] But some regional differences continued. See Ch. 7 below.

be taken into account in any study of other parts of the Roman empire.

The topic of children and childhood is, I believe, of intrinsic interest, but it is also important for what it can reflect of a society's values and priorities. The treatment of children has, in recent years, been increasingly used as a barometer of a society's humanity, sense of justice, and general standard of civilization.[17] Since the 1960s there have been a number of books written from this point of view, e.g. De Mause (1974), Shorter (1976), and Stone (1977), which cast an eye (that of non-specialists) on Roman society. Their use of a limited range of evidence, and sensationalism in misinterpreting such evidence, led to sweeping generalizations about the cruelty and misery experienced by Roman children in antiquity. No doubt such experiences were widespread, but not for the reasons advanced in such books. More recently a French scholar, who is indeed a specialist in Roman society, has proposed an opposite view: that in the second century CE children benefited from a new development of family love which was due to Roman men's turning inwards to domestic life in reaction to a loss of political power to the emperor (Veyne 1978). This view too is ill based. Veyne's political, upper-class men were a small minority of the Roman population, whereas much of the family sentiment being expressed came from lower classes, especially slaves and ex-slaves. And elite men themselves continued to have active public lives, were ambitious and competitive for political office and in the lawcourts and the army, and often found new opportunities for public advancement in the administration of a growing, more complex empire. Moreover, some of the features identified by Veyne to support his view had already existed in Roman society for a long time: funerary inscriptions, for example, from the first century BCE already attested marital bonds and family virtues.

More recently, excellent new work has emerged which gives a better chance of understanding Roman children and childhood

---

[17] A recent example of this in Australia has been the emotive debate about the treatment (real and alleged) of refugee children by either their parents or the Australian government. When in October–November 2001 Afghan asylum-seekers in boats were alleged to have thrown their children overboard (a claim later proved to be false) the Prime Minister proclaimed that if this was the way they treated their children 'they are not the sort of people we want in Australia'.

through detailed and expert use of a wide range of evidence. The intensity of scholarship on ancient demography has provided new opportunities to understand family relationships and a child's life cycle. Studies of housing and domestic space help locate the child in one of its most formative environments. Epigraphy and iconography have yielded insights into the widespread representation and memorialization of children. Roman law is now recognized as a fruitful source for social attitudes as well as for technical juristic problems even when one acknowledges the difficulty of identifying formal law, or even jurists' comments, with everyday behaviour.[18] Studies of slavery have provided a context for better understanding the condition of slave children and the role of slaves in family life (their own and that of others). All of these developments have enriched family studies in the last generation or so and can now be drawn on for childhood studies. Many of them are subsequent to the publication of Wiedemann (1989), and Golden's excellent work on Athenian children (1990) did not have the wealth of evidence to draw on which is available to Roman scholars. At a late date in writing this book, I became aware of Orme's work (2001) on medieval children, which sets new standards in the publication of extensive visual evidence. The entry of new and young scholars into the field of Roman Family studies, and now Roman Childhood, has been a source of pleasure and stimulation for me. They bring their own viewpoints, sometimes a different kind of training, and they foreshadow a healthy and lively future for such studies.[19] Very late in my writing I came into contact with Jeannine Uzzi, who completed her Ph.D. (Duke University) in 1998 on the representation of children in Roman public art. She generously made her dissertation available to me and discussed with me her projected book on this topic. Similarly, Lesley Beaumont, an archaeologist at the University of Sydney, made available to me a pre-publication copy of her paper on Greek childhood. I have been able to incorporate the work of these two scholars only briefly, but I have

[18] Crook (1967) was the path-breaker in such studies; and he pointed out that, although formal law was less relevant to some people than others, its implications were inescapable in some areas (e.g. status).

[19] Jeanette McWilliam, Leslie Shumka, and Fanny Dolansky have all done interesting work in their postgraduate theses, from which I have profited, and I look forward to seeing further results of their work in print.

benefited from their insights and scholarship, and have been
warmed by the collegial dialogue that followed our exchange of
work. Beaumont's paper will be associated with an exhibition on
'Coming of age in ancient Greece', and a conference with wider
scope, to be held at Dartmouth College in 2003—another indi-
cator of the wealth of material and new modes of communication
in our field.[20]

All of the recent work cited above is on specialized themes.
The aim of this book is to be more comprehensive, to offer a dis-
tillation of specialized work (my own included) as a basis for my
own current understanding of what it meant to be a child, and to
have children, in Roman Italy. I hope that it will be of interest
not only to classicists and ancient historians in many fields, but
also to other historians, educationalists, and the large section of
the general public which continually attests to the fascination of
the Roman world by buying books, watching films and other
drama set in that world, and attending exhibitions of art and artefacts from that world. Some parts of this book will of necessity
be more specialized than others, but the discerning reader will
know when to skim: there is usually a general summary provided
for such sections. All Latin in the text has been translated into
English, and I have used the titles (Latin, Greek, or English) for
ancient works which I think will be most intelligible and accessible. Occasionally the Latin in more specialized footnotes has
been left untranslated. I have used the Latin of the source material extensively, to convey the flavour of the sources better to those
who know Latin and to achieve more precision and authenticity
than any translation can hope to achieve.

The structure of the book is two parts, 'Representations' and
'The Life Course'. As we have virtually no first-hand sources
from children themselves, we cannot contrast 'how others saw
them' with 'how they saw themselves'. It was tempting to contrast 'Representations' with 'Reality' or 'Real Life'. But the whole
thrust of Part I subverts such a contrast. 'Reality' is to some
extent in the eye and mind of the viewer or reader or listener.
This is recognized now even of photography, which was once
seen as an objective image replicating reality ('the camera never

---

[20] A predecessor, in the field of Roman women, was Diana Kleiner's *I,
Claudia* at Yale University and other museums in the USA.

lies'), by contrast to, for example, a painting. Cannon's cross-cultural study of nineteenth-century funerary monuments (1989) has shown the role of cyclical change in display ostentation, including fashion and class. Nevertheless, a certain amount of generally applicable 'real life' can be deduced to produce a picture of the life course of children. I note that Pomeroy's recent book (1997) on Greek families does not shy away from the 'reality' word, but she uses it in the plural: her subtitle is *Representations and Realities*.

Children's identity was shaped by their membership of a family—at first, biological, and then sometimes surrogate family in the form of some kind of fosterer. A range of carers might supplement the family in raising a child: wet-nurses were commonly used, and other nurses and attendants participated according to the resources of the family. Toys, games, and story-telling were part of a child's early years. These began to shape the child's perception of the world, and subsequent forms of education built on this. Formal education—in literacy, numeracy, and higher levels of communication, reasoning, and imagination—was much prized and obtained by more children than those of the elite, although the great majority learnt from apprenticeships, the streets, and the great array of festivals, ritual, and visual culture which were part of urban society in Roman Italy. Deaths and funerals were a familiar experience, including those of the very young. Romans attached considerable importance to proper burial and commemoration, and these were provided even at quite modest levels, although again the anonymous masses have left no record. Infants, too, received less formal burial and commemoration than others, but the law took account of how they should be buried. The existence of real grieving can be recognized in some Roman literature and epitaphs and through the experience of modern anthropologists. The very existence of numerous representations of young children is in itself a testimony to real-life recognition and appreciation of children. These are the themes of the chapters which follow.

PART I

Representations of Children
in Roman Italy

I

Representations

Sacred to the departed spirit of Q. Sulpicius Maximus, son of Quintus and of
the Claudian tribe, a native of Rome. He lived for eleven years, five months and
twelve days. He performed at the third celebration of the Competition, amongst
52 Greek poets, and the favour which he attracted through his young age was
turned to admiration by his talent: he acquitted himself with honour. His
extemporaneous verses are inscribed above, to show that his parents have not
been carried away by their affection. Q. Sulpicius Eugramus and Licinia
Ianuaria, his desolate parents, have set this up for their devoted son and for
themselves and their successors.

DEIS MANIBVS SACRVM

Q SVLPICIO Q F CLA MAXIMO DOMO ROMA VIX ANN XI M V
D XII | HIC TERTIO CERTAMINIS LVSTRO INTER GRAECOS
POETAS DVOS ET L | PROFESSVS FAVOREM QVEM OB TEN-
ERAM AETATEM EXCITAVERAT | IN ADMIRATIONEM INGE-
NIO SVO PERDVXIT ET CVM HONORE DISCESSIT VERSVS |
EXTEMPORALES EO SVBIECTI SVNT NE PARENT(ES)
ADFECTIB SVIS INDVLSISSE VIDEANT | Q. SVLPICIVS
EVGRAMVS ET LICINIA IANVARIA PARENT(ES) INFELICISSIM
F PIISSIM FEC ET SIB P S

THE monument of the 11-year-old Maximus (Fig. 1.1), on which
this epitaph appears (*CIL* 6. 33976), is grander than many, but the
way in which the boy was represented was familiar to many
Romans at the end of the first century CE. His intellectual
achievements and professional promise are the main focus of his
Latin epitaph, reinforced by the supplementary text in Greek (*IG*
14. 2012), by his physical stance as a budding orator, by the scroll
in his left hand, and by his dress as a Roman citizen (the toga).
The secondary focus is on the affection and pride of his parents
and their grief at the loss of their devoted son. Education was an

FIG. 1.1 Altar of Q. Sulpicius Maximus, aged about 11, as budding orator, with epitaph and inscription of his poem. Rome, 94–5 CE.

aspect of childhood and adolescence much prized and advertised by Romans, especially for boys, reflecting parents' hopes for sons' future success and often an improvement in the family's social standing. Frequently too it was the dashing of such hopes by a child's early death which was proclaimed and lamented: in this society of high mortality rates, testimonials to children were often funerary commemorations.

Maximus' full-length statue gazes out at the viewer from its niche on a large altar of fine marble, the text of the Greek poem which he had composed and recited inscribed on either side of his statue and extending onto his scroll. His Latin epitaph, of good lettering, sits below the statue, and then below the epitaph the parents provide more Greek text with further personal details, including the fact that their son died of exhaustion from studying too hard. The boy's expression is serious, and he is represented as somewhat older than his years—proleptically as the accomplished orator which he was expected to become.[1] The altar was set up in a public place, on a main road leading out of Rome (the Via Salaria), where countless passers-by saw it for many years. It was substantial enough to be incorporated into a gateway of the new (Aurelian) wall of the third century, where it remained until the twentieth century. The statue and inscriptions are now in the Capitoline Museum at Rome.

The date of this monument can be established as soon after 94 CE, since that was the year of the third celebration of Domitian's Capitoline festival, when Maximus performed with great credit in the Greek poetry section amongst fifty-two competitors, many of them adults. It is fortunate that for this monument we can put together contextual details—material, location, date, sculpture, and inscription—all of which contribute to an appreciation of the memorial as a whole. Many of these details are lacking for other monuments. Internal evidence of a lone inscription, however, can often provide context for the way in which a child is represented. A great many of the epitaphs from Roman Italy were dedicated by close family members, especially spouses and parents. Sometimes children themselves were, at least in name, the

---

[1] The expression may not be true to the original, as the face has been partly damaged and restored (Kleiner 1987: no. 45). See below, Ch. 5, for further details of oratorical training and prospects and competitive festivals; and Ch. 8 for premature deaths of children.

dedicators. Children were thus represented as sons or daughters or some form of foster-children (as we shall see in Chapter 6 below). The structure of Roman nomenclature and the epithets used can throw light on the nature of the child's relationships. Q. Sulpicius Maximus was presented to the world as a young freeborn Roman citizen by his clothing and by the presence in his name of filiation (Q. f.) and tribe (Cla(udia)). His parents' names suggest that he was a first-generation freeborn citizen: Q. Sulpicius Eugramus and Licinia Ianuaria do not have the indicators of freeborn status which their son's name does, their *cognomina* are names most likely to be borne by slaves, and they supplement the Latin epitaph with an epigram in Greek; so there is a strong probability that they are freed ex-slaves. Through education they hoped to help their son build on his superior status to achieve social standing, wealth, and influence higher than their own. The boy's status and his epitaph represent him as well on his way to this goal: he attracted the *fauor* of his audience by his tender years ('ob teneram aetatem'), and turned this to admiration by his talent (*ingenium*), a performance which won him honour (*honor*). The transcription of his poem is intended to provide impartial evidence of his talent. Only towards the end of the last line of the epitaph are the parents themselves represented with an epithet, that of great grief: *infelicissimi*. Their son has been represented as the encapsulation of their hopes, their love, and their pride, and now he is the source of their great suffering.

This example is typical—if rather grander than many—of one way in which parents sought to represent their children in art and inscriptions: as precocious achievers, loved, and dutiful (*piissimi*). Males were more often commemorated than females. Girls had, however, been represented in free-standing portrait sculpture for at least as long as boys had,[2] and George (2001) sees the girl in an early tomb-relief (mid-first century BCE) of mother and daughter (Fig. 1.2) as sharing some of the symbolism discussed above for Sulpicius Maximus. There is no inscription to establish

---

[2] Gercke (1968: 150–77). Representations of boys became more frequent in the Julio-Claudian period, with many statues and busts of boys of the imperial family and copies of these for private citizens. The young Antonine princes— Marcus Aurelius, Lucius Verus, and Commodus—were portrayed as boys and youths in the mid-2nd c. (Fittschen 1999), but the influence of this on private portraiture is not so clear.

FIG. 1.2 Relief sculpture of mother and daughter. Rome, mid-first century BCE.

name, relationship, or status, but on stylistic grounds George sees the girl, aged about 5 or 6, as being 'simultaneously laden with both the servile past of her parents and the social expectations awaiting her as an *ingenua* [freeborn female]'.

As we shall see when we discuss 'Public Life' in Chapter 7, individual viewers form their own particular image of their city, its monuments, its messages, and its history. Similarly, there was no single image of Roman children. The maker or commissioner of a child's image chose to represent the child according to his or her own wishes and perceptions; but the message was received in a variety of ways, mediated by the viewer's personal characteristics (such as age, sex, status, or knowledge of that child) and by the location, medium, and material of the image itself. This applies to representations not only in art and inscriptions but also in literature and the law. Nevertheless, some readings became widespread through the repetition of certain kinds of images, sometimes through their association with authority (as in imperial propaganda), and their embedment in individual and collective memory.

Thus, in inscriptions children are sons, daughters, or foster-children, often prematurely dead; in art, individuals who play and go to school and learn lessons and pose with other members of their families; in law, individuals who have rights to be protected, and, as age increases, responsibilities. In literature they are not prominent but are sometimes symbols of family life and sometimes of all the defects of immaturity. They appear in public and private monuments with increasing frequency from the first century BCE.

Busts and statues of children—girls and boys—are known from the early first century BCE, but it is only with the inscribed funerary reliefs later in that century that we can identify individual children. From an earlier period (from at least the fourth century BCE) there had been votive figurines of women and children in central and southern Italy, suggesting a native Italian interest in representations of infants and motherhood. The interpretation of these is difficult, but they appear to be Italic rather than Greek.[3] They include representations of wombs, of babies in swaddling clothes, of married couples, and of mothers breast-feeding infants. Greek representations of women suckling infants (*kourotrophoi*) were usually of goddesses or personifications, rather than of real-life mothers. Often the *kourotrophos* figure was not

---

[3] Bonfante (1984, 1985, 1997). Bonfante makes a distinction between suckling figures and other mother-and-infant pairs.

the natural mother but one who fostered the infant. Bonfante (1997) names Latona and Demeter as the only goddesses who are represented in Greek art as natural mothers nursing their own children. This suggests that the Romans' choice of the Hellenistic statue of Latona, nursing the newborn Apollo and Diana, for the temple of Concord at Rome was not arbitrary: it fitted well into the Italic tradition in the first century CE.[4]

The development of this tradition does not seem to have derived directly from any part of the Greek world. There had been representations of human children in Greek art, and from the latter half of the fifth century there had been increasing interest in human children (in addition to gods) and an increasing facility in representing the young child's body,[5] but these do not seem to have been transferred directly to Rome. Until the later fifth century BCE, figures of children in Greece had appeared almost entirely on inexpensive material such as terracotta and pottery. When monumental funerary stelai were revived late in fifth-century Athens, and continued for much of the fourth, children found a place on them (which they had not had on the stelai or in free-standing sculpture of the sixth century). These representations are individualized but only rarely have inscriptions to identify them. Relationships are seldom specified. K.R. Bradley (1998b) has noted the representations of children which Romans must have seen in their travels in the Hellenistic East, especially in the second and first centuries BCE. Such types, however, were by no means a major part of Greek sculpture at that time. Moreover, expensive funerary monuments were banned at Athens (again) in 317/316 BCE, and funerary stelai were semi-private monuments, located away from the central areas of public life.[6] Some Athenian wall-paintings had scenes involving

---

[4] Pliny the Elder knew this statue in the 1st c. CE (NH 34. 77: 'Latona puer-pera'). There is no suggestion that this statue had been recently installed there, but we do not know how long before Pliny's time that took place. The temple of Concord had been restored by Tiberius between 7 BCE and 10 CE, following a fire in 9 BCE (Dio 55. 1. 1, 55. 8. 1–2; *LTUR* 1: 317).

[5] Kleiner (1978); Pollitt (1986); Golden (1990, 1997); Pomeroy (1997: 128–34); and Beaumont (forthcoming), who details changes from the 6th to the 3rd centuries BCE.

[6] The few tombstones with inscriptions in Clairmont (1970: 22, 23), from late 5th-c. BCE Athens, show that what appear to be 'obviously' mother and child representations can commemorate other relationships, so interpretation of those

children (Pliny the Elder, *NH* 35. 66, 70), but there is no evidence of their survival or of their interest for Roman travellers. What survives of Roman wall-painting has only rare representations of children, such as the frescoes of a boy and a girl from the house of M. Lucretius Fronto in Pompeii (Rawson 1997*a*: Fig. 9.7). There is no parallel in Roman Italy, except in the southern parts known as Magna Graecia, for the painted pottery of Greece which included scenes of domestic life. Even in Magna Graecia representations of children are not frequent. Nor did Etruscan pots, which survive in considerable quantity from the eighth to the third century BCE, use scenes involving children (Beazley 1947). A few Hellenistic statues of children were much copied by Romans,[7] but the date of the copies is uncertain, which makes it difficult to establish just when Greek art became a factor in Romans' developing interest in representations of children. We also do not know enough about the context, setting, and purpose of the originals. One model of the popular 'boy strangling goose' was a votive offering in a temple of Asklepios. The figure was known to Pliny the Elder (*NH* 34. 84), who also tells us that his contemporary, the emperor Titus, owned a statue of two boys playing dice which had originally been sculpted by a fourth-century Greek artist (*NH* 34. 55). The statue of a seated boy extracting a thorn from his foot is known in bronze, marble, and terracotta forms.[8] None of these representations is intended as an individual portrait: they were genre types. They do reflect an interest in sentimental representations of children, but it seems to have been mostly in the imperial period that Romans made

without inscriptions is difficult (see B. Rawson 1995: pls. 1.1, 1.2). And inscriptions seldom give more than the name of the dedicatee. The illustrations in Pfuhl and Mobius (1997–9: pl. 64 nos. 392, 395, 397–9, 402) are from Asia Minor. There is a problem in interpreting the small female figures which sometimes accompany women on these monuments: it is not clear whether they are slaves or children.

[7] Smith (1991: 136–7). Vermeule (1977: 7) also comments on the limited number of Greek originals which were copied many times by Romans: this activity was at its height in the first three centuries of the Empire, and the originals were mostly gods, athletes, and elite individuals. See Ridgway (2000: 251–3) on the problem of many versions of the 'Boy strangling a goose'.

[8] Bronze: mid-1st c. BCE? Helbig[4] (II no. 1448); Stuart Jones (1968: 43–7, no. 2, pl. 60).

copies of these and displayed them, when their own representations of children in various forms of art were increasing.

Greek influences can be identified in the art of the late Republic, and there was a passion for collecting Greek art (see Chapter 7 below), but there is little attention at that stage to children. In the late Republic the taste of Roman collectors of Greek art was more for classical Greek pieces than for Hellenistic, and contemporary artists were working in a 'classicizing or "neoclassical" style' (Pollitt 1986: 161–2; Smith 1991: 258–61). The works of art discovered in the Villa of the Papyri at Herculaneum have been analysed by Pollitt as an example of Roman taste of that time (approximately mid-first century BCE to mid-first century CE). There are no representations of children, and the portraits are of men as political or literary figures or philosophers.

Roman art in the Republican period reflected public life rather than private and focused on individual adult male Roman citizens—as generals, magistrates, priests. There is the togate statue from Perusia of an orator ('Arringatore'), there are the busts of men like Crassus, Pompey, and Julius Caesar,[9] there is the prolific coinage of the late Republic advertising family history but increasingly glorifying individual contemporary men, and there is the so-called 'Ahenobarbus altar' from Rome, a sculpted relief depicting magisterial duties—a forerunner to the later *curriculum uitae* reliefs on sarcophagi and other monuments—and perhaps a mythological genealogy.[10] There was also in the late Republic an increasing number of statues in public places of notable men, on foot and on horseback. There were occasionally statues of women erected in public places, representing qualities intrinsic to the ideal Roman character. The bravery and patriotism of Cloelia, a young Roman woman of the late sixth century BCE, were honoured with an equestrian statue of her in a much frequented spot on the Sacred Way.[11] The statue of Cornelia, mother of the

[9] Examples in Zanker (1988: figs. 4–7). Walker (1995: 100 and fig. 74) gives a date of 100 BCE or earlier for the 'Arringatore'.

[10] Zanker (1988: 12–14 and figs. 10a and b). Cf. Ch. 7 below for some of this art.

[11] Livy (2. 13. 11) implies that the statue was contemporaneous with Cloelia herself, but its original date is unknown. It was seen not only by Livy in the Augustan period, but also by Seneca the Younger in the middle of the 1st c. CE (Seneca, *Consolation to Marcia* 16. 2).

Gracchi and daughter of Scipio Africanus, was set up about the end of the second century BCE, probably for political reasons, and seems to have been moved by Augustus, perhaps with its inscription recut, to increase its impact as a representation of the ideal mother.[12]

In the very early Republic, a consul of the distinguished Claudian family included representations in miniature of children of his family on shields commemorating his ancestors, attached to the temple of Bellona. Pliny the Elder commented on the popular favour which such representations attracted. It was a fine practice to decorate shields with ancestors' images and names, he said, 'especially if this is balanced by a crowd of children in miniature form representing a sort of nest of fledglings—such shields inspire universal pleasure and favour in viewers'.[13]

Occasionally an individual child (a boy) was honoured in this way. M. Aemilius Lepidus was commemorated in the late third century BCE by an equestrian statue in honour of his heroism as a boy. His descendant Lepidus, the future triumvir, chose this statue to commemorate on his coinage of 61 BCE (Fig. 1.3). Lepidus' motivation was probably more to recall the long public distinction of his family than to focus on a boy as such; but about this time children were beginning to appear, probably as members of families, on funerary monuments.[14] The statue commemorated an incident in the Second Punic War when the 15-year-old Aemilius was said to have ridden into battle, killed one of the enemy, and rescued a Roman citizen.[15] A 15-year-old could conceivably have been serving with the army in that period, in the retinue of a relative; but one would expect that he had taken on the garb of adulthood (the *toga uirilis*). The statue, however, shows him wearing the *bulla*, the pendant worn by freeborn boys before their coming-of-age ceremony. This made explicit that it was a child who had performed this feat: children had a role in

---

[12] Coarelli (1978); Hillard (2001: n. 41) for uncertainty of date. See also Ch. 7 below; and B. Rawson (1997*a*: 212).

[13] Pliny the Elder, *NH* 35. 12: Appius Claudius, consul 495 BCE.

[14] See Zanker (1975) and Kleiner (1977) for examples. Children on these early monuments are either unnamed or their family connections are unclear.

[15] Valerius Maximus 3. 1. 1. The coinage (*RRC* 419/1a–e and pl. 51) recorded an inscription attesting this deed: AN. XV PR(ogressus) H(ostem) O(ccidit) C(iuem) S(eruauit).

FIG. 1.3 Equestrian statue of M. Aemilius Lepidus, aged 15 in the late third century BCE, on Roman coin of 61 BCE.

public life and were capable of great things. As we shall see below (Chapter 7), children were frequently before the eyes of the Roman public in ceremonies and festivals. They had long been used to enhance the parade of triumphing generals—the generals' own sons young enough to ride with them, or conquered kings' children marching as captives to make dramatically visible the humiliation and extinction of other powerful and wealthy nations—and to give sanctity to public rites and ceremonies. In the late Republic, the honours conferred by the senate on Ser. Sulpicius Rufus included provision for his children to have a reserved space round his statue in the Forum on certain public occasions. Cicero moved the decree in the senate in 43 BCE:

A bronze statue of Seruius Sulpicius on foot should be set up on the Rostra, according to the vote of this body, and around that statue there should be a space of five feet on all sides for his children and descendants to view the games and the gladiatorial shows. This is for his death in the service of the state, and that reason should be inscribed on the base.

The senate also voted a public funeral and an allocated space for burial which would be available for Sulpicius' children and descendants (Cicero, *Philippics* 9. 16–17).

Children marked out in these ways in the public eye were exemplars for other children, and they both reflected and

conditioned the perspective of adults. In the imperial period children continued to be used in this way, and visual representations
of them became more frequent. Children of the imperial family
had a further, dynastic purpose. Augustus' adoptive son Gaius
Caesar appeared on coins in Gaul when he was about 12,
mounted on a horse and wearing a boy's *bulla*[16] (Fig. 1.4) in much
the same style as that of the statue of the young Aemilius. There
appears, however, to have been little visual record made of ceremonies in which children took a prominent part. So children
were visible in public life and could have a significant role, but
Republican art did not record such occasions. Mythological
scenes were much more frequent than historical ones until well
into the imperial period, and the representation of children was
not an important part of these mythological scenes.[17]

FIG. 1.4   Equestrian statue of C. Caesar, aged 12, on Roman coin,
Lugdunum, 8 BCE.

[16] Gold and silver coins from Lugdunum (*RIC*[2] 1. 54 nos. 198–9; *BMCRE* 1.
85–6 nos. 498–503). Gaius was sent to Gaul in 8 BCE, aged 12, to take part in
cavalry exercises with the army fighting on the Rhine (Dio 55. 6. 4).

[17] We know little of painting of this period, but the remains of Pompeii give
no reason to think that domestic or public paintings were historical rather than
mythological and scenic. See Ch. 7 below on the development of historical
reliefs and representations.

The Basilica Aemilia in the Forum, refurbished and embellished by the Aemilii family over many generations from the second century BCE, combined family and national history in its
decoration; and the statue of the boy Aemilius, on the Capitoline
hill above, was a reminder that children could have a role in such
history. In 14 BCE Augustus incorporated into the Basilica a
portico in honour of his grandsons Gaius and Lucius Caesar. The
dynastic motive was already strong. The relief sculpture inside the
Basilica, extant in part, has scenes from Roman legend: Aeneas
escaping from Troy; the punishment of Tarpeia; the rape of the
Sabine women.

It is surprising that Romans of the Republican period, with
their demonstrable interest in their history[18] and their application
of it as models for behaviour of young and old, did not use public art (other than coinage) to illustrate and exploit that history.[19]
Individuals honoured with sculptured representations were, as
noted above, mostly important historical figures, but they were
not part of any historical narrative. These statues and busts were
honorific rather than funerary. It was funerary art, associated with
burial places (monuments for cremation urns), which began to
record a wider range of private individuals and groups from the
early or mid-first century BCE. Children quickly had a place in
these memorials.

One of the earliest of the funerary reliefs to include a child
specifically, as a member of a family, is the marble relief of 30–20
BCE for the Seruilii,[20] representing the freeborn son (*f(ilius)*)
P. Seruilius Globulus, his father (*pater*) Q. Seruilius Hilarus,
and the father's wife (*uxor*) Sempronia Eune, the last two both
of freed status (Fig. 1.5). The boy's image is set apart from that
of the adults by a pillar, and he is further differentiated by the
signs of his freeborn status: the filiation in his nomenclature (Q.
f.) and the locket (*bulla*) round his neck. The adults wear the

[18] e.g. the Roman annalists, and Cato, Sallust, Cicero, Caesar, Livy.

[19] Little Republican art remains to us, but literary evidence helps reconstruct
some picture of what art was available in private and public places. Pliny the
Elder devoted several books of his *Natural History* to this material (Books 34–7).
Greek art which was imported, looted, or copied for Rome consisted essentially
of representations of gods, goddesses, and heroes.

[20] *CIL* 6. 26410; Kockel (1993: 141–2 and pl. 51a); Kleiner (1977: no. 71) (with
date of 13 BCE to 5 CE); Zanker (1975: fig. 19).

FIG. 1.5 Relief of Seruilii family: freeborn son and freed couple. Rome, 30–20 BCE.

dress of Roman citizens, but their nomenclature (*Q. l.* and *C. l.*) shows that their free status was won by manumission and not by free birth. The representation of the child advertises his superior status and the family's upward mobility. There are other, similar examples from this period (B. Rawson 1997*a*: 211). An interest was developing in representing groups, including children, in private portraiture. This seems to be connected with the large number of slaves and ex-slaves in Italy who were being integrated into Roman society and were seeking ways to advertise their improving status and wealth. They had few of the trappings of official life to advertise, so they memorialized their family relationships, often using children to represent the family's upward mobility.

Augustus, that master of propaganda, of seizure and exploitation of the public mood, picked up this trend and developed it for his own public policy purposes. The Ara Pacis (Altar of Peace), begun in 13 BCE and dedicated in 9 BCE, offered Romans a 'new deal', but this built on pre-existing ideals and ceremonies. After the first decade of his sole rule, Augustus had turned his attention more to social issues rather than justifying and regularizing his political position. He himself and the wider Roman society were concerned for stability and continuity: family life and children were a strong symbol of this. The funerary reliefs which we saw above were being erected by families who were establishing and improving their position. The need for such memorials was often brought on by the early death of a child, which interrupted a family's progress, but at least there was a public record of its existence and its hopes. Sometimes the memorial was set up in advance of death, making proper provision for future burial and commemoration. Augustus himself began his own mausoleum early, in 28 BCE, when he already had an 11-year-old daughter (Julia) and might still have hoped for more children, especially sons (this time from Livia). In 20 BCE his first grandson was born—Gaius, the son of Julia and her husband Agrippa. A second grandson, Lucius, followed in 17, and Augustus then adopted both boys as his own sons as C. Iulius Caesar and L. Iulius Caesar. In succeeding years these boys were widely advertised in Italy and beyond, and their images became very familiar: busts and statues (much copied, making it difficult for us to identify them as for princes or private children), and on coins as future heirs,[21] 'leaders of youth' (*principes iuuentutis*),[22] and future military leaders (cf. Fig. 1.4 above).[23] They were seen in the flesh at public festivals in Rome, such as the Secular Games, the Troy Game, and the dedication of the temple of Mars Ultor in Augustus' new forum, all of which gave a special role to children (see Chapter 7 below); and Gaius was sent on a tour of duty to the provinces at a young age. The imperial children were highly visible, in imagery and activity; and new legislation in 18 BCE, 4 and 9 CE (the *lex Iulia de maritandis ordinibus*, the *lex Aelia Sentia*, and the *lex Papia Poppaea*) gave an important role to children more generally.

Before Augustus had developed this focus on children, Vergil (who died in 19 BCE) was writing his epic poem, the *Aeneid*, in which *pietas* (loyalty to gods, country, and family) was the central virtue. The image of Aeneas rescuing father Anchises and son Ascanius from the burning city of Troy, a symbol of family devotion, became ubiquitous. Julius Caesar had capitalized on the associations of Aeneas and the Julian house, and Octavian represented the legend on his coinage before 31 BCE. In his new forum the Aeneas legend took its central place in Augustus' representation of national and family history, and the statuary here set the legend in its received, official form. Before the dedication of Augustus' forum in 2 BCE, the usual representation was of Aeneas carrying his father out of Troy. The statuary in the new forum added Ascanius, and it was the trio that was normally represented thereafter. It was endlessly reproduced, on jewellery, lamps, and other artefacts. It reached such a point of saturation that it was the subject of caricature.[24] But it became so internalized as a dominant ideal of the age that it was diffused from the political to the private sphere as a generalized representation of *pietas* as family devotion and duty. There was little that could be done to incorporate a mother into these images: the legend was clear that Creusa had been lost in the flight out of Troy: Vergil, *Aeneid* 2.

---

[21] e.g. with their mother Julia in 13 BCE: *RIC* I². 72 nos. 404, 405; B. Rawson (1997*a*: 214–15 and fig. 9.3).

[22] *RIC* I². 55–6 nos. 205, 212: 2 BCE; B. Rawson (1997*a*: fig. 9.4).

[23] e.g. Gaius on horseback during military exercises in southern Gaul in 8–7 BCE: see above.

[24] Zanker (1988: fig. 162) gives an example from Stabiae.

740. On a private tombstone from northern Italy, however, the family trio has been adapted to make the child a girl rather than a boy (Fig. 1.6), perhaps to accommodate or allegorize the family history of the dedicator, a freedwoman Petronia Grata, who set

FIG. 1.6   Relief of Petronia Grata, adapting legend of Aeneas–Anchises–Ascanius. Aquae Statiellae (Liguria), probably first half of first century CE.

up the stone for herself and her mother (also a freedwoman of the same name).[25]

On the precinct wall of the Ara Pacis, parents and children were represented both realistically and symbolically. On one of the long sides Augustus' family, in procession, includes some of the children (boys and girls) of the imperial family, interacting with parents (both mothers and fathers) and spilling out of the foreground over the frame of the frieze. The garb of two other boys (*camilli*, 'altar-boys') signifies the religious character of this procession to sacrifice. On the other long side the senatorial procession includes the children of one of the senators.[26] The polysemic nature of the representation of children on the Altar is well discussed by Currie, who summarizes thus: '(The child's body) could stand simultaneously for past, present and future.'[27] On one of the ends a fecund female figure (whether she be Pax (Peace) or Tellus (Earth) or Italia) holds infants ready to suckle, surrounded by other symbols of fertility. Individual family memorials became more frequent in the years around and succeeding the dedication of the Ara Pacis. Increasing stability and prosperity, and the continuing manumission of slaves, explain some of this; but the influence of Augustus' ideology and imagery also contributed.

Augustus' representation of children on the Ara Pacis and on his coinage had a clear dynastic motive.[28] Dynastic continuity was a dominant concern for his successors, and emperors' representations of children until the end of the first century almost all had dynastic implications. Members of Augustus' family took the message to the provinces in person, as mothers and fathers, sons

---

[25] *CIL* 5. 7521, originating from Aquae Statiellae, in Liguria, between the modern cities of Turin and Genoa. The trio is sculpted on one side of the stone. All four sides bear sculpture, which includes a man and a woman, both helmeted, and symbols of hunting and the countryside. I am unable to interpret the symbolism, but the composition of the figures of the trio is unmistakably that of the Aeneas–Anchises–Ascanius trio.

[26] Identification of some figures is still controversial. See e.g. Pollini (1987, esp. 21–32); C. B. Rose (1990).

[27] Currie (1996: 159). She accepts earlier views on the priority ('spectacular debut') of the Ara Pacis in the representation of children in Roman public art, but it is not clear whether she includes in such art funerary art, some of which, as we have seen, pre-dates the Ara Pacis.

[28] The dynastic motive is well documented for the Julio-Claudian period by C. B. Rose (1997).

and daughters. Once Agrippa and Julia had young children to display, they travelled *en famille* to the East. This began a trend often followed in subsequent periods by members of the imperial family and other Roman dignitaries.[29] It reflected a growing recognition of the status of the provinces as partners in the Roman empire, and of the role of children and family in winning the favour of provincials. In 16 BCE Agrippa and Julia set out with their sons Gaius and Lucius and probably their daughter Julia, the eldest child about 4 years old and the youngest scarcely 1. Before their return in 13 they had produced another daughter, Agrippina (the Elder). Over twenty years earlier (in 39), when Octavian and Antony were trying to heal the wounds of Rome's civil war in the East, the birth of a daughter in Athens to Antony and Octavian's sister Octavia was the occasion for much celebration and consolidation of support for Rome. Coins were issued in Athens bearing Octavia's portrait.[30] Now again there were celebrations and hopes for the future, this time more personally focused on Augustus and his family. Statue groups representing various combinations of Agrippa's family were set up in Greek cities. One group, from Thespiae (in Boeotia), has been reconstructed from its inscription as showing Julia and Agrippa and three of their children, one of them the infant Agrippina in her father's arms. There is no known Greek model for this: children of Hellenistic rulers had never been represented as infants. This was surely commissioned from Rome, or from Agrippa's own staff. Agrippa was busy in the East commissioning Roman-style public works, and the family group represented a Roman concept and furthered Roman propaganda.[31]

In the next generation Agrippina herself, now married to Germanicus, travelled widely with him and gave birth to at least three of their children in the provinces. The way in which her pregnancies were handled, and the presentation of her toddler son Gaius ('Caligula') in miniature military costume to win

---

[29] Agrippa had not travelled with family before. Tacitus (*Annals* 3. 34) includes a claim that Livia travelled widely with Augustus, but there is little specific evidence of this. In any case, they had no children to take with them.

[30] Gold in 38 BCE: *RRC* 533; Sydenham 1200.

[31] Cf. above on the native Italian interest in infants and motherhood, and on the nature of Greek *kourotrophoi* statues. See C. B. Rose (1997: 13 and Catalog 82) on the group statue from Thespiae.

popularity with the troops, are classic examples of manipulation of the role of motherhood and children. In the face of mutiny on the lower Rhine in 14 CE, Germanicus persuaded Agrippina to leave the camp to go to the safety of a nearby town. In Tacitus' graphically visual account of the farewell scene, Germanicus 'wept profusely, embracing his pregnant wife and their son'. 'There filed out of the camp the line of pitiable women, the wife of the commander a refugee, her little son held in her arms, amid lamentations of the wives of the commander's staff officers, who were leaving with her.' Tiberius' suspicions were aroused by many aspects of Agrippina's role on the Rhine: 'as if there were not enough currying of favour in parading the commander's son in a private's uniform and wanting a Caesar to be called "Little Boots" (Caligula)' (Tacitus, *Annals* 1. 41, 69).

Agrippina's child-bearing ability (*fecunditas*: Tacitus, *Annals* 1. 41) was one of her claims to distinction. Augustus himself had been glad to exploit it when he met opposition to his pro-family legislation. He ostentatiously sat in public with Germanicus, each with one of the infant children of Germanicus and Agrippina in his lap (Suetonius, *Augustus* 34). Germanicus' fatherhood was presented as a model (*exemplum*) for dissenting male citizens, and the children were symbols of future prosperity for families and the nation. In his triumphal parade in 17, Germanicus loaded his chariot with his then three sons and two daughters.[32] The centrality of children, and other family connections, to Germanicus' image was confirmed by the senate's posthumous honour to him, a triumphal arch in the Circus Flaminius dedicated by the senate after his death in 19. Statues of twelve members of his family were placed in the attic of the arch, including all six children whom he had by then, aged 1 to 13. Germanicus himself was represented riding in his triumphal chariot, surrounded not only by the children but also by parents, siblings, and wife. The smallest children may have been in the arms of adults.[33]

---

[32] Tacitus' language brings out the splendid excess: 'currusque quinque liberis onustus' (*Annals* 2. 41).

[33] Details of the arch, which is no longer extant, have been reconstructed from the contents of an inscription, the Tabula Siarensis, found in Seville in 1982—the most complete copy known of the senatorial decree originally set up at Rome. See C. B. Rose (1997: Catalog 37).

In the year of Germanicus' death, twins were born to Tiberius' son Drusus and Drusus' wife Livilla (Iulia Liuia). Tiberius exulted over the birth of twin grandsons. Years later, Tacitus reported this acerbically in his *Annals* (2. 84):

This is a rare and joyful event even in humble homes, but it so elated the emperor that he did not resist boasting to the senate that never before in Roman history had a man of such high rank had twins born to him. Thus he turned everything, even chance events, to his own glorification.

Tiberius shared the glory by allowing Drusus to issue coins in 23 in his own name, celebrating dynastic continuity and bringing out associations with fecundity and the favour of the gods, both of which augured well for Rome. The obverse represented the twins emerging from cornucopiae on either side of a *caduceus*. The cornucopiae, 'horns of plenty', were a symbol of prosperity and of the fruitfulness of Tiberius' line; the *caduceus* was the staff carried by Mercury as the messenger of the gods and the bringer of good fortune.[34] Claudius was the first of the emperors to have a child born to him during his reign. His accession to power was irregular, and he had not been marked out as the successor of the childless Gaius, so the birth of a son (Germanicus, later called Britannicus) soon after his accession offered hopes of a new beginning and a natural successor. The bronze coinage of 41 CE celebrating the son's birth carried the figure and name of Spes, 'Hope'. Spes was later used by Vespasian too, early in his reign (70 CE), to symbolize the hopes vested in his sons and heirs, and, more than a century later, by Septimius Seuerus for his sons Caracalla and Geta.[35] In this connection Spes carried also the message of youth (Clark 1983: 82–3). When Claudius' stepson Nero supplanted Britannicus as the primary heir in the year 50, he was not an infant: the 13-year-old was represented on Claudius' coins (gold and silver) as *princeps iuuentutis* ('leader of

[34] *RIC* 1². 97 no. 42; B. Rawson (1997a: fig. 9.6). The boy in the wall-painting in the house of M. Lucretius Fronto in Pompeii (see above) is represented as Mercury.

[35] Claudius: *RIC* 1². 118–19, 128–30 nos. 99, 115; Zanker (1988: fig. 190). Vespasian: *RIC* 2. 63 no. 396. The same type (without the specific name Spes) was used in 74/5 in association with Vespasian's younger son Domitian as *princeps iuuentutis*: *RIC* 2. 41 no. 233. Septimius Seuerus: *RIC* 4. 212 no. 5, 314 no. 4.

youth'), and a shield and spear on the coins symbolized his military prowess and promise. On these coins Nero was associated with Agrippina the Younger, the mother who had made this heir possible.[36]

Nero's celebration of his newborn child, even though she was a daughter and not a son, reflects the potency of the image of fatherhood and children in public perception. At her birth in 63, the infant daughter received the title Augusta (as did her mother Poppaea): although she could not succeed Nero as emperor she was intended to take her place amongst the imperial women and have her role to play in dynastic strategies. Nero celebrated extravagantly, and when his daughter died a few months later he was inconsolable. The child received the title of deification, Diua. The birth of a child in the imperial family augured well for the continuity of the dynasty and stability for Rome. Nero stimulated hopes for more children in his vowing of a temple to Fecunditas ('Fertility').[37] The temple project was probably not carried through, but this association of the emperor's wife with such a personification, and the timing of the title 'Augusta' for her, to celebrate the birth of her child,[38] foreshadowed a more consistent use of such imagery in the second century (see below on the Antonines).

In the year of civil war in 69, during Vitellius' brief reign, he added to his initial coinage types representations of his two children, to boost confidence in his position and hopes of stability. Within a few months before this, the Roman world had seen the violent deaths of three childless emperors. (The elderly Galba had tried, without success, to use the adoption of a distinguished young man to remedy his position.) Vitellius had two children, one a very young son and the other a daughter who was not

---

[36] *RIC* I[2]. 125 nos. 75, 78, 79: 50–4 CE.

[37] Poppaea did conceive again, in 65, but died pregnant and was deified (Tacitus, *Annals* 16. 6, 21). After Poppaea's death, a bronze coin or medallion from an Eastern mint celebrated the daughter who had died in 63 as DIVA CLAVDIA NER(onis) F(ilia), 'the deified Claudia, daughter of Nero', with Poppaea on the reverse as DIVA POPPAEA AVG(usta) (Cohen 1.315). But there was no representation of the infant as such: a woman was represented standing in a round temple. An eastern medallion of lead, of more doubtful authenticity (Cohen 1. 316), bore the legend CLAVD(ia) AVGVSTA, with Nero's head on the reverse. But the type was that of a woman's bust, not that of an infant.

[38] Tacitus, *Annals* 15. 23, for titles of the child and Poppaea.

beyond her early teens. Their portraits were displayed on gold and silver coinage, the legend explicitly identifying them as 'the children of the emperor Germanicus'.[39] The use of the young son was particularly exploitative and pathetic. The boy had a speech impediment and seems to have been weakly, and the sources hint that in other circumstances Vitellius might have preferred to keep such a son out of the public eye. But when Vitellius had established his position at Lugdunum he called for his son to join him there. To impose such a journey on a very young child (an *infans*) in conditions of civil war demonstrates the importance attached to the presence of a child, especially a son, with a father claiming imperial power. Vitellius conferred honours on the child, including the title 'Germanicus', wrapped him in a military cloak, and held him in his arms as the army paraded before them. By the end of the year Vitellius' cause was lost, and his son was part of the abject public surrender first attempted by Vitellius: Vitellius led his household out onto the streets of Rome, his tiny son carried in a small litter. Perhaps it was sympathy aroused by this sight which prompted the crowd to resist the surrender, leaving Vitellius a little longer to survive before the Flavian troops captured, humiliated, and executed him. Early in the new year (70) the son too was put to death: the honours claimed for him by his father made him too dangerous (it was alleged) to survive. The daughter had been a useful pawn in her father's plans for power, but her sex prevented her from being a political or military threat in her own right and she survived.[40]

Vespasian was undaunted by the fate of Vitellius' son. His sons Titus and Domitian were already adults and he made clear from

[39] The daughter was engaged or married during the year 69 to strengthen Vitellius' position. She survived her father's death and was later provided with dowry and a new husband by Vespasian: Tacitus, *Histories* 1. 59; Suetonius, *Vespasian* 14. Coins from Tarraco, Lugdunum, and Rome: *RIC* 1². 268, 271–3, pls. 30 no. 57, 31 no. 78, with legend LIBERIS IMP. GERMANICI or some variation of that. Vitellius took on the title Germanicus to identify the original basis of his support, as commander of the Roman legions in Germany.

[40] Suetonius (*Vitellius* 6) describes the son as 'stammering, all but dumb and tongue-tied' ('titubantia oris prope mutum et elinguem').Tacitus (*Histories* 2. 59) describes Vitellius displaying the *infans* at Lugdunum as 'paludamento opertum, sinu retinens'; and (3. 67) the son in the attempted surrender parade as 'ferebatur lecticula paruulus filius'. See also Tacitus, *Histories* 1. 75, 2. 47–8, 3. 68–86, 4. 80; and Suetonius, *Vitellius* 18.

early in his reign that he intended them to be his heirs, forming
a Flavian dynasty. He issued coinage bearing their two heads on
the reverse, each as Caesar and son of the Augustus (*RIC* 2. 15 no.
2). There were no infants in Vespasian's or Titus' households during their reigns, but they used the image of children to signify the
emperor's protective role over the Roman world[41] or to advertise
the quality of *pietas*.[42] Domitian was the only Flavian to come to
power as father of a very young son, but this prospective heir died
prematurely in 82 or 83 at the age of 9 or 10 (Desnier 1979).
Domitian grieved as extravagantly as had Nero for his daughter:
he deified the boy and issued coins of gold and bronze commemorating him as DIVVS CAESAR. The reverse of the gold (*RIC*
2. 180 no. 213) represents the child as much younger than his
years, more like an infant, seated naked on a globe, lifting arms
and head towards the seven stars above him. It has been
suggested that this representation was influenced by the sentimentality associated with the death of a very young child and by
the engraver's wish to depict the child in the heroic nudity of
divinity. The mythological allusions of this reverse (a son translated to heaven as the star Arcturus to join his spiritual mother,
the constellation The Great Bear, and summoned by his father
Jupiter) illustrate Domitian's talent for manipulating the 'politics
of religion'.[43] On the bronze coinage (*RIC* 2. 209 nos. 440, 441),
the reverse focuses more on Domitia as mother of the deified heir
(DIVI CAESARIS MATER, with Domitia accompanying the child),
and the child is represented more realistically, as somewhat older
than the one on the gold coin. The choice of metal was not arbitrary: each metal targeted one section of the population more
than another and was an essential part of the message.

Domitian continued to use children in his imperial symbolism.
The Secular Games of 88 had a prominent role for children, and

---

[41] TVTELA AVGVSTI on Vespasian's coins of 70 and 71, with a female figure
protecting two children whose hands are raised to her: *RIC* 2. 63 no. 398; 72 no.
480.

[42] *Pietas* and a small child, associated with Titus' deified sister Domitilla,
whose progeny were intended to continue the Flavian line, on his coin of 80.
Under Domitian, the same image was associated with Domitian's wife Domitia,
on coins in 81–3/4 and 91–2: *RIC* 2. 124 no. 73.

[43] See Desnier (1979) on the suggestion and these allusions. See Ch. 8 below
for heroization and similar imagery for other dead children.

coins of 88 commemorating these games (LVD(i) SAEC(ulares)) had
representations of children. For instance, a child and an adult citizen are depicted as recipients of Domitian's distribution of largess;
and three children take part in a procession before Domitian (Fig.
1.7).[44] This wider use of children in official imagery, beyond the
purely dynastic, heralds developments of the second century, when
representations of children were used to symbolize broader aspects
of policy, especially the emperor's generosity (*liberalitas*) and his
care for all his people as *pater patriae* ('father of his country').
Trajan extended the lists of those eligible for handouts of grain and
money (*congiaria*) to include children from the time of their birth
('ab infantia': Pliny, *Panegyric* 26), and there seems to have been no
minimum age for eligibility for the child-support scheme known
as the *alimenta*. These programmes benefited parents as much
as children, but the inclusion of very young children in visual

FIG. 1.7   Secular Games procession, boys preceding men. Roman coin,
88 CE.

[44] *RIC* 2. 201 nos. 376, 379.

representations of such programmes was a recognition of them as
individuals, as recipients in their own right. Young children are the
continuing, connecting theme in a long series of coinage and monuments celebrating second-century emperors' liberality and concern for their people (see below).

Children represented in private art are only rarely infants.
Inscriptions and iconography show most of the children to be
aged above 2, usually 4 or 5 years or older. In most societies,
infants have been regarded as only marginal members, and the
high infant mortality rates in ancient Rome increased this mar-
ginality. As we shall see below (Chapter 8), this reduced their
funerary commemoration. Even in modern societies, death
notices and formal burial have been rare for infants, but modern
technology and commerce make it possible and inexpensive to
keep detailed family records of infants, in photographs, video-
tapes, and 'My Baby' diaries. It was a different matter, psycho-
logically and economically, to commission a statue or painting of
an infant in an ancient society, and literary preoccupations did
not encompass the minutiae of infant activities and development.
We shall see, however, glimpses of such interests in the correspondence of Fronto with the emperor Marcus Aurelius.

The Ara Pacis had used infants on one end of its precinct wall
as symbols of fecundity and hope for the future, and from
Augustan times sculpted marble portraits of infants are known,
albeit of very small size.[45] Bonfante (1997: 183) places the Ara
Pacis image of the mother figure (Tellus) with infants in the Italic
tradition of private terracotta votive figurines which was noted
above. The earliest specifically identified infants of which I am
aware are the two boys with their mother Maena Mellusa on an
altar of not insignificant size, probably from the Claudian
period.[46] The mother is represented seated and veiled, holding
one infant against her body and extending a hand to the other
child standing in front of her (Fig. 1.8). The inscription around

---

[45] An infant's head in the Metropolitan Museum in New York is dated to
the Augustan period: *Roman Portraits, Metropolitan Museum of Art* (1948: pl. 33
and n. 33). Another, in the Vatican, is dated to the Claudian period: *Bildkatalog-
Vatican* (1995: pls. 136–7). They are respectively 0.095 m and 0.17 m in height.

[46] Dimensions of the altar are: height 1.00 m, width 0.54 m, depth 0.46 m.
This is now in the Vatican: *Bildkatalog-Vatican* (1995: pls. 422–3); see also
Boschung (1987: cat. no. 964, p. 114).

FIG. 1.8 Altar of Maena Mellusa and two infant sons. Rome, probably Claudian period.

the sculpture gives the infants' ages as eleven months and three
months. The monument was dedicated by the infants' father
C. Oenucius Delus.[47] The inscription alone, without its sculptural context, might suggest that the monument was essentially
for Delus' wife and himself. The first two lines are led by the
couple's names, reading 'For Maena Mellusa (freedwoman of
Lucius), my wife; C. Oenucius Delus—and for himself also.' The
infants' names, with ages, come at the end. But the sculpture
highlights Mellusa's role as mother, with individuated figures of
the children corresponding roughly to their different ages at
death. The infant children are an integral part of this family's history. Their names suggest slave status, whereas the mother is
explicitly an ex-slave. She could form a proper Roman marriage
with Delus only after gaining freedom. The boys, if slaves, were
born before their mother won freedom. Perhaps they predeceased
both parents, and Delus took the opportunity to prepare a burial
place for his wife and himself while commemorating the infants.
If the infants had lived they might have won freedom too, but
their deaths ended any such hopes. Delus was not the slave-
owner of Mellusa (their family names are different), so not the
owner of the sons if they were slaves. How he retained connection with Mellusa and the boys can only be guessed at, but it is a
remarkable monument, and tribute to family solidarity and
dashed hopes, for such a society at such a time.

The only other first-century example of a representation of a
specific, named infant, of which I am aware, shares some of the
same characteristics. A *cippus* from a columbarium of probable
Flavian date[48] is explicitly for a 2-year-old, dedicated by his parents, and the parents' names suggest ex-slave status. The boy's
name, C. Aurunceius Primitiuus, heads the epitaph, followed by
that of his mother Aurunceia Threpte and then his father
L. Rasticanus Felix. The boy's figure stands nude below the
inscription, holding a bird to the left side of his body and pointing with his right hand to a large *bulla* round his neck. The *bulla*
advertises the boy's freeborn status, but he takes his family name
from his mother, not his father. Moreover, it is in the columbar-

---

[47] Not 'Genucius' as in *CIL* 6. 21805. The reading of 'Oenucius' is supported
by Fig. 1.8, the photograph in Boschung, and the text in Helbig[4] I no. 299.

[48] *CIL* 6. 13410; Stuart Jones (1969: 60 no. 25, pl. 10).

ium of his mother's *familia* (the Aurunceii) that the child is buried. The parents were not in a formal Roman marriage at the time of the boy's birth, probably because the mother had achieved freedom before the father did. The precedence of her name over his strengthens the probability of her superior status. The father did achieve free status after his son's birth, and the (freed) parents might have looked forward to a bright future for their freeborn son. At his death they recorded his existence as a playful infant, with his pet bird, but also with the symbol of free Roman birth round his neck.

For young children, older than infants, busts and statues were produced in the Julio-Claudian period under the influence of representations of Gaius and Lucius Caesar and then other young members of the imperial family. A favourite style for boys was as a budding orator or an accomplished scholar: the papyrus scroll was the attribute for such accomplishments, as we saw above for Q. Sulpicius Maximus. The statue in Fig. 1.9 contains all the essential features: scroll in right hand, left hand stretched out with fingers splayed in one of the gestures of oratorical style, draped toga, and *bulla* round the neck of a boy aged about 10 years.[49]

Girls were seldom represented with such attributes. They had access to education at various levels, as we shall see (Chapter 5 below), but the roles in public life for which an oratorical education prepared young males were not open to females (for example political office, the army, or conducting cases in the major lawcourts). They were seldom commemorated for their intellectual accomplishments, but rather with conventional, domestic qualities. We shall see in later chapters that women were capable of a wide range of responsibilities, exercising their judgement in many aspects of social and financial life, but modes of female representation preserved more limited, traditional ideals and values. (See Dixon 2001*b* on many aspects of this, e.g. 73.) Such dissonance between ideals or stereotypes and the lived lives of females is not unfamiliar in our own society. A rare example of commemoration for intellectual qualities is the large, handsome

---

[49] *Musée du Louvre, Catalogue des portraits romains* I, cat. no. 92, pp. 196–7. The statue is dated to the Julio-Claudian period, perhaps that of Claudius. The head has been restored, and is not certainly of the same date as the statue, but it is the stance of the body which is of interest here.

FIG. 1.9   Statue of young orator. Probably from Rome, Julio-Claudian
period.

epitaph from Rome for the 7-year-old Magnilla (Fig. 1.10), who was 'learned beyond her years' ('super annos docta'). This quality is wedged into a list of otherwise conventional epithets, but *docta* ('learned') gains prominence by its placement at the beginning of a line in a carefully composed metrical text, its separation from its related phrase 'super annos', and its position first in a trio of alliterative epithets.[50]

FIG. 1.10   Epitaph for Magnilla, aged 8, 'learned beyond her years'. Rome.

The first monuments to girls as named individuals in their own right, with portraits, of which I am aware date from the second half of the first century CE. An elaborate altar for the 8-year-old

[50] *CIL* 6. 21846: 'FORMOSA ET SENSV MIRABILIS ET SVPER ANNOS | DOCTA DECENS DVLCIS GRATAQVE BLANDITIIS' ('beautiful and sensitive and learned beyond her years, honourable, sweet, and delightful in her caresses'). I am grateful to Rob Baker, of the University of New England, for his insight into this text.

Iunia Procula, from the Flavian period, yields an interesting family history[51] (Fig. 1.11). On the front of the altar, below the portrait of the girl and quite elaborate sculptural decoration, is the
epitaph for Procula, dedicated by her grief-stricken parents ('she
left her wretched father and mother in grief'). Both parents'
names had been inscribed, but the mother's was later erased. The
reason for this is contained in the inscription added on the back
of the altar—this was a free-standing altar, meant to be seen from
all sides. The family history can be reconstructed as follows.
M. Iunius Euphrosynus had freed his slave Acte, as a gift, and
married her; so she bore his family name as Iunia Acte. Their
daughter, born after this, was freeborn: Iunia M. f. Procula. At
some time after the daughter's death, however, Acte ran away
with Zosimus and some of her husband's slave staff, leaving the
aged husband bed-ridden, robbed, and in despair. The husband
had her name chiselled out of the front of the marble altar, and a
blood-curdling curse inscribed on the back against the perfidious
Acte, the adulterous Zosimus, and those who ran away with
them. What the state of mind of husband and wife was after the
child's death, besides grief, is unknowable; but the representation
of their child remains as a fashionably coiffed girl with a good
Roman name and a status better than that of at least her
mother.[52] A handsome monument testifies to the dashing of
hopes for the future—initially the hopes of child and parents, and
later the hopes of a husband for his marriage and perhaps future
children.

Sometimes children were associated with mythological or
divine figures. Diana, as the virgin goddess who represented
women's interests, was an appropriate choice for girls. A representation of a girl in the guise of huntress like that often used for
Diana, striding out with bow and quiver and dog, was sculpted
on the front of the second-century altar of Aelia Procula, with an
explicit dedication also to Diana.[53] The dedicators were the girl's
parents P. Aelius Asclepiacus and Vlpia Priscilla: the father's status as a freedman of the emperor Hadrian is highlighted by the
larger lettering of his title AVG(usti) LIB(ertus). Less explicit is the

---

[51] *CIL* 6. 20905; Kleiner (1987: no. 23, pl. XV.1–2).
[52] And probably her father, whose *cognomen* suggests slave origin.
[53] *CIL* 6. 10958; Kleiner (1987: no. 104, pl. LX.1).

FIG. 1.11   Altar of Iunia Procula, aged 8. Rome, Flavian period.

altar for Iulia Victorina, who died at 10 and was commemorated by her parents.[54] She is associated with lunar imagery, which sometimes symbolized a translation to another life in the heavens (cf. Domitian's young son, above). This will be discussed below, in the context of changing views of death and the after-life, in Chapter 8.

Funerary altars, which came into use from the middle of the first century CE, continued to be popular into the third century. The earlier funerary reliefs usually recorded groups, whose accompanying inscriptions identify them as members of the same *familia* or of a biological family. The nature of reliefs allowed only limited space for inscriptions—seldom more than the names of those commemorated. Altars provided greater scope for both image and inscription, and these focused on a married couple or on an individual rather than a group. Children commemorated on known altars range in age from infants to 11 years: the earliest example from Roman Italy is that of A. Egrilius A. f. Pal. Magnus, a 5-year-old from Ostia (50–60 CE). His epitaph (*CIL* 14. 4899) gives only his name and age. His image is that of a full-length standing figure, clothed in formal Roman toga, the *bulla* round his neck confirming the evidence of his nomenclature that he is a freeborn citizen. In his left hand he holds the ubiquitous scroll, with his right he holds the horn of a pet goat.[55] His expression is serious, which applies to almost all the representations of children known to us from Roman Italy. Some commentators have been tempted to describe these children as 'sad', but the expression is surely part of the genre and a function of fashion. Many of us have in our own family albums similarly serious studio photographs of children and of wedding couples, whereas informal holiday snapshots show the same people laughing and playful. We lack these informal images of Roman children, except for a few literary references (see below) and the hints of epithets

---

[54] *CIL* 6. 20727; Kleiner (1987: no. 15, pl. X.3–4).

[55] *CIL* 14. 4899; Kleiner (1987: no. 12, pl. IX.1–3); B. Rawson (1997a: fig. 9.8). Goette (1989: 460) dates the altar to the Trajanic period, without explanation, but the nomenclature and the full form of 'Dis Manibus' suggest an earlier date; and Kleiner gives stylistic grounds for the earlier date. She also suggests that the goat may have symbolic significance, associated with the after-life; but at one level it is part of the Roman fondness for pet animals and birds on their funerary monuments, on which see K. R. Bradley (1998b).

such as *dulcissimus*. Children who were commemorated as *dul-cis/dulcissimus* ('sweet', 'most sweet') tended to be younger than those who were *carissimus* ('very dear') or *pientissimus* ('very devoted'). Up to the age of about 5, children were most remembered verbally as sweet and playful, before they began to take on the greater responsibilities inherent in *pientissimus* and *bene merens* ('well deserving').[56] But visually Roman children, even very young ones, took their image seriously—or the dedicators and artists presented a serious image consistent with the status of a Roman citizen or with aspirations for citizenship, and with promise of a successful adult life.

The portrait of another 5-year-old (Fig. 1.12)[57] typifies these aspirations, and the nomenclature of the boy and his parents underlines the generational improvement in status. P. Albius P. f. Memor was represented by a fine bust above his epitaph: his hairstyle copies that of the emperor Trajan (helping us date the altar to the early second century), and his clothing of tunic, toga, and *bulla* reinforces the freeborn status advertised in his name. His parents, however, who dedicated the altar 'filio dulcissimo', are less likely to be freeborn: P. Albius Threptus and Albia Apollonia share the same *nomen* and have *cognomina* often borne by slaves, and have no status indication, all of which suggests that they may be ex-slaves freed in the one household. The handsome altar for their son is not only a tribute to their loss and love for him but also a statement about where they have arrived in their life course: it advertises their free status and some considerable wealth, and their son's name symbolizes the higher levels of society to which they could aspire through freeborn children.

As noted above, images of children of the imperial family were widespread in the first century, being used largely for dynastic purposes. They signified hope for the future, the favour of the gods, stability, and continuity. Sometimes foreign children were used in the public sphere for a different purpose. Specially favoured sons of foreign rulers were sometimes brought to Rome—in effect, as hostages, but they could be presented as honoured guests, raised and educated with coevals in the imperial

---

[56] See Sigismund Nielsen (1997) for detailed analysis. Cf. Cicero and Pliny below on 'cheerfulness' in children.

[57] *CIL* 6. 11346; Kleiner (1987: no. 51, pl. XXXII.1–2).

FIG. 1.12   Altar of P. Albius Memor, aged 5. Rome, early second century CE.

family, socialized to become Romans and loyal allies of Rome, symbols of Rome's policy of peace, harmony, and stability for the empire. Augustus followed this practice with 'many of the children' of foreign rulers, having them brought up and educated with boys of his own family (Suetonius, *Augustus* 48). Herod the

Great sent several of his sons to Rome, apparently to stay with
Jewish friends (Josephus, *Jewish Antiquities* 17. 20–21). Herod
Agrippa (future king of Judaea) lived in Rome under Augustus
from early boyhood and made good use, over a long period, of his
bonds with Drusus (Tiberius' son) and other members of the
imperial family.[58] In the second century, Herodes Atticus was
sent by his prominent Greek family to spend some of his boyhood at Rome with a prominent Roman family. The daughter of
that family, Domitia Lucilla (later to become the mother of
Marcus Aurelius),[59] was approximately the same age as Herodes,
and the association and mutual benefit continued in the next
generation when Herodes became one of Marcus' tutors. Such
boys will have been seen in public company with boys of the
imperial family and sons of senators, confirming in the public
consciousness the ideological message of Roman imperial policy.

Less fortunate foreign children were seen in more abject roles,
especially as captives in Roman triumphal processions and celebrations. Here they were the mirror image of Roman children:
they too were the new generation, their people's prospects for the
future, but these hopes and prospects were extinguished—or at
least transformed—by Roman victory and integration into a
dependent empire. Such scenes were not frequent in Rome under
the *pax Romana* of the imperial period, but, like the triumphs of
which they were part, they reminded Rome of the importance of
military victory and provincial administration in maintaining that
'Roman Peace'. We shall return below (Chapter 7) to the question of the impact on Roman children of such scenes: did they
sometimes arouse pathos and fellow-feeling as well as pride and
patriotism? Women and children were used to great visual effect
on the columns of Trajan and Marcus Aurelius, as symbols of
Rome's power and her enemies' humiliation. The significance of
these symbols had already been reflected in the text of a monument of the 70s CE: the memorial to the senatorial commander
Ti. Plautius Siluanus Aelianus. His civil and military achievements were inscribed on a large slab in front of the Plautii
family tomb beside the Anio river near Tibur (Tivoli). His

[58] Josephus, *Jewish Antiquities* 18. 143–6, 235–7. His mother Berenice was a
friend of Antonia the Younger, mother of Claudius and grandmother of Gaius.

[59] Fronto, *Letters* (Marcus Aurelius, as Caesar, to Fronto) 3. 2 (41 N, 61 H).

achievements included protection of his province of Moesia on the Danube, 'in which he brought across the river more than 100,000 from the population of Transdanubians to pay tribute, along with their wives and children and leaders and kings'.[60] The impact of this mass forced movement of people, its procession into Moesia, and associated ceremonies, on the now settled but still vulnerable province is not difficult to imagine. The submissive leaders, and the women and children who represented the future of their people, personified the end of a separate, independent people.

Such a use of foreign women and children was translated into durable visual form by Trajan and then Marcus Aurelius on their memorial columns. In between their reigns, Hadrian used female figures on his coins to represent various provinces, but these were in the form of recipients of Hadrian's benefactions. With the exception of Judaea, the provinces were not the scenes of warfare. That Judaea too was represented as a beneficiary is striking in view of Hadrian's particularly ruthless suppression of two rebellions in Judaea. Moreover, Judaea is represented accompanied by children, the only province so represented.[61] In the long roll-call of provinces in the ADVENTVS series (provinces welcoming Hadrian) and that of 'the provinces' characterized by geographical attributes, none is represented with children. The addition of children for Judaea cannot be by chance. There is also a bronze medallion (Cohen 2. 179 no. 871) representing Judaea as a female figure surrounded by children and kneeling at the emperor's feet. Hadrian's gesture of reaching out to raise her up is consistent with his other representations of Italy and provinces rescued and helped by him (e.g. in the RESTITVTOR series). Judaea had been represented on Roman coins before, but Hadrian added the children: he introduced the concept of the mother country with her progeny. This use of children is consistent with what else we know of the development of official iconography in the first half of the second century. Flavian coins had represented Judaea as a female figure, more abject than on Hadrian's coins and explicitly

[60] *CIL* 14. 3608. 11. See Eck (1997: fig. 4.1) for photograph of the tomb and its associated inscriptions.

[61] With the exception of a few of the NILVS coins (for the river Nile). Judaea is represented, like the other provinces, standing facing Hadrian across an altar; several children accompany her: *RIC* 2. 448 no. 853; 454 nos. 890–4.

conquered ('CAPTA'). She was usually alone, but sometimes accompanied by a male figure. Hadrian's portrayal is more optimistic, and must pre-date the 'final solution' of 132 to deal with the uncooperative Jews by founding a new Roman colony, Aelia Capitolina, on the site of Jerusalem.[62] Coins minted in the East represented the colony as a new start: no figure of a suppliant or grateful Judaea, and no children, but symbols of the foundation of the new colony (Hadrian ploughing the perimeter with a bull and cow, and a military standard in the background).[63] Representations in modern media of allied campaigns in wartime and post-war settlements have been the subject of much analysis to reveal the emphases chosen for home consumption. Hadrian's first version will have been aimed at Rome itself, but the Aelia Capitolina coins were probably intended more for reception in the provinces.

The two columns[64] portray Roman victories on the northern frontiers. Whereas, however, Trajan's wars against the Dacians went well for the Romans and a new province strengthened the north-east of the empire, Marcus' wars against Germans and Sarmatians went much less well and the northern frontier problems remained unsolved at his death. There is much bloody detail on the columns, but also the pathos of families separated and dispossessed. There is dispute about how much detail spectators could see from the street (or even from the upper levels of Trajan's libraries),[65] but those who commissioned and crafted the friezes of these columns were men of second-century society, who personally registered such details and considered them worth recording on their columns. There was a long tradition of Roman generals taking artists in their entourage, whose paintings from

[62] *RIC* and *BMCRE* both date all these provincial coins to the end of Hadrian's reign, e.g. after 136, as a retrospective view of his travels. But Mildenberg (1984: 97–9) dates the 'Judaea' coins, as I do, to before the destruction and renaming of Jerusalem. He also dates the 'Aelia Capitolina' coins to before the Bar Kokhba revolt in 132, on the grounds that the new colony was a cause of the revolt rather than its result.

[63] Legend of COL(onia) AEL(ia) KAPIT(olina) COND(ita): *BMCGC* 'Palestine' 82 no. 2.

[64] See Becatti (1982, 1957); Kleiner (1992: 214–20, 295–301, with further references); and, most recently, Scheid and Huet (2000).

[65] See Beard (2000) for the fluidity of spectators' views of any scene, depending on the angle and position of their viewing.

life provided the material for commemoration at Rome. On
Marcus' column there are many more scenes of pursuit and brutality towards foreign women and children than on Trajan's column. These include scenes of a young girl pulled away from her
mother[66] by a huge soldier, a mother holding a boy close to her
but away from the soldier grabbing her, another mother caught
between two soldiers while her son clings to her front (Fig. 1.13),
an infant grabbed from a mother by a soldier while two other
children (the infant's siblings?) shrink away from the scene to the
other side of their mother, and of young women fleeing or being
pulled along by soldiers.

A recent project which brought together an international
group of scholars to focus on Marcus' column has considerably
illuminated the iconography and ideology of this column (and
made many comparisons with that of Trajan).[67] They recognize
the significant stylistic differences between the two columns, and
agree that pronouncements of artistic 'decadence' are neither useful nor valid. They are cautious, however, about attributing the
differences to a changed mentality in the later second century and
they recognize, as others have, that one cannot apply to official
public policy any supposed evidence of Marcus' personal human-
itarianism to be found in his *Meditations*. Zanker (2000*b*) brings
out the great pathos of scenes involving children; but he believes
that the message of such scenes is political and ideological rather
than humane or sentimental. The rape and enslavement of
women, and their separation from their children, destroyed all
social cohesion for a people: opposition to Rome could lead to the
annihilation of a whole people. 'Women are represented as the
personification of a subjugated people' (Zanker 2000*b*: 173). And,
according to Zanker, the subjugation was proper and correct in

---

[66] I take each example of an adult woman with a child as a mother, but she
could be some other relative or carer. In the traditional numbering for Marcus'
column, the scenes referred to in this sentence are, respectively, scenes 97, 85,
104, and 69. In the upper register of Fig. 1.13 the women being herded on are
accompanied by an infant and a child: here it is the separation from their men-
folk which symbolizes enslavement and the destruction of the identity of a
people.

[67] Scheid and Huet (2000). The precise dates of designing and building
Marcus' column (e.g. how much is due to Commodus) do not affect the
argument which follows, especially as any 'humanitarian' influence of Marcus is
discounted.

FIG. 1.13   Relief of foreign woman and son taken captive by Roman soldiers. Column of Marcus Aurelius. Rome, late second century CE.

Roman eyes: Roman soldiers were perceived as doing their duty against Rome's enemies; the Roman emperor was doing his duty in punishing such enemies and protecting the Roman people.[68] One has to concede too that in the private art of some sarcophagi in the late second century the scenes of abject foreign captives, including women putting their children forward as a token of submission, are almost incidental to the main action, which centres on the person of the deceased: it is hard to see the foreign figures as the focus of much attention or pathos.[69] It comes back to context and intention. The sarcophagi commemorate the careers of soldiers and generals, and the submission of foreign captives (scenes which are not explicitly brutal) is but one incident in this. The scenes on Marcus' column are more numerous, more brutal, and more eye-catching in their places on the spiral.

The dangers of retrojecting modern sentiments to the past must indeed be recognized. And yet—did all Romans remain unmoved by the eloquent images on Marcus' column of the suffering of women and children? Did they so easily make the distinction between Romans and foreigners? The images portrayed more of these sufferings than had earlier monuments, including Trajan's column. That the images, and the use of children in them, were designed to present a horrific picture and to arouse pathos is clear—whether in a context of Roman self-righteousness or in one of greater empathy is less clear. I am inclined to believe more in empathy than some scholars allow for, but, whatever the purpose and the viewers' reception, the figure of the child and the depiction of its emotions were powerful symbols recognized by Roman viewers: they were key instruments in achieving the column's effects. The extent to which Romans, including children, were moved by such scenes depends on the extent to which foreigners, 'barbarians', and Rome's enemies were dehumanized and demonized in Roman perceptions. The comparatively harmonious co-residence of many diverse nationalities in Rome suggests that xenophobia was not a serious problem. But real fear for Rome's

---

[68] Cf. Robert (2000: 190–1); and Pirson (1996: 158–77), who discusses 'the message of absolute Roman superiority' in the context of an increased external threat to Rome's northern borders.

[69] Examples, all dated c.170–80 CE, are from the Vatican (Andreae 1977: fig. 501; Kleiner 1992: fig. 270); Portonaccio in Rome (Kleiner 1992: fig. 269, especially the lid); and Mantua (Kleiner 1992: fig. 271).

security and her ability to ward off hostile invasion may have been developing in the late second century. In our own recent times civil wars, refugee crises, and terrorism have engendered mixed emotions in stronger, more prosperous nations; and sentiment at Rome was surely also complex and individualized.

Uses of Italian children in official art and inscriptions of the second century were, however, more benign. Domitian had begun to extend the visual symbolism of children on coins beyond the dynastic context, and this was further extended by his successors. A partial explanation is that no successor until Marcus Aurelius, sixty-five years later, had a young son or daughter to promote for dynastic purposes; but there were other forces at work to heighten perceptions of children more widely in Roman society. Currency was given to the concept of a new age beginning in the second century.[70] Already in 100 CE Pliny the Younger was applauding and shaping the image of a generous and blameless emperor, and linking this to the importance of children in Roman society and parents' increased willingness to raise them. Addressing Trajan in his inaugural consular speech, Pliny said,

May the gods give you the age which you deserve, Caesar, and preserve the spirit which they have given you: how much greater will be the crowd of infants which you will again and again order to be inscribed on the lists![71] That crowd grows daily and goes on increasing, not because children have become more dear to parents but because citizens are to the emperor. You will give *congiaria* if you wish, you will provide *alimenta* if you wish, but those children are born because of you. (*Panegyric* 28)

Trajan's child-support policies are often put down to a simple wish to raise more potential soldiers for the army. But Pliny acknowledges twin motives: the birth of new citizens is encouraged 'as resources for wars, and as the ornament of peace (*subsidium bellorum ornamentum pacis*)'.[72] 'They learn to love their

[70] This section draws on two of my earlier publications (B. Rawson 1997*a* and 2001).

[71] Lists of recipients of *congiaria*, which were now distributions of money rather than grain.

[72] Cf. *Panegyric* 22, where women are claimed by Pliny to have a great desire for more children, perceiving 'for what an emperor they raised citizens, for what a general they raised soldiers' (with war and peace in the reverse order from the later passage).

country not only as their country but also as their nurturer (*altricem*).' This image of children as the nurslings of their country was reinforced by Trajan's position as universal father—of his country, of its citizens, and of their children. He constructed this image carefully, beginning with generous handouts to adults and children but declining to take on the title of *pater patriae* ('father of his country') until he felt truly worthy of it. This modest reluctance had been overcome by the time that Pliny gave his speech in 100, so that Pliny could declare him the only emperor to be really father of his country before becoming *pater patriae* formally. This construction of identity as the modest, generous, benevolent father figure is mirrored perfectly in Pliny's language: '(Before you accepted the title of *pater patriae*) that is what we knew you to be, in our hearts and minds, and it made no difference to public loyalty what you were called, although it seemed grudging to call you emperor and Caesar rather than "father" as our experience showed you to be' (*Panegyric* 21). The language of parent and children is sustained: 'You live with your citizens like a parent with his children.'

Trajan himself was still expressing the concept of 'the spirit of our times' towards the end of his reign. In more general contexts about justice and humanity,[73] Trajan conjured up such phrases: 'nec nostri saeculi est', 'non est ex iustitia nostrorum temporum'. One of his biggest public-relations efforts was to promote the *alimenta* (literally 'nourishment') scheme for the support of children in various parts of Italy. The scheme is illustrated in a variety of media—imperial art and coinage, legislation, and administrative detail (some of which is recorded in inscriptions). Trajan developed this scheme, whereby farmers took out loans from an imperial fund (administered locally) and the interest was directed to the support of freeborn boys and girls.[74] Coinage celebrating the scheme extended over most of Trajan's reign and was issued in gold, silver, and bronze, reaching all levels of the population.[75] The earliest coins represented Trajan himself making a handout

---

[73] Anonymous accusations against Christians, and financial duress (Pliny, *Letters* 10. 97 and 55 respectively, Trajan's replies to Pliny's queries from Bithynia).

[74] Both legitimate and illegitimate. For the status implications of these terms, rather than moral implications, see below (Ch. 6).

[75] For detailed discussion and photographs, see B. Rawson (2001).

to the female figure of Italia, who holds one child on her left arm and extends her right hand over another child standing at her side. It is an image of imperial generosity, and the health of Italy is personified in the maternal figure with children. The imagery developed over the years, but children remained the essential ingredient in the advertisement of Italian welfare, especially agricultural productiveness (*fecunditas*, a term applicable to both female fecundity and agricultural fertility). Children were symbols of Italy's future, not only as soldiers to protect her frontiers, as citizens to hold office and contribute to a productive workforce, but also to populate Italian towns and work on the land. Trajan's foresight (*prouidentia*) in such policies is made explicit in an inscription on an altar from Tarracina, on the Italian coast south of Rome, associated with sculptures of a boy and a girl grasping the emperor's hand (*CIL* 10. 6310). Furthermore, eloquently sculpted scenes on Trajan's arch at Beneventum, another Italian town, at an important crossroads, reflect the elaborately intertwined symbolism of the caring and generous *pater patriae*, the welfare of Italian towns, and the presence of children with their fathers (Fig. 1.14). Moreover, on this arch the Seasons are represented, for the first time on Roman monuments, in childish form, as *putti*. In Currie's words (1996: 175), 'It was now the male child's body rather than the adult woman's body that was the prime denoter of a perpetual and natural cycle.'

Children continued to be an important part of Rome's cultural symbolism for most of the second century. Trajan and his wife Plotina had no children of their own, but his niece Matidia (the Elder) had two daughters who took an honoured place with her on the coinage, associated with PIETAS AVGVST(a) (Fig. 1.15; *RIC* 2. 300–1 nos. 759–61). One of those daughters, Sabina, was wife of the next emperor, Hadrian, and although she had no children of her own she figured in similar representations on Hadrian's coins.[76] Children were an essential part of imperial ideology by now, and, just as a childless emperor could be *pater patriae*, so a childless empress could project the qualities and attributes to be most desired and aimed at by Roman women.

Images of children in the public sphere continued to have these associations for most of the rest of the second century. The

[76] See B. Rawson (1991*a*: pl. 2b) for an illustration.

FIG. 1.14 Trajan offering children to Italy. Trajan's arch at Beneventum, 114 CE. Top of right pylon of 'the country' façade.

FIG. 1.15   Matidia protecting two girls; PIETAS AVGVST(a). Roman coin,
112–17 CE.

alimenta scheme continued, and Antoninus Pius' addition to it,
benefiting girls in order to honour his wife Faustina (the Elder),
who died early in his reign, was celebrated on coins and in sculpture. His coins showed girls (the *puellae Faustinianae*) and their
parents as part of a distribution scene, with the emperor presiding.[77] Marcus Aurelius' wife, Antoninus' daughter, was also a
Faustina (the Younger), and the scheme for girls continued in her
name during Marcus' reign. When their daughter Lucilla was 16
she was married to Marcus' co-emperor Lucius Verus, and in
honour of the marriage a new scheme for both girls and boys was
established.[78] On a fine pair of marble reliefs recording the *puellae Faustinianae* under Marcus, it was the imperial wives Faustina
and Lucilla who presided over the distribution to the girls who

[77] *RIC* 3. 74–5 nos. 397–9; Rawson (1997*a*: fig. 9.10). Faustina is represented
on one coin as sharing the platform with Antoninus Pius, but her title DIVA
shows that the coin is posthumous and it may be more honorific than recording an actual distribution. *Hunter Coll.* (2. 253 no. 9) and *BMCRE* (4.48 no. 325)
identify the standing female figure as Faustina; *RIC* (3. 75 no. 399*a*) says only 'a
woman'.

[78] SHA, *Marcus* 7, which says that a new name was given to this category
of children, who seem to have been included in grain distributions: 'pueros et
puellas nouorum nominum frumentariae perceptioni adscribi praeceperunt'.

processed towards them. This time the girls were represented more as adolescents than as children:[79] motherhood had returned to the imperial palace, with the wives of both Marcus Aurelius and Lucius Verus producing children. Those imperial children were themselves advertised as infants on Marcus' coinage, but the representation of the *puellae Faustinianae* as almost nubile reinforced the role of females as mothers as part of the ideology of *fecunditas* and *felicitas temporum* ('fecundity' and 'the happiness of the times'). Faustina the Younger had begun producing children while Antoninus Pius was still emperor, and Antoninus celebrated these grandchildren as representing 'the happiness of the age' (*saeculi felicitas*). Two of them were portrayed as infants playing on a throne, with a star over each head.[80] The obverse bore the head of Faustina, who had received the title AVGVSTA with the birth of her first child in 147, the first woman to receive the title before her husband himself became emperor.[81] Marcus was awarded tribunician power for the first time, a clear mark of his intended succession, to mark the auspicious occasion. These titles, and the coinage, clearly represented children as a legitimating and celebratory factor in imperial power. The first-born child, a daughter, died very young, but children kept coming with great regularity for twenty-three years, including two sets of twins, not all of whom survived.[82] Successive births were celebrated with various images, including the cornucopia type with twins (used by Tiberius for the birth of his grandchildren) and Pietas with two children. Juno was represented as the goddess of childbirth, IVNO LVCINA, holding a child on one arm and associated with two small girls at her sides (*RIC* 3. 270 no. 692).

The theme of *saeculi felicitas* and the associated image of two infants playing on a throne were repeated on Marcus' own coinage after he became emperor (Fig. 1.16; *RIC* 3. 271 nos.

[79] Helbig[4] IV no. 3234; Reinach (1912: iii. 147); Rawson (1997a: fig. 9.11) for one of the reliefs. The *alimenta* scheme set upper age limits for the support of boys and girls: 18 and 14 respectively (*D.* 34. 1. 14. 1, Ulpian, with a suggestion that age limits were sometimes thought of in terms of puberty).

[80] *RIC* 3. 95 no. 509.

[81] The husband of Antonia the Younger, Drusus the Elder, never became emperor, and it was her grandson Gaius who conferred the title on her in the last year of her life.

[82] On the children of this marriage, see Birley (1987: App. 2 and Stemma F).

709–12; 346 nos. 1665–6). Probably five children were born after his succession in 161, including a son Commodus and his twin (who did not survive). In the triumph celebrated by Marcus and Lucius Verus in 166 for eastern victories, Marcus had all his non-adult children, boys and girls, ride with him in the procession (as we saw Germanicus do in the year 17).[83] Some of these children seem to have been in the East in 166 with Faustina and Lucilla: Fronto, writing to Lucius Verus, sent greetings to Verus' mother-in-law and the children in terms ('uestros liberos') which must refer to children of both empresses (*To L. Verus* 2. 4 = 132 N, 236 H). It is also possible that Marcus had some of his children with him at the northern warfront in 168, in the campaign against the Marcomanni.[84] If so, this would strengthen the comparison with Germanicus. We have already seen the importance of having imperial children before the eyes of the soldiers. Commodus was certainly with his father Marcus at the warfront in 172, when he got the title 'Germanicus', and in 175 to receive his *toga uirilis* (Dio 72. 22. 2). Commodus' two older sisters were probably also there.[85] Faustina herself was there by 174, when she received the title *mater castrorum* ('mother of the camp': Dio 72. 10. 5). She had brought with her their youngest child, a daughter of not more than 3 years old. This is revealed by an anecdote about Marcus' diplomatic dealings with some distinguished Athenian citizens who were in conflict with another citizen, Herodes Atticus, and who had come to Marcus' base at Sirmium in Pannonia to engage his support. Marcus showed them courteous hospitality, 'in which he was encouraged by his wife and by his little daughter who still had her baby lisp—she was the one particularly who with much sweet talk threw herself at her father's knees, pleading with him to save the Athenians for her' (Philostratus, *Lives of the Sophists* 2. 1. 560–1: *Herodes Atticus*). To have a child of this age in a rugged province, in wartime and with plague spreading widely, is striking. Being a daughter, she carried little of the political and military symbolism which we have seen attached to sons of earlier generals on the warfront, and which made Commodus' presence important. It is not unreasonable to suppose that Marcus wanted

[83] These were probably two daughters, aged 7 and 6, and two sons, aged 5 and 4.

[84] Halfmann (1986: 92 n. 330), on the basis of a votive inscription.

[85] Birley (1987: 174), on the basis of two inscriptions.

to enjoy the last of his 'babies'. All of his other surviving children were now teenagers or older. He had fairly recently (in 169) lost a 7-year-old son. All his previous sons except Commodus had died (mostly in infancy, and Commodus' twin at age 4), and the 7-year-old had borne the title 'Caesar' for several years as a sign of his father's hopes for him. The little Vibia Aurelia Sabina surely brought some consolation and joy to Marcus.

FIG. 1.16   Two infant sons of Marcus Aurelius, playing on a throne; SAECVLI FELICITAS. Roman coin, Marcus Aurelius.

The fact that Marcus chose to have Commodus' ceremony of the *toga uirilis* at the warfront and not in Rome is eloquent testimony to the importance of audience and spectators in such symbolic acts. At this moment, in the context of Marcus' ill health, the spread of the plague from east to west through the empire, the northern war proving difficult, and the outbreak of a revolt in Syria (led by Auidius Cassius), the army's reception of Commodus' passage from boyhood to manhood, and to a viable role as partner and successor to his father, was crucial. So too was the reception by provincials and nearby foreign powers. Not that the population of Rome was left out of this construction of continuity, stability, and well-being. Coins of 175 CE, which must pre-date Commodus' departure for the northern front, record a distribution made in Trajan's forum by Commodus. The representation of Commodus, still in the toga of boyhood (*toga praetexta*) but performing an emperor's duties, was symbolically rich.[86] It must have prepared the ground for a warm send-off soon after, when Commodus began his journey north to his father and to his future career (it was hoped) as heir, soldier, and protector of his people.

Lucilla's marriage to Lucius Verus seems to have produced only one surviving child, a daughter.[87] Coinage issued in Lucilla's name celebrated childbirth and motherhood. Diana was represented with her torch as the patron of childbirth (LVCIFERA, 'bringer into light'), and the images of Fecunditas and Iuno Lucina were both associated with the figures of children.[88] Marcus also had hopes of grandchildren through his son Commodus, who had married Crispina in 178. Coins in Crispina's name advertised gods of marriage and childbirth (DIS CONIVGALIBVS, DIS GENITALIBVS) and specifically Juno and Venus, but there were almost no images of children themselves. Nor is there evidence of the birth of actual children. Commodus issued no such coins once he became sole emperor in 180: the change in tone is palpable.[89] His interests were more in military types,

---

[86] SHA, *Commodus* 2, for *congiarium* and *praetexta puerilis*. *RIC* (3. 262–3; 334 no. 1516) for coins. The coin legend is LIBERALITAS AVG., so the distribution is in the name of Marcus and not Commodus himself. Liberalitas stands on the platform, with abacus and cornucopia, behind the seated Commodus; a citizen climbs the stairs to the platform, holding out the fold of his toga for the distribution.

[87] An inscription of 166 CE (*CIL* 6. 360) is a dedication to Iuno Lucina in honour of the two emperors and their families (the *domus Augustorum*), which is defined as Marcus Aurelius, Lucius Verus, Faustina, Lucilla, 'and their children' (*liberorumque eorum*). If this is the date of the birth of Lucilla's child, it would explain why the infant was not in the joint triumphal procession along with Marcus' children. If Lucilla had already borne one child (in the East), it would still have been no more than a year old.

[88] *RIC* 3. 274–5, 352–3.

[89] Crispina was sent into exile in 183. Some of her coins (*RIC* 3. 398–400, 442–3) may have been issued in Marcus Aurelius' reign. She had the title

Hercules, and gladiators, although care for the grain supply (Annona) continues to be noted, and there is emphasis on Concordia (in the face of threats to his position and internal military conflict), and general references to prosperity.[90] He was, of course, not much more than 30 years old when he was killed; so, apart from his personal tastes, he was hardly of an age to present himself as a father figure. Septimius Seuerus was a more mature man, already with two sons, when he became emperor in 193, and he knew the importance of using these sons to proclaim a new, ongoing dynasty. For an appearance of continuity he claimed the family name of Aurelius (allegedly by adoption), and his elder son, later nick-named 'Caracalla', bore the official name of M. Aurelius Antoninus. Caracalla was still a child (7 years old) in 195 when he received this name and the title 'Caesar' and had his image on the obverse of his father's early coins, clearly advertising dynastic hopes. He became *princeps iuuentutis*, and reverse types on the coinage issued for him proclaimed ongoing hope and confidence and public good fortune.[91]

Similar types and titles were subsequently associated with the younger son Geta (although Geta was always the junior partner). The two boys' images appeared together in 201–2 associated with the eternity of the empire (*Aeternitas Imperii*: *RIC* 4. III no. 155). Echoes of Augustus continued with the Secular Games in 204, which included celebration of the Troy Game. Septimius' wife Julia Domna had coinage in her own name, appearing with husband and both sons to celebrate *Aeternitas Imperii* (*RIC* 4. 166 nos. 539–41) and with her sons celebrating *Felicitas Saeculi* (*RIC* 4. 115 no. 181). She proclaimed the same concept on a different coin where the figure of Felicitas carried a cornucopia and was

Augusta from the time of her marriage to Commodus, before he became sole emperor. Her only coins which include children are some rare bronze coins on which Fecunditas holds a child. Some scholars doubt that emperors were directly responsible for the types and legends on the coinage of their reigns, but the coinage of the 2nd c., especially, seems to me to reflect well what we know from other sources of those emperors' interests and policies. See B. Rawson (2001: 38–9 n. 7).

[90] Types such as Fortuna, Prouidentia, and Salus are used but not made explicit in the legends, which on these coins record only Commodus' titles and offices.

[91] *RIC* 4. 212–13: *Spes Perpetua, Securitas Perpetua, Felicitas Publica.*

accompanied by six small girls (*RIC* 4. 204 no. 827). The imagery here suggests some distribution or support for girls.[92] These types all appeared early in the third century, and although the *saeculum* had been celebrated previously in the happiness and security of 'the age', the pending Secular Games gave a special emphasis to the concept of the turn of another 110 years. Choirs and rituals needed to be prepared and rehearsed, and children had an important role in all of that. Septimius took advantage of the Secular year to give Geta his *toga uirilis*, and it was about this time that the 16-year-old Caracalla was married to Plautilla. Both sons were consuls-designate for the following year (205), and, as with Commodus, there was no suggestion that the boys should wait until their twentieth year actually to hold office—as had been required by Augustus for Gaius and Lucius Caesar (*RG* 14).

Julia Domna's coins associated her with some other types representing motherhood and children, such as Luna Lucifera and an image of Juno (as IVNO AVGVSTAE) holding a child,[93] but they are not the dominant types and Julia herself did not bear any more children after her husband became emperor (nor, it seems, did Plautilla bear any children to Caracalla). Septimius' use of children is limited to his own sons as part of a dynasty. Other aspects of his coinage showed no official interest in matters of family or support for children. Nor is there much evidence in the legal codes of such interests or activity. Most of his rescripts are in the joint names of himself and Caracalla ('Seuerus et Antoninus'), but the early ones which might be more closely associated with Seuerus himself include a comment on the mutual *pietas* between father and son, and another on the disinheriting of children.[94] Seuerus was absent from Rome for long periods, but so too was Marcus Aurelius, yet Marcus is said to have made a point of dealing personally with legal responses and policy, even at a distance (Dio 72. 6), and this activity included significant matters of policy concerning children.

The second century gave a prominence to children which was unknown in later periods of the Empire and more highly

---

[92] Probably a continuation of some form of the *puellae Faustinianae*: we know of no new scheme.

[93] *RIC* 4. 131 no. 316; 273 no. 379; 310 no. 587.

[94] *C.* 5. 25. 4: 197 CE; *C.* 6. 28: 204 CE. Cf. *D.* 27. 1. 1. 4 and 27. 1. 2. 4 (Modestinus) for guardians and the interests of minors.

developed than in any previous period. This is most easily demonstrated from the visual evidence, so that one can at least say that it was important to emperors to be perceived to have a concern for the interests and welfare of children, from infancy onwards, and their parents. Beyond visual evidence, and the perceptions fostered by it, Roman law gives an important place to children[95] and helps us expand our understanding of how children were perceived. Our major source for Roman law is late: the *Digest* is a compilation and editing of earlier law, carried out in the sixth century under Justinian. It does, however, cite many earlier jurists and emperors, enabling us to form some picture of legal activity and preoccupations at different periods. Intense interest in Augustus and his period has led modern scholars to reconstruct Augustus' social legislation in some detail. Children had an important place in the marital legislation of 18 BCE and 9 CE, as the means by which parents could win political and financial rewards. The focus was on adults (the parents) and their interests rather than on children themselves, although children were thereby represented as a social good to be encouraged. The *lex Aelia Sentia* of 4 CE did cater more directly for children's interests in that it opened up ways for slave children to be manumitted at ages younger than the legal norm (see Chapter 6 below).

The most important jurist of the first two centuries CE was Gaius, whose work belongs to around the middle of the second century. His textbook, the *Institutes*, sets out classifications of status and rules of property and procedure. Children figure frequently here in contexts of *patria potestas*, emancipation, guardianship, and inheritance. In the early third century, the great Roman jurists then working organized and interpreted the large body of legislation and judgments which had by then accumulated, especially from the second century. In the *Digest* children are represented as having rights and obligations; age differentiations are noted; children's bonds with their mother's family are increasingly recognized, replacing in practice the former priority given to the agnate (paternal) line; they are vulnerable in many ways, especially in the context of parental mortality rates which left them needing financial and other forms of protection and nurture.

[95] See e.g. Gardner (1998).

Many children lost one or both parents before puberty (Parkin 1992; Saller 1994). The law recognized a non-adult child as an orphan (*pupillus/-a*) if a father died: a surviving mother might have ongoing responsibilities, but she could not exercise the legal rights and powers of a *paterfamilias*. She was obliged to see to it that the child had a guardian (*tutor*) to administer the child's property and oversee its interests until puberty. Thus, in this context, a child was perceived as its father's child, and, in the absence of a father, in need of the care of another adult male. This did not preclude a mother's role in the choice of a *tutor* before or after her husband's death. The law applied, in theory, to all citizen children, but was not likely to be invoked for children with few financial or educational interests. Nevertheless, the image of children needing an adult male 'protector' no doubt influenced family relationships at all levels and affected the choice of whom mother or child turned to for support. The concept of an immature child's vulnerability was enunciated early, by Seruius (Sulpicius Rufus) in the middle of the first century BCE: 'Guardianship (*tutela*) is for the purpose of protecting a person who because of his age cannot defend himself in his own right.'[96]

Although the original aim of guardianship was to protect property, the child's interests came to be perceived more broadly. By the early third century the *tutor* could be represented as the protector of a child's character (*mores*) as well as of property (*res*): D. 26. 7. 12. 3 (Paul). This obliged the guardian to undertake a range of duties, such as paying a decent salary to the child's teachers, appropriate to the size of the estate and the child's family standing: the *tutor* will, in the first place, 'decide on the wages of the teachers, not the lowest he can, but those in accordance with the resources of the inheritance and in accordance with the rank of the family; he will provide maintenance for the slaves and freedmen, sometimes even for those outside the household if this will be advantageous to the *pupillus*, and he will send the customary gifts to parents and relatives'.[97] When a praetor had to make a

[96] D. 26. 1. 1, Paul, citing Seruius: 'ad tuendum eum, qui propter aetatem sua sponte se defendere nequit'.

[97] D. 26. 7. 12. 3, Paul, translation edited by Alan Watson (1985): '(tutor) inprimis mercedes praeceptoribus, non quas minimas poterit, sed pro facultate patrimonii, pro dignitate natalium constituet, alimenta seruis libertisque, nonnumquam etiam exteris, si hoc pupillo expediet, praestabit, solemnia munera

decision on where children should be reared or reside, he normally took into account a broad range of criteria: the child's character, station in life, and the period of guardianship.[98]

The image of the *tutor* as a surrogate father is found in literature and in law. Pliny the Younger lost his father young, and paid tribute to the 'fatherly commitment' which his *tutor* Verginius Rufus gave him.[99] In the early third century the jurist Callistratus saw the *pupillus* as having a right to the same care (*diligentia*) from a *tutor* as a *paterfamilias* would exercise over his own affairs (*D.* 26. 7. 33 pr.). He cited a ruling by Marcus Aurelius which shows Marcus' interest in the transition of responsibilities from *tutor* to *curator* (the trustee of a post-pubertal boy to the age of 25). Marcus' concern for the interests of orphans and other children is reflected in various sources.[100] In 178 a new measure (the *senatus consultum Orfitianum*) made it possible for children to have priority of succession to an intestate mother's estate, even though formally she belonged to a family different from theirs. In a different, non-legal context, Marcus showed his concern for the welfare of children: during the entertainment at his triumph in 166, a boy tightrope-dancer (a *funambulus*) fell, prompting Marcus to order the equivalent of a safety-net to be provided, a

parentibus cognatisque mittet'. The term *parentes* here cannot include the father, who is dead—unless funereal and commemorative offerings are envisaged; it signifies mother, grandparents, and further ascendants in paternal and maternal lines (*D.* 50. 16. 51, Gaius; and see Wilkinson 1964 for further extensions of usage).

[98] *D.* 27. 2. 1. 1, Ulpian: 'solet ex persona, ex condicione et ex tempore statuere'.

[99] *Letters* 2. 1. 8: 'ille mihi tutor relictus adfectum parentis exhibuit'. The relationship continued into Pliny's adulthood, with Verginius helping to induct and support Pliny in many aspects of public life. Cf. Pliny's comment (*Letters* 8. 14. 6) about the ancient tradition of boys being inducted into public life by a father, 'or, if a father were lacking, by the most important and long-standing male connection'.

[100] SHA, *Marcus* 9. 7–12. 6, summarizes much of Marcus' legislation and administrative activity. This included new arrangements for the *alimenta* and a requirement for registration of freeborn children at birth in Rome and in the provinces. Stanton (1969) agreed that more than half of the 324 law-texts by and about Marcus Aurelius had a bearing on women, children, and slaves; but he believed that Marcus delegated much of the legal activity to others and argued that his legislation was similar to that of his 2nd-c. predecessors.

reform which became established practice.[101] Some commentators are sceptical about the individual contribution which emperors could make to legislation and judicial decisions, but a close study of texts relating to the second century (Williams 1976) presented persuasive arguments for 'the active interest of the reigning emperor'. We have seen Marcus' personal role in decision-making, even when distant from Rome (the affair of Herodes Atticus), and jurists after his time attributed a special quality to his legal knowledge, justice, and humanity.[102] The area of his interest which related especially to children was that of guardianship for under-age orphans. He established a special office, that of *praetor tutelaris*, to oversee the interests of *pupilli* more carefully (SHA, *Marcus* 10. 11).

In the law, then, children are represented as requiring the affection and care of a parent or a parent-substitute (and, for some purposes, only a male will do in that role). They are also represented as having a variety of interests which must be protected: financial, emotional, educational, and an interest in maintaining a certain social standing.

Even slave children who are non-adult (*impuberes*) are represented as having legitimate interests which the law should protect, such as the promise, in a will, of freedom and an inheritance. The appointed heir (*institutus*) may wish not to take up the inheritance, but already before the time of Hadrian a senatorial decree could oblige him to, so as not to frustrate the young slave's hopes and expectations. Hadrian extended the scope of this ruling (*D.* 26. 5. 13, Papinian). The slave's interests here are in status and property. There is no mention of the wider range of interests acknowledged for free children, but emancipation and money would make many opportunities available to the ex-slave, including the possibility of freeing other members of his natural family (e.g. parents, siblings) and, later, of

---

[101] SHA, *Marcus* 12. 12. The *culcitae* provided were bags of soft stuffing, sometimes used as mattresses.

[102] e.g. Papinian (*D.* 31. 67. 10) described him as 'prouidentissimus et iuris religiosissimus'; and when the emperor Gordian made a humane ruling to protect the testamentary manumission of a slave it was noted that that had been the view of Marcus, 'consultissimus princeps' (*C.* 7. 2. 6).

contracting a Roman marriage and producing freeborn children of his own.[103]

The age of puberty was obviously crucial for the perception of a child's (comparative) autonomy: before this he was represented as requiring protection and help of various kinds. He was not, however, represented as completely helpless or useless before that age. After the age of 5 a slave could have a monetary value set on his services in an assessment of his master's estate (*D*. 7. 7. 6. 1, Ulpian). Persons below the age of 5, or infirm, or otherwise unable to provide services, are all exempt from the *aestimatio*.[104] Ulpian goes on to speak of slaves as possible objects of a master's affection or pleasure, but no monetary value was to be set on this.

Other age distinctions within childhood were perceived by the law. A *possessor* of property who was *infans* (and one who was insane) could not be held liable for damage (*D*. 6. 1. 60, Pomponius). Children below the age of puberty could not be prosecuted for forgery (*falsum*) because below that age they were perceived as not capable of criminality or criminal intent (*dolus malus*: *D*. 48. 10. 22 pr., Paul). But it was Julian's view that a child was liable to charges of theft if he was 'doli capax' (*D*. 47. 2. 23, Ulpian).[105] Again, *infantes* were expressly excluded. No one below the age of puberty could be tortured, according to a ruling by Antoninus Pius, except in a case of treason (*maiestas*: *D*. 48. 18. 10, Ulpian). (The age of puberty was defined at 14 years by the late jurist Arcadius Charisius.) An infant who caused the death of anyone could not be held responsible under the law on murder (*lex Cornelia de sicariis et ueneficiis*) because he was seen to be incapable of homicidal intent ('innocentia consilii', *D*. 48. 8. 12, Modestinus).

Children past infancy were thus perceived as responsible for some of their actions, e.g. theft, vandalism (Thomas 1975). But probably no rigid age of liability was imposed. As early as Labeo

---

[103] Only in exceptional circumstances would a slave under 30 who was freed by will become a Roman citizen immediately. But from Latin status he had opportunities to achieve full citizenship. See Weaver (1990: 278).

[104] Cf. *D*. 7. 1. 12. 3, Ulpian, in a discussion of usufruct, where potential value is posited for slaves who are at present unproductive, including an *infans*, whose services can have no monetary value set on them.

[105] 'Capable of guile'. The principle and terminology of 'incapax doli' still exist in most Western law systems.

(under Augustus) it was implicit that a child's capacity to appreciate wrongdoing should be taken into account: thus physical and intellectual capacity were taken into consideration. There was flexibility in assessing this on an individual basis. There is some suggestion that earlier law might have accepted 'mental wickedness' at a younger age than did more developed classical law (Thomas 1975: 26). In late antiquity, the transition from *infantia* to the ability to speak and comprehend was represented more specifically as happening at the end of the seventh year (Knothe 1982). The age of 7 had already been perceived as a milestone in intellectual development;[106] but the more rigid imposition of age categories, with assumed qualities, is a feature of late antiquity.

The concept of *pietas*, so strong in Roman culture, involved 'reciprocal affection and obligations shared by family members' (Saller 1991). The law code represented children as deserving—indeed, having a right to—parents' care and a share of their property as well as having obligations to respect and care for their parents and, if children died young, to have their property (if they owned any) go to parents. Thus the concept of an 'undutiful will' (*inofficiosum testamentum*) could work both ways: 'Children's inheritance is not due to parents on grounds of parents' wishes and their natural affection towards their children; but, when the natural order of mortality is disturbed, *pietas* demands that an estate should be left to parents just as much as to children' (*D.* 5. 2. 15 pr., Papinian). As Saller has shown (1991: 149), parental *pietas* toward children is as frequent in the *Digest* as is filial *pietas*. This is part of nature rather than 'a creation of civil law'. It was recognized even where natural children had been emancipated and for slave families.

The familial context in which children were perceived is reflected in the law's attitude to *spurii*—'illegitimate' children in that they were not born of a marriage recognized by the state, but not having the negative moral associations which have attached to illegitimacy for much of European history. The key issue is the lack of a *paterfamilias*. *Spurii* are represented not only in the law code but in inscriptions and occasionally in literature. (See

---

[106] e.g. Quintilian 1. 1. 15. Cf. Seneca, *On Benefits* 7. 1. 5, where one of the observable phenomena which are hard to explain is 'why every seventh year makes its imprint on one's life' ('aetati signum imprimat').

Chapter 6 below.) They are represented as giving and receiving the normal, or expected, qualities of family affection and obligation. But their primary point of reference is the natural mother: they do not belong, in the fullest sense, to a family, as they are 'not subject to the web of rights and responsibilities involved in *patria potestas*' (B. Rawson 1989).

In the second and third centuries, children continued to be represented as members of families, especially as sons and daughters or surrogate forms of these relationships. The dedications in epitaphs were largely focused on these relationships (Saller and Shaw 1984). When private funerary monuments for children, such as altars and urns, carried sculpted images, the space was usually devoted to the image of an individual child, but the dedication was, more often than not, from a parent. Newer forms of memorial, such as the *kline* (a kind of funerary couch, usually in marble) and the sarcophagus, provided greater scope for groups or for narrative. This must have been part of their attraction, with several sides and a lid available. The increasing use of inhumation rather than cremation in Italy from the early second century CE is too early to be due to Christian influence. Indeed, some sarcophagi seem to have been receptacles for ash urns, retaining the practice of cremation but making use of a new medium for visual display. There are often children in the scenes of these reliefs, commemorating either the brief life of a prematurely dead child or childhood stages in the life of an adult. Regular features in these stages are birth, play, and education. Death might be represented by a funeral scene or a form of apotheosis. The birth scene often contained considerable detail, representing mother, infant, midwife, and sometimes other female attendants. A birth scene had been an important part of the mythology and iconography of Dionysus' birth, but Greek representations of it seem to have been strikingly different from Roman ones, especially in that it was the miraculous birth from father Zeus' thigh which was the focus, not a natural birth from mother Semele (who, in most versions of the myth, had been killed by lightning before being able to deliver her child). Moreover, the attendants present when Dionysus leaps forth are, in pride of place, Hermes ready with formal clothes, and behind him three female figures who may be Nymphs or Moirai (or the single figure of Eileithyia, a goddess who facilitated childbirth). There is an example of this version on a classical (fifth-century BCE) bowl, and at least one Roman copy of this version is known (on a marble relief), from the period of Hadrian.[107] On other reliefs, however, and on sarcophagi the Romans favoured their own version of the newborn Dionysus. In this version the mother-figure takes pride of place, receiving the infant from one of the female attendants.[108] In the mythological context, two men are present (a Silenus and a Satyr), but representations of human births usually include only females.[109] Occasionally the actual birth is shown (see Chapter 2 below), but more commonly it is the midwife's handing-over of the infant to the mother, or the first bath, which announces the new arrival. Although stories of the births of gods were common in Greek and Roman mythology (Loeb 1979), the Roman use of such scenes now in human contexts reflects a popular interest in the first stages of infancy and recognition of this phase in people's own lives. Turcan (1966: 430) identifies the spirit of the times as having a 'familial tonality', a very Roman taste for domestic scenes: 'cette tonalité, ce goût—d'ailleurs très romain—de la scène d'intérieur'.

Representations of groups on sarcophagi are often lively, full of movement and interaction. They often embody close observation of the development and personalities of children. Scenes of children (boys and girls) playing games—with nuts, dice, hoops—were popular. One of the earliest sarcophagi for a child, which dates from Trajan's reign,[110] includes scenes of a child riding in a carriage with his parents, learning to walk, playing with a pet goose, and finally taking another carriage ride which symbolizes the end of his life and some form of apotheosis. Such series of scenes are, at one level, a metaphor for the child's life cycle, but they also reflect real-life activities. Huskinson has collected 320 examples of sarcophagi from Roman Italy which by their size can be defined as children's. She classifies the scenes on them into ten

---

[107] Bowl: *LIMC* 667. Relief: *LIMC* 668; Helbig⁴ I 91 (Vatican).

[108] A relief dating probably to Marcus Aurelius' reign: Turcan (1966: pl. 14); Helbig⁴ (I no. 350).

[109] A partial exception is the father-figure who is depicted gazing at the newborn infant in its mother's lap on the sarcophagus of M. Cornelius Statius (Fig. 2.2).

[110] Helbig⁴ (III no. 2394); Huskinson (1996: 1. 29, pl. 1.3).

categories,[111] but warns that such categories can be 'too rigid to make the most of the multi-layered imagery' of this funerary art (1996: 7). Scenes of education or reading more often featured boys than girls. The theme of the precocious orator continued, but on sarcophagi he is more often in a group of boys. These boys are sometimes in the guise of Muses, such as the nine figures accompanying the central boy (presumably the deceased) who sits enthroned like a philosopher (Fig. 1.17).[112] On the lid, the boy reclines, this time in a tunic but again holding texts from which to read. His pet dog leaps towards him.

Although this sarcophagus was found in a late third-century catacomb from Rome, there are no signs on it to associate it with Christianity. It may have been bought 'off the shelf' without regard to its decoration, or because its decoration was not inappropriate to a Christian.[113] Scenes of education are amongst the few scenes of everyday life which continued from earlier sarcophagi onto those of Christians. Christians preferred biblical scenes, but learning and teaching were important elements in the practice and promotion of Christianity. Zanker discussed this continuity of imagery under the heading of 'Christ as the teacher of the true philosophy' (1995: 289–97). From the late third century the dominant visual image of Christ in catacomb paintings and on sarcophagi was as the teacher of wisdom. Epitaphs, too, continued the praise of child prodigies for their precocious learning: a father Dalmatius, for instance, commemorated his 7-year-old son (also Dalmatius) for his complete *ingeniositas* and *sapientia* (*ICUR* 1978 = *CIL* 6. 33929). The further details of the boy's study of Greek and Latin literature are reminiscent of earlier non-Christian epitaphs. Only the date of death, and the reference to his being snatched away from human affairs ('ereptus est rebus humanis'), indicate his Christian connection. Even the naming of the father here is more typical of non-Christian than Christian children's memorials. Christian children and

[111] The categories are: Everyday Life, Mythological Subjects (excluding Dionysiac), Dionysiac Themes, Marine Themes, The Muses, Cupids, Cupid and Psyche, Season Sarcophagi, Decorative Schemes and Subjects, Christian Sarcophagi.

[112] Huskinson (1996: 5. 5, pl. 10.2; and ch. 5, 'The Muses').

[113] Or it may have been an earlier sarcophagus re-used by a Christian. I am grateful to Janet Huskinson for discussing these matters with me.

FIG. 1.17 Sarcophagus of boy with symbols of learning, such as philosopher's garb, Muses, scroll. Rome, c.280 CE.

adults were all brothers and sisters with only one father, God; hence their earthly, biological family relationships, like details of their daily life, were less important for recording.[114]

Girls on Christian memorials are less often represented with these qualities. In Christian iconography, the female *orans* (standing figure with hands outstretched or clasped high in prayer) is frequent, and such figures are sometimes accompanied by a scroll; but this represents religious piety rather than scholarly achievement. One small sarcophagus from a fourth-century catacomb in Rome, however, has on its front a bust portrait of a girl (not an *orans*) clasping a scroll (Fig. 1.18).[115] Other figures on the sarcophagus include Cupid and Psyche and the Good Shepherd. Another, for a girl (Optata) of about 3 years of age, shows an *orans* figure with a box at her feet which might hold scrolls. Her epitaph praises her for sweetness of speech as well as of gesture.[116] A rare glimpse of a scholarly profession for girls—or at least training in literacy and calligraphy—comes from a story about the third-century Christian writer Origen (Eusebius, *Ecclesiastical History* 6. 23). He had considerable resources put at his disposal in Caesarea in Judaea for taking dictation and copying his commentaries on the Scriptures. These included 'girls trained for beautiful writing'. Haines-Eitzen (2000) has shown how references to these female calligraphers has been suppressed or trivialized in ancient and modern sources: they have been ignored or represented as lowly and low-skilled workers. Commentators have assumed a gender hierarchy or a hierarchy of training and skills which shaped their images of the team used by Origen for his work. Female scribes and secretaries, however, had long been known in the Roman world. Treggiari (1976) has discussed women's epitaphs commemorating their titles of *a manu* or *libraria* (see Chapter 5 below), and one of the best known, the ex-slave Caenis, held a position of trust and responsibility on the staff of Antonia the Younger. As we saw above, there can be dissonance between representations in some genres and lived lives recorded in other genres.

[114] For more detailed discussion, see B. Rawson (2003), on which this section is based.

[115] Huskinson (1996: 10. 8); *RS* 381.

[116] Huskinson (1996: 10. 13): HIC OPTATA SITA EST QVAM | TIRTIA RAPVIT AESTAS. | LINGVA MANV NVMQVAM | DVLCIOR VLLA FVIT. | IN PACE.

FIG. 1.18 Sarcophagus of a girl with scroll; Cupid and Psyche, Good Shepherd, to right. Christian. Rome, early fourth century CE.

Portrait images on the sides of sarcophagi became popular
from the middle of the second century. An early example (from
the latter half of Hadrian's reign) portrayed a boy of about 10
years of age.[117] His bust is surrounded by Erotes and griffins—
symbolism particularly associated with children's memorials at
this time. Griffins were the guardians of the underworld, the
guides of souls (*psychopompes*), and the accompaniment of Erotes
and torches suggested some form of apotheosis. The 'Isis curl'
behind the right ear also suggested apotheosis, perhaps associated
with initiation into the cult of Isis. More explicit apotheosis language is that of the final carriage ride, as we saw above.[118]
Apotheosis symbolism, in epitaphs and art, is associated particularly with children (but sometimes with women), and in Chapter
8 below there is discussion of possible implications of this for
changing views of death and the fate of prematurely dead
children.

Many of the representations of children in art and epigraphy
are related to their deaths. As we have seen, child mortality rates
were very high, especially in the years from infancy to about 5, but
the frequency of such deaths did not dull sensitivity to the individual experience (see Chapter 8 below). Roman literature (with
a few exceptions), however, had little to say about children's
deaths, and indeed children are seldom portrayed in any guise.
The many genres of Roman literature have other preoccupations.
Like any artefact, literature must be assessed according to its purpose, who produced it, who was the purchaser, patron, recipient,
or audience.

Romans' familiarity with children in the family circle and with
their daily activities enabled some Roman writers to use them as
symbols and similes. These passages do reflect close observation
of infants and children in Roman society, and a sentimental
pleasure in their behaviour; but, for the most part, they are not
concerned with individual children in their own right but with
children as generalized symbols. Lucretius and Catullus are the
two Republican poets who have the most eloquent images of
children of this kind. Most literature of the Republican period
was public rather than personal, with history the preferred genre.

---

[117] Getty Museum: Eberle (1990); B. Rawson (1997a: fig. 9.14).
[118] Cf. B. Rawson (1997a: 229–30 and fig. 9.13) for other examples.

Cicero's extensive writings reveal a concern on the part of himself, his wife, and his brother's family for the education and material welfare of their children, but this is largely for their adolescent and adult children. Cicero pays little attention to the birth of his grandchildren, both of whom died at or soon after birth.[119] Cicero did share the pleasure of his friend Atticus in the birth of Atticus' daughter, quite late in Atticus' life, and followed the child's development with interest. His references to Attica are playful and affectionate, and he names cheerfulness as the best quality in little children: 'Please give Attica a kiss from me for being such a merry little thing (*hilarula*). It is what one likes to see in children.'[120]

For Lucretius, in the first half of the first century BCE, in his tirade against the fear of death and the supposed deprivations to be suffered after death, a prime symbol of what men fear most to lose is the joy of children and a loving wife. They are the emblem of all that makes life worth living (*praemia uitae*), so he tells men that they fear that, after death, 'No longer, now, will your home greet you with joy, nor will your best of wives or sweet children run to snatch your first kisses, nor will they move your heart with unspoken pleasure.' But, adds Lucretius, nor will there be any more longing (*desiderium*) for such things (*On the Nature of Things* (*De rerum natura*) 3. 894–901).

Catullus' wedding-hymn (poem 61) also enshrines the family group. The poem greets the bride and then the bridegroom and leads up to a wish for the fulfilment of their marriage in the birth of children. The procession accompanying the bride to the groom's house includes girls (*integrae uirgines*), who are also to expect marriage in their future lives. Marriage makes possible

---

[119] Both were the progeny of Tullia's marriage with P. Cornelius Dolabella. The second, born in 46 BCE, brought about the death of Cicero's much loved daughter, which must have added to Cicero's indifference or hostility to the grandson who did not long survive his mother.

[120] *Att.* 16. 11. 8; 44 BCE, when Attica was about 7 years old; translated by Shackleton Bailey. On an earlier letter, *Att.* 6. 1. 22 (50 BCE), Shackleton Bailey dismisses as 'persiflage' Cicero's game of pretending that a less-than-1-year-old was giving her father serious instructions about sending her greetings to Cicero; but it is a game familiar to most of us, establishing affectionate communication with a small child. Cicero's references to Attica run from 51 to 44 BCE: see Index Nominum of Shackleton Bailey's *Correspondence with Atticus* under 'Caecilia Attica'.

legitimate children, who are the satisfaction and support of their
parents (lines 61–9) and the protection of their country (71–4).
Boys in the procession include a pubescent lover (*concubinus*) of
the groom who must now be set aside: he is wretched ('miser o
miser | concubine') at the looming loss of his privileges and the
need to turn to more orthodox pleasures. The scattering of nuts
provides a game for the boys and the symbolism of fecundity. The
poem leads up to the wish for children, to continue the venera-
ble family line—a son who will look like his father, proving his
father's paternity and his mother's honour. The cameo of the
babe-in-arms is an attractive family scene, but the infant's tenta-
tive smile is directed to the father: 'My wish is for a little
Torquatus, stretching out his baby hands from his mother's lap,
to turn a sweet smile on his father, his tiny lips half open' (212–16).

   Images of children playing games come to hand as vivid similes. Vergil conveys the frenzied flight of a suicidal woman with
the image of a spinning top (*turbo*) which boys lash on through
the empty *atrium* of their house: as the top spins in ever-
widening circles they are full of amazed fascination at the effect
of their game (*Aeneid* 7. 378–83). Seneca compares the undisci-
plined excesses of some adult men with the undiscriminating
make-believe of children playing games (*On Firmness* (*De
constantia*) 12. 1–2):

Children are greedy for knuckle-bones or nuts, and for small change;
men for gold and silver, and for cities. Children play amongst themselves at holding magistracies, with pretend robes of state and lictors'
rods, and official platform; men play the same games in earnest in the
Campus Martius and the Forum and the senate-house. Children on the
beach use sand castles to raise up imitation houses; men, as if engaged
in some great enterprise, concentrate on piling up stones and walls and
roofs, thus creating a hazard out of what was meant as a protection for
the body.

These are scenes conceived from life.

   Quintilian's large work on education gives considerable space
to early childhood, recognizing its importance in the formation
of the older child. He represents young children as needing to be
coaxed with games into learning, as enjoying stories being told to
them, and as eager to learn if the right incentives are in place. He
knew small children at first hand, as a father, and wrote in mov-

ing detail about the death of his two young sons (see Chapters 6 and 8 below).

Children in any society are recognized to be less than fully formed—mentally and emotionally, as well as physically. Law codes represent them in their early years as incapable of distinguishing right from wrong, or of knowingly inflicting harm on others. This can be represented negatively as a kind of stupidity or positively as innocence. The passage from Seneca quoted above is introduced by negative comments about the defects (*mala*) of childhood, which is characterized as changeable, uncertain, undiscriminating in its appetite for pleasures, and timorous. We are familiar today with the concept of 'innocent children', a phrase often used to focus condemnation on those doing some kind of harm to society at large. There is little evidence of Romans' use of *innocens* or similar epithets for children:[121] *innocentia* is the virtue of blamelessness or integrity which adults might achieve by effort and discipline. Pliny the Younger comes closest to this concept when he characterizes childhood as open and uncomplicated: the best qualities of each age are *simplicitas* in childhood, *comitas* for men in their prime, and with advancing years *grauitas* (*Letters* 6. 26).

Pliny's letters, like Cicero's, show an interest in his friends' families, but young children get little attention. He looks forward to children being born from marriages of friends' sons and daughters, but primarily to continue a name and to bring distinction from a future public career. When he congratulates a friend on a prospective son-in-law (*Letters* 6. 26) his wish is that the grandchildren be as like their father as possible. There is a glimpse, however, of the vicarious joys of grandfatherhood for the childless Pliny, and an interest in a small child for its own sake, when he ends his letter with: 'What a happy day it will be for me when I can take his children, your grandchildren, from your arms as if they were my own children or grandchildren and hold them with equal right.' One girl gets an eloquent testimonial (*Letters* 5. 16), but she is on the brink of womanhood (not quite 13,[122] and

---

[121] But see below, Ch. 8, for the Greek-language epitaph of 2-year-old Eutychos who 'knew neither good nor evil' in his short life. See Sigismund Nielsen (2001: 170–3) for more frequent use in epitaphs of Christian children.

[122] Pliny says 'not yet fourteen', but an epitaph (*CIL* 6. 16631) registers her age as 12 years, eleven months, and seven days. The epitaph also gives the girl's name.

engaged to be married). Pliny does not even give her name, although he clearly knew her well: she is simply 'the younger daughter of Fundanus'. She was Minicia Marcella, daughter of Minicius Fundanus, one of Pliny's fellow-senators. She died after what seems to have been a long illness, during which she was strong-minded, quietly resigned, and considerate of others, according to Pliny's account. Pliny characterizes her as a lively and affectionate child before this illness. Like Cicero, he appreciated cheerfulness in a child ('nihil umquam festiuius'), and he represents other virtues of childhood, for a girl, as sweetness (*suauitas puellaris*) and modesty (*uirginalis uerecundia*). Her image, perhaps idealized by Pliny, is also of a seriousness and maturity beyond her years, which may well have been the result of a long illness.[123] She showed uninhibited affection for her father and his friends, and respect for her nurses, attendants, and teachers. She studied conscientiously and with intelligence (and we saw, above, that studiousness was not rare in girls at various levels of society). She was not uninhibited in her games: her restraint and moderation here again suggest an ailing child. The image is perceptive and affectionately drawn. Yet Pliny's summary of what the father had lost, and what explains his grief, is that the daughter was 'a replica no less of his character than of his appearance, a wonderful likeness of her father in every way'. No more could have been said of a son of that age, although hopes for the future, and for a public life, would have been different.

Letters to friends—whether or not they were intended for publication—are more likely to represent and report daily life than are other genres of literature. Seneca's letters were really philosophical essays to a young man, and some of the correspondence of Marcus Aurelius and Fronto is like that, but other letters between this pair contain the most personal and intimate images of children in Latin literature. They may be brief, but they convey a real and continuing concern for their own and each other's children—so many of whom suffered ill health and early death. Fronto was a senator and one of Marcus' tutors, and their correspondence extended over most of Marcus' adult life. From the birth of Marcus' first child, a daughter in 147, they were exchang-

---

[123] 'She already had the wisdom of an old woman and the authority of a matron': 'iam illi anilis prudentia, matronalis grauitas erat'.

ing reports on their children's health and daily activities. Marcus wrote to Fronto that the infant ('our little Faustina') had had diarrhoea and fever, but there were signs of recovery, although she was very emaciated and still had a bit of a cough.[124] This child died in 151, by which time another daughter had been born, and Fronto's letters send greetings to later daughters as 'our little ladies'.[125] After Marcus became emperor, he had heavy duties, but he snatched time to write brief letters on personal matters, such as:

I have just received your letter, which I shall enjoy as soon as possible. At the moment I have inexorable demands on my time. In the meantime, my dear master, here is what you want to know—briefly, as I am busy: our little girl is in better health and is running around the bedroom   (H 2. 8, N 230).

Marcus showed concern too for Fronto's health and that of his family. 'I wish you continual good health for many years, and much joy in the well-being of your daughter, grandchildren, and son-in-law' (H 2. 32, N 94). In this letter Marcus also plays the game seen in Cicero's letters, of passing on earnest good wishes from his young children: 'The occupants of our little nest, each according to his capacity, offers prayers for you.'

There is much more of this kind, over many years, exchanging comments on illness and health, birthdays, pet birds, grandchildren. Death is ever-present, and Fronto, in spite of his philosophical training, rails against the injustice of the premature death of children. We shall return to this below (Chapter 8). Here, we note that for Fronto children are a source of joy and love. One puzzling comment, in another context (*Letters to L. Verus*, H 2. 154, N 133), is that Romans lack real warmth of affection: the Greek term *philostorgia* has no Latin equivalent, he says. What provoked this comment in this particular letter cannot be known, but it is in the context of adults. It may reflect class

[124] *Letters* 4. 7 = H 1. 202, N 72. Fronto's response to this revealed that relationships with children, for all the affection which they might inspire, were of a quite different depth from those with close, adult friends. Some ambiguity in the beginning of Marcus' letter made Fronto think at first that it was Marcus who was ill, which dismayed Fronto, who was then relieved to find that it was 'only' the infant daughter.

[125] *Letters* 5. 42 = H 1. 244, N 88: 'matronas nostras meo nomine exosculare'.

sensitivity;[126] or it may refer to the self-discipline preached by upper-class men in their philosophical discussions. Marcus himself counselled such control in his *Meditations*. He presents the illness and loss of children as one of the sufferings which reason should help men endure with composure (1. 8); and the 'power of positive thinking' should help men rephrase their prayers from 'How may I avoid losing my child?' to 'How may I avoid dreading to lose my child?' In the letters, however, children, and their parents interacting with them, are represented as overflowing with warm affection—to a cloying degree, according to some tastes. A recent study of representations of childhood death in various modern genres has discussed the ways in which Ralph Waldo Emerson, the nineteenth-century poet and philosopher, presented his grief at the death of his 5-year-old son. In the journals and letters written at the time of the boy's death, the death 'was not met with "manly" stoicism or faithful resignation; his father could "comprehend nothing of this fact but its bitterness" '; but in a later poem the loss was commemorated more formally, as the loss of a future great poet. 'The immediacy of the journal entries is gone, . . . The father's powerful sense of desolation is subsumed in the poem, and the dead child offered as a signifier of collective poetic loss' (Avery and Reynolds 2000: 4–5). The importance of genre and temporal context can hardly be more clear.

Life-cycle reliefs on funerary monuments, especially sarcophagi, often give an important place to phases of childhood, as we saw above. One might have looked to literary biography to portray something of this stage of life. Modern, post-Freud biographies often recognize the significance of childhood in their story (E. Erickson's *The Young Luther* was an early example of this). Ancient biography, however, had other preoccupations. It usually accepted that character was fixed at birth: there might be

---

[126] Fronto addressed the adult Marcus as *philostorgos*: H 2. 19, N 230, but he saw Marcus as an exceptional man and their relationship was particularly close. Marcus refers to this view of Fronto's in *Meditations* 1. 11 as applying to aristocrats (*eupatridai*), a category into which Fronto himself did not fit. It might be significant that Fronto concedes this quality in a close friend, Gauius Clarus, who is explicitly of lower rank (and age) than Fronto: 'senator aetate et loco minor maiorem gradu atque natu senatorem probe colit' (*To L. Verus* H 2. 150, N 133).

various influences on it during its development, but it was always essentially the same and would ultimately reveal itself in full adulthood. So it was the mature adult which was the object of study. Tacitus' portrayal of the Julio-Claudian emperors illustrates this. Quintilian's work, however, did accept the role of education and other influences in changing character; but, as we shall see below (Chapter 5), Quintilian was more flexible and more thoughtful about such matters than some of his contemporaries.

Pelling (1990) has canvassed some of these problems in his discussion of Greek biography. He points out that Hellenistic encomium, invective, and the biographical novel showed an interest in their subject's childhood, but Greek political biography (Plutarch) eschewed this except sometimes for the subject's education.[127] As he says (1990: 231), 'For all his stress on education and character development, Plutarch's own presentation of the childhood of particular heroes is often extraordinarily banal.' The lack of complexity of his characters does help the exemplary nature of Plutarch's biographies. Latin biography, too, aims to teach a lesson, illustrate a moral, just as briefer tales of heroes and villains served this purpose in Roman education. K. R. Bradley argued perceptively that the main theme of the imperial biographies written by Suetonius is 'the image and the reality of the Roman emperorship' (1991b: 3729). There is an ideal standard of imperial conduct against which individual behaviour and performance are implicitly judged. If, then, these biographies are about emperorship rather than emperors, the focus will understandably be on the mature man and his office, rather than on early experience.

Most of the images and perspectives discussed above come from the centre, from Rome. We shall see below that the capital city became a magnet for the rest of Italy (and, to some extent, the rest of the empire) and that many aspects of Roman and Italian culture interacted. Nevertheless, regional differences remained. The nature of some of the media available to us from Roman Italy, especially literature and law, precludes a reflection of such differences: they belong very much to the centre. Inscriptions may record individual details from all over Italy, but

---

[127] 'Education' tends to be moral education, carried out by parents at home, rather than formal or technical education carried out by professional teachers.

they do so within a set form.[128] For children, their inscriptions are usually epitaphs, and although the sentiment behind these may be genuine and heartfelt it is not expressed in forms that vary regionally. There are sculpted images of children from most parts of Italy. Of the approximately 500 images of children which I have collected from Roman Italy,[129] about eighty are from out-side Rome and Ostia. It is difficult to identify any characteristics which differentiate regional Italy from Rome-Ostia. There are fewer handsome memorials and fewer with inscriptions, which might indicate a lower level of prosperity and artistic skill avail-able in regional towns. The poorer state of preservation might indicate fewer resources available to regional sites and collections for their maintenance. One example, from Capua, is a funerary stele of the Florius family, dating probably to the first century CE (Fig. 1.19). Made of travertine, its images and inscription are quite worn. Four persons are represented in a niche: the three adults are ex-slaves and the child is still a slave. The dedicator of the mon-ument, Q. Florius Q. l. Liccaeus, is second from the left, sharing the marital gesture of linked hands (*dextrarum iunctio*) with Titia C. l. Dorcha, who is on the left of the stele. Between the couple and the man on the right is a girl, Fausta, described as a *delicium*, 'little darling', a term often used of favourite child slaves (see Chapter 6 below). The man on the right, Q. Florius Q. l. Faustus, shares the dedicator's *nomen* and seems to be his fellow-freedman; and his *cognomen* is the same as the child's, but rela-tionships cannot be further identified.[130]

---

[128] See Gallivan and Wilkins (1997) for a project attempting to differentiate the kinds of family relationships commemorated in various parts of Italy. See K. R. Bradley (2000) for the kind of regional picture of the Mediterranean to be found in Apuleius.

[129] The digitized images and catalogue notes have been entered on a CD which I have used for my own research and made available to a few colleagues as work-in-progress; but unresolved problems of copyright have so far prevented my giving it wider circulation. It is a collaborative work with Edyth Binkowski and Michael Greenhalgh.

[130] He could be the child's older brother or her father; or the similarity of personal name (a common one for slaves) is fortuitous. The grouping and poses of the figures put the child closer to the couple than to the other man. The threesome to the right of the woman is identified more by the bonds of slavery in the one household than by biological bonds; Titia Dorcha is present as a wife, freed by a different master whose relationship with the Florius household is

FIG. 1.19 Funerary stele of Florius family (three adults and child). Capua, first century CE.

unknown. *CIL* 10. 4370; Eckert (1988: no. 17, pl. 17). The frieze of animals at the bottom may reflect the agricultural character of Capua and its environs.

Pliny the Younger expressed the malleability of representations when he sent to his friends Vestricius Spurinna and Cottia a draft of his proposed memoir of their dead son. He invited 'additions, alterations, or omissions'. 'If a sculptor or painter were working on a portrait of your son, you would indicate to him what features to bring out or correct; and so you must give me guidance and direction as I, too, am trying to create a likeness which shall not be short-lived and ephemeral, but one you think will last forever. It is more likely to be long-lived the more I can attain to truth and beauty and accuracy in detail.'[131] The interest in observing the detail of individual children, either as author/artist/ legislator or as reader/listener/viewer/carer, made children potent signs and symbols which could be used to shape private emotions or exploited in the advertisement of national qualities, public policy, and the promotion of imperial dynasties. This chapter has been concerned not so much with the question 'What was it really like for children?' as with the diversity of ways in which children were perceived and represented—by a variety of people and a variety of sources. In the following chapters we will be more concerned with trying to reconstruct children's life courses and their experiences as they progressed through life as children. Throughout, however, we shall have to bear in mind these questions of the commissioning agent, authorial intention, and reader reception.

[131] *Letters* 3. 10, trans. Betty Radice (Penguin). This passage is quoted by Leach (1990) in a wide-ranging discussion of literary and visual representations and, in particular, Pliny's self-presentation.

PART II

The Life Course

Welcoming a New Child

PROCREATION of children was the explicit aim of Roman marriage (Gellius 4. 3. 2, 1. 6; Treggiari 1991: 3–13). This was a wife's
prime duty and her husband's prime expectation of her. We have
no direct evidence about what a woman expected of marriage, but
the public expectation must have strongly coloured her private
expectation. This did not, however, exclude sentiment. A proper
marriage had to involve partners' intention to regard each other as
husband and wife, not as fleeting partners in a merely sexual or
reproductive exercise.[1] Even when partners were not eligible for a
formal Roman marriage (*matrimonium*) they borrowed much of
the language and symbolism of that institution; and family bonds,
affection, and expectations are often attested for what might be
called *de facto* unions (B. Rawson 1966, 1974). The first divorce
recorded on grounds of the wife's alleged sterility[2] dates from
*c.*230 BCE, but at least by the early Empire there was difference
of opinion as to whether desire for children should outweigh
conjugal devotion.[3] Already during Augustus' Principate an elaborate inscription recorded a husband's refusal to accept his
wife's earlier offer of a divorce to enable him to remarry to have
children.[4]

Women married young (by our standards): probably in their
late teens for most people but somewhat younger (early to mid-
teens) in the upper classes (Parkin 1992: 123–4). Their husbands

---

[1] *Maritalis affectio* is the phrase used by the jurist Ulpian in *D.* 24. 1. 32. 13,
and although it cannot be translated as marital 'affection' it does involve some
feelings about marriage beyond sex and procreation—the intention to enter an
enduring relationship with many shared activities. In a non-legal text Quintilian
uses the phrase *mens matrimonii* (5. 11. 32) for the same complex of expectations.

[2] That initiated by Spurius Caruilius Ruga: Gellius 4. 3. 1–2.

[3] Valerius Maximus 2. 1. 4, written under Tiberius. Valerius places the origin of this difference of opinion earlier.

[4] The so-called *Laudatio Turiae* 2. 31–40: *CIL* 6. 1527.

were generally about ten years older (Shaw 1987; Saller 1987). But fecundity was low for very young women, and children did not usually come until the late teens and beyond. Pregnancies before the mid-teens are more risky for mother and child than later pregnancies. Miscarriages and infant mortality resulted in the loss of some children before serious account was taken of them. Soranus, in the second century, argued against very early inter-course, in the interests of women and future children (1. 33). Cicero's daughter Tullia married young but it was only in her third marriage, aged about 30, that she produced her first child, which was premature and did not survive. The second child, born nearly four years later, was a weak infant who died within a month, not long after his mother's death in childbirth.[5] When Quintilian's wife died at the age of 18 she had borne two sons, one of whom then died at the age of 5 and the other not long after. Quintilian's report of this (6 pr. 4–16) is a moving account of his tribulations through this succession of events. Pliny and his wife Calpurnia are a well-known example of childlessness: we know of it because of Pliny's expressions of concern and his report of her miscarriage. He attributes the miscarriage to Calpurnia's youth and inexperience (*Letters* 8. 10). Eventually, still childless, he accepted the honorary rights of three children (*ius trium liberorum*) from the emperor Trajan (*Letters* 10. 2).

In Augustus' legislation on marriage and inheritance (*lex Iulia de maritandis ordinibus* and *lex Papia Poppaea*), the ages at which citizens were expected to be parents in order to have full inheritance rights were 20–50 for women and 25–60 for men, which must reflect a realistic expectation of the age span of child-bearing and rearing. The legislation took account of infant mortality by an elaborate calculation of how many children sur-

---

[5] The first child, a seven-month weakling (*perimbecillus*) boy, was born in May 49 BCE (Cicero, *Att.* 10. 18. 1). Cicero was grateful that Tullia had come through the birth safely and does not mention the death of the child, which we have to infer from contextual evidence. The second son, born in January 45, is dignified with a name (Lentulus), but Cicero shows little interest in the infant which had caused his own daughter's death (Cicero, *Att.* 12. 28 and 30). Tullia's husband, P. Cornelius Dolabella, was out of Rome at the time of each of the births, fighting on Caesar's side in the civil war, first in the Adriatic and then in Spain; and by the time of the second birth Dolabella and Tullia were divorced. On deaths of mothers and children, see Ch. 8 below.

viving to what age could count for eligibility for inheritance.[6] It has been calculated that, to maintain population levels, a woman would need to give birth to an average of five or six live children during her child-bearing years. This average allows considerable variety of family sizes within it. Fertility could extend over several decades: Soranus (1. 34) thought that women's period of fertility extended from age 15 to 40. Some notable examples of high fertility and high mortality were Cornelia, Agrippina the Elder, and Faustina the Younger and their children (Parkin 1992: 94).

Multiple births might multiply the achievement and joy of parenthood, as when twins were born to Tiberius' son Drusus and Livilla in the year 19 CE. There were dynastic overtones in that event, as the twins gave double hope of extending the imperial succession by another generation. We saw above (Chapter 1) Tiberius' celebration of the event and Drusus' coin representing the twins as symbols of fertility and prosperity. Ordinary families, too, would hold similar hopes at a more modest level. For them, multiple births provided two or more prospective heirs to continue the family name, to care for aged parents, and eventually to bury them and see to their commemoration and continued memory. Such hopes were all too often dashed, sometimes at birth or soon after. Elite and non-elite shared such experiences. One of Livilla's and Drusus' twins died in 23, as did Drusus himself (aged about 36). (The other died, through non-natural causes, at the instigation of the emperor Gaius, in 37 or 38, i.e. in his late teens.) At the other end of the social scale, a slave woman in the period of Augustus bore quintuplets at Laurentum, but they survived only a few days and the mother died soon after delivery. Augustus gave instructions for a monument to be erected beside the road to Laurentum, the Via Laurentina, recording the number of children born (Gellius 10. 2).[7] He was

---

[6] e.g. three infants who survived to their naming day (eight or nine days) or one to puberty counted for inheritance rights. Cf. Ulpian, *Reg*. 15, where a spouse can inherit an additional tenth of the other's estate for each child of the couple who had died since the naming day; and *Reg*. 16 for further elaboration on child-bearing which allowed a spouse to inherit the whole property. See Astolfi (1970: 174) and Introduction above on *ius liberorum*.

[7] In the mid-1st c. Pliny the Elder wrote (*NH* 7. 33–5) that multiple births beyond triplets were considered portentous. As an example he gives the

willing to incorporate into his social ideology (promotion of the family) as wide a range of material as he could find. This is consistent with his bower-bird approach to reading both Greek and Latin literature. He kept the equivalent of a card-file system, noting down examples which could be used later for whatever purpose came to hand. 'He particularly sought out precepts and examples which were for the good of the public or private individuals and he often used to copy these word for word and send them to members of his household or those in charge of armies or provinces or city magistrates according to their needs for guidance' (Suetonius, *Augustus* 89. 2).

The importance and dangers of child-bearing are reflected in the considerable attention given in medical and technical literature to pregnancy, childbirth, and early childhood. There was a well-developed body of medical knowledge at Rome by the late Republic.[8] There had long been discussion of the roles of male and female parent in the conception and characteristics of a child born to them. By the time of Galen, in the late second century, the existence of an effective female contribution had been confirmed, although there were still discussions of the relative strength and dominance of male and female 'seed' (Blayney 1986; Bestor 1991).

Early in the second century, Soranus wrote an extensive work entitled *Gynaikeia* (*Gynaecology*), which gave considerable attention to pregnancy, childbirth, and care of the infant. Much of the 'theory' and almost all of the practice of gynaecology and obstetrics, however, were in the hands of female midwives. Soranus set a high standard for them, but one must wonder how widely such a standard was met. Superstition, magic, and religion continued to play a large part in general thinking about health. Soranus himself explicitly required freedom from superstition in a midwife (1. 4). Early in the third century the jurist Ulpian excluded from the definition of a *medicus* anyone who used incantations, imprecations, or exorcisms although there were people, he conceded,

birth of quadruplets (two males and two females) to a lower-class woman, Fausta, at Ostia on the day of Augustus' funeral: this was seen, after the event, as portending the food shortage which followed.

[8] See below, Ch. 3. See now Flemming (2000) on many aspects of childbirth, medicine, and midwives.

who claimed to have benefited from these (*D*. 50. 13. 1. 3).[9] The evidence available on pregnancy and childbirth reveals little of the taboos and segregation attested in many other pre-industrial societies—beliefs and practices which anthropologists see as antagonism and tensions between the sexes (e.g. Paige 1981: 30–1, 212).

The law took an interest in the outcome of pregnancies in various ways besides the inclusion of new citizen children in the census and, later, birth registrations and declarations. If a woman died while pregnant, her burial was forbidden until the foetus had been removed from her body, to ensure that no potentially live offspring was buried (accidentally or criminally) with her (*D*. 11. 8. 2, Marcellus, citing a law going back to the regal period, i.e. before the late sixth century BCE). This confirms other evidence that Caesarean section deliveries were known from an early date (but perhaps not from live women), although the procedure does not appear in medical texts until the fourteenth century, and the association with the birth of Julius Caesar is doubtful (Blumenfeld-Kosinski 1990: 24, 145–53). The concern of the law was probably as much protection of a potential heir as protection of life. Ulpian recognized that a child 'taken from the womb by means of a surgical operation' was a proper heir (*D*. 28. 2. 12 pr.). The law also recognized the prospective inheritance rights of a child in the womb by providing explicitly for posthumous children.[10]

The birth will have taken place at home (usually the marital home, but in the case of the widow below she was not to be trusted in her own house and had to move to a properly supervised house). Soranus is our best source for details of the actual

---

[9] See Pliny the Elder, *NH* 28. 59, for an example of sorcery (sitting near a pregnant woman with fingers interlaced, especially round a knee), corroborated by Ovid's account of Alcmena's birth of Hercules (*Metamorphoses* 9. 281–315). Cf. McDaniel (1948) on comparable superstitions and use of amulets and charms in 20th-c. Italy. Sered (1994) discusses the persistence of older folk-religious practices in modern Jewish society, where pregnant women might, for psychological reasons, observe rituals and wear amulets which in earlier times were thought to win divine assistance and ward off misfortune. She also discusses the importance of kin-related women in pre-modern society as psychological support for pregnant women.

[10] e.g. *D*. 28. 2. 4, Ulpian; 10, Pomponius; 29. 11–15, Scaeuola on the *lex (Iunia) Velleia* of the year 26. Cf. Gaius, *Institutes* 2. 132–4.

birthing.[11] He has detailed prescriptions for the size of the birthing room, the people who should be present, necessary equipment, and postnatal care (e.g. 2. 70). Some of this is confirmed by legal texts, such as the Praetorian Edict (*D*. 25. 3–4) in which are set down rules for supervision of a widow's labour. For a widow or divorced woman there could be legal dispute about the status of the child to be born. Thus the Praetorian Edict made the following stipulation:

The woman must give birth in the house of a woman of excellent reputation who will be appointed by me. Thirty days before she believes that she is due for delivery the pregnant woman must notify the interested parties, inviting them, if they wish, to send persons to witness her pregnancy. The room in which the birth is to take place must have no more than one entry; if there are more they must be boarded up, inside and out. At the entrance to this room, three men and three women of free status must keep watch with a pair of companions. Whenever the woman enters that room or any other, or goes to the bath, those keeping watch may, if they wish, inspect that place first and search those who enter it. Those on watch at the entry of the delivery room may also, if they wish, search all who enter that room or the house. When the woman goes into labour, she must notify the interested parties, or their representatives, to send persons to witness the birth. Women of free status, up to the number of five, should be sent, so that in addition to two midwives there are not more than ten free women in the delivery room and no more than six slave women.[12] Those women who are going to be present in the room should all be searched to ensure that none is pregnant. There should be no fewer than three lights in the room (obviously because darkness is suitable for substituting a child).[13] The newborn infant must be shown to interested parties, or their representatives, if they wish to inspect it. (*D*. 25. 4. 1. 10, Ulpian)

Although in the widow's case some of the witnesses present might have been hostile or suspicious, the group of those present would normally provide a supportive atmosphere. There are references in literature to the presence of the woman's mother or

---

[11] His work and influence survived for many centuries, into the 16th c. (Temkin 1956 p. xxv). He wrote on a wide range of medical topics, of which gynaecology was only one.

[12] Soranus specifies three women helpers in addition to the midwife. The maximum in the Praetor's Edict would be invoked only in suspicious cases where a legal challenge was possible.

[13] The parenthesis is Ulpian's, to explain this part of the Edict.

aunt. But specific relatives would not always be still alive, and a woman was probably glad of whatever family and friends were available. This initial network of those with a specially intimate relationship with the newborn child consisted of women. We hear of a mother who had been present at the difficult delivery of her daughter's baby and who was in charge of getting wet-nurses immediately afterwards (Gellius 12. 1. 1–5). There is another story of a father hurrying to get a midwife for his daughter who was in labour (Seneca, *Letters* 117. 30), but those present at the actual birth were almost always women. A male doctor might be brought in if there were complications. There are two reliefs known which seem to represent male doctors assisting, or being ready to assist, the midwife,[14] and a passage in Galen suggests that a doctor (at some remove, perhaps in the next room) might get a running commentary from the midwife and offer advice. The midwife is clearly in charge of the birthing process and instructs the parturient; but she answers the doctor's questions from time to time, for instance about the extent of the dilation of the orifice of the uterus (Galen, *On the Natural Faculties* 3. 3). There were obviously conventions of female modesty which normally applied.[15] Even the female midwife had to be aware of these: 'The midwife should beware of fixing her gaze steadfastly on the genitals of the labouring woman, lest being ashamed, her body become contracted' (Soranus 2. 70).

The methods and physical setting of childbirth are portrayed in a few very specific monuments. On a relief over the entrance to a tomb at Isola Sacra, near Ostia, a midwife is shown at work and commemorated in an inscription.[16] The midwife sits on a low stool in front of the parturient, who sits, naked, on a higher chair with solid arm-rests which seem to have gripping-handles built into them. We know from other sources that there was a

[14] French (1986: pl. III): a marble relief from a private collection which shows two men with medical implements behind the parturient. Cf. the ivory relief from Pompeii in her pl. II. Hanson (1994) discusses male participation further. There is evidence of female doctors: Treggiari (1976); list in Flemming (2000).

[15] Cf. Sered (1994) on reasons of modesty or masculinity which keep some Jewish husbands (ultra-orthodox or from more eastern cultures) aloof from the pregnancy and the birthing process.

[16] 2nd c.: Kampen (1981*b*: 69–72); Thylander (1952: A 222). The inscription is set up by a woman for her mother Scribonia Callityche (who seems to be the midwife) and for her own husband, who may be the doctor represented on the relief.

crescent-shaped opening in the seat of the chair, through which the midwife would pull the baby. Behind the parturient is a female assistant whose arms support the upper body of the woman giving birth. One might be surprised that there are any representations on public monuments of the act of childbirth, which was a personal, intimate, and often painful experience for the woman giving birth (even if it was not an entirely private occasion). The monuments do not, however, record the parturient mother so much as the midwife at her profession. The Isola Sacra relief is of terracotta and of rough workmanship and commemorates a working woman, the midwife, not an upper-class mother.[17] The first moments after birth, such as the first bath, are often recorded on life-cycle monuments. Fig. 2.1 depicts a mother and attendants soon after the birth. The mother, now clothed, watches while a nurse sees to the bath.[18]

FIG. 2.1 Sarcophagus of adult male: first bath of infant, with nurse and mother. Rome, late Antonine.

[17] Cf. Demand (1994: ch. 7) for Greek evidence.
[18] Amedick (1991: cat. 64, pl. 62.1): one end of an adult male's sarcophagus. Cf. Ch. 1 above for birth scenes of Dionysus.

If the birth was irregular, such as a breech birth ('feet first', the Romans said), it was considered a bad omen. When Nero turned out badly, people remembered that he had been born this way. His great-grandfather Agrippa survived such a birth reasonably well (Pliny the Elder, *NH* 7. 45–6; Gellius 16. 16. 1–4). We know nothing of how Nero's mother fared, giving birth in this way. One finds it difficult to envisage Agrippina the Younger being slowed up much by Nero's birth. At 22 she was vigorously active in the public life of the new emperor, her brother Gaius—so much so that he found cause to exile her for plotting against him two years later.

Loss of mother or child or both in childbirth was not infrequent, and this would make the occasion a tragedy rather than a celebration. The death in 54 BCE of Julia, daughter of Julius Caesar and wife of Pompey (followed soon after by that of the newborn infant), was a political as well as a personal disaster. When two sisters (daughters of Helvidius) died in childbirth at almost the same time early in the second century, Pliny grieved for them, their husbands, and the motherless infants (*Letters* 4. 21). He spoke of their brother as the last pillar of the house of Helvidius, obviously not considering newborn infants seriously in this category.[19] These children did survive, but many newborns did not. Infant mortality was much higher than that of mothers in childbirth. French's estimate (1986) that 5 mothers in 20,000 died in childbirth is surely too low,[20] but the figure is likely to have been much lower than the 5 per cent of all live-born babies

[19] The children of Helvidius' daughters would not automatically continue the name of Helvidius; but the maternal name could be incorporated in a child's name, and other grandchildren were considered valued posterity even through the maternal line. (See Salway 1994 on nomenclature.) Pliny emphasized this about the hoped-for children of his own wife Calpurnia: her grandfather was anxious for great-grandchildren to continue his line (*Letters* 8. 10). So it was essentially the young age of the children of the Helvidia sisters, and the adulthood of the women's brother, which influenced Pliny's outlook on this occasion. But the fact that they were female did further restrict their ability to transmit a *nomen*.

[20] Schofield (1986) acknowledges that maternal deaths in childbirth were much more numerous in the pre-modern era than today. (He quotes 10 per 1,000 in the period before 1750.) But he argues that child-bearing might have been 'a rather less mortal occasion than we may have been inclined to believe'. Today maternal mortality in childbirth is 0.1 per 1,000 in the developed world, but Schofield quotes 17 per 1,000 for Bangladesh.

who died in their first month. If we include foetal and in-childbirth deaths the infant mortality rate for the first month increases to about 8 per cent. Close to 30 per cent of babies died in their first year.[21] But only 1.3 per cent of epitaphs in Rome and Italy are for infants under 1 year of age (Garnsey 1991: 51–2). This under-representation must reflect a lack of confidence in their survival and an infant's lack of full identity. (See Chapter 8 below for further discussion.) Legal prescriptions for mourning periods indicate the mortality probabilities at different ages. If a baby died in its first year, no formal mourning was prescribed. Dixon (1988: 136 n. 3) gives examples from the eighteenth century of similar practice, e.g. 'court mourning was not observed for small children of the English royal family' and, more generally, parents would not necessarily attend the interment of a very young child. Romans did not consider full mourning appropriate for children under 10 years: between 3 and 10 the mourning period was grad-ually increased. The young child therefore did not qualify for full recognition of its existence and individuality until the age of 10. It is probable that the census of Roman citizens from 28 BCE onwards included men, women and children but not infants under the age of 1 year (Brunt 1971: 43). Cicero (*Tusculan Disputations* 1. 93) balances the formal prescriptions against sen-timent: 'Some think that if a small child dies this must be borne with equanimity; if it is still in its cradle there should not even be a lament. And yet it is from the latter that nature has more cruelly demanded back the gift she had given.'[22]

Midwives' responsibilities extended beyond the time of deliv-ery: they supervised those first fragile days following birth. Soranus is very aware of the delicacy of the newborn infant and recommends treatments for this and for the care of the new mother. Large, wealthy households probably had their own

[21] Hopkins (1983: 225); Parkin (1992: 92–4). Parkin gives an infant mortality figure (in the first year) for the modern developed world of less than 1%; for poorer countries 5 to higher than 20%. Jalland (1996: 5) shows the rapid improvement in such rates in England from 154/1,000 in the latter half of the 19th c. to 132 early in the 20th c., declining to 105 and then 100 in the early decades until it was 16/1,000 in 1983.

[22] In *Moralia* 612 A, consoling his wife for the death of their 2-year-old daughter, Plutarch presents a similar view of Greek law and practice. It is tra-ditional, he says, not to celebrate public funerary ritual for an infant; but this does not exclude private sentiments of grief.

midwives. Of the sixteen midwives attested in the inscriptions of Rome, nine are from *columbaria*, the collective burial chambers of dependants of the imperial family or of upper-class families.[23] Midwives had a certain professional standing. The jurist Ulpian included them with doctors in a list of persons to be recognized by governors of provinces as belonging to liberal professions, because 'they seem to practise a sort of medicine' (*D*. 50. 13. 1. 2). They were entrusted with the medical responsibility of establishing pregnancy and had heavy moral duties of honestly attesting what went on in the delivery room: there was, for example, severe penalty for smuggling in a supposititious baby (Paul, *Sententiae* 2. 24. 8–9).

The baby's father was involved soon after the birth. The father of Octavian (the future Augustus) was late for an important senate debate (on the Catilinarian crisis) in 63 BCE, and Suetonius (*Augustus* 94. 5) says that this was because of his wife's labour. The midwife would, immediately after the birth, have set the baby on the floor to inspect it and thus be able to offer advice on its physical condition and prospects. It was the parents, however, who decided whether or not the child should be reared. This decision would have to be made promptly; it did not involve any formal ceremony. The responsibility for the decision has traditionally been attributed to the *paterfamilias*,[24] but surely the mother was involved in the decision. There would have been times when the father was absent and the effective responsibility was left with the mother. There must have been prior assumptions, before birth, about these matters, and unless there were serious factors militating against it (such as extreme poverty, perhaps a husband's suspicions of adultery[25]) the expectation would be that the child would be reared. One envisages Octavius hovering outside the

---

[23] See French (1986: 72, 82 n. 28) for a list of inscriptions and discussion of midwives.

[24] Corbier (1999*c*) and Shaw (2001) have convincingly shown that the phrase *tollere liberum* ('to raise a child') did not denote any physical formal act of the father raising the child from the floor, carrying legal implications of recognizing the child as his own. The decision to rear was not necessarily an avowal of paternity, but it did entail an obligation to give the child proper maintenance.

[25] See Ch. 3 below, under 'Rejecting a New Child'. Even with suspicions of adultery, there are suggestions that husbands might recognize a child as their own because of the prestige and material benefits of fatherhood, e.g. in Juvenal's satires below. See Ch. 3 also for female infanticide.

delivery room (as many expectant fathers have done for centuries until recently), waiting to see the child and take it in his arms. In Fig. 2.2 a father is represented holding a newborn baby, immediately after a scene of mother and infant in a life-cycle series on a mid-second-century sarcophagus from Ostia.[26]

A father's friends seem to have gathered quickly, on news of the birth, to congratulate him. Nero was born at the family villa at Antium, down the coast from Rome, but there was soon a gathering of friends (Suetonius, *Nero* 6). We have already seen that this was an irregular birth, and doleful predictions and intra-family tensions made this something less than a completely joyous occasion. Often, however, the birth was the occasion for an impromptu party[27] (the more formal party for the naming day coming eight or nine days later). Our reports make such gatherings sound very masculine affairs: men friends gather, congratulations are offered to the father, and the men pontificate about the child's future and what arrangements—immediate and longer term—should be made for it. Pliny tells us how much in demand he was to attend family occasions of this kind.[28] But we should remember those women present in the delivery room: they might well have been having their own party, near the new mother, and offering practical advice and making practical arrangements. One report of a post-delivery gathering in the first half of the second century gives a role to a woman, the new mother's own mother (Gellius 12. 1. 1–5). News of the birth of a son to this distinguished senatorial family had reached some of the father's friends, including his rhetorical and philosophical professor Favorinus and fellow-students, so they ceased studies for the day and went off to the father's house 'to see the [newborn] boy and congratulate the father'. The father's mother-in-law took a forceful part in the discussions: in response to arguments about the virtues of

[26] Paris, Louvre MA 659, marble sarcophagus of M. Cornelius Statius. Cf. Amedick (1991: 140); *CIL* 14. 4875.

[27] Festus (144 L) lists occasions of celebration for Romans—occasions which can reduce the grieving for someone less closely related to the family: birth of children, higher rank to a member of the household, return home of a prisoner-of-war who is parent, child, husband or brother, and betrothal of a girl.

[28] *Letters* 1. 9. But the celebration of a birth is not included in this particular list, which mentions coming-of-age ceremonies, betrothals, weddings and witnessing a will—occasions involving older 'children'.

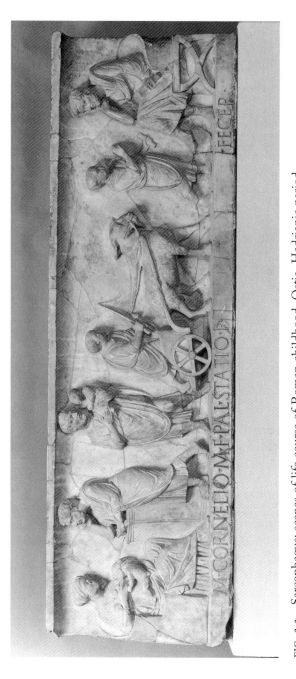

FIG. 2.2   Sarcophagus: scenes of life course of Roman childhood. Ostia, Hadrianic period.

breast-feeding over wet-nursing she declared that her very young daughter (*puella*) was far too exhausted by the birth to sustain breast-feeding, and she set about engaging wet-nurses immediately.

That a wife's delivery of a child was the occasion for celebration is clear from Seneca's inclusion of it in the events which are commonly thought to give joy, along with a friend's consulship and his marriage (*Letters* 59. 2). In philosophic mode, however, Seneca warns that these are not occasions for true joy (*gaudium*), which can be achieved only by the truly wise and which can never be changed into its opposite. The other events listed are often, he warns, the beginning of future unhappiness.

The political, social, and inheritance value of a child, especially a son, is clearest for the upper classes. Senatorial men probably had most to gain. The senator Pliny writes to his wife's grandfather (*Letters* 8. 10) that both men have equal hopes for children from Pliny and Calpurnia: both father and maternal grandfather can hand on reputations and well-established ancestry, which should make the road to office easy. These advantages applied to the imperial family to an even greater degree. The provision of an heir gave greater stability to any regime, offering hope for an undisputed succession, and strengthening the emperor's ability to capitalize on the ideologies which had been built up around family and children since at least the time of Augustus. Augustus used a wide range of media for this purpose, such as the Altar of Peace, the Secular Games and other festivals, and coinage. As we saw above (Chapter 1), Augustus had no son of his own, but he celebrated the birth and development of his daughter Julia's sons, Gaius and Lucius Caesar, whom he adopted as his own sons. Successive emperors used representations of children (their own or more generally) to underpin their reigns, tapping into the sentimental attachment to young children and their symbolism for the future. Faustina the Younger was the most prolific of imperial mothers, bearing at least fourteen children, only a few of whom survived to adulthood. Imperial publicity closely associated her with fecundity, especially in association or identification with Juno Lucina, Diana Lucifera, and Venus Genetrix.

A consistent element in celebrations for the arrival of a new child was the decking of the front door with laurel wreaths (Statius, *Siluae* 4. 8. 37–40; Juvenal 6. 78–80, 9. 85). Pliny the

Elder (*NH* 15. 127–38) provides information on the symbolism of laurel. It was sacred to Apollo, provided protection from lightning, and was used for purification. It celebrated victory and joy, hence was used in military triumphs and as house decoration to symbolize domestic happiness ('gratissima domibus'). Its use on the front door was a sign to the wider world of the good fortune of the family, and if the family had clients they would offer congratulations at the next *salutatio*. Juvenal (6. 78) describes long benches being set up by the proud father in the narrow streets outside his house. These may have been for notices and representations associated with the birth, but they were more likely for refreshments for passers-by and the less intimate acquaintances who were thus encouraged to join in the celebrations, creating a virtual street-party. It is a nice picture of the mixture of public and private in Roman life.[29]

Fires were lit on altars to give thanks to the gods for a birth. This happened in friends' homes (Statius, *Siluae* 4. 8. 37–40) and in the parents' home. Anniversaries of birthdays were celebrated, when there was similar ritual.[30] Birthday celebrations of an adult man focused on his *genius* (his vital spirit, life-spark), which is often represented (e.g. in serpent form) with the *Lares* above the family altar. A child's *genius* was not normally celebrated, but it must have come into being at birth. 'Our ancestors attributed to each of us a Genius and a Juno' (Seneca, *Letters* 110. 1). The concept of the *iuno*, the female counterpart of the *genius*, is attested from early imperial times. Whether the child's *genius* or the father's was being celebrated when fires were lit on altars at a new birth is not certain.

An array of divinities and spirits was associated with birth and the newborn child. The origin of much of the ritual and superstition is difficult to establish, but the general thrust seems to be propitiation of superhuman forces, protection of the infant at a time of great danger, and cleansing of pollution.[31] Juno Lucina and Diana Lucifera were goddesses whose role was to assist women in childbirth: their epithets suggest the bringing of the

---

[29] The fact that these Juvenal references are heavily satirical does not detract from their value as evidence of common forms of celebration.

[30] See Ch. 4 below.

[31] For more detail on the rituals below, see B. Rawson (1991*a*: 13–15) and, at much greater length, Köves-Zulauf (1990).

child into the light of day. Ovid gives a vivid impression of the
travail of childbirth and the superstition and superhuman forces
associated with it in *Metamorphoses* (9. 294), where Alcmena tells
of the birth of Hercules.[32] The Carmentes goddesses had individual names of Prorsa (sometimes Porrima) and Postverta,
reflecting the importance attached to having the baby properly
positioned for the birth.[33] From the time of childbirth, Cunina
was called on to watch over the cradle (*cunae*). After a safe birth,
a *lectisternium* (a couch and a meal for the gods) was arranged in
the *atrium*. The location of the *lectisternium* here, in the most
public part of the house, is appropriate as the focus for family and
friends in the first few days, for congratulations and consultations
of the kind which we have seen above.

Within eight days (for girls) or nine (for boys)[34] the infant was
thought to have reached a new stage of its existence. One indication of this was its ability to open its eyes and focus them and
perceive separate objects and persons. Juno watched over this
stage.[35] The end of this stage was associated with the end of the
period of greatest danger and pollution, and the ceremony to
mark this was the *lustratio*. On the eve of the *lustratio* a ceremony
was held, which included a vigil in the house to protect the
infant. The ritual associated with this eve is usually taken to symbolize driving off evil spirits. Three men approached the house,
two of them striking the threshold with axe and pestle and a third
sweeping it with a broom. Köves-Zulauf (1990), however, says
that the symbolism is that of stages of the care of the newborn:

[32] Other divinities noted by Marchi (1896–1903; 1975: 165–6) included the di
Nixi, Diespiter, Mater Matuta, and the Carmentes.
[33] Varro in Gellius, 16. 16. 4. Plutarch (*Romulus* 21) mentions the childbirth
association of the Carmentalia but also reports the tradition of Carmenta being
a goddess of prophecy. The latter interpretation is in Ovid (*Fasti* 1. 633–6) and
Servius (on *Aeneid* 8. 336).
[34] The difference presumably reflects the slightly better chances of survival
for female infants.
[35] L. and P. Brind'Amour (1971) read Persius 2 in the light of this. They
believe that at the *lustratio* the maternal aunt performed the role of Juno in
opening the child's eyes. She touched the brow and lips of the infant with a
finger moistened with saliva, to stimulate it to life (by opening the eyes and
inducing breathing). Ritual abstinence and purity were required of her. The
authors see her as a kind of godmother and make comparisons with Christian
baptism.

cutting the cord, determining its soundness, and cleansing. To what extent most families performed these ceremonies or thought about the symbolism is hard to say. Probably more conservative, upper-class families with long family traditions were more likely to do so. The placing of a *bulla* and other charms on a child's body to ward off evil spirits may have been more common. Various kinds of lockets and charms, worn by children and adults today, have similar superstitious or religious overtones. The *bulla* (a pendant containing an amulet) had particular significance, as a sign of free birth. It was placed around the child's neck and was worn until adulthood. For boys, this was until the ceremony of the *toga uirilis*, when the boy exchanged his bordered toga for the white toga of manhood. Evidence for girls wearing the *bulla* is sparse. If in fact only boys wore it, it had a significance beyond protection from evil spirits. The *bulla* was gold for those who could afford it; otherwise it was leather.[36]

The *lustratio* was the first of many stages along the child's path to an individual identity. On this day it was given a name (thus the *dies lustricus* or *dies nominis*). The convention was that the maternal uncle gave the child its name (for instance, the emperor Gaius, maliciously, to Nero: Suetonius, *Nero* 6). One assumes that any such person was an agent of the parents, who must have had firm ideas about their child's name. There was, however, an expected pattern to naming (see Salway 1994), which did not allow completely free scope to parents. Slave children belonged to their mother's owner, who might sometimes have exercised his or her right to name the child; but not infrequently a slave child's name reflects that of a parent, so parents seem to have had some say.

The Roman nomenclature system signalled a child's legal and social location: with father, or mother, or mother's owner. Within thirty days of the naming day a child's birth could be entered on an official register, from the time of Augustus (see Gardner 1986*b*: 144–6). Previously one awaited the five-yearly census (which was not always held regularly) to get new citizens and property registered. Several pieces of Augustus' legislation, such as the *lex Aelia*

---

[36] For illustrations, see Figs. 1.5, 1.9, and 1.12 above. Cf. Gabelmann (1985: 510–22), who accepts that the *bulla* was worn only by boys, arguing from the lack of any artistic evidence for it on girls and from the existence of a single literary reference, which is Plautus (*Rudens* 1171).

Sentia and the *lex Papia Poppaea*, required evidence of age and status. So he introduced a system of registering births of freeborn children of regular Roman marriages. Marcus Aurelius extended the registers to all freeborn Roman children, irrespective of the nature of the union which produced them, i.e. 'illegitimates' as well as legitimates (SHA, *Marcus* 9).

Official declarations of birth were made at the Temple of Saturn at Rome (the location of the Treasury). In the provinces they were made to the governor or his representative.[37] They were usually made by the father, but could be made by mother or grandfather (*D.* 22. 3. 16, Terentius Clemens). An official declaration (a *professio*) was kept in the public archives. Juvenal (9. 84) satirizes the husband who celebrates his manhood and access to financial privileges by registering his children in the public record ('in libris actorum'), even though these children are the fruits of his wife's adultery. Individuals could have private copies made for their own use. Some people who did not qualify for the official register recognized the potential importance of such a record and made a private declaration which they took care to have witnessed and recorded (a *testatio*).

Amongst the most numerous private records which have been discovered in the Roman world are the extracts which military veterans had made of their official discharge documents. Emperors legislated to give veterans certain benefits on discharge, such as Roman citizenship, recognition of marriage, citizenship for their children. The general terms were inscribed on official bronze tablets at Rome but individualized copies (bronze, or papyri, or waxed tablets) recording relevant specific details have been found at several sites around the Mediterranean. It is soldiers' 'marriages' (not recognized as such during their service) which account for some of the birth declarations which have been found, dating from 60 to 242 CE.[38] Soldiers' children, not being born of a regular Roman marriage, had no place on the official Roman birth register before Marcus Aurelius, but one parent or the other often took care to make a *testatio* which could be useful later to corroborate age or free birth (although the declarations

---

[37] Examples from the 3rd, 1st and 2nd c. respectively may be found in *FIRA*² 3 nos. 1–3.

[38] These have all come to light in the 20th c. See Lévy (1952) for details and bibliography.

had no absolute evidentiary value and the witnesses to the declaration would not normally have been present at the birth).

In Egypt in 127, a cavalryman M. Lucretius Clemens declared
in Greek the birth of a son Serenus by Octauia Tamusta. He
stated that he made the *testatio* because of the impediment (to
legitimate fatherhood) imposed by military service, 'propter dis-
trictionem mil(itarem)' (Bell 1937: 30–6). In 145 it was the mother,
Sempronia Gemella, who recorded twin sons M. Sempronius
Sarapio and M. Sempronius Socratio (*FIRA²* 3. 4). Not from
military circles but apparently from an ex-slave whose form of
manumission did not give him Roman marriage rights is a dossier
of tablets from Herculaneum, dated to 60 and 61, concerning
L. Venidius Ennychus. He declared the birth of a daughter by
Liuia Acte.[39] The child is not named, but she apparently survived
her first year because in a later document her first birthday is
presented as argument for her parents' being granted Roman
citizenship.

Those who attended a birth registration or declaration, like
those who had attended the *lustratio* and the birth and any other
associated activities, were potential or actual witnesses to the
child's existence. Relatives and friends of its parents, they formed
its first social network. This could have been extensive in families
of substance. It might have been less so in more modest families,
but 'the neighbourhood' often made up for the lack of powerful
relatives and friends.[40]

[39] Arangio-Ruiz (1974: 535–51). See Weaver (1997: 68–9) for further details of
this family.

[40] See Gardner (1986a) on the use of neighbours as proof of identity and
status. The discussion of *tatae* and *mammae* in K. R. Bradley (1991a: ch. 4)
recognizes that the physical living conditions of sub-elite families was conducive
to 'a collaborative style of child rearing' (p. 90). See Ch. 7 below on 'the
neighbourhood'.

3

Rearing

THERE were family situations where the prospect of a new child was not welcome. These would include poverty, other financial considerations, the pregnancy of an unmarried girl, adultery, and a wife's more general wish to limit her pregnancies (cf. B. Rawson 1986c: 11–12).

Contraceptive substances and methods were known.[1] The economy of Cyrene benefited from export of silphium, a plant used widely for its medicinal properties but especially for contraception. Substances were of varying efficacy and availability, and it is probable that educated, well-off women were better able to achieve contraception than were others. As Hopkins (1965) has shown, contraceptives were sometimes confused with abortifacients. Since, however, there were no intrinsic moral or philosophical principles against contraception or abortion or about the sanctity of the embryo, this confusion was of little consequence. Conscious abortion in later stages of pregnancy would have been more dangerous. If none of these methods succeeded, or if the newborn child proved unacceptable, infanticide and abandonment (usually referred to as 'exposure') could be resorted to.[2]

The Greek text which has come down to us as the Hippocratic Oath includes five promises, one of which is not to administer any deadly medicine or to provide a woman with an abortifacient. Yet the rest of the Hippocratic corpus discusses various methods of abortion in a neutral context, without indication that these are contrary to medical ethics. Soranus (1. 60, 65) advised abortion for very young wives who became pregnant, and he stated that doctors should assist requested abortions unless the pregnancy

---

[1] See Riddle (1992) for detailed discussion of substances, methods and medical writers.

[2] See Garnsey (1991); W. V. Harris (1994); and Corbier (2001).

was the result of adultery or solely a woman's wish to preserve her looks. This and other evidence make clear that medically assisted abortions were not uncommon in Greek or Roman society.[3] There seems not to have been strong public prejudice against abortion, except where a married woman resorted to it without her husband's knowledge or permission. Roman law did not make abortion, as such, a crime; but a wife could be prosecuted for depriving her husband of an heir if she underwent an abortion without his agreement (*D.* 47. 11. 4, Marcianus). This ruling is attributed to the early third century (the emperors Septimius Seuerus and Caracalla),[4] but Cicero had already expressed the same moral principle two and a half centuries earlier.[5]

The Hippocratic Oath therefore does not reflect any deep-seated societal view that abortion was wrong in principle. It reflects, as Murray (1991) argues, a doctor's need to assure the (male) head of household that he will not use his medical knowledge or his entry into the privacy of the household against the interests of the family, especially the interests of the *kyrios* or *paterfamilias*. There would have been situations where abortion was agreed by the family to be desirable or necessary, but it was not for a pregnant wife, with or without collusion by a doctor, to make such a decision. Riddle (1992: 15) concludes, from a variety of evidence (literary, skeletal, comparative), that 'classical peoples were somehow regulating their family sizes'. As Shaw (2001) has shown, the father's unfettered right to decide on life or death for his child at the time of birth is largely a social construct of the imperial period, not mirrored in formal law or actual practice. A

---

[3] The date of the Oath is uncertain, but is usually attributed to the 5th or, more probably, the 4th c. BCE. It seems to have been in continual use, although with modifications, ever since. See Murray (1991) for extensive discussion, to which I am indebted here. See also Hopkins (1965) for a range of ancient medical writings mentioning or describing methods of abortion. Some discussions of the Hippocratic text stress that the only abortifacient mentioned is a pessary.

[4] But Tryphonius (*D.* 48. 19. 39) attributes this ruling to a case where a woman procured an abortion after a divorce, so as not to bear a child to a man who was now her enemy.

[5] *In Defence of Cluentius* 32, concerning a woman of Miletus, whose self-abortion he condemned because 'she had robbed the father of his hopes, his name of continuity, the family of support, the house of an heir, and the state of a prospective citizen'.

husband might well, however, have put pressure on his wife, or decided with her, that a pregnancy should be terminated. The motives attributed to parents by the ancient literary sources vary: they include personal selfishness and financial greed, political fear and uncertainty, and female vanity (the last motive recognizing a possible independent role for women).[6]

Apart from direct human intervention, other factors militated against the birth and survival of infants. Miscarriages must have been frequent: Pliny's wife Calpurnia is a well-known example of one because of Pliny's letters to her aunt and grandfather about it (*Letters* 8. 10, 11). Natal and neo-natal mortality rates were high. Wealthy and aristocratic families were not immune, for example in the second century BCE Cornelia bore twelve children to her husband but only three survived into adulthood;[7] in the second century CE Faustina the Younger bore at least fourteen children to the emperor Marcus Aurelius but few survived.[8] Even when a pregnancy went full term and there was a live birth, the condition of the infant might be a reason not to rear it.[9] It was considered by some to be in neither the public interest nor that of the family to raise a badly deformed baby. Religious scruple probably reinforced fears for the child's health and for its contribution to society, so as to sanction leaving it to die or hastening its death. Cicero (*On the Laws* 3. 8. 19) cited the Twelve Tables as an early source for this, and Seneca (*On Anger* 1. 15) argued that it was rationality, not anger, which motivated such an act: it separated the sound (*sani*) from those who could make no contribution to society (*inutilia*). The language used by both Cicero and Seneca, however, indicates that they were discussing extraordinarily deformed babies: 'insignis ad deformitatem puer' (Cicero: 'a boy notably deformed') and 'si debiles monstrosique editi sunt' (Seneca: 'if they have been born weak and monstrous'). In the

---

[6] e.g. Seneca, *Consolation to Helvia* 16. 3; Pliny, *Letters* 4. 15. 3, *Panegyric* 22. 3; Juvenal 6. 594.

[7] The Gracchi brothers and a sister (Plutarch, *Tiberius Gracchus* 1).

[8] The one surviving son, Commodus, was the first natural son to succeed an emperor for nearly a century.

[9] See Williamson (1978) for an anthropological perspective on the almost universal occurrence of infanticide in human societies, and Wrightson (1982) for the history of infanticide in European history. Both agree that there has been a variety of motives, but that 'the welfare of the larger group' (Wrightson, p. 2) has usually been a consideration.

early third century jurists debated whether badly deformed or monstrous babies should count as children for the benefit of parents. They inclined to give the benefit of the doubt, so as not to deprive of the privileges of parenthood any parents who had produced a child in good faith. This did not necessarily imply a commitment to its rearing, but the law did differentiate between degrees of deformity and disability and implied that those infants not actually 'some kind of monster or prodigy' might be reared.[10] By the time of the *Sententiae* (probably fourth century) attributed to Paul, infanticide and abandonment were considered murder (*D.* 25. 3. 4).

Whether infanticide and abandonment were more frequent for girls than for boys is still debatable. Riddle (1992: 11–13) gives a summary of the literature and arguments, and concludes that the evidence for this form of discrimination against females is weak. He admits, however, that second-born or female children might sometimes have suffered some neglect in their upbringing, so 'sexually biased child care' might have acted against the survival chances of girls. As we shall see later, girls were valued in Roman society and there is no evidence of the serious dysfunctional effects on society which a major imbalance in sex ratios would create. We shall also see (Chapter 8 below) that practices of infanticide and abandonment are not inconsistent with high valuation of children, and even when high mortality rates were to be expected parents could grieve deeply for lost children.[11] Scott (2000) has recently queried some of the assumptions in discussions of infanticide and has suggested that the evidence for alleged bias against females and the disabled in infant deaths is weak. She argues that infanticide should be seen as one of several means of birth-control available in antiquity, against the view that 'societies in the past routinely disposed of particular types of infant because they manifested a biological commodity which we modern observers have arbitrarily decided is inherently "unvalued" or "unwanted" '.

[10] *D.* 1. 5. 14, Paul; 50. 16. 135, Ulpian. Cf. *D.* 28. 2. 12. 1, Ulpian, where a child born physically deformed (physically incomplete, 'non integrum') but 'cum spiritu' (thus a real, living being) is considered a proper heir.
[11] e.g. see Garnsey (1991) and Golden (1988). On 18th-c. France, McManners (1981: ch. 13 and n. 57) notes the evidence which suggests 'the desire to have fewer children, but to look after them better'.

Infants who were abandoned did not necessarily die. There were well-known locations for deposit of abandoned babies, e.g. a column in the *forum olitorium* (the vegetable markets beside the Tiber river in Rome),[12] the water tanks near aqueducts (Juvenal 6. 603), temples, crossroads, and rubbish-heaps, just as now church steps and orphanage front doors are favourite places. In late twentieth-century Italy concern about deaths of abandoned babies led to an advertising campaign to persuade mothers to choose a hospital or safe shelter for their babies rather than rubbish bins, and a Catholic organization has revived the medieval 'wheel of the innocents' to allow mothers to abandon their infants safely without being identified.[13] Those who rescued abandoned babies could raise them as slaves or free, but the Roman legal view was that a person's legal status at birth was not thereby changed and could be reclaimed later if adequate evidence could be produced. Roman law until the fourth century did not require repayment of the costs of rearing, as did the law of some Greek cities.[14] The plots of Hellenistic and Roman comedy often turn on the sudden and timely discovery of freeborn status (usually of a girl), often through amulets or other objects which had been attached to the abandoned infant, but the chances of this happening in real life must have been slim. Some cases are, however, recorded. One of the teachers in Suetonius' collection *De grammaticis*, M. Antonius Gnipho, a teacher of Julius Caesar, was reclaimed as freeborn by his mother after he had been raised as a slave and earned his freedom by manumission, but he rejected his mother and preferred to retain the freed status in which he had made good as a teacher and acquired a

---

[12] 'quod ibi infantes lacte alendos deferebant' (Festus 105 L): 'because they brought infants there to be suckled with milk'. This can be interpreted as a place for hiring a wet-nurse (Corbier 2001: 63).

[13] *Sunday Times*, Canberra, 5 July 1998.

[14] Pliny had difficulty with the different local rulings on this in the East: *Letters* 10. 65–6. In 331 Constantine conceded the right of those who rescued and raised abandoned children to keep them in the status in which they had been raised, e.g. as slaves, irrespective of any claims by those who originally abandoned them (*CTh.* 5. 9. 1). He had already (in 313) declared that parents who sold their children must pay to reclaim them (*Frag. Vat.* 34; cf. *CTh.* 4. 43. 2). He also declared that state help should be provided for parents who might be forced by poverty to kill or sell their children (*CTh.* 11. 27. 1, 2).

valuable network of patrons and friends.[15] Quintilian (7. 1. 14)
suggests that cases about exposed children, their status, and their
natal father's rights were frequent enough for students to learn to
exploit the emotional as well as the legal dimensions of such
cases. Seneca devoted one long example in his *Controuersiae* (9. 3)
to a debate between a foster-father and the natural father who
had abandoned two sons but then wanted to reclaim them. Less
fortunate were babies born to women in the imperial family who
were suspected of adultery. Augustus forbade the rearing of the
newborn infant of his granddaughter Julia,[16] and Claudius
ordered the abandonment of the child of his divorced wife
Urgulanilla even though the infant had already begun to be reared
(Suetonius, *Claudius* 27. 1).

The extent of involuntary childlessness should not be underestimated. Again, Pliny is the best-known example of a man who
desperately wanted children and failed in three marriages. There
were rituals and festivals which provided opportunities for childless women to seek fertility and for pregnant women to seek a
successful birth.[17] Artefacts from an early stage of Italian history
include votive offerings representing the part of the body for
which a cure is desired or has been obtained. Parts associated with
pregnancy and childbirth are a common element in these
votives.[18] Medical writings which deal with women and children
concentrate on pregnancy and very early childhood.

[15] *Gramm.* 7. Cf. C. Melissus, under Augustus (*Gramm.* 21).

[16] Suetonius, *Augustus* 65. Julia could have been in the *potestas* of Augustus
only if he had adopted her, as he did her two brothers Gaius and Lucius Caesar.
Her father Agrippa was long since dead when she was exiled in 8, and her husband L. Aemilius Paullus had almost certainly already fallen into disgrace after
a failed plot against Augustus (Suetonius, *Augustus* 19). Augustus may, of course,
have been acting simply as emperor and *de facto* head of the imperial family.

[17] In Propertius 4. 1. 101 a woman is delivered from labour by vows to Juno
Lucina. Juno Lucina and Diana Lucifera were the most important deities for
these purposes. Juno Lucina was the focus of the festival of the Matronalia on
1 Mar., an occasion when men gave gifts to their wives (D. 24. 1. 31. 8,
Pomponius on Sabinus). Her temple on the Esquiline dated from the early 4th
c. BCE (Dury-Moyaers and Renard (1981: 149–51); see also Ovid, *Fasti* 2. 425–52
and commentary by J. G. Frazer, ii. 383–9).

[18] Bonfante (1984, 1985); Turfa (1994).

MEDICINE AND NURSING

There was a long tradition of magical and religious elements in health-care in the ancient world. Herbal cures were popular. Medical 'science' which had developed in Greece was brought together in a variety of works known as the Hippocratic corpus, and these works were known at Rome and medical scholarship was added to by later physicians who practised at Rome. Medical practitioners at Rome were at first Greeks and usually slaves. They must have been itinerant rather than resident, as Julius Caesar felt it necessary in the 40s BCE to offer Roman citizenship to physicians who would establish themselves at Rome (Suetonius, *Julius Caesar* 42). Asclepiades of Prusa, who died around 40 BCE, was a medical writer who spent some time at Rome. Native-born Romans of high status showed an interest in medical matters, including those relating to children. Varro wrote about the diet of young children (Gellius 4. 19), and Celsus' wide-ranging treatise on medicine used children as examples under various topics.[19] Bertier (1996: esp. part V) points out that the medical writers pay attention to both psychological and physical needs of children.

Romans continued to attach importance to availability of health-care in the towns and cities of Italy and the empire, and physicians who were officially recognized had access to various privileges and exemptions. The reputation and social standing of physicians increased and in the second century they attracted large audiences at Rome as leading intellectuals of their day. Of greatest interest to us is Soranus (early second century): from the wide scope of his writings on medicine, what remains is largely the *Gynaecology*, which deals with pregnancy, midwifery, and care of infants. Writings from the Mediterranean world of the first two centuries CE show considerable interest in child care, e.g. Pliny the Elder, Plutarch, Tacitus, Rufus of Ephesus and Alexandria, Galen.[20] Rufus and Galen discuss methods of achieving pregnancy and a safe delivery.

Soranus' *Gynaecology* was probably aimed at a variety of readers, including doctors, educated laypersons, and midwives.[21]

[19] e.g. 2. 1. 18–20, 3. 7. 1b, 5. 28. 15d, 6. 11. 3–4.
[20] See the texts collected by Oribasius in his compilation of the 4th c.
[21] See Jackson (1988: 86–111).

Midwives were expected by Soranus to be literate, and their profession covered many aspects of women's and children's health. Although there must have been many levels of competence and professionalism in midwifery, including, at the lowest level, amateur back-street practitioners, Soranus (1. 3) envisaged formal training. Prerequisites for success were for the midwife to be 'literate, with her wits about her, possessed of a good memory, loving work, respectable and generally not unduly handicapped as regards her senses, sound of limb, robust, and, according to some people, endowed with long slim fingers and short nails at her fingertips'.[22] Soranus explains the need for each of these qualities. The best midwives would be 'trained in all branches of therapy (for some cases must be treated by diet, others by surgery, while still others must be cured by drugs)' (1. 4). As noted above, a century later the jurist Ulpian recorded that midwives had a certain professional standing, as being seen to practise medicine, and thus they were recognized by the governor of a province as belonging to the liberal professions (*D.* 50. 13. 1. 2).

Topics listed by Soranus (2. 9) under 'the care of the newborn' include: 'which of the offspring is worth rearing, how one should sever the navel cord and swaddle and cleanse the infant which is to be reared, in what manner one should bathe it, how one should bed it and what kind of a nurse one should select, and which milk is best and what one should do if it gives out, and when and how one should wean the newborn; teething, and the mishaps which at times befall them'. The judgement about the infant's prospects of successful rearing relied not only on observation of its own physical features but also on the history of the mother's pregnancy (2. 10). The midwife made the judgement and recommendation, but the decision was made by the parents (see Chapter 2 above). If the new child had no *paterfamilias* present, the decision on rearing must sometimes have had to be taken by the mother herself. If, however, the mother was a slave, then her child was born a slave and there was a master to make such decisions.

Swaddling was considered a way of keeping the infant's hands under control, thus protecting the delicate eye area (2. 15), but the feet appear to be free on some figurines. Swaddling was also intended to develop a strong, well-formed body (2. 42),

---

[22] Translation and commentary by Temkin (1956).

supplemented by massage and gentle manipulation (2. 32–4), with gradual release from the bonds during the second month of life. Swaddling is generally condemned today, but there might seem to be a parallel between the Romans' concern with physical perfection and other practices in modern societies, such as teeth-bracing for young teenagers, at an age when there is not only physical discomfort but also much more psychological sensitivity than in infancy.

Wet-nursing was frequent in Roman society, apparently at all levels. There had been a long tradition of wet-nursing in the Greek and Roman worlds. An early text from Italy gave advice on choosing a wet-nurse.[23] Soranus (2. 18) accepts that it is desirable for the mother to breast-feed her newborn infant. But he also accepts that this is likely to be an undue strain on the mother and might delay further child-bearing, so he gives attention to the choosing of a suitable wet-nurse. Indeed, he advises providing several wet-nurses, to give the infant a variety of milks, because one wet-nurse might become ill and die and the infant might suffer trauma in transferring to a different milk from one to which it had become accustomed (2. 20). The best wet-nurses, according to Soranus (2. 19), were aged between 20 and 40 ('in their prime'), had already given birth two or three times, were generally healthy, robust, sober and even-tempered, and practised good hygiene. There is a suggestion that a wet-nurse might be feeding more than one child at a time. The best time for hiring her was when she had had milk for two or three months, so she could already have suckled her own infant if it had survived birth and been retained by her; but such a child is likely to have had a lesser claim on its mother after she began wet-nursing the child of an owner or employer. Tributes to affection between fellow-nurslings (*conlactei*), however, suggest that the nurse could manage to juggle the physical and psychological demands of both obligations, engendering a sibling-type bond between the infants—a bond which endured, perhaps through continued raising together.[24]

It is clear from Soranus and other writers that the wet-nurse was expected to have some affectionate interaction with the

---

[23] 3rd–2nd c. BCE. Thesleff, *Pythagorean texts*, in Lefkowitz and Fant (1992: 187–8 no. 250).

[24] See K. R. Bradley (1991*a*: 149–55) on *collactanei*, and Ch. 6 below.

infant, and the preference for a Greek-speaking woman who would accustom the infant to 'the best speech' implies chatter and, a little later, story-telling. Wet-nurses might stay on as general nurses or nannies even after the child was weaned, and there are instances of long-lasting affectionate bonds between nurse and nursling.[25] Loyalty and affection were the expectations which slave owners had of the slave women who nursed their children, and these expectations are reflected in the literature. Literature and legal evidence give examples of grateful owners who rewarded nurses with freedom and material gifts: Pliny, for example, records his gift of a farm to his former nurse (*Letters* 6. 3). The nurse was one of those closely bonded to a person whose early manumission was approved by the *lex Aelia Sentia* (*D*. 40. 2. 13, Ulpian), and the law has examples of nurses as heirs of grateful nurslings (*D*. 33. 2. 34. 1, Scaeuola). Nurses in epitaphs receive dedications approximately as often as they dedicate to others. Joshel (1986) warns us that we know little of the nurses' emotions: loyalty may have been no more than self-interest or self-protection.[26] Nevertheless, if it was the nursling's perception that he or she was the focus of real affection and good care from a nurse, that would have been a more positive factor in development than neglect and cruelty.

In the upper classes, where women married earlier and the family could afford wet-nurses, it became rare for the mother to breast-feed her own child. Some male intellectuals might protest at this (e.g. Vipstanus Messalla in Tacitus' *Dialogue on Orators*), but that seems to have had little effect on the women. The protesters might not even have been representative of mainstream male thinking: Favorinus, for example, whose protests are reported in Gellius 12.1 (protests overridden by the new mother's own mother), was a rhetorician and philosopher from Gaul (Arelate) who spoke Greek and was said to be a hermaphrodite. He might have been respected for teaching young men the finer

---

[25] e.g. *CIL* 6. 16450, dedicated to his ex-slave nurse ('nutrici et mammul(ae)') by Ser. Cornelius Dolabella Metillianus, who seems from *CIL* 9. 3152–4 to have been a notable citizen of Corfinium in the early 2nd c.; and 10229. Joshel (1986: 20) says that only three epitaphs are dedicated by senatorial or equestrian nurslings. See K. R. Bradley (1986; 1991a: ch. 2) for nurses in Rome and nurses in Italy and the provinces.

[26] See further on nurses and their relationships in Ch. 6 below.

points of philosophy and oratory, but could he be expected to identify with the needs and emotions of members of a family with a new baby?

In large households slave mothers must often have been obliged to be productive workers, without distractions of breast-feeding, soon after the birth, and the household could provide other lactating slave women to take on nursing responsibilities. There is evidence of using country estates to rear newborn slave infants before returning them to the city household.[27] How the mass of other women and their infants fared is uncertain. An inscription on a sarcophagus from Rome, honouring the 24-year-old Graxia Alexandria for nursing her own children (*CIL* 6. 19128), might suggest that this was a fairly rare event. Her husband, an imperial freedman, praised her as a notable model of proper womanly virtue, 'insignis exempli ac pudicitiae'. Comparative evidence tells us that even quite poor women have used wet-nurses, largely because of their poverty and necessity to work outside the home, as in France until the 1920s (G. Sussman 1980: 224–52).

The use of a wet-nurse did not necessarily mean that the mother took no interest in her newborn child.[28] When her own mother was available she too might be involved in early care. We saw above a grandmother seeking out appropriate wet-nurses for an infant and arguing for the need of them (against the academic Favorinus). Persius (2. 31) mentions a grandmother and a maternal aunt, as does Propertius (2. 31–40), who shows them performing ritual at the infant's cradle. An epitaph (*CIL* 6. 20938) dedicated to the 2-year-old Iuuenalis was set up by the grandmother Canuleia Tyche and the nurse Erasena Libas. The epitaph is also for themselves and their families ('et sibi et suis'). This, with the nomenclature which is suggestive of slaves and

[27] This comes from a legal source (*D.* 32. 99. 3, Paulus) which is establishing definitions for urban and rural property and equipment. The case is raised of a child born to a slave woman in an urban household and then sent to a country estate for nursing. Does such a child belong to the urban or the rural house-hold? The best opinion is that it belongs to the urban. This implies that the early period of rearing, before weaning, is a temporary, transient stage and that the child will soon be returned to the urban household and perhaps even to its mother.

[28] Nor indeed the father. Note the sculpture of a father, holding a newborn infant, on the sarcophagus of M. Cornelius Statius in Fig. 2.2.

slave origin, makes it likely that the child was being raised in the
familia of a large household by surrogate parents. The trio of
nurse, mother, and grandmother is recognized by Ulpian (*D.* 26.
10. 1. 7) as having the best interests of a child (probably not an
infant) at heart (through *pietas*) after a father has died: they thus
merit a role in prosecuting an unworthy *tutor*, although women
would not normally have such a role.

Mothers must often have been left with much responsibility
for young children, with the early death or absence of a father.
The law said that a *tutor* must be appointed when a minor's father
died,[29] and it is clear that in the propertied classes such an
appointment often happened. But even then the mother was left
with much day-to-day responsibility, and in other classes the
mother would just have 'got on with it', calling on whatever
friends or family were available to help but essentially coping
alone. If a propertied father provided for an infant child by leaving the management of the estate to the mother, the child and
mother could benefit from that immediately: 'His wife (Seia) was
to receive the whole inheritance, and he passed on a trust to her
in these words: "I want you, Seia, to pass on all of this . . . to our
darling baby girl (Maeuia). Seia is not to be required to provide
sureties, as I know she will increase the estate rather than detract
from it" ' (*D.* 32. 1. 41. 14, Scaeuola).

ILLNESSES

Infant mortality was high, as we saw in the previous chapter.
Medical writings concentrate on the early neo-natal period and
attach high value to the healthy, unimpaired body. There is a concern to maximize the survival chances of the strong, rather than
to tend the weak and struggling. Garnsey (1991: 65) considers it
likely that there was 'a high incidence of undernourishment and
disease' amongst children under age 5, but stresses that this
should be seen in the context of 'the social norms and cultural
practices of a preindustrial society'. He specifies wet-nursing,
inadequate nutrition, and early weaning as threats to infants.
From writers of the early imperial period such as Celsus, Pliny
the Elder, and Rufus we can compile a list of childhood illnesses

---

[29] Cf. Ch. 1 above for representations of children in Roman law.

and recommended treatments, as K. R. Bradley (1994: 144–5) has done. Soranus too is useful (e.g. 2. 51–6). Probably half of all children born had died before the age of 10.[30]

WEANING

The recommended age for weaning in Rome of the second century was about 2 years (Soranus 2. 46–8), but there is evidence of earlier and later ages (Fildes 1986: 354). Soranus gives advice on gradual weaning, suitable food and drink, and the best season of the year. If the infant is 'too heavy and short of breath' the wet-nurse must watch her diet and give the infant exercise by means of a little push-cart. Some children's mothers or wet-nurses would have died or lost their milk before the child was ready for weaning, which made bottle-feeding necessary. There is a wide range of feeding vessels known from Greek and Roman antiquity, which are usually associated with weaning but which could also have served for bottle-feeding in other circumstances.[31]

STORIES, GAMES, AND PETS

Story-telling and game-playing are usually associated in the literary sources with nurses.[32] This might be because those sources (especially Soranus) are specifically discussing nurses and nursing. The iconographic evidence does not associate such activities closely with any person or group. The educative role attributed to mothers of young children suggests that they were involved in all these activities. But it was the nurse who was most constantly with the young child and who would have had to be adept at entertaining and comforting it and singing it to sleep. She slept close to the infant, sometimes in the same bed (but the risk of suffocation of the infant made a separate crib desirable: Soranus 2. 37). No doubt other members of the family and the child's early network visited and interacted with it, and we can deduce from prescriptive and descriptive literature an atmosphere of considerable stimulus and activity for the development of the young child.

[30] Saller (1994: 25); K. R. Bradley (1994: 143); Garnsey (1991: 51). Cf. above, Ch. 2, for mortality estimates for infants.
[31] See Fildes (1986) for illustrations of these.
[32] See K. R. Bradley (1994: 148–51).

Resources for this were more likely and more diversified in urban settings than in the country.

Even in cities and large towns parents who could afford little time away from jobs and who did not have a nurse might have had to leave their young child lying fairly passively and neglected for long periods, which would retard its development and socialization. But attention and stimulation were not restricted to children whose families were comfortably off and with good social networks. In large slave households and in the teeming apartment blocks and crowded streets of poorer Rome, and in a society where we can see considerable interest in young children, there would be no shortage of child-minders, playmates, and adults ready to spend a few moments shaking a rattle or gurgling over an infant. In these settings, however, the attention and care were less structured, less driven by any set of ideas or policies, and, as the child developed, potentially more dangerous and socially undesirable. The differentiation between haves and have-nots would become more marked from the age for formal education.

Quintilian believed that learning through play was to be cultivated from an early age. He had argued that from the earliest years some forms of learning should be encouraged. The young child had a retentive memory, so take advantage of it, he said: aphorisms, famous sayings, and selections from poetry could all help children retain moral principles.[33] Again, it was the constant presence of the nurse which helped develop elementary ethics and literacy. But, he said, he was not ignorant of age differentials (*aetates*); so the very young should not be pressed too hard or asked to do real work. 'For our highest priority must be that the child, who cannot yet love learning, does not come to hate it and carry beyond the early years a fear of the bitterness once tasted. So let the child play (*lusus hic sit*)' (1. 20). Rewards and various kinds of stimulation are recommended. Modern anthropologists have developed theories of informal learning, recognizing different processes such as mimesis, identification, and co-operation: 'in play mimesis and identification reinforce the skills and the cognitive schemata on which learning and development depend'.[34]

---

[33] Quintilian 1. 1. 15–17, 26, 36–7.
[34] Goody (1982: 262–3), based on Meyer Fortes.

A large range of toys is known from Roman antiquity, revealed through archaeological and literary evidence.[35] Many kinds of rattles existed—expensive, elaborate, plain and simple. These amused the baby and were probably thought to keep off evil spirits. Dolls provided scope for role-playing, as they always have. Most of the dolls known seem to be for girls rather than boys. Their association with pre-adult girls is reflected in the ceremony in which girls on the eve of marriage dedicated their dolls to Diana or Venus (e.g. Persius 2. 70 and scholiast). Dolls have also been found in the tombs of girls who died before reaching adulthood. The dolls were usually articulated human figures, on average 15–16 cm tall, and made in a range of materials including wood, terracotta, and ebony but especially bone and ivory. Manson (*Jouer* catalogue, 1991: 55) sees a development in doll manufacture in the Antonine period, corresponding to better socio-economic conditions and greater attention to children's needs. He seems to assume some commercialization of the manufacture of dolls, reflected in the numbers and elaborateness of dolls found. I can find no explicit evidence of a doll-making or toy-making industry. The few ivory-workers (*eborarii*) commemorated in inscriptions at Rome give no hint of specialization in their products. There is, however, an impressive monument (second century) for the *collegium* of ivory-workers and inlayers, detailing strict scrutiny of membership and the privileges due to members (*CIL* 6. 33885). Perhaps the structure of wooden and pottery dolls and toys was simple enough for any handyman, and more elaborate, expensive ones could have been special commissions from craftsmen in ivory, silver, and other precious substances. Dolls might also have been an offshoot of another trade, such as the making of cult statuettes (as Manson suggests).[36]

Hoops, spinning tops, and push-carts were frequent, encouraging physical activity and helping toddlers learn to walk. Ball games were popular, and games played with nuts, knucklebones

[35] See *Jouer* catalogue (1992: 44–51); Martial 14. 54. Shumka (1997) contains a valuable catalogue and discussion; she sees little gender differentiation in the toys used by boys and girls.

[36] Thomas Wiedemann suggested to me that in the long winters of northern Europe, when children had to be entertained indoors for more hours, the toy industry was more likely to flourish.

and dice must have had an element of the gambling which was popular in adult Roman society.[37] They seem also to have had a combative element, not unlike the rough-and-tumble of children's games everywhere. Boys are more prominent than girls in these games, but there are representations of girls playing games with nuts and balls. On one of the earliest sarcophagi known, the scene of a child using a wheeled frame to learn to walk is in a series of familial scenes, including the child riding in a carriage with parents (first as a swaddled infant and last as a toddler at his death) and the child with a pet goose. Other representations depict the child alone, pushing a wheeled walking-frame.[38] Scenes of children playing games are frequent, as statuary, on murals, on a *kline* frieze and especially on sarcophagi, in Roman art from the first to the third centuries. Single figures are boys, groups are usually boys but sometimes girls. They hold knuckle-bones, they box and wrestle, they throw balls and nuts, drive hoops, and ride in carts drawn by rams or goats.[39] Goats are among the various pets associated with children in art and literature (K. R. Bradley 1998*b*).

Animals—real or their representations—were a frequent part of children's games, and toys were often in the form of animals. Animals and birds were also popular as pets with Roman children. We shall see below (Chapter 7) the growing taste for exotic animals in Roman entertainment and art, as Rome's foreign conquests from the second century BCE provided increasing

[37] Seneca (*De constantia* 12. 2) refers to children's appetite for dice, nuts, and small change, and their games of playing at being magistrates and building sandcastles on the seashore: these are all games, but adult men take similar interests to serious levels. See Ch. 1 above on literary representations of children playing games. Martial (5. 84) refers to nut games which schoolboys reluctantly leave after the Saturnalia holiday, and he characterizes such a boy as a gambler (*aleator*). Horace (*Satires* 2. 3. 247–9) describes being in love as even more irrational than children's games of 'let's pretend'. Phaedrus (3. 14) uses the example of Aesop and other boys in Athens playing with nuts to draw the moral that adults too need recreation, so that they can return fresher to serious things.

[38] Sarcophagus of early 2nd c.: cf. Ch. 1 above on sarcophagi. A tomb painting of a boy alone, from the Via Portuense in Rome, of the 2nd c., is described by Felletti Maj (1953: 40–76), who identifies several similar scenes, one on a *chous* of the 4th c. BCE from Capua and another a terracotta from Hellenistic Egypt.

[39] Girls: Amedick (1991: no. 116 pl. 98.1). Frieze: Berczelly (1978: 63 n. 13). Many illustrations are available in Amedick (1991) and Huskinson (1996).

wealth and an expanded perspective on the Mediterranean world and beyond. An example of the range of domestic pets of an older, indulged boy in the late first century CE is given by Pliny (*Letters* 4. 2): Regulus' son had had ponies, dogs, nightingales, parrots, and blackbirds. K. R. Bradley (1998*b*) has provided an illuminating analysis of Roman children's pet-keeping. Pets mentioned frequently or represented in art (public and funerary) include birds, dogs, cats, goats, sheep, rabbits, and geese. In the light of Regulus' pets, and what we shall see below (Chapter 7) of a 'cavalry culture', horses must have been popular too, although limited to those who had access to the means and space for agistment. Bradley discusses modern views on various functions of pet-keeping—educational, moral, emotional, or psychological. He suggests that three aspects may have been important for Roman children: pets provided them with 'strong ties of affection'; children drew a 'sense of mastery and control from their experiences of pet-owning'; and pets provided 'consolation . . . at times of emotional distress'. The experience of animals was not all, however, 'at the level of the warm and the affectionate'. Experience of animal sacrifice in religious ritual may have been ambivalent—gory, but for a noble purpose. But animal hunts as entertainment, although often involving considerable skill, were not for the soft-hearted. Bradley points out that the bloodsport of cock-fighting was not uncommon at Rome, and children (perhaps only boys) were exposed to it. The brutality involved, and the promotion of male bravado, were hardly positive aspects of children's interest in animals. And counterbalancing the representations of children playing co-operatively and harmoniously with animals, including a goose (see Chapter 1 above), is a version where the boy appears to be strangling the goose (Fig. 3.1).

CARERS

A wet-nurse might stay on as a child-carer even after weaning, for example the *nutrix assa* Volumnia Dynamis (*CIL* 6. 29497), whose nursling Volumnia C. f. Procla later gave her freedom and provided an epitaph claiming that the nurse was 105 when she died. If the family could afford it, there would be other carers, such as *educatores* and *nutritores*, both fairly general terms for 'bringers-up' (K. R. Bradley 1991*a*: ch. 3). Even for infants other

FIG. 3.1 Sarcophagus: boy's life course, infancy to death. Rome, early second century CE.

carers were known, such as male and female cradle-rockers.[40] We should remember, too, that children could be exposed to the influence and example of many slaves beyond those with speci-fied duties relating to children.

The nurse of children is the only professional nurse known in Roman society. There is no visual or textual record of any other kind of trained nurse, such as for sick adults or wounded soldiers or the dying (Kampen 1988: 7–16). Family members usually took responsibility for the sick and dying. That specialized health-care developed only for childbirth and early childhood indicates something of the priorities of Roman society, or at least of those levels which could afford these trained helpers. Poorer persons used whatever help was available and could be afforded. In wealthier and upper-class families the role of the husband/father was important in providing care. Not only was there emotional concern for mother and infant, there was concern also for lineage and inheritance. Birth and early childhood were times of danger for mother and child, and expert care was required to give them the best chance of survival and good health.

A propertied child would need financial assistance and advice as he or she was growing up, especially if the father was not avail-able. Because of high mortality rates and the fairly late age of marriage for males (towards 30 years of age for the sub-elite), about a third of Roman children lost their father before the child reached puberty.[41] In one will, a man provided for his 9-year-old son to have the services of an accountant (*dispensator*) and an estate manager and his wife (*uilicus* and *uilica*), all slaves, until the son was 17, at which time the slaves were to be given their freedom (*D*. 40. 5. 41. 15, Scaeuola).[42]

Mortality and divorce rates in Roman society meant that many children were reared by surrogate parents, such as step-parents, more distant relatives, or (for slaves) other members of the *familia*. These situations will be considered below in Chapter 6. Slave carers who remained with a child in these circumstances would provide an element of continuity and stability and would

---

[40] *Cunarius* for the infant Nero, *CIL* 6. 37752; *cunaria*, *CIL* 6. 27134.

[41] Saller (1994: 189). See Ch. 6 for orphans and guardians.

[42] Champlin (1991: 139–41) discusses 'conditional' testamentary manumission of slaves: these were usually slaves with particular skills who had to put their skills at the service of another for a fixed period before obtaining freedom.

be more likely to feature prominently in their affections and development. The law (*D.* 40. 2. 13, Ulpian) recognized these special relationships in granting exemptions from the age rules for manumission of a variety of carers, including an *educator*, a *paedagogus* (see Chapter 5 below), a nurse (or child of any of these), a book-carrier (*capsarius*), and a slave whom a young person wanted to be his financial administrator (*procurator*).

4

Ages and Stages

By celebrating the anniversary of their birthday every year, Romans marked the passage of time. They gave thanks for the past year and prayed for divine protection for the coming year. Usual elements were fire on the domestic altar, incense, ritual cakes, wine, garlands of flowers, and white robes.[1] These celebrations, and the ritual associated with them, were essentially Roman. There seems to be no Greek parallel for this tradition of annual celebrations of personal birthdays.[2] The birthday poem, as a celebration and a birthday gift, is a Roman genre, attested over three centuries from the Augustan period.

We have seen that there were celebrations and religious ritual when a child was born: fires on the domestic altar and garlands on the front door. All of our evidence for later birthdays is for adults' birthdays. As the focus of the celebrations was a man's *genius* or a woman's *iuno*,[3] and these were fully developed only in adults, that is understandable. But it is inconceivable—in the light of parents' initial celebrations, their frequent recording of precise ages for children, and their consciousness of various stages in a child's development—that children's birthdays were not celebrated in the home, at the domestic altar. What is striking about Roman birthday celebrations is that they were essentially a ceremony carried out by an individual on his or her own behalf. Family and friends might join in, offering gifts and even performing ceremonies on that individual's behalf in other homes, but it was principally the individual who gave thanks for having

---

[1] e.g. Ovid, *Tristia* 3. 13. 13–18; Martial 10. 24.

[2] See Argetsinger (1992) for Roman birthday ritual and its natural development into celebration of the emperor's birthday.

[3] The *iuno* (Juno), the female equivalent of the *genius*, is first heard of in the Augustan period (Argetsinger 1992: 176). Argetsinger has a good discussion of the nature of the *genius*, as being 'both part of a man as well as an external deity' (1992: 186).

had 'many happy returns' and who prayed for many more. In modern Western society, it would be unusual for a person to celebrate his or her own birthday in this way. We expect others to take the initiative and we might well let the birthday pass unmarked if others do not provide the celebration. Even if we throw our own party, we invite others and it is their participation and good wishes and, often, gifts which make it a 'real' birthday. For the Romans there was a sense of self which was at the core of birthday celebrations, and the essential ritual was between the individual and the divine forces which protected the individual. Part of a child's socialization must have been to learn this ritual and to develop this sense of self. During childhood there were the birthdays of parents or other closely associated adults to observe and learn from.

Funerary monuments sometimes represent life as a journey. This is particularly so in the 'biographical' or 'life course' sarcophagi.[4] The life course is sometimes a competitive race, which involves a starting point, turning points, and a finish post. Death in childhood truncated this journey, depriving the individual of the variety of stages and experiences which might have been expected. Cicero expressed the stages of the full journey when philosophizing about old age: each age has its own interests, then one moves on to other interests, until eventually all are played out and we are ready for death (*On Old Age* 76).

Particular stages of life of which the state took note were birth, coming-of-age (for males), and death. Taxes or financial offerings had been due on these occasions since early (regal) times at the temples of Juno Lucina, Iuuentus, and Libitina respectively (Dionysius of Halicarnassus 4. 15. 5). It was from Augustus' time that formal state records of these occasions began to be developed. These occasions were also the major *rites de passage* marked by ritual in Roman society, along with marriages. (The state took no formal note of marriages, although it did have an interest in the outcome of marriages.) Such *rites de passage* marked stages, or occasions, rather than ages. There was little rigid age demarcation within childhood in Roman society until late antiquity: Romans depended more on individual development and perceived capacity to determine fitness for responsibilities.

---

[4] See Whitehead (1984); Huskinson (1996: 110–11), 'Frameworks for life'.

Quintilian enshrined this principle in his work on education in the latter half of the first century (e.g. 1. 3): he emphasized the need for flexibility, according to the individual child's abilities, development, and character.

The number 7 had magic or superstitious connotations, and many systems of dividing the life cycle were based on this number.[5] There were other systems, such as that of Varro, based on the number 5, calculating five stages of fifteen years each: *puer* to 15, *adulescens* to 30, *iuuenis* to 45, *senior* to 60, *senex* thereafter (Censorinus, *De die natali* 14. 2). Horace (*Ars poetica* 156–78) presented four stages of the life-span: childhood, youth, adulthood, old age.[6] Such systems were based on numeric symbolism rather than any well thought-out theory of psychology and development. There was considerable flexibility in observing the age distinctions, and it was only in late antiquity that stages of the life cycle were firmly set at a specific age, such as the end of infancy at 7, the age of puberty for girls and boys at 12 and 14 respectively.[7] The variety of age classifications may not have much intrinsic absolute value for insights into child development. But the very variety shows at least two things about Roman attitudes to childhood. First, there were few rigid age barriers to any stage of development: children moved on according to their individual growth and talents and their parents' wishes and resources. Second, there was considerable discussion of and interest in the development of children, spawning different views of age groupings, but all sharing the basic essentials of development, allowing for infancy, childhood, and adolescence.[8]

There was a great array of divinities associated with children. French (1988: 1361) lists some of these and comments that they show Romans' awareness of the difficulties and dangers of childhood. It is possible that they also reflected something of how Romans conceptualized the child and envisaged its development.

---

[5] Eyben (1973: 228) has examples.

[6] Cf. Marcus Aurelius (*Meditations* 9. 21. 2), who presents the change from each of these stages to the next as a 'death'.

[7] Knothe (1982). Cf. Ch. 1 above on representations of children in Roman law.

[8] Manson (1978: 283) suggests that the identification of infancy as a differentiated part of childhood may date from the late Republic, with the use of *infantia* for the years before *pueritia*.

They included, for example, Educa, Potina and Rumilia (associ-
ated with a baby's eating and drinking), Abeona, Adeona,
Statulinus (associated with walking), Cunina (sleeping),
Fabulinus (speaking), Pauentia (fearfulness), Vagitanus (crying),
Ossipaga (growth of bones).

Cicero specified the qualities of different ages as these: *infir-
mitas* for children, *ferocitas* for *iuuenes*, *grauitas* for men in the
prime of life, *maturitas* for old men (*On Old Age* 33, 76). In
another work (*De finibus* 5. 15. 42) Cicero described in more detail
the characteristics of young children as they developed: after
infancy they learn to stand upright, use their hands, recognize
their carers; they enjoy the company of their peers, play games
with them, and enjoy hearing the telling of stories; they are generous, curious about activities at home, they begin to learn, and
are competitive with their peers. Horace's description (cited
above) of each stage of life is vivid in its perception of the qualities and characteristics of each. He began his work *The Art of
Poetry* with advice on style and tone. Language should be appropriate to the character of the speaker (lines 112–18), for example
god or hero, mature old man or passionate young man in full
bloom, influential lady of rank or a fussing nurse, and so on.
Aristotle (*Rhetoric* 2. 12–14) is sometimes cited as comparable, but,
unlike Horace, Aristotle omits childhood in his stages. Horace
begins with the child not long out of infancy, one 'who can repeat
words and stand firmly on the ground'. This child is anxious to
play with his peers, is quick to anger, and just as quick to change
moods. At a later stage the young man, not yet with a beard
grown, freed from supervision, rejoices in horses and dogs and the
grassy, sunny field of the Campus Martius; as impressionable as
wax, he is easily influenced to vice, sharp with any who reprimand
him, slow to see what will be beneficial, prodigal with money,
high-handed, full of desires, and swift to leave aside the objects
of his desire.

Seneca (*Letters* 121) elaborated in some detail on the principle
that each age (such as infancy, boyhood) has its own *constitutio*
(121. 15): the infant is toothless, then its teeth grow, and it adapts
to each condition. He stressed (121. 3) that one must understand
one's own nature in order to know how to act. We must know
what is suited to the human animal. Whereas other animals are
born with an instinct for their own nature and abilities, humans

have to learn this and be trained (121. 6). This leads to a graphic picture of a child learning to walk (121. 8): 'The infant, thinking about standing up and scarcely used to that, begins at the same time to try its strength further, and falls down; there are tears, but time and time again he pulls himself up, until, through painful practice, he has mastered what is required by his own nature.'[9]

As we saw above (Chapter 1), Roman law gave some attention to discussing and defining ages at which a child could be considered socially, morally, or criminally responsible. Economic and political responsibility did not come (for a male) until his mid-twenties.[10] Military responsibilities, or at least training, began about age 17 (for males). Within childhood various kinds of responsibility were attached to different ages. Modern systems of law have also to face such questions, and there is a striking similarity with what can be expected of a 10-year-old in ancient and modern societies.[11] In general, the age of 14 or puberty is critical for the perception of a child's greater responsibility. Below this age, the child is regarded as *doli incapax* (incapable of criminality or criminal intent), but those over 10 years of age might be considered capable if they could be shown to have understood the nature of their deed. Julian (mid-second century) expressed this view (D. 47. 2. 23, Ulpian), and in the words of today's law 'the capacity to commit crime . . . is not so much measured by years

---

[9] 'infans, qui stare meditatur et ferme se adsuescit, simul temptare uires suas coepit, cadit et cum fletu totiens resurgit, donec se per dolorem ad id, quod natura poscit, exercuit.' Cf. his *Letters* 118. 14, where *infans* becomes *pubes*: the one is *irrationalis*, the other *rationalis*.

[10] In the Republic, political office (a formal magistracy) was not available before the age of 30. Augustus reduced this to 25. Males and females could technically own nothing while they had a *paterfamilias* alive, although in practice they often had considerable freedom in use of resources as they became adults. They could own property at any age if they were *sui iuris* but even these persons were, if male, under the guidance of a *tutor* until puberty and then under the looser influence of a *curator* until age 25. Females were under a *tutor* for life, unless specifically exempted, but the control of a *tutor* became very loose for many women in the imperial period. The *lex Plaetoria* which protected a young male or female from being taken advantage of financially was quite early (*c.*200 BCE).

[11] Rogoff *et al.* (1975: 356) cites Blackstone (1765–9) for the view that a child of 7 is capable of knowing right from wrong and of standing trial. Cf. Catholic canon law for sin, confession, and communion.

and days as by the strength of the accused's understanding and judgment'.[12]

Before 10 a child could be expected to assume various other responsibilities. An ethnographic project, based on the Human Relations Area Files at Harvard, covering fifty cultures, concluded that 'in some respects, at least, diverse human cultures assign new roles and responsibilities to children in the five-to-seven-year age range' (Rogoff *et al.* 1975). This is consistent with Cicero's observation that early childhood ended at an age of about 6 or 7 (*De Finibus* 5. 15. 42). The ethnographic study is worth quoting at some length:

> From our data it appears that in the age period centering on 5–7 years, parents relegate (and children assume) responsibility for care of younger children, for tending animals, for carrying out household chores and gathering materials for the upkeep of the family. The children also become responsible for their own social behaviour and the method of punishment for transgression changes. Along with new responsibility, there is the expectation that children between 5 and 7 years begin to be teachable. Adults give practical training expecting children to be able to imitate their example; children are taught social manners and inculcated in cultural traditions. Underlying these changes in teachability is the fact that at 5–7 years children are considered to attain common sense or rationality. At this age also, the child's character is considered to be fixed, and he begins to assume new social and sexual roles. He begins to join with groups of peers, and participate in rule games. The children's groups separate by sex at this time. Concurrently, the children are expected to show modesty and sex differentiation in chores and social relationships is stressed. All of these variables indicate that at 5–7 the child is broadly categorized differently than before this age, as he becomes a more integral part of his social structure.   (Rogoff *et al.* 1975: 367)

The age of 7 was taken by the Romans as approximately the end of 'infancy' in some technical ways.[13] It was at about this age that a child lost its milk teeth and got its permanent teeth. Therefore before this age children were not cremated; but from this time of physical change they joined the adult world for the

---

[12] See further in B. Rawson (1997*b*). The quotation is from contemporary Australian law. Cf. Ch. 1 above.

[13] But this age was not codified (as the upper limit) until late antiquity: *CTh.* 8. 18. 8.

purpose of funerary ritual.[14] The stage of *infantia* was literally the stage of not having the capacity for speech (Varro, *On the Latin Language* 6. 52). Where this was associated with the age of 7, it must have embraced the ability to understand speech. Thus at the end of *infantia* a child was eligible for betrothal, when the parties were supposed to understand the proceedings.[15] Romans did recognize the first year of life, however, as a significant stage even if they did not apply the word 'infancy' to it. During that year the first teeth appeared (at about seven months: Soranus 2. 49). A child who reached its first birthday (an *anniculus*) qualified its parents for various legal privileges: for instance, from early in the first century a Junian Latin parent of such a child could apply for full Roman citizenship.[16] The sources contain considerable discussion of the needs and characteristics of infants in their first year, but when they died they were not commemorated as frequently or with the ceremony devoted to children a little older.[17]

Within the first seven years some differentiations were made. The 2-year-old is referred to in literature and inscriptions. The best-known and most eloquent picture in literature is that of Catullus (17. 13), where the *bimulus* is represented as sleeping, rocked in its father's arms.[18] The *bimus* is found in inscriptions of

---

[14] Pliny, *NH* 7. 16. 69–70. Rogoff *et al.* (1975: 354) reports that the age of getting second teeth (6½ to 7½ years) is recognized as a new stage in development by the Ngoni people of Malawi in central Africa.

[15] Knothe (1982). Members of the imperial family were occasionally betrothed soon after birth. Meillet (1920) points out that there is no single Indo-European term for 'infant': there is a variety of ways of rendering this concept, and it is characteristic of only Latin to use 'not yet speaking'. The term *infans* seems to have been used as an adjective until the late Republic. Lucretius (1. 186) might provide the first usage of *infantes* as a noun, thus recognizing a particular age group with particular characteristics. The first such use in the singular, *infans*, seems to be that of Cicero in *On Divination* 1. 121.

[16] The age of 1 is taken as the defining age for a surviving child in a judgment quoted by Papinian at the end of the 2nd c. (*D.* 23. 4. 26). By an agreement between a woman's father and her husband, the husband was to keep the whole dowry if she predeceased a child who had reached the age of 1.

[17] See below (Ch. 8) on formal mourning and commemoration for infants and the relationship between formal, public action and personal, private experience.

[18] The reference is also used here to ridicule an opponent. See Manson (1978), who argues for the meaning of 2-year-old for this term rather than two-months-old. As he points out (1978: 281), the child has passed two winters.

Rome and other parts of Italy, sometimes with complaints about premature death. The boy Ephebus (probably a slave), son of Auctus, lived for two years, three months, and fourteen days (BIMVS | ET MENSVM III DIES XIIII | VIXIT). His epitaph told his parents not to grieve: his death came too soon, but this was his destiny (*fatum*).[19] The 3-year-old in Lucretius (5. 884–5) has not yet been weaned. Pliny (*NH* 7. 16. 73) claims that at age 3 a child has reached half its ultimate height. Three years is one of the markers in Roman law for deciding how many surviving children give parents the capacity for inheriting from each other under Augustus' legislation: three children surviving to their naming day give that capacity, but two are sufficient if they have survived to age 3.[20] At 5 a slave child can be expected to render services (*operae*) to its master.[21]

As we have seen, the age 7 had particular significance. Educational thought and practice saw children moving on to a new phase around the age of 7. Quintilian (1. 1. 18) saw this as the end of *infantia*. He also thought that by then children would have imbibed some stories and their morals, but he stressed that the extent of this depended on the individual child, who should not be pressed. (Cf. Chapter 3 above for story-telling.) The fact that this age marked the beginning of public school-going for many children, and that this probably affected more boys than girls, makes this age a stage in gender separation. Ten, too, was a significant transition point. We have already seen changes in responsibilities about that age, and it was at that age, for a long time, that male citizens became eligible for the grain dole at Rome, a recognition of a kind of adulthood.[22] Celsus (2. 1. 17–21) claimed that most childhood illnesses disappeared by the time of a boy's puberty or first intercourse. This suggests that the two events, puberty and first intercourse, were thought to be not far apart. What sexual partners were available to well-born boys, given that girls of their own class were not generally available? Slaves and

[19] *CIL* 6. 17196; cf. 26544.
[20] Ulpian, *Reg.* 16 (*FIRA*[2] 2. 278). One child was sufficient if it survived to 12 (for girls) or 14 (for boys). Cf. Ch. 2 above.
[21] Knothe (1982: 254). Cf. Ch. 5 below for jobs performed by children.
[22] Trajan abolished age restrictions, making children eligible from infancy: Pliny, *Panegyric* 26–8. See Garnsey and Saller (1987: 83–5) on ages of eligibility.

prostitutes[23] are the obvious answers. If Cicero's picture of Clodia is more widely applicable, liberated society ladies might also have provided this service.

At 12 and 14 respectively, girls and boys were eligible to marry. The ages must have been associated with the onset of puberty, although they were not so defined until late antiquity. There is evidence for such early marriages in the upper classes, but they do not seem to have been the norm in wider society.[24] From that age, however, a boy might go through the ritual of attaining manhood by changing his boyhood garb (the *toga praetexta*) for the *toga uirilis*. Ages known for this ceremony range from 13 to 18. Parents' freedom in deciding when the boy was ready and when there was an appropriate occasion is another example of the flexibility of concepts of stages of development in Roman society. This contrasts with the uniformity decreed by the state in our own societies for ages marking some forms of adulthood, such as the age for voting, the age for purchasing alcohol or tobacco.

During Cicero's governorship of Cilicia in 51–50 BCE he had with him his teenage nephew (Quintus) and son (Marcus). They were getting provincial experience, but were still students and not involved in active service.[25] However, with civil war looming, there seems to have been some urgency about giving them the adult toga. At the Liberalia festival in 50, on 17 March, the traditional (but not obligatory) date for this ceremony, Cicero saw to it for Quintus at Laodicea.[26] Quintus was about 16 years old, and the fact that the ceremony was held in the province rather than in Rome, and in the absence of Quintus' father (who was in winter quarters with the army[27]), suggests some urgency. In the next year Marcus, some months short of 16, went through the same ceremony in Italy. Cicero could not enter Rome, still holding *imperium* from his proconsular command, so he welcomed the

---

[23] For literary references to prostitutes, see Cicero, *In Defence of Caelius* 48: 'Youths have always used *meretrices*'; Horace, *Epodes* 5. 58; Persius, 31. 32.

[24] Saller (1987); Shaw (1987).

[25] Cicero, *Att.* 5. 17, Aug. 51 BCE; 6. 1. 12, Feb. 50. For military purposes, boys remained *pueri* until their seventeenth birthday, when they might begin service as *iuniores* (Gellius 10. 28, quoting Q. Tubero).

[26] *Att.* 6. 1. 12. Ovid, *Fasti* 3. 771–88, speculates on reasons for this choice of date for the toga ceremony.

[27] *Att.* 5. 20. 5, Dec. 51.

opportunity to induct his son at Arpinum, the family's home town south-east of Rome, as the next best choice.[28] Both young men were then active in the civil war which broke out between armies led by Caesar and by Pompey.

Octavian was just too young (13), when civil war broke out, to participate. He was sent to the country for safety. Soon after his sixteenth birthday, however, he took on the *toga uirilis*. Even after that, his mother tried to maintain close supervision of his movements and behaviour, and opposed his joining his great-uncle Caesar when Caesar set out for the African campaign later in 47. But Octavian had already performed in public life at the age of 12 (51 BCE), when he gave the funeral eulogy for his grandmother Julia, Caesar's sister; and in 47 he was appointed Prefect of the City at the time of the Latin Festival (an important element in Caesar's plans for stability and continuity at this time). He also became a *pontifex* in that year, no doubt sponsored by Caesar as part of his plans for Octavian's future. Octavian shared in the celebrations and honours at Caesar's triumphs in 46, and not long afterwards he took the first opportunity after his seventeenth year to join a military campaign, following Caesar to Spain (though arriving belatedly).[29]

At age 14 Britannicus, son of the previous emperor Claudius and stepbrother of the new emperor Nero, was still sitting amongst the children (as a *puer*) at dinner, rather than reclining amongst the adult men (Tacitus, *Annals* 13. 16, for the year 55); but he may have been held back in his development in favour of Nero, who was three years older and had already assumed the toga of manhood at age 13. This age was considered premature, but, with Claudius ailing, Nero's supporters (including his mother Agrippina the Younger) were anxious to mark Nero's fitness to rule. The senate conferred on Nero special honours and rank, including that of consul-designate, although they provided

---

[28] *Att.* 9. 19, Apr. 49. Dyson (1992: 76) discusses the importance of local networks and connections. Marcus became aedile at Arpinum in 46.

[29] The main sources for Octavian's early to mid-teens are Nicolaus of Damascus' biography (especially 4–5) and Suetonius' *Augustus*. Inconsistencies between these are discussed in Jane Bellemore's edition of Nicolaus and John Carter's of Suetonius. *CIL* 10. 8375 preserves the day and month (18 Oct.) of Octavian's assumption of the adult toga. See also Broughton (1951–2), under relevant years.

that he was not actually to enter the consulship until his twentieth year. Claudius had presided at Nero's coming-of-age
ceremony as his adoptive father, but, according to Suetonius,
Claudius looked forward to the time when he could do this for
his natural son. Nero would have been in no hurry to bring this
event on when he became emperor in 54.[30]

There was considerable ceremony associated with the donning
of the *toga uirilis*, at least in families of some standing in the
state.[31] Coming to full adulthood was a staged development, but
this point in the early to mid-teens was recognized as significant,
socially and politically. The wearing of the white toga, without
the purple band of childhood, was one visible sign. At the same
time, freeborn boys put aside the locket (*bulla*) which they had
worn from birth, had their facial hair shaved off, and their hair
cut short.[32] This was part of the religious ritual in the home early
in the morning, before the boy set out for the Forum, accompanied by his father and his father's friends and supporters, to
perform further religious ritual on the Capitol and to be inscribed
in the roll of citizens in the Public Records office in the *tabu-
larium*.[33]

---

[30] Tacitus, *Annals* 12. 41: 'uirilis toga Neroni maturata quo capessendae rei
publicae habilis uideretur'. At the games, popular favour was cultivated by
Nero's wearing of *triumphalis uestis*, while Britannicus wore the *toga praetexta*.
Nero could be seen in the splendour of command, while Britannicus was in a
boy's outfit. Suetonius, *Claudius* 43.

[31] Dolansky (1999) treats the ceremony and its associations at length. See also
Ch. 7 below, including the transfer of the public part of the proceedings to the
forum of Augustus.

[32] Martial 1. 31. 6 and 10. 42. 2 for the cutting of the hair. Some foppish
young men cultivated long hair or little beards, to Cicero's disgust (*On the
Agrarian Law* 2. 58, of the son of King Hiempsal of Numidia in 63 BCE; *Att.* 1.
14. 5, of Clodius' supporters in 61; *In defence of Caelius* 33, of Clodia's young men
in 56).

[33] Cicero, *In Defence of Murena* 69, refers to the readiness of male citizens to
join the early morning procession of such boys, even those of humble rank: this
would be one of the reciprocal duties of friends and of patrons and clients. On
the morning of the fateful Ides of March (44 BCE) senate meeting when Caesar
was murdered, Cassius' fellow-conspirators gathered at his house to accompany
him and his son to the Forum as part of the *toga uirilis* ceremony (Plutarch,
Brutus 14). A century and a half later Pliny the Younger wrote of the claims on
his time of ceremonies such as that of the *toga uirilis* (*Letters* 1. 9. 2). Iuuentas
is the deity (of youth) to whom offerings were made in the temple of Jupiter on
the Capitoline (Dionysius of Halicarnassus 4. 15. 5). Festus (p. 32 L) defined the

There was no comparable ceremony to mark the coming-of-age of girls. For them, the significant transition was from virginity to marriage. Marriage was the expectation for most members of the population, and for upper-class girls it came early. On the day before their marriage they dedicated dolls and toys to their household gods or to Venus.[34] This practice had been observed by girls in classical Greece, but the more elaborate puberty rites, such as those associated with Artemis and practised in the Arkteia festival at Brauron in Attica, seem to have no counterpart in the Roman world.[35]

These concepts of a child's stages of development underlay the theory and practice of Roman education. They were most explicitly developed and articulated by Quintilian, in the latter half of the first century CE, but we have seen evidence from a wide range of time and genre of Romans' observation of them and consequent treatment of children based on that observation and understanding.

(golden) *bulla* as the insignia of *pueri praetextati*, hanging down their chests. It was reported that at Caesar's funeral mothers threw onto the pyre their own jewellery and their children's *bullae* and *praetextae* (Suetonius, *Iulius* 84. 4).The poets Propertius and Persius both refer to the toga and the *bulla*. Propertius' father had died before Propertius came of age, so his ritual took place before his mother's family gods. He represents himself as receiving advice about his future from Horus when his golden *bulla* had been removed from his young neck and the adult toga put on: he was to be an elegaic poet, not a man for military or political life, and Apollo would guide him (4. 1. 131–2). Persius (5. 30–5) marks his transition to the freedom of manhood by the removal of *bulla* and childhood toga, which are draped over the *Lares*. Seneca reminded Lucilius of Lucilius' joy at putting on the adult toga and being conducted to the Forum (*Letters* 4. 2).

[34] 'pupas, manias, mollis pilas, reticula, strophia': Varro in Nonius 863. 15 L; Persius 2. 70.

[35] See Demand (1994: 88) for details. She speculates (113–14) on the potential psychological effect of these rites on the participants. Some girls, being pre-pubertal, may have fallen short of society's expectations of girls preparing for marriage. This would have raised anxieties, contributing to the 'illness of maidens'. There is no indication of such systemic anxiety in Roman girls, but their preparedness for marriage must have depended on the quality of advice received from their mother (if alive) and other adult female relations and friends.

5

Education

'EDUCATION' is here interpreted broadly. Details of the rhetorical education of upper-class adolescent boys are well known[1] and they go some way to answering the question of how children were socialized and trained to fill a role in society, to deal with relationships, and to achieve intellectual and personal development. But they tell us little about younger children, girls, the lower classes, or slaves. We thus need to look also at schooling at all levels, formal and informal education in the home, apprenticeship, other forms of practical experience and role-modelling, and experience in the public sphere.[2] We need too to understand something of the cultural milieu which provided the context for all this.

The question of the extent of literacy in Roman society is still much debated. W. V. Harris (1989) takes a pessimistic view, estimating that literacy levels were low, perhaps less than 15 per cent in Italy, with no general provision of education. He admits, however (1989: 326), that the Romans used writing for a wide range of functions, such as business, political slogans, army records, state records, political announcements, letters, literature, epitaphs. Other scholars give more weight to such functions to present a less pessimistic picture.[3] Nevertheless, orality continued to be an important feature of Roman society.

---

[1] Major works by Cicero, Quintilian, and Tacitus which deal with this stage have contributed to this familiarity. Bonner (1977) provides useful details on many aspects of Roman education, but is limited in scope (not going beyond the early 2nd c. CE and dealing mostly with the upper classes) and does not sufficiently explore the cultural milieu. See E. Rawson's criticisms of its limitations in her review in the *Times Literary Supplement*, 24 Feb. 1978. The recent collection by Too (2001) now offers a more pluralistic account of ancient education (Greek and Roman).

[2] See below (Ch. 7) for the educative and socializing effects of festivals and other elements of Roman public life.

[3] e.g. contributors to Beard *et al.* (1991), especially Nicholas Horsfall,

RHETORIC

Rhetorical education was provided for boys of good family in their early to mid-teens (or sometimes younger) who expected to be active in public life, especially in the senate, the lawcourts, and in high military and administrative offices. Its normal age catchment therefore puts it largely outside the scope of a work on childhood. Some aspects should, however, be discussed here, not only because some boys in our age range did participate in rhetorical education[4] but also because the highest stage of education often influences and explains what is taught earlier, and how it is taught, and it often encapsulates the aims and ideals of a society's whole educational philosophy.

The ability to speak well—to persuade, to inform, to please an audience[5]—was essential to many aspects of public life, especially in a society with limited circulation of the written word and none of the modern mass media (newspapers, printed books, radio, TV, to say nothing of other electronic media). Considerations of morality were always an important element in the preparation of a speaker: in a simpler, earlier Rome (second century BCE) Cato the Elder could describe the orator as 'uir bonus dicendi peritus', ('a good man skilled in speaking').[6] This thread continued in pedagogical theory and practice for centuries. Already, however, more specialized teachers were visiting Rome from Greece and introducing a more complex system of rhetoric. The senate tried to suppress such teaching in 161 BCE,[7] but it quickly gained

'Statistics or states of mind', pp. 59–76, who attaches more importance to informal and non-school education and to interrelations between various forms of practical literacy and jobs; Woolf's chapter on orality in Bowman and Woolf (1994); Solin, Salomies and Liertz (1995).

[4] Cicero's son Marcus was embarked on it by the age of 11, studying with his 13-year-old cousin Quintus under the rhetorician Paeonius (*Q. fr.* 3. 3. 4, 3. 1. 4, late 54 BCE).

[5] Cicero, *On the Orator* 2. 115, *Brutus* 185. Cf. his *On the Best Kind of Orators* 3: the best speaker 'docet et delectat et permouet' the minds of his listeners ('teaches and delights and stirs').

[6] Quoted in Seneca the Elder, *Controuersiae* 1 pr. 9.

[7] Suetonius, *Rhet.* 1 and Gellius 15. 11. 1 record the *senatus consultum* banishing philosophers and rhetoricians from Rome. In this same year, one of the consuls brought in a sumptuary law, so there seems to have been a mood to preserve the old morality. No fattened poultry was to be served at banquets: this veto was continued in later legislation (Pliny the Elder, *NH* 10. 139).

ground to become the orthodoxy by the end of the century. It was seen as providing the broad-based liberal education which a public figure required: philosophy, literature, language (with a heavy emphasis on Greek branches of these, in which study and scholarship were much more advanced than in Latin). Cicero quotes the censor of 92 BCE as characterizing it as providing not only linguistic skill, but also 'doctrinam aliquam et humanitate dignam scientiam' ('a certain training and a field of learning fit for developing humane qualities', *On the Orator* 3. 94). Over a century later, Tacitus (*Dialogue on Orators* 35) was nostalgic for this breadth, claiming that the rhetors' schools were full of boys and youths, all equally ignorant (*imperitus*).

When rhetoric teachers using only the Latin language began setting up schools in Rome and attracting many young men, the censors of 92 BCE expressed strong disapproval of these 'Latin rhetors'.[8] They stopped short of evicting them or closing them down, but the censors' edict was meant to be equivalent to a black ban. (The young Cicero, aged 12 or 13, had already been warned off: he had been attracted by the new teaching but took the advice of his elders not to attend.[9]) The basis of the censors' opposition, expressed in the text of their edict, was that there were dangers in departing from ancestral tradition, and that young men were spending long hours with these teachers unproductively. Apparently the young men were fascinated by the skilful use of language and argument, but were seen not to be developing the wider intellectual skills and insights which would give depth and meaning to their oratory. Crassus, who claimed that as censor in 92 BCE he did close down the Latin rhetors, envisaged the possibility of a Latin system of rhetoric in the future, but there were not yet men of sufficient learning (*eruditi*), he said; when they did appear, they would be preferable to the Greeks.[10]

At first sight this opposition to a Latin system of rhetoric is strange, especially the identification of a Greek system (barely a century old in Rome) as ancestral tradition. It could not have

---

[8] Suetonius, *Rhet.* 1; Gellius 15. 11. 2.

[9] Suetonius, *Rhet.* 2. Seneca the Elder, *Controuersiae* 2 pr. 5, reports that the first Latin rhetorician at Rome was Plotius, 'in Cicero's boyhood' (*puero Cicerone*).

[10] Cicero, *On the Orator* 3. 93–5. Cicero was writing this in 55 BCE: perhaps with hindsight, after Latin rhetoric had become established.

been simply 'cultural cringe'. The Romans had long been adapting Greek culture to their own needs and melding it with native traditions. And the censors arc unlikely to have taken up the senate's time with a purely cultural issue: one has to suspect wider social or political motives. Nevertheless, it is worth noting these strong senatorial stands in 161 and 92 BCE on educational issues, especially in the light of the pronouncement of Polybius, a Greek commentator and historian of Roman society in the mid-second century BCE, that the Roman government took no formal interest in the education of its young (Cicero, *On the Republic* 4. 3). The edict of 92 BCE reveals a deep conviction that young men entering public life required an education which could draw on broad cultural understanding and which was anchored in firm philosophical principles. The only philosophy available was Greek. Ironically, it was Cicero, who was wedded to the Greek rhetorical education, whose own writings contributed much to popularizing Greek philosophy and presenting it in Roman form, if not creating a Roman system of philosophy.

The Romans, then, valued the long tradition inherent in Greek rhetoric and the body of scholarship which had been built up around it. They valued the discipline of not only learning a second language (Greek) but being able to use it as effectively as their own. The Latin rhetoricians must have been seen to be too utilitarian and narrow, using only Latin and aiming mainly at linguistic cleverness. Such criticisms of oratorical training continued, even after the Latin rhetoricians became established, and the tension between rhetoric and philosophy continued for at least two centuries. Cicero criticized a Latin-trained orator of his own day, C. Titius, for his lack of Greek learning and experience: 'sine Graecis litteris et sine multo usu' (*Brutus* 167). A century and a half later Pliny the Younger criticized half-baked young men who were so self-assured in the lawcourts but who had too narrow an education and little practical experience (*Letters* 2. 14). Quintilian addressed the problem and argued for a remarriage of philosophy and rhetoric.[11] The argument is familiar in modern discussions of higher education for the professions. Not all systems have the policy of US institutions of requiring liberal arts or

---

[11] 1. pr. 9–20. The orator must be a *uir bonus* with all intellectual qualities ('omnes animi uirtutes'): the principles of virtue do not belong only to philosophy—philosophy and oratory are intertwined.

generalist degrees as a preliminary to Law, Medicine, and other professions. The Romans succeeded in resisting specialized professional schools for many centuries. In the third century a law school, probably the first such, was established at Berytus in Syria.

The Latin rhetoricians, however, were not to be denied and within a generation of the censors' edict against them they seem to have been an accepted part of the educational scene. For many, like the future Augustus, Latin rhetoric was additional to Greek rhetoric, not a substitute for it (Suetonius, *Rhet.* 4). Tiberius cultivated the liberal arts (*artes liberales*) in both languages (Suetonius, *Tiberius* 70. 1). But Latin rhetoric must have opened up the study of oratory (and hence public life) to a wider clientele, and this may well have been the political fear, the fear of extending access to power and reducing exclusivity, which motivated the censors in 92 BCE. A similar fear of the vernacular has been seen in other elitist institutions, for instance the long battle to replace Latin with the vernacular in the Roman Catholic mass. By Quintilian's time, in the late first century CE, the Latin system was widely accepted: Quintilian (2. 4. 42) refers to it in neutral terms, stating simply, on the authority of Cicero, that it began in Rome towards the end of (the orator) Crassus' time, with Plotius being the most distinguished of the practitioners.

Even the traditional rhetorical education was not confined to a tightly controlled, restricted elite. To some extent, any parent who could pay could put his child through this form of education, and there are examples of ambitious parents who did that. For the Romans, as for so many other societies, education was an instrument of socialization and social mobility. The father of the poet Horace was an ex-slave, who took his son from their country town, at whose school centurions' sons were taught, to Rome, to have the education of the sons of senators and equestrians. This earned Horace status in cultural circles close to the emperor Augustus (Horace, *Satires* 1. 6. 65–78). Other future poets and other country boys also moved to Rome for a superior education (see below under 'City and Country'). Hermeros, in Petronius' *Satyricon* (58), taunts the young Giton with being ignorant in spite of his education in rhetoric: 'I'll show you that your father wasted his fees.' The ex-slave Echion, an old-clothes dealer, had ambitions for his son, who already had some competence in

Greek and Latin, arithmetic and literature, was studious, and liked painting. Echion had bought him some books: he wanted him to have a taste of law so that he could manage property. One of the occupations open to him was that of a *causidicus*, a lower-level pleader in the courts (Petronius, *Satyricon* 46). Masurius Sabinus (*PIR²* M 358) and Pegasus rose to be heads of their respective law groups ('schools') in the first century through their legal scholarship, in spite of their origins in non-elite families. Sabinus came probably from Verona and Pegasus from the eastern Mediterranean (*PIR²* 512; Champlin 1978).

An education was probably not enough, however, in the Republican period if one did not have a patron or family friends to take one under their wing and guide one through the early stages of a career. This might explain why Horace and Ovid did not move on to public careers. But, as the Principate developed, the emperor and his bureaucracy provided the necessary patronage and opportunity, and careers opened up for a wider range of men. Flavian and later emperors patronized and advanced education. The public career structure which developed required, especially at senior equestrian levels, a broad education. Syme has written (1958: 607–8) of the high expectations of the bureaucrats of the imperial household. 'Court officials shine as men of letters, the secretariat bristles with erudition, and the procurator abroad will alternate fiscal duties with scientific research.' Equestrian and senatorial careers moved in and out of military and civilian posts: there were not separate career paths for these posts. Their holders had shared educational backgrounds in law, oratory, literature, and—sometimes—philosophy. In full career they shared similar intellectual interests, attended lectures and readings, and dabbled in their own literary compositions. There were opportunities in the lawcourts, in spite of the occasional intervention and always potential influence of the emperor. There were thus, as Hardie (1983: 48) has pointed out, many opportunities for provincial youths to rise by merit at Rome. 'Immigrants could place themselves in the mainstream of the capital's culture' and they adopted Roman culture. The career opportunities help to explain the temptation to cut corners to get qualified quickly. Pliny, as we saw above, deplored the over-confidence of young men in the lawcourts who had not been guided by a senior patron or prepared themselves with a broad education, and other authors deplored the pressure on young boys to move on prematurely to rhetoric and public competitions such as the Alban festival.[12]

The increased participation in a broad liberal education (*liberalia studia*) and the opening up of career opportunities reflect something of the movement from a 'closed' to an 'open' society as described by Laurence Stone (1969: 73–4) in his discussion of literacy and education in England for the seventeenth century. He points out the monopoly of all key positions in society by those who had a classical education. We might compare the minority in England who commanded 'the cultural medium of Latin' with the elite in Republican Rome who had a command of Greek language and culture. The minority in England, says Stone, was able 'to assert, and to impose upon the rest of the community, a sense of its own natural superiority'. It was not an entirely closed system. By 'a system of "sponsored mobility", regulated by scholarships, the recipients of which are selected and controlled by upper-class patrons', new members (sons of the new monied class) were incorporated into the elite: this 'gave them a sense of common identity with the old ruling class over and against the rest of the population'. Stone compares this 'regulated trickle' from one educational level to another with the 'competitive trickle' in eighteenth- and nineteenth-century France and contrasts these with the 'competitive flood' of twentieth-century North America. It might be an overstatement to speak of a 'flood' into the influential classes in imperial Rome, but society did become more 'open' through wider career opportunities in public service and the courts, and access to these continued to be through the traditional (but modified) rhetorical education, which was remarkably broad and similar for all those aspiring to positions of influence. The hierarchical nature of the bureaucracy provided positions at more modest levels for which a more restricted, functional education sufficed, such as in accountancy, clerical skills, shorthand.[13] It is not clear what *artificium* young Marius Vitalis was so passionate to learn, but he persuaded his parents to give him this education and was on his way from Rome

[12] Cf. below, under 'Schools, Teachers, Curriculum', which includes child prodigies.

[13] e.g. Martial (10. 62) wishes a *magister* well by wishing that he will be able to compete successfully for pupils with any *calculator* or *notarius uelox*. See below on 'Professions and Trades'.

on the emperor Hadrian's staff, still a student, when he died at 17, leaving his grieving mother to set up his epitaph.[14]

By the late Republic the cultural milieu in Rome was conducive to a lively interest in education, literature, and philosophy for those who had the means to enjoy it. The stream of visiting intellectuals increased, many of them took up residence at Rome (often in the homes of leading citizens), Romans became more active in literary composition, the physical embellishment of the city and private homes provided space and facilities for intellectual discussion and creativity, and significant collections of books were being gathered together in private and then public libraries.[15] The active debate about Greek and Latin rhetoric was but one feature of this milieu.

Since much of this activity centred on the home, children in such homes could not have failed to be aware of it from an early age. There is a long list of famous pairs of Roman patron and Greek intellectual, known from at least the second century BCE onwards, e.g. Scipio Aemilianus (Africanus the Younger) and both Polybius and Panaetius, Lucullus and Antiochus of Ascalon, Pompey and both Theophanes of Mytilene and Posidonius, Cicero and Diodotus, Piso and Philodemus of Gadara.[16] These are the best known, but the phenomenon seems to have been much more widespread. These intellectuals were advisers, tutors,

---

[14] *CIL* 6. 8991. L. Marius L. f. Vitalis was freeborn; whether his mother, Maria Malchis, was freeborn or freed is unknown. He was 'consummatus litter(is)' and the final phase of his short life is described in verse thus: 'discessi ab | urbe in praetorio | Hadriani Aug. Caesar. | ubi dum studerem fata | inuiderunt mihi raptum | que ab arte tradiderunt | hoc loco' ('I left Rome in the retinue of the emperor Hadrian. While I was still a student the fates decided against me: they tore me from my learning and dispatched me here').

[15] For details of library resources in Rome, see M. H. Harris (1995: 56–67) and Marshall (1976).

[16] Suetonius gives examples of resident or consultant intellectuals (*Gramm.* 3, 6, 10, 14, 15, 16, 20, 21). Balsdon (1979: 54–8) has a list of Greek intellectuals resident with Romans from the 3rd c. BCE to the end of the Republic. Cf. Treggiari (1969: 110–28) for freedmen scholars, teachers, and writers. Rowland (1972) provides a catalogue of Cicero's contacts with Greek intellectuals and artisans of various social levels, arguing that such relationships were motivated by 'culture, services . . . and governmental efficiency' (p. 459).

librarians, or just general 'resource persons' to grace a family's
dinner table, or to discuss specific issues at other times, or to provide the steel on which members of the family—especially the
father—could sharpen their own minds. Their status might be
slave, freed, or freeborn. The relationship between Cicero and
Tiro shows that even when the Greek was a slave there could be
a relationship of warmth and mutual respect.[17] Such slaves had
good chances of being rewarded with manumission and Roman
citizenship. At a lower level there were slave entertainers who
were hired or employed on the household staff to perform, especially at dinner time. There seems to have been a long tradition
of entertainment at Roman dinners, such as singing, dancing,
instrument-playing, poetry-reading, acting. In early days the
children of the family sang songs with historical or mythological
themes at dinner time. But by the late Republic children, dining
with their family, were part of the audience for such performances.[18] Families which had villas in the country or at the coast
were particularly likely to use their greater leisure time there in
such activities. As many villas were in the area of Campania and
the Bay of Naples, Romans could draw on the long-established
Greek cultural climate there.[19]

An example of the role played by such intellectuals in individual households and in forging links between households and
cementing a common, cosmopolitan culture is that of Apollonius,
the freedman of Publius Crassus, younger son of the 'triumvir'
Crassus. Apollonius was a frequent visitor in the houses of Cicero
and Julius Caesar, and Cicero's wording (in a letter of 45 BCE to
Caesar, *Fam.* 13. 16. 4) suggests that as a slave child Apollonius
visited in the train of the older Stoic scholar Diodotus, absorbing
the intellectual conversations and discussions until he established
his own scholarship and literary career, winning freedom from
Crassus along the way. In 45 BCE he was planning to record

---

[17] See Christes (1979) for details of Tiro and other slave or freed teachers and
scholars in Rome.

[18] Varro, *De uita populi Romani* fr. 84, for early days. Fr. 83 reports that
at private dinners the boys and girls of the family served (*ministrabant*).
K. R. Bradley (1998a) discusses 'the Roman family at dinner' in more detail. He
is sceptical of the frequency of children's participation, and points out that non-
adult children sat apart from adults. See below, Ch. 6.

[19] See Hardie (1983: 40, 59) and d'Arms (1970, e.g. pp. 165–7) for examples.

Caesar's achievements in Greek. It is worth noting that Cornelia, daughter of Metellus Scipio, who married Publius Crassus in 55 and Pompey in 52, was said to be a young woman of well-developed intellectual interests: these must have been fostered by the atmosphere in the sort of household being described above. Plutarch (*Pompey* 55) describes her as 'well versed in literature and in playing the lyre and in geometry, and she had been accustomed to listen to philosophical discourses with profit'. She was probably still in her teens, perhaps even early teens, when she first married. This suggests that she had already acquired a good education in her father's home,[20] and that she continued to participate in the intellectual and cultural activities in the houses of her husbands. Calpurnia, last wife of Julius Caesar, was the daughter of Calpurnius Piso who had a splendid library of Epicurean philosophical works, probably the one discovered in the charred remains of his villa at Herculaneum.[21] Again, there is a common thread of intellectual interests in natal and marital homes.

Dionysius was another accomplished slave (and later freedman) on the staff of Atticus but he taught Cicero's son Marcus for a period. In 54 BCE (Marcus was 11 years old) Dionysius was absent in Greece with Atticus, and Cicero wrote anxiously to Atticus about Dionysius' return to Rome: he wanted him to continue Marcus' education, and indeed said that he himself would profit intellectually from Dionysius' presence (*Att.* 4. 15. 10). Cicero owed much to a slave of his own called Dionysius who had helped him build up and organize his (expensive) library. In 46 BCE the slave absconded, apparently with some of Cicero's books, and Cicero had friends and agents pursuing him in the East (without success, it seems) for quite a long time, more anxious perhaps to recover his books than to inflict punishment on the

---

[20] There was criticism of the age disparity between her and Pompey (Pompey was 54 in the year 52 BCE). It was said that Pompey was old enough to be her father, and her age was compared with that of Pompey's sons. Gnaeus Pompeius was born probably between 80 and 77 BCE and Sextus between 71 and 67. On the basis of Cornelia's father's career, she is unlikely to have been born much before 70 BCE.

[21] The original J. Paul Getty Museum at Malibu in California was built as a reconstruction of Piso's villa. The booklet *The J. Paul Getty Museum. Guide to the Villa and its Gardens* (1992) provides useful detail about the villa.

slave.[22] Cicero's close relationship with his daughter Tullia suggests that she would have had access to Cicero's library during her girlhood and have had discussions with her father about its contents.

Atticus had a reputation for raising and training his own slaves (Nepos, *Atticus* 13). Whatever their duties, they received a good grounding in literacy. Some specialized as readers (*anagnostae*) and copyists (*librarii*). The large number of copyists helped him supply copies of books for other people's libraries. His daughter Caecilia was born into this household in 51 BCE. Her mother, Pilia, died in Caecilia's childhood[23] and Atticus probably took an interest in his only child's education and development. He was instrumental in organizing an excellent marriage alliance for her later (probably 37 BCE), to Agrippa, due to become Augustus' most powerful associate and already consul and active ally and officer of Octavian. A girl growing up in Atticus' house, in the ambience described above (libraries, book production, resident and visiting intellectuals, and a range of cultivated, powerful, and wealthy friends), could hardly have failed to profit educationally and socially.

The patronage of intellectuals and the fostering of libraries continued in the imperial period, with many emperors taking the lead and providing new opportunities for intellectual activity. (See 'Role of the State' below.) Pliny's *Letters* (e.g. 1. 13) attest the frequency of public readings (*recitationes*) and he praises the strength of intellectual activity (*studia*) at the end of the first century and early in the second. Much of this applied to only a minority of Roman society, although how small that minority was is difficult to say. There were always hopeful parents and children who saw the advantages of the education and cultural trappings of elite families and sought to emulate their practice. By the late Republic, wealth was increasing and spreading more widely in society, and there was increasing public exposure to art, theatre, visiting intellectuals and ambassadors, and a diverse cultural and demographic environment. Even for those who did not share directly in the intellectual culture which has been described

---

[22] Dionysius was an *anagnostes*, trained to read texts aloud for others' entertainment and edification. In 50 BCE, he was in good favour (*Att.* 6. 1. 12). See *Fam.* 13. 77. 3 and 5. 9. 2 for the 40s.

[23] Probably 44 BCE: Cicero, *Att.* 16. 7. 8.

above, there was some indirect educative and socializing role in more popular entertainment and public ritual, as we shall see below (Chapter 7).

EARLY EDUCATION

Elementary education was carried out in the home in a child's early years. By Quintilian's time, there were well-developed views—one might almost talk of a 'theory'—on the appropriate education for very young children. There is little evidence of any attention to this age in Greek thinking, even in the Hellenistic period when art seems to reflect a greater awareness of small children.[24] Quintilian (1 pr. 4–5) argues that early education is like the foundations of a building: one must give the most careful attention to it, to ensure a satisfactory superstructure (the fully educated orator) which is seen and admired as the final product. He thus recommends attention to education from a child's infancy (*ab infantia*).

During this early period there was no one person responsible for imparting the elements of speaking, reading, writing, and counting. These elements were acquired informally from various members of the household (such as nurses and both male and female carers), many of whom would be slaves, and from child playmates. The mother usually had some supervisory role,[25] but Quintilian stresses the importance of having both parents involved from the time of the child's birth and the desirability of their both being well educated themselves. Earlier, Cicero (*On the Laws* I. 47) saw parents and nurse as the earliest source of children's *opiniones*. There were famous mothers often cited as having influenced their children's education (Cornelia, Aurelia, Atia, Iulia Procilla[26]), but there was also a long line of fathers acknowledged for their active contribution (such as Cato the

---

[24] Cf. Ch. 1 on children in Greek art.

[25] Tacitus (*Dialogue on Orators* 28. 5) sees a role for an older woman relative here. In Messalla's nostalgic picture of an idealized past, such a woman was a kind of superior nanny for all the children of a family, regulating the propriety of their words and deeds and overseeing their recreation and games.

[26] Tacitus, *Dialogue on Orators* 28. 6. These were the mothers of the Gracchi, Julius Caesar, Augustus, and Agricola respectively.

Elder and the fathers of Cicero, Atticus, Horace, and Statius).[27] There was a tradition of fathers dedicating didactic books to their sons. LeMoine (1991) provides a list of examples of such dedications and of written dialogues between fathers and sons: they include Cato, Cicero, Seneca the Elder, Apuleius, Aulus Gellius. These educational and religious books extend from 200 BCE to 500 CE. LeMoine shows that this was a particularly Roman tradition, not common in the earlier Greek world, and that Roman father-authors drew their didactic authority from their family role. Even if there was an element of literary convention in these dedications and dialogues, 'they reveal what kind of relations were considered appropriate between father and son' (p. 339). They also reveal the ethical emphasis in Roman educational thinking. Cicero reflects this in his pronouncement (*On Duties* 1. 123) that older people must be good role models for the young. If adults are self-indulgent, this will make young men's lack of discipline (*intemperantia*) more shameless. Livy's story (7. 4–5) of the trial of Manlius (Imperiosus) in 362 BCE for the neglect of his son's education also reflects the ideal of the father as educator and role model (see Chapter 6 below). Juvenal refers to the role of parents and nurses in a satirical account of their insidious influence (14. 190–3, 208–9). They are anxious for children to begin study as early as possible, but parents' own behaviour exemplifies the overwhelming importance of getting rich. Nurses (*assae*) din this lesson in, and girls learn it even before their alphabet.

SCHOOLS, TEACHERS, CURRICULUM

The age usually specified for passing out of the elementary stage of education is 7, but some moved on to formal education earlier than that. Marcus, Cicero's son, was being taught by Aristodemus

---

[27] Plutarch, *Cato Maior* 20; Cicero, *On the Orator* 2. 1. 1; Nepos, *Atticus* 1; Horace, *Satires* 1. 6. 72–88; Statius, *Siluae* 5. 3, e.g. 209–14; cf. Valerius Maximus 2. 7. 6 for Postumius Tuber and Manlius Torquatus. Cicero himself took a close interest in the education of his son Marcus and his nephew Quintus (see K. R. Bradley 1991a: ch. 8). In 49 BCE he criticized their tutor Dionysius (Atticus' freedman) but, rather than change *magister*, he supplemented the boys' teaching by teaching them himself on the side (*subdoceri*): *Att.* 8. 4. 1.

of Nysa before he was 6,[28] and a 6-year-old named Marcianus is depicted in an inscription and sculptured relief of the early second century CE as a schoolboy with appropriate equipment (a book satchel at his feet, Fig. 5.1). Marcianus' epitaph, in the first person, laments his early death and the crushing of his parents' hopes: the Muses had endowed him with early signs of eloquence, and when he died the whole street wept and an 'immense crowd' attended his funeral.[29] As we saw above (Chapter 4), modern research indicates that in the age range 5 to 7 'broad changes in information-processing' occur (Rogoff 1975: 367). Quintilian recognizes this, recommending that children start the study of literature as soon as they show capacity for it, as memory is especially retentive in small children (1. 1. 15–19). There is an assumption that they are teachable: they are ready for

FIG. 5.1   Relief and epitaph for Marcianus, aged 6, going to school. Rome, early second century CE.

[28] K. R. Bradley (1991a: 104). Aristodemus came from a family of *grammatici* of the same name. This Aristodemus also taught Pompey's children. Another, a cousin, trained Pompey. Strabo 14. 650.

[29] *CIL* 6. 7578; Gordon (1983: 140–1 no. 60). For a translation of the inscription and further details, see B. Rawson (1999).

school,[30] or, at a lower socio-economic level, ready for work. Ulpian, in *D.* 7. 7. 6. 1, sets 5 as the age below which a slave does not count as an income-producing part of its master's estate.[31] From that age there was a range of jobs which small children could be set to do. (See 'Professions and Trades' below.)

The choice between public school or a private tutor at home was much discussed (by those who could afford either and could choose between the two). When Pliny wrote to his friend Corellia Hispulla about her son, who had had teachers at home in his early years, he recognized that the boy should now (in his early teens) go to school, but they needed to choose a school which would 'combine a strict training (in Latin rhetoric) along with good manners and, above all, moral standards' (*seueritas, pudor, castitas*). The fear of sexual seduction of a pretty boy had, no doubt, been a factor in keeping him at home till now; and that danger still needed to be guarded against. So the man whose school was chosen had to be 'more than a teacher; a guardian (*custos*) and mentor (*rector*) must be found' (*Letters* 3. 3. 3). An inscription from Campania is an eloquent testimony to such virtues in Furius Philocalus, an elementary-school teacher (*magister ludi litterari*). He lived his life modestly and decently ('parce pudensque') and behaved towards his pupils with the highest morality ('summa quom castitate in discipulos suos'). The sculptures at the bottom of the large marble slab depict him seated between the standing figures of a boy and a girl (Fig. 5.2).[32]

---

[30] In modern Western societies there are now earlier stages of 'schooling', e.g. kindergarten and pre-school. This may be a recognition that formal learning can take place earlier, but in many ways these institutions provide opportunity for peer learning and group activity which were available to the pre-5 or -7 year-old in the larger households and more open neighbourhoods of Rome but which are less available in the small, self-contained households of modern Western societies.

[31] Cf. K. R. Bradley (1991*a*: ch. 5, e.g. pp. 115–16).

[32] *CIL* 10. 3969, translated in B. Rawson (1999). The teacher and the boy are holding what appear to be writing tablets. The inscription also records that Philocalus wrote wills reliably (presumably as a second-string to his trade), doing justice to all, and that he went through the course of his life trustworthy and without fear ('fidus sine metu'). Some kind of *collegium* saw to his burial. Marrou (1938: no. 16) says that the figures are not school pupils but rather a slave and a female relative of the teacher. He later (1956: 430 n. 8) revised the date of the monument from mid-2nd c. to Augustan but did not discuss further the people represented.

FIG. 5.2 Epitaph and relief for teacher Furius Philocalus, with two students. Capua, Augustan period.

A private tutor might still teach children in a small group rather than one-to-one. References to girls' tutors suggest individual tutoring (e.g. Caecilia, daughter of Atticus, and Minicia Fundana), although some girls went to public schools (see below). We know more about the education of boys of the imperial family than others, and these were sometimes in groups which included boys from other upper-class but not imperial families. The *grammaticus* who taught Augustus' grandsons Gaius and Lucius, the freedman M. Verrius Flaccus, was allowed to move his school into the imperial household (Suetonius, *Gramm.* 17). Claudius' son Britannicus had Vespasian's son Titus (from age 7 to about 15) as fellow-pupil.[33] The grandfather (M. Saluius Otho) of the future emperor Otho was brought up in Livia's house (Suetonius, *Otho* 1). From the little that is known of the grandfather's career (he was *monetalis* in 11 BCE) we can deduce a probable birth date in the 40s BCE. This would make him approximately a coeval of Livia's sons Tiberius (born 42 BCE) and Drusus (38 BCE). As their father Drusus died in 33, it was after that that they and M. Saluius Otho (and perhaps other boys)[34] were brought up together in Livia's house. These examples reflect a recognition of the importance of peer learning and interaction in preference to a cloistered, individual tutorial education. There was a similar socializing motive in Augustus' bringing foreign princes to Rome to be educated with members of his own family.[35] The acculturation would be two-way and useful for both sides in the future.

Quintilian emphasizes the importance of group learning, for its pedagogical and socializing benefits, in his lengthy discussion of schools versus private tutors (1. 2). He addresses the two main arguments against schools: a child's morals are especially at risk at a young age in the company of many other children, and a teacher who has to divide his time amongst a number of children cannot give the individual attention to one which a private tutor

---

[33] Suetonius, *Titus* 2. Vespasian and Vespasian's brother had played a part in Claudius' invasion of Britain.

[34] The emperor Galba had reason to be grateful for Livia's patronage: did this include education?

[35] Suetonius, *Augustus* 48. E.g. the Jewish prince M. Iulius Agrippa (Agrippa I) was reared at Rome with Tiberius' son Drusus and his nephew Claudius: Josephus, *Jewish Antiquities* 18. 143. Cf. below (Ch. 6) for Antonia's role in this.

can. He admits that there is evidence of bad influences on boys
at schools, but argues that such influences can occur at home too
(from tutor, household slaves, or over-indulgent parents). A
trustworthy chaperone (usually a *paedagogus*) is recommended to
accompany the child to school and remain with the child there.
As for personal attention in teaching, he shows how that is possible in a schoolroom: pupils need a certain amount of time for
individual initiative and study, and the explication of texts
requires a teacher to give a lecture, which all pupils can profit
from simultaneously. Moreover, says Quintilian, a boy who is
going to live a public life needs to become used early to the glare
of publicity and to the stimulus and competition of his peers; he
needs to form friendships which may be life-long; he needs to
develop an understanding of his fellows; and both teacher and
pupil will benefit from performing to a largish audience. Some of
these benefits can be seen in the career of Atticus in the late
Republic. Of equestrian family himself, he went to school with
Cicero, also an equestrian but due to become the first senator in
his family and to reach high office, and with the Younger Marius,
who would become a second-generation senator, and with
L. Manlius Torquatus, of long-established patrician family, who
became consul in 65 BCE.[36] Schools, then, were to be preferred (in
Quintilian's view) and parents should choose a school according
to the quality of the teacher and the quality of the other pupils.
There was obviously a wide range of choice by Quintilian's day.

Schools for young children seem to have existed in Rome and
Italy from an early period. Various cities in Greece had taken an
official interest in the education of the young. Sparta put boys
from the age of 7 under a state magistrate and by the age of 12
they were in collective barracks away from their families, a system aimed at developing the soldier-citizen. Athens took an
interest in teenage citizen boys, and by the fourth century the
institution of the ephebeia had developed, under the supervision
of city-appointed magistrates, most notably the gymnasiarch.
This essentially aristocratic system spread to many other Greek
cities and gradually became less military and physical and more
intellectual. In the later Hellenistic period, when the city was no

---

[36] Nepos, *Atticus* 1, 4. Cf. Millar (1988: 46), who speaks of 'the variety of
social levels within the Senate' and the mingling of senatorial and equestrian
families.

longer the chief source of political power, individual benefactors established foundations to fund public schools, i.e. schools which were open to anyone who could pay a fee but which were privately funded. The city assumed some responsibility for the administration of the school, as envisaged later by Pliny for his school at Comum (*Letters* 4. 13).

There are no contemporary records for Roman schools before the first century BCE, but later authors refer to children at classes in public areas from an early period. There is enough circumstantial detail in the two accounts of the ordeal of the girl Verginia, in the fifth century BCE, to suggest that they are based on a long tradition. Livy (3. 44, dealing with 449 BCE) has Verginia entering the Roman forum, on her way to school, when she attracted the lustful attention of Appius Claudius. Dionysius of Halicarnassus (11. 28. 3) has her already in school (that of a *grammaticus*), reading. Verginia was about 15 years old at the time and ready for marriage. Her mother had died, but she had women attendants (nurses or chaperones) to accompany her. Schools at Tusculum in the early fourth century are mentioned by Livy (6. 25. 9).[37] The first teachers recorded by name date from the middle of the third century BCE. Suetonius (*Gramm.* 1–2) gives the poets Liuius Andronicus and Ennius[38] this role, but names the Greek Crates of Mallos (168 BCE) the first to introduce the systematic study of *grammatike* to Rome.[39] Plutarch (*Roman Questions* 50) says that the first to open a school and charge fees was Spurius Caruilius, a freedman *c.*230 BCE.

By the late Republic schools were a common feature of life in Rome and Italian country towns. They were by no means, however, universal: Pliny the Younger was shocked to find that there was not a school in his native town of Comum at the end of the first century. Although modern textbooks often delineate a hier-

---

[37] I find the detail persuasive. It might, however, merely be part of Livy's idea of what a normal town would be like: shops open, craftsmen at work, schools operating. Cf. evidence for youth organizations (for girls and boys) at Tusculum later: Jaczynowska (1978) below.

[38] Both from Magna Graecia, but the former an ex-slave and the latter free-born.

[39] Crates did not, however, open a school for children. He held audience for adults who gathered to hear him expound on Greek literature, and they used him as a model for how to impart this to children.

archy of schools, from primary (that of the *litterator* or *magister*) to secondary (that of the *grammaticus*) to tertiary (that of the *rhetor*),[40] there is no such sharp distinction in the ancient sources. Some teachers taught at two levels, offering overlapping curricula according to their pupils' needs and abilities. The rhetorician did stand much higher, in reputation and fees, than other teachers, and his students were more select in that rhetoric was studied by those who had some ambition for a public career—this would eliminate girls and many boys.

Flexibility of curriculum was made easier because of little reliance on specialized equipment. Schoolrooms were austere and sparsely furnished, located in public areas and operating out of ad hoc space such as booths or shops on the edge of the forum. We know of no permanent physical buildings for schools and there were not the material resources and equipment familiar in many modern schools.[41] Details which recur in literary descriptions of schools include their noisiness, the early hour at which they started classes,[42] the severity of corporal punishment, and the low status and payment of most (but not all) teachers.[43]

The *paedagogus* was an important element in the school-going process. He was usually a slave but had to be carefully chosen for moral integrity,[44] conscientiousness, and, if possible, some intellectual ability. He was not a teacher, but as he accompanied the child to and from school and oversaw the child's lessons and learning he inevitably imparted some informal education (and acquired some himself, which enabled him to better himself later). Quintilian (1. 8–11) required the best-quality *paedagogus* possible and implied some role in elementary teaching or tutoring.

I would urge that *paedagogi* should either be thoroughly educated—that should be the first consideration—or should realize that they are not.

---

[40] Booth (1979) and W. V. Harris (1989: 234) are valuable correctives to this rigid view.

[41] See Bonner (1977: ch. x, pp. 116–25) and W. V. Harris (1989: 236–7).

[42] Probably in common with all aspects of public life, although Juvenal (*Satires* 7. 222) says that schoolchildren had to get out of bed while others, even workmen, slept.

[43] Some examples of literary references: Martial 9. 29. 5–8, 9. 68, 12. 57, 14. 223; Juvenal 7. 222.

[44] There was a recognition of the danger of sexual molestation of boys at school or on their way through public places.

Nothing is worse than those who have progressed a little beyond the alphabet and delude themselves that they have real knowledge. They think that the role of tutoring is beneath them, and as if by some right of authority (a frequent source of vanity in this sort of men) they become imperious and sometimes brutal and indoctrinate the child with their own fatuousness. Their misguidedness is no less harmful to the child's morals . . .

If, however, it proves impossible to have the ideal nurses, schoolmates and *paedagogi*, there should be at least one constant attendant with some command of speaking who will immediately correct any imperfect expression used by these others in the presence of the pupil and prevent its sinking in. But be clear that what I previously set out is the ideal, and this latter is only a remedy.

In Augustus' childhood he had had a slave *paedagogus*, Sphaerus, who performed his duties so well that Augustus later freed him and gave him a public funeral when he died (Dio 48. 33. 1). The mid-first century BCE was a stormy time in the city of Rome, when *paedagogi* had to be especially vigilant for their charges. During the proscriptions of 43 BCE, children who lost their parents and inherited wealthy estates were particularly vulnerable. Appian (*Civil Wars* 4. 30) writes of one *paedagogus* who refused to surrender his young charge, which resulted in the death of both *paedagogus* and orphan. The close bond between *paedagogus* and child was recognized by the law, which allowed early manumission of a *paedagogus*. Included in the list of such favoured slaves was the more lowly slave who carried a student's satchel (for texts or writing materials), the *capsarius*.[45] One who was recorded in an epitaph was L. Volusius Heracla, who had risen from satchel-carrier to win his freedom and be his master's chamberlain. He purchased or was given the slave woman Prima whom he freed to be his wife: as Volusia Prima she set up his epitaph (*CIL* 6. 7368).

Of the four female *paedagogae* recorded from Rome, three were attached to girls and belonged to large households which could afford extra staff of a more specialized kind. The female *paedagoga* probably worked with male colleagues who could carry out

---

[45] *D.* 40. 2. 13, Ulpian. For others in this list of favoured slaves, see Ch. 6 below.

the 'bodyguard' responsibilities of the job.[46] Most of the girls for whom we have details had male *paedagogi* (see below).

By the time children came to school they had already had some exposure to myths, stories, and pieces of poetry (Quintilian 1. 1. 36). We have seen the role of nurses in story-telling, and although Tacitus (*Dialogue on Orators* 29. 1) criticizes the misleading nature of some of this (slave carers, male and female, fill infants' minds with rubbish, 'fabulis et erroribus') the stories nevertheless laid a foundation of moral *exempla* and sketchy history on which later education could build. Quintilian takes a more positive attitude than Tacitus to these early experiences: by memorizing aphorisms, famous sayings, notable historical personages, and selections of poetry the young child will retain the moral element in these and they will help form his own character. In the early years it is mainly memory which is being trained, and that is not a trivial accomplishment but one which will stand the future orator (i.e. public person) in good stead.

The emphasis on the moral lessons of history continued throughout a broad liberal curriculum, but for older children it was not necessarily a mindless memorizing of historical examples and acceptance of their morals. Valerius Maximus, who published a collection of famous deeds and sayings in the early imperial period (under Tiberius), saw that the study of the past could help in understanding how contemporary society and prosperity came about and could thus make a contribution to present-day behaviour (Book 2, preface). Beard (1993) has helped restore the credibility of the declamation exercises practised by older boys, pointing out that their subject-matter is not trivial but concerns 'central problems of human behaviour'.[47] And these problems were debatable: they were not capable of simple resolution. Thus, after the earliest stage of education, historical precedents could be

---

[46] A male *paedagogus* is named along with the *paedagoga* for the two Sulpiciae Galbae girls (*CIL* 6. 9754). These girls may have had some connection with the future emperor Galba. *PIR* S 742 postulates that they may have been daughters of C. Sulpicius Galba, consul in 22 and oldest brother of the future emperor. Two other *paedagogae* were attached to a Messallina (4459) and a Statilia (6331) in big family *columbaria* (the *monumenta* of the Marcelli and the Statilii respectively). (See below on *paedagogi* of girls.) For Urbana (9758), nothing is known beyond her job title and her age (25).

[47] Kennedy (1972: 334) had already pointed out the preoccupation of declamation with 'the relationship of children to parents'.

used critically rather than to present rigid, prepackaged models of behaviour.[48]

The post-elementary stage of education, conducted by a *grammaticus*,[49] might last until the age of 14 or 15 (but the stages were flexible and some boys moved out of this stage earlier). In this stage the aim was to develop further the ability to read, write, and speak well. It was heavily based on literature (originally Greek literature, then Latin translations of Greek, and then gradually, in imperial times, Latin authors as they became available, especially Vergil). Books (papyrus rolls) were produced in very limited copies; thus much depended on aural learning and students' memorizing. The comparative rarity of texts made Rome a very aural and visual society. Literature itself was made known largely through the *recitatio*, the public reading which became so frequent in imperial society. Visual representations of education scenes often show the teacher seated or standing, reading and dictating to his pupils from his one copy of a text (see Figs. 2.2 and 5.2),[50] although there are also representations and references which show that pupils sometimes had some texts of their own.[51] The teacher's explication of a text provided material for a wide range of subjects, such as linguistics, grammar, pronunciation, lit-

---

[48] Cf. Roller (1997), who stresses the importance of ethical argumentation in declamation. He discusses the way in which declamation 'generally places two or more accepted social values into competition': the conflict between the values is 'the basis for deliberation'. Moral criteria are privileged. Thus 'a moral understanding of events is the primary mode of understanding' (pp. 112–13). Cf. Kaster (2001) for the practical lessons inherent in even the most lurid rhetorical exercises. Bloomer (1997) sees the practical lessons as those of empathy and acculturation—youths learning to enact different characters in their training as future administrators.

[49] There is no satisfactory translation of this term ('grammarian' is too narrow), so the Latin term will be used throughout.

[50] Cf. Berczelly (1978: 63 ff.); and examples in Marrou (1938: 28–147, figs. 1–186). A marble statue of the teacher Orbilius was set up on the Capitol at Beneventum, showing him seated, clad in a Greek mantle, with two book-boxes (*scrinia*) at his side (Suetonius, *Gramm.* 9). Sometimes it is not clear whether we have a schoolroom scene or a father–son scene. The Pompeian relief cited below (De Franciscis 1988), which might show a scene in a book-copying business or a schoolroom scene, could also depict an author-father's gift of a text which he has dedicated to his son (cf. LeMoine 1991).

[51] Juvenal 7. 226–7 (see text below, at n. 74). On Marcianus' memorial the boy has a book satchel (Fig. 5.1).

erature, history, ethics. In Tacitus' words (*Dialogue on Orators* 30, spoken by Messalla), the child would become familiar with *res*, *homines*, *tempora* ('the natural world, human nature, and the civic world'). The curriculum usually included also some geometry, astronomy, and music.

Cicero spoke of all these subjects and the divisions of rhetoric: once disparate, they now formed a coherent curriculum (*On the Orator* 1. 187). He did not here mention philosophy, although we know that he acquired an extensive knowledge of philosophical systems and principles. That probably came at a later stage. We know that at the age of 18 he was enthused by the Greek philosophers flocking to Rome (partly as refugees ahead of King Mithridates' push into Greece), especially Philo, the head of the Academy.[52] Quintilian (1 pr. 9–20) associated the study of philosophy with that of rhetoric, insisting that they were intertwined and that philosophy did not have a monopoly on teaching principles of virtue. Here again is Cato the Elder's old definition of the orator, 'a good man skilled in speaking', but the technical skills were now much more sophisticated: an excellent orator must not only be of excellent moral character but must also have excellent intellectual qualities ('omnes animi uirtutes'). The study of philosophy was now more sophisticated too, and therefore more suitable to the teenage years than to the school of the *grammaticus*. But from the earliest stages of education moral principles were being inculcated. The Romans' way of doing this, especially for younger children, was to provide concrete examples rather than theoretical analyses. Valerius Maximus is most explicit about this. In the preface to his chapter on 'Poverty' (4. 4) he gives the example of Cornelia, mother of the Gracchi brothers, responding to a woman friend's display of expensive jewellery by pointing to her own children as her *ornamenta*. This concrete example of her real wealth was worth far more, says Valerius Maximus, than a disquisition on the nature of wealth, and his own message would be conveyed better by personalities and historical examples (*personae*) than by mere words (*uerba*). He then proceeds to give other examples of how specific people dealt with poverty and wealth. In a later section of his work (8. 14) he says that others (implicitly Greeks) have discussed the nature of *gloria* theoretically, but he

---

[52] Cicero, *Brutus* 306; cf. *Fam.* 13. 1. 2, written from Athens in 51 BCE.

wants to illustrate human actors by their deeds and vice versa (*auctores* by *facta* and *facta* by *auctores*).

Plutarch, writing in Greece (and in Greek) in the late first and early second centuries, identifies the moral aim in students' reading of poetry: they will in this way learn early about virtues and vices, e.g. the virtues of moderation and magnanimity (*Moralia* 35C, 'How to study [listen to] poetry'). Such lessons complement philosophy and are a good preparation for the philosophical study which will shape the wise man (*Moralia* 35F–36D). For the Romans, however, the aim was not to develop a philosopher (*sapiens*, literally 'a wise man') but to enhance learning about ethics, partly because of the moral element in the ideal public man and partly because the public man (the fully trained orator) needed to be exposed to many fields of knowledge. This broad command of many subjects would stand him in better stead than any specific training for a particular case. He could apply his broad knowledge of many matters and many ways of thinking to any issue, yielding insights and understanding. Tacitus claims (*Dialogue on Orators* 31–2, Messalla) that this is recognized and appreciated in the best orators not only by the well-educated part of an audience but also by the more general population (*populus*). This might be something of an overstatement by Tacitus, but it does reflect the wide display of oratorical talents in Roman public and cultural life (see Chapter 7 below) and the tincture of oratorical training even in lower levels of education open to a wider range of students. Musonius Rufus, a philosopher-teacher of the latter half of the first century, who—we shall see—directed some of his philosophical discussions at family questions, defined the purpose in learning ethics, and being able to distinguish good from evil, as a happy life (7. 58. 14–15: τὸ εὐδαιμονεῖν καὶ ζῆν μακαρίως εἰς τὸ λοιπόν).

The emphasis on practical applications is seen in Roman attitudes to the study of music, a broad term embracing singing (and poetry), playing an instrument, and dancing. These had been important elements in much Greek education. Nepos warns his Roman audience, in his biography of Epaminondas (1. 1–2), not to judge other peoples by Roman tradition and habits. Epaminondas' education included singing, dancing, and instrument-playing, and these accomplishments were praiseworthy in Greece, but are considered frivolous and contemptible by Romans

(2. 1–3). Nepos claims that music is inappropriate for a leading Roman citizen, and dancing is considered a vice. But in Nepos' own lifetime a consul-elect, Murena, was adept at these.[53]

Quintilian (1. 10. 9–22) acknowledges the long history of respect and almost religious awe attributed to music (*musice*) by Greeks and Romans, and its close association with poetry. He then emphasizes the importance to oratory of learning from music (especially singing) how to stir emotions by means of gesture, arrangement of words, and inflexion of voice (1. 10. 22–30). His preferred music is, however, the patriotic music of old, not the modern, effeminate, lascivious music of the stage. In the previous generation Seneca the Elder had similarly condemned the modern style of singing and dancing as degenerate and effeminate and connected it with a decline in Roman oratory since Cicero's day.[54] Quintilian argues (1. 11. 15–19) that gymnastics teachers (*palaestrici*), whose lessons might include dancing, could be useful in teaching graceful and appropriate gestures,[55] and he cites the long Roman tradition of using dance in religious ritual. But none of these skills should be developed to professional levels.[56] This tension between the attractiveness and usefulness of music on the one hand and its potential subversiveness of morals and national values on the other hand had a long history in Rome. Scipio Aemilianus, Africanus the Younger, was reputed to have deplored in 129 BCE the craze for dancing lessons which had gripped freeborn boys and girls in Rome (Macrobius 3. 14. 7).[57] Macrobius says that this taste for dancing (*saltatio*) had developed amongst young men and women of good family since the beginning of the second century BCE (after the end of the Second Punic War) and that the practice had brought no dishonour. Perhaps it was more highly developed skills, and more foreign steps, which

---

[53] Cicero, *In Defence of Murena* 13, has to rebut Cato's charge that Murena is a *saltator*, and his rebuttal is very tendentious.

[54] *Controuersiae* pref. 8: 'cantandi saltandique obscaena studia effeminatos tenent', and young men vie with women in effeminacy of toilette and voice.

[55] Epaminondas, the 4th-c. Theban statesman and soldier, used *palaestra* exercises to prepare himself for athletics and war (Nepos, *Epaminondas* 2. 4).

[56] 1. 12. 14. Cf. Cicero, *On the Orator* 3. 86–7: professionals, e.g. *scaenici*, would sing every day, but a man of practical affairs (a *paterfamilias*, an *eques Romanus*) sings only when it suits him, having learnt it in childhood.

[57] *ORF* fr. 30. Cf. Cato's judgment on a senator: Macrobius 3. 14. 9–10, *ORF* frs. 114–15.

alarmed Scipio later in the century.[58] Sallust's criticism of Sempronia, wife of an ex-consul in 63 BCE, was not so much that she danced and played the lyre but that she did it too well (*Catilinarian Conspiracy* 25. 2).

Attitudes towards musical skills and performance were probably shifting, if slowly, in the late Republic and in the Principate. Already in the second century BCE, as we have seen, good families were allowing their sons and daughters to learn dancing; singing had long been popular within Roman families, mainly of traditional songs; at the end of the Republic Cicero, Sallust, and Nepos still saw dancing, for males and females, as disrespectable but it was obviously practised in high society. In Augustus' time Vitruvius (*On Architecture* 6. 8–9) recommended music in the curriculum for architecture students, because of its usefulness in some aspects of the profession, such as the design of ballistic weapons, for acoustics in theatres, and for making water-engines. Columella (*On Agriculture* 1 pr. 3 and 5) lists music and dancing amongst the skills for which there was no lack of formal training. Nero's efforts to recruit young people of good family to his musical activities met with an eager response;[59] and although Nero was much criticized for his attempts to 'go professional', and Quintilian had reservations about some kinds of musical performance, such activity was obviously fairly widespread and popular by then. Suetonius was able to report in neutral or favourable tones on Titus' instrumental and vocal accomplishments.[60]

As in other matters of education and culture, we need to be cautious about generalizing from the criticisms of upper-class

---

[58] There may also have been political undertones which we can no longer read. Scipio's criticism was expressed in a speech attacking a proposed law to restructure the lawcourts. This law is attributed by Macrobius to Ti. Gracchus, but Gruen (1968: 58) shows that there must be confusion with C. Gracchus.

[59] e.g. Tacitus, *Annals* 14. 14–15. Tacitus also reports (*Histories* 3. 62) that a man of high rank, Fabius Valens, who died in the civil wars of 68, had developed into an enthusiastic and skilful (if indecent) performer of mimes at the Juvenalia under Nero, although he claimed at first to be participating unwillingly.

[60] But these were not excessively polished: he was only 'not unaccomplished' (not *rudis*) in music (*Titus* 3). This follows a report on Titus' physical skills (arms and horsemanship) and fluency in Greek and Latin oratory and poetry composition. It is the sort of package of accomplishments reported by Nepos for the Athenian Epaminondas of five centuries earlier.

male writers who may have been conservative and may not have reflected widespread practice. Funerary monuments sometimes show the practice of musical skills, as depicted by children in the guise of Muses (see Fig. 1.17). Was it thought that such skills brought about immortality? They had long been associated with gods and heroes, and this view might have persisted in popular religion and culture. This is the way in which Toynbee and Ward-Perkins (1956: 92 and 103 n. 91) interpret the representations on a sarcophagus in the Vatican Cemetery.[61] In each of two scenes a seated girl is accompanied by a standing attendant. In one scene the girl appears to have held a scroll (like the one held by her attendant) and in the other she is about to play the lyre. Toynbee and Ward-Perkins suggest that 'the moral of the picture is that devotion to the arts and sciences wins for the soul a blessed here-after' and that 'such representations suggest that music played a more honourable part in Roman education and culture than Quintilian's words . . . might lead us to expect'.[62]

This curriculum then had breadth, but with a functional and practical emphasis. This emphasis was not intended to lead to a narrow range of subjects or skills. It was what we would call 'applied' rather than theoretical, although there was a theoretical underpinning. It aimed at public activity and performance rather than internalized cultural development. The process might be called *educatio*, or *institutio*, but it aimed at *humanitas*.

Much of the curriculum relied on the use of both Latin and Greek. By Quintilian's time he actually recommended (1. 1. 12–14) that a child should learn Greek as its first language in infancy, because all Latin disciplines had their roots in Greek counterparts and because Latin would be acquired easily enough as being the native language. But Latin should not be long delayed, for fear of late learning breeding bad habits. Thus the two languages would continue simultaneously. Because of the desirability of learning Greek correctly early, families who cared about their children's education were advised to choose a wet-nurse carefully: she should be a Greek native-speaker, 'so that the infant nursed by

[61] Tomb R, apparently one of the earlier parts of the cemetery, perhaps early 2nd c. CE.

[62] Cf. Marrou (1938: Part II, ch. IV, pp. 231–57) for the association of 'hero-isation' and intellectual accomplishment.

her may become accustomed to the best speech'.[63] Such nurses (usually slaves) would have spoken the colloquial Greek of the day, not the scholarly, Atticizing Greek of literary and oratorical studies. Thus contemporary pronunciation and usage were important for anyone who was going to be active in the multicultural society of Rome and her provinces in the late Republic and the Empire. Greek was spoken by a wide variety of the population at Rome—foreign residents (*peregrini*), traders, many Jews (and, later, some of the Christian community), and many slaves and ex-slaves. In the early second century Juvenal (3. 61) deplored the 'Greek city' which Rome had become. Already in 64 BCE Quintus Cicero was reminding his brother Marcus (a candidate in the consular elections for 63) that Rome was a seething mixture of customs, talk and feelings, a city formed from a conglomeration of many peoples, 'nationum conuentus' (*Commentariolum petitionis* 54). In the middle of the next century Seneca wrote[64] of the very mixed populations in many cities of the Roman world. Into Rome there had been an influx from all over the world, people drawn by ambition, public duty, love of luxury, desire for education (*liberalia studia*), the public entertainment available, friendship, the opportunity to work hard and achieve success, the market for one's services (sexual or oratorical). For many of these, Greek (albeit sometimes a dialect) was the *lingua franca*. It is clear from Cicero's correspondence that men like him were fluent in this colloquial Greek.[65]

Slaves who won their freedom in time to have freeborn children tended to give these children Latin names rather than Greek (B. Rawson 1966), and there must have been an attempt by the upwardly mobile to acquire and use Latin as a mark of Romanness. For the upper classes, however, colloquial Greek was complemented by scholarly Greek as they moved into formal education. This was the language of high culture, although colloquial Greek was much used in popular entertainment. Julius

[63] Soranus 2. 19, trans. Temkin; cf. Quintilian 1. 1. 4.

[64] *Consolation to Helvia* 6. 2–5, minimizing some of the effects of exile, to comfort his mother Helvia during his own exile.

[65] See Dubuisson (1992) for an excellent discussion of bilingualism at Rome in Cicero's day. He suggests that slaves were normally addressed in Greek. The text above owes much to Dubuisson's discussion. See also Leiwo (1995) for the concept of mixed-language communities and code-switching.

Caesar sponsored actors (*histriones*) of all languages in the theatre (Suetonius, *Iulius* 39. 1), and Cicero refers to *Graeci ludi*, which appear to be plays in the Greek language, at the opening of Pompey's theatre in 55 BCE.[66] The emperor Tiberius was fluent in Greek, but was a purist about using only Latin in formal Roman situations, such as in the senate and for soldiers' testimony (Suetonius, *Tiberius* 71). The literary teaching by the *grammaticus* drew heavily on Greek literature. Ovid (*Tristia* 2. 369–70) cites Menander as being studied by boys and girls and lists a great many other Greek authors who he assumes are familiar to his readers. As we have seen, Greek-speaking intellectuals were frequent visitors and even residents in upper-class Roman homes. Cicero's son Marcus, at an age of about 19, is depicted as seeking a Latin version of what he has already learned in Greek about rhetoric (Cicero, *De partitione oratoria* 1).

The teaching of literature relied heavily on dictation by the teacher and memorization by the student. This was not infrequently reinforced by the rod and other forms of corporal punishment. Many writers confirm this aspect of schooling, and there are some visual representations, as in a wall-painting from Pompeii showing the beating of an almost-naked boy slung over another boy's shoulders, his feet held by yet another boy.[67] Quintilian, with his usual humanity and perceptiveness, argued more in favour of inducements and persuasion than compulsion. He saw that excessively severe criticism made children depressed,

---

[66] *Fam.* 7. 1. 3. There were also Oscan plays, and there must have been many different languages spoken in Rome. But a widespread familiarity with Greek is apparent. Cf. Cicero's dismissive comment on 'Greek plays' in 44 BCE: *Att.* 16. 5. 1. Cf. Ch. 7 below.

[67] Bonner (1977: fig. 11 p. 118), the *catomus* position. This representation is frequently reproduced in modern discussions, but, as far as I can establish, it was not a frequent motif in ancient art. Berczelly (1978: 64) claims that the two themes of *lectio* and punishment 'appear in art closely related to each other', but his only example is the punishment of a young satyr by Silenus in scenes of Dionysus' childhood, which he admits probably has symbolic religious significance. There may be a metaphorical reference in Cicero to the form of punishment depicted in the Pompeian wall-painting. In a letter to a friend in 45 BCE (*Fam.* 7. 25. 1) he jokingly refers to fear of punishment for eulogistic works on Cato. The 'schoolmaster' (Caesar?) has returned earlier than expected: 'I'm afraid our *Cato* books will get the *catomus* treatment' (see Shackleton Bailey's commentary). See above, n. 50, and below, for other visual representations of school scenes.

lose morale, come to hate studies, and give up effort (2. 4. 10). He argued that corporal punishment was humiliating and counter-productive (1. 3. 13–17). It was, he said, fit only for slaves; even for slaves it does not work if they are of the worst kind, as they become hardened to blows, and similarly it will not work with a child if he is so mean-spirited (*illiberalis*) that he cannot be improved by reproof (*obiurgatio*). It will be at best of short-term benefit because it cannot be used on older youths, so it is better to use other methods[68] from the beginning. Moreover, psycho-logical trauma can result from thrashings, and there is potential for child abuse. (Quintilian clearly has sexual abuse in mind.) Quintilian's analysis is particularly pertinent in the climate of many of today's 'advanced' societies, where the full dimensions of child abuse (including abuse in schools) are only now being recognized. Quintilian sums up, 'No one should have excessive power over those who are at an age when they are helpless and easily victimised' ('in aetatem infirmam et iniuriae obnoxiam nemini debet nimium licere'). More than half a century earlier, M. Verrius Flaccus, a freedman and *grammaticus* who taught Augustus' grandsons Gaius and Lucius and who ran a school from the imperial household, used incentives to stimulate his stu-dents' efforts. He rewarded students with gifts of handsome books (Suetonius, *Gramm.* 17).

Horace (*Epistles* 2. 1. 70–1) remembered his teacher Orbilius as *plagosus*, 'the flogger', drumming literary texts into the small boy. A fellow-pupil who also became a well-known poet in Augustus' reign, Domitius Marsus, recorded the same reputation for Orbilius.[69] Other anecdotes about Orbilius suggest that he was an embittered, sharp-tongued man with a chip on his shoulder; but it should be noted that he had had a difficult life. He was orphaned young in tragic circumstances, had to earn a living before he could resume higher education studies, and taught in a municipal town (Beneventum) for many years before going to

[68] e.g. 'stick and carrot', 'reproof and encouragement', as advised by Seneca in *On Clemency* 1. 16. Cf. *On Clemency* 16. 3: the best teacher of *liberalia studia* does not rely on thrashings but 'monitionibus et uerecundia emendare ac docere'.

[69] Suetonius, *Gramm.* 9, quotes Domitius Marsus' line, 'si quos Orbilius ferula scuticaque cecidit', as well as Horace's adjective. See Suetonius for other details on Orbilius.

Rome, where he earned a good reputation as a teacher but little money (having to live in a garret). Moreover, he was probably over 60 years of age by the time Horace and Domitius Marsus were his pupils,[70] and presumably there was no end in sight to having to cope with often disruptive and untalented pupils and mean, uncaring parents. Hardly an old age to sweeten the temper! (He lived to almost 100, but mercifully (?) had lost his memory before then. How he supported himself in his last years can only be guessed at.)

Other references to corporal punishment are scattered through the literature of the imperial period. Ovid (*Amores* 1. 13. 17–18) upbraids Dawn for waking boys early, and sending them off to their schoolmasters, where their tender hands will suffer savage blows (*uerbera saeua*). In the mid-first century Seneca (*Letters* 94. 9) used the angry schoolmaster as an example of those who preach against a vice (anger) but cannot practise what they preach. In the early second century Martial and Juvenal both associated schooldays with an early start to the day and fear of blows,[71] and such references were still to be found in Christian writers of the fourth and fifth centuries (Bonner 1977: 143–5). The usual weapon was a cane (*ferula*), but sometimes the more savage *scutica* was used, 'the Scythian hide, thonged with bristling lashes'.[72] It was usually the schoolmaster who administered such punishment, but sometimes the *paedagogus* enforced discipline with a cane.[73]

The sufferings of the schoolmaster are graphically expressed by Juvenal at the end of his seventh satire. He has been complaining about the lot of intellectuals, and the need for patronage. His lament for the *grammaticus* (7. 215–43) begins with the teacher's low pay and the need to give a cut to the child's attendant and to the father's paymaster. He then continues:

---

[70] Orbilius was in his fiftieth year in 63 BCE, and Horace—born 65 BCE—will not have joined his classes until the late 50s BCE.

[71] Martial 9. 68, 14. 80; Juvenal 1. 15, 7. 222.

[72] Martial 10. 62. 8–10 for this and references to the *ferula*.

[73] But see Saller (1991, esp. 157–65) on the contrast between slaves and freeborn children in the nature of their punishment. It is implicit there that slaves would not normally have administered severe corporal punishment on freeborn children.

Better give in, then: bargain, be beaten down
For a lower fee, like a hawker peddling blankets
And winter rugs—so long as you get *some* recompense
For presiding, before it's light, in a hell-hole any blacksmith
Or wool-carder would refuse to train apprentices in;
So long as you get *some* return for enduring the stink
Of all those guttering lanterns—one to each pupil,
So that every Vergil and Horace is grimed with lampblack
From cover to cover. Yet, nine times out of ten,
You need a court order to get even this small pittance.
In return, what's more, such parents demand quite impossible
Standards from any master; his grammar must be above cavil,
History, literature, he must have all the authorities
Pat at his fingertips. They'll waylay him *en route*
For the public baths, and expect him to answer their questions
Straight off the cuff—who was Anchises' nurse, . . .
. . . They demand that the teacher
Shall mould these tender minds, like an artist who shapes
A face out of wax, with his thumb. He must, they insist,
Be a father to all his pupils, must stop them getting up to
Indecent tricks with each other (though it's no sinecure
To keep check over all those darting eyes—and fingers).
'See to it,' you're told, 'and when the school year's ended,
You'll get as much as a jockey makes from a single race.'[74]

In the course of the satire, Juvenal has claimed that rhetoric
teachers get paid much less than those who teach wealthy boys
music and singing. There seems to have been a variety of specialist teachers in the imperial period, offering 'enrichment'
courses or more functional, applied courses against which the
generalist teacher had to compete. Martial (10. 62) mentions the
teacher of arithmetic (*calculator*) and one of shorthand (*notarius*).
In spite of the complaints of low and irregular pay, we know of
some well-paid teachers in the late Republic and early Empire.[75]
Already in the 40s BCE Julius Caesar provided incentives for
teachers (and doctors) to practise at Rome. They became recognized by Roman law and the imperial administration as members

[74] Juvenal 7. 219–43, trans. Peter Green (Penguin, 1967).
[75] Pliny, *NH* 7. 128; Suetonius, *Gramm.* 3. Pliny says that the highest price
for a slave before his own day was the 700,000 sesterces paid for a *grammaticus*
named Daphnis; but in his own day slave actors (*histriones*) fetched higher
prices.

of the learned professions which qualified for privileges and exemptions (*D.* 27. 1. 6. 1–12, Modestinus; 50. 4. 18. 30, Arcadius Charisius; both citing earlier authorities).

Advice abounded on how to choose the best teachers. Pliny the Younger took seriously the quest to find teachers for his friends' children: he gives a full account of this in *Letters* 3. 3, where he stresses the technical and moral qualities necessary in a teacher of rhetoric. The recommended teacher (Julius Genitor) was a man of serious and excellent character, even rather austere, and had the highest reputation for oratory. Quintilian (2. 2. 1–8) emphasized that character (*mores*) was important for teachers at all levels, but especially at the level of rhetorician the teacher's role *in loco parentis* was crucial.

It might cause surprise that Romans were prepared to entrust care of their children to people (e.g. wet-nurses, other carers, *paedagogi*, teachers) of a class inferior to their own. This does not indicate that Romans attached little importance to these aspects of their children's rearing and development, but it might reflect their respect for special skills and their willingness to pay for them. Is this very different from modern parents' willingness to entrust children to staff of kindergartens, child-care centres and schools, to nannies and sports instructors, many of whom would stand lower on the socio-economic ladder than at least some of the parents?

The low social status of teachers is acknowledged by Seneca the Elder, when he draws attention to Rubellius Blandus as the first Roman knight to open a rhetoric school: this had been in the early first century CE. Previously, says Seneca (*Controuersiae* 2 pr. 5), 'it was dishonourable to teach what it was honourable to learn' ('turpe erat docere quod honestum erat discere'). Nevertheless, the importance of the teacher's role was recognized, and we know by name a large number of *grammatici* and rhetoric teachers. Suetonius has preserved many of these in his works *On Grammatici* and *On Rhetoric Teachers*, but other names recur in a range of other writings.[76] Cicero spoke appreciatively of his teachers and mentors,[77] and in 54 BCE he reported to his brother (*Q. fr.* 3. 3. 4) that young Quintus was devoted to his rhetor

[76] There is a useful list of *grammatici* and 'philologues', with discussion and source references, in Christes (1979).

[77] *In Defence of Plancius* 81; *In Defence of Archias*, e.g. 1, 5, 7.

Paeonius, whom Cicero described as a well-trained and morally good man ('ualde exercitati et boni'). Cicero respected Paeonius' expertise: although the rhetor's system was different from his own, he was unwilling to disturb Paeonius' teaching. The Stoic Diodotus taught Cicero geometry, music and, later, dialectic. When he was old and blind he came to live in Cicero's house. Perhaps we can judge his success and standing, as well as his gratitude to Cicero, by the fact that when he died in 59 BCE he left Cicero 100,000 sesterces (the financial qualification for equestrian rank) (*Att.* 2. 20. 6). Busy men of affairs sometimes showed their continuing interest in teachers' activities and skills by sitting in on lessons in their schools. Cicero was praetor in 66 BCE when he attended lessons in the school of M. Antonius Gnipho, who had previously taught the young Julius Caesar in Caesar's house (Suetonius, *Gramm.* 7). Atticus' freedman Caecilius Epirota, who taught Atticus' daughter Caecilia but was dismissed after a falling-out, was able to take up residence with the distinguished equestrian and poet Cornelius Gallus and live with him on close terms (*familiarissime*: Suetonius, *Gramm.* 16).[78] In more general and philosophical terms, Seneca (*On Benefits* 6. 15) discussed the value of teachers (and doctors). A teacher (*praeceptor*) was worthy of great affection (*caritas*) and respect (*reuerentia*), he said, and could move from the position of employee to that of friend.

Many life-cycle funerary monuments include scenes of education as important stages in the life of the deceased. The monument of Marcianus (Fig. 5.1), a 6-year-old on the way to school, is a large marble tablet (approximately 53 cm wide, 37 cm high, 11.5 cm thick, including inscription and sculpture). His clothing shows his freeborn status (tunic, toga, *bulla*). Attributes associated with education (such as the papyrus roll) are frequent on memorials. The 5-year-old A. Egrilius Magnus is represented at Ostia on a fine altar of the mid-first century holding such a roll.[79] (See further in Chapter 1 above.)

---

[78] Germanicus, a man of flamboyant gestures, presented his teacher (*praeceptor*) Cassius Silanus with the expensive gift of two chased cups (Pliny, *NH* 34. 47). But Silanus was much more of a social equal: cf. Ovid, *Letters from Pontus* 2. 5.

[79] Kleiner (1987: 12); B. Rawson (1997a: 220). Kleiner suggests that although the roll is intended to show the boy's erudition he was probably too young to be able to read.

The early stages of education, even when harsh and severe, did not crush all desire for learning, as 'higher education' teachers often attracted much favourable attention. Already in the second century BCE groups of young men were attracted by visiting scholars and teachers (e.g. Crates of Mallos in 168 BCE), creating an informal school or college of eager students. Three centuries later Pliny, a mature man, wrote enthusiastically of the performances of the visiting rhetorician Isaeus, urging a friend to make the effort to come to Rome from the country to hear him (*Letters* 2. 3). The high public profile of rhetoric teachers, their higher standing compared with that of the *grammaticus*, and the glittering prizes attached to success as an orator, all provided an incentive for boys (abetted by their parents) to hurry on to rhetoricians' classes. Some rhetoricians had a 'star' quality about them and their performances attracted large audiences from elite levels of society.[80] Some rose to senatorial rank and other high office (Suetonius, *Rhet.* 1). Adolescent boys who could claim a classroom link with such figures, and who aspired to the same level of clever argument, deft turn of phrase, and polished delivery, would bask in the reflected glory of such teachers at their public presentations. Younger brothers who attended would be inspired to move up to that stage of education as quickly as possible.

There was none of the modern lock-step programme of education: as with the legal system, individual judgements could be made about a young person's maturity and fitness to perform certain acts.[81] But this very flexibility had its drawbacks: some boys were pressed too hard in their education, and some youths advanced too quickly through their studies, making a premature beginning in public life. From the Flavian period there is criticism of this pressure and of the youths who entered public life overconfident and under-prepared. Pliny (*Letters* 2. 14) represents

[80] As pointed out by Beard (1993: 53): 'glamorous rhetoricians, enjoying a sparkling reputation among the Roman elite'. Pliny, *Letters* 2. 18, refers to the presence of 'senior senators' in a rhetoric teacher's classroom.

[81] In later antiquity, the ages for holding magistracies were much reduced (Wiedemann 1989: ch. 4). Although this was due largely to the difficulty of filling magistracies, Rome's flexibility about age eligibilities made it easier. Most of the examples in Wiedemann are from the 3rd c. onwards, but the epigraphic record for Italy provides evidence for a few child magistrates, in addition to members of the imperial family. Cf. Ch. 7 below.

young barristers in the courts as half-baked know-alls who have moved rapidly through the curriculum but who have acquired none of the experience (and humility) which Pliny claims for the older apprenticeship system.[82] Quintilian (12. 6. 1–7), balanced as ever, shares some of these concerns but argues that the age at which youths should start pleading cases should depend on individual capacity (*uires*). There are dangers in delaying entry too long, and he is aware of reported precedents for youths able to plead even before receiving the toga of adulthood (while still *praetextati*). Boys of distinguished families sometimes had to give public speeches at a young age, if they were the appropriate person to give the funeral eulogy for a deceased member of the family. The future Augustus was 11 (in 51 BCE) when he delivered the eulogy from the Rostra (in the Roman Forum, in probably the most public spot in the whole city) for his grandmother Julia.[83] Tiberius was only 9 in 33 BCE when, also from the Rostra, he delivered the eulogy for his father Nero (Suetonius, *Tiberius* 6). Gaius was 16 when he gave the eulogy for his grandmother Livia (Suetonius, *Gaius* 10. 1; Tacitus, *Annals* 5. 1). Nero too was 16 when he spoke at Claudius' funeral, but he had already been groomed and given opportunities for speech-making. Once he was married to Claudius' daughter Octavia and thus seen as heir presumptive to Claudius, he gave a series of elegant speeches to obtain privileges or assistance for various communities: these were aimed at polishing his reputation ('utque studiis honestis et eloquentiae gloria enitesceret').[84]

These examples come from elite families, but they tell us something about Roman education and Roman society's perception of children. The boys' education helped fit them for a public role; and society recognized this role, perceiving children as having an important part to play in *rites de passage* such as family funerals. What we do not know is what effect this early exposure had on the boys themselves. In Nero's reign Petronius has one of his characters (Encolpius) deliver a tirade against parents who try to force eloquence on boys scarcely out of the cradle ('pueris nascen-

---

[82] Cf. Tacitus, *Dialogue on Orators* 35, above.

[83] Suetonius, *Augustus* 8. 1: 'in his twelfth year'. Cf. Quintilian 12. 6. 1; Dio 39. 64.

[84] Tacitus, *Annals* 12. 58, 13. 3. There was a suggestion that Seneca had written Nero's speech for Claudius, but Nero knew how to deliver it.

tibus': *Satyricon* 4). Half a century later Tacitus (*Dialogue on Orators* 30) presents Messalla in the Flavian period as nostalgic for the good old days, when Cicero received a broad, well-paced education, as opposed to his own time[85] when there is indecent haste to get to the rhetoricians' schools.

One of the best-known and imposing monuments to a child prodigy whose intellectual achievements outstripped his age is that of Q. Sulpicius Maximus, discussed at the beginning of Chapter 1 above (Fig. 1.1). Here we see the pressure, by parents and children themselves, for children to perform beyond their years. In this case there seems to be further pressure for an upwardly mobile family to make its mark through educational achievement. The boy was freeborn, but his parents seem to have been ex-slaves. Their grief at the loss of their son is for social as well as personal reasons. Education has in many cultures been an avenue for ambitious, newly prosperous parents (especially migrants) to improve the standing of their children, and, through them, their own. Maximus' home city was Rome, but others flocked in to Rome to compete. L. Valerius Pudens came in from an Italian country town and won first prize in Latin poetry in 106 when he was 13 (see below, on 'City and Country'). These young competitors had to compete against mature performers. The poet Statius, for example, was a married man at the time of his victory at the Alban festival and his defeat in Latin poetry at the Capitoline (*Siluae* 3. 5. 28–33). There seem to have been no age categories, no concept of junior or senior competitions.

Lane Fox (1994), in his discussion of the importance of texts for Christianity and Judaism, emphasizes the specific role of the Reader (*lector*) in Church hierarchy. Sometimes very young children performed this role: epitaphs attest boys from the ages of 5 to 18. He comments (p. 144) that 'In the early Church, the holy innocence which Christians nowadays ascribe to choirboys rested on boys who were reading God's word aloud to their audience.' In other contexts children were increasingly represented with adult qualities in late antiquity.[86]

---

[85] The dramatic date is probably the year 75.

[86] There was a blurring of the categories of *puer, adulescens senilis*, and *senex* (the boy, the elderly youth, and the old man). See Eyben (1993: 10); Wiedemann (1989, e.g. references to '*puer senex*'); Carp (1980).

ROLE OF THE STATE

It is clear that the state had an interest in the education and training of at least some of its population. At the upper levels of public life, the ability to communicate and argue orally and to draw
on a broad background of ethical, linguistic, and other cultural
studies was crucial. At other levels a wide range of skills was in
demand. The state had an economic and administrative interest
in the acquisition of such skills and education, and individuals
had personal fulfilment interests in various aspects of a broad
liberal education. The state was slow, however, to take any direct
role. We have seen Polybius' surprise at this, but Cicero's comment (*On the Republic* 4. 3) was that the Greeks had served no
useful purpose in their attempts to regulate public education and
that Rome had chosen better in not having an official, public,
uniform system. Roman schools were privately funded, although
there was sometimes a municipal responsibility for the administration of the funds.[87]

In spite of this caution about direct state involvement, we have
seen incidents where the Roman senate chose to comment or act
on existing schools or modes of teaching (161 and 92 BCE), citing
the public interest. Suetonius' account (*Rhet.* 1) of the censors'
decree of 92 BCE claims that it stated that 'Our ancestors established what they wished their children to learn and to what
schools they wished them to go.' As we saw above, there were
privileges and exemptions to encourage teachers to practise from
at least the time of Julius Caesar, and as the Principate developed
there was closer state supervision to protect teachers' salaries and
conditions.

It is from the Flavian period that we see more direct involvement of emperors in education and associated activities.[88]
Vespasian allocated state funds for a public post for the teaching
of rhetoric (first held by Quintilian). Domitian receives a bad
press from Pliny, Tacitus and Suetonius, but through their attribution to him of dissembling and bad motives we can see some
positive actions. Martial and Statius present Domitian in a more
favourable light, and although their poetry has the taint of sub-

---

[87] Cf. Pliny's arrangement for hiring teachers for a school at Comum: *Letters*
4. 13.
[88] See Hardie (1983: 45–9); d'Espèrey (1986: esp. 3053–4).

servience to a patron it does reflect Domitian's interest in literature. As a young man at the beginning of his father's reign he felt rebuffed by Cerialis, one of his father's senior officers, and withdrew into the study of literature, indulging his love of poetry and giving public readings. Both Tacitus (*Histories* 4. 86. 2) and Suetonius (*Domitian* 2. 2) claim that these interests were a camouflage for his real feelings and interests. As emperor, however, Domitian devoted attention to public libraries[89] and he established the Alban and Capitoline festivals, which provided scope for intellectual as well as athletic competition. His interest in religious tradition required considerable scholarly advice, such as that of the college of *quindecemuiri* (which included Tacitus), which interpreted documents recording ancient Roman tradition. An inscription from Pergamum (*AE* 10 (1936) no. 128) records Vespasian's edict of 74 (in Greek) granting privileges to doctors, *grammatici*, and rhetoricians who practised in their own city, with Domitian's rescript (in Latin) of 93/4 added, withdrawing privileges from doctors and teachers who took fees for educating slaves. Domitian condemned such scholars, whose learning (*ars*) should be transmitted to freeborn youths, but who were motivated by greed instead of culture (*humanitas*) to increase their income by teaching slaves who were on their masters' intimate staff (*serui cubicularii*). See below, 'Slave Children', for the distaste for giving slaves a liberal education.

Pliny (*Panegyric* 47. 1) praises Trajan for reviving *studia* and treating teachers and philosophers with respect. In his contrast with Domitian, Pliny grants Domitian a certain respect (*reuerentia*) for these intellectuals but claims that it was this respect, and thus his fear of their influence, which motivated his exile of them from Rome rather than animosity (*odium*) towards their profession. Certainly Domitian supported privileges and exemptions for philosophers and other scholars elsewhere, as seen in the inscription cited above and in other sources.[90] Other emperors

---

[89] See above on the private and public libraries of the late Republic. Augustus developed these further. Suetonius (*Domitian* 20) tells of Domitian's rebuilding of libraries which had been destroyed by fire and his efforts to replace texts by having them copied and emended in Alexandria and other places. Other sources specify the libraries on the Palatine (in the temple of Apollo) and in the temple of the Deified Augustus at Rome: see B. W. Jones (1992: 82 and references there).

[90] e.g. Pliny, *Letters* 10. 58. See B. W. Jones (1992: 121–2).

maintained festivals which included intellectual or cultural competitions, and in the second century emperors endowed and supervised the affairs of philosophical schools at Athens.[91] They also continued the tradition of having intellectuals as advisers and close associates.[92] In some modern societies in some periods governments which employed and maintained close liaison with intellectuals have also been associated with respect and support for the education system in their country.[93]

Roman law took care to protect some children's right to an education or some form of training. Again, this was probably on grounds of public interest, but it is also consistent with the growing sensitivity, from the second century, to children's individual needs and personalities. There is considerable provision in the law for the interests of *pupilli*, children who had become fatherless while still minors. One section of the *Digest* (27. 2) deals with where a *pupillus* ought to be brought up and what resources should be made available to support him ('ubi pupillus educari uel morari debeat et de alimentis ei praestandis'). Ulpian reports (*D. 27. 2. 2 pr.*) that a guardian can claim reasonable expenses for maintenance or education (*disciplinae*) and (27. 3. 5) that the praetor decides on the amount to be allocated from an estate for the education (*instructio*) of male and female *pupilli* even up to their twentieth year (i.e. beyond the technical ages of wardship). Already in the second century Scaeuola (*D. 33. 1. 21. 5*) had speculated on the situation whereby two sons were orphaned, one above and one below the age of puberty, and left equal heirs of their father. The older son was instructed to make available to his mother the costs of a liberal education for the younger son between the ages of 12 and 14, when the younger son would be able to inherit properly (although still under the supervision of a *curator*). Children of divorced parents also had their financial and

[91] e.g. Hadrian and the Epicurean school at Athens in 121: *CIL* 3. 12283 = *FIRA*[2] 1. no. 79; Marcus Aurelius and chairs in philosophy and in rhetoric: Dio 71. 31. 3; Philostratus, *Lives of the Sophists* 2. 2 (= 566).

[92] Millar (1977) discusses literary men (pp. 83–93), jurists (94–7), and orators and other intellectuals (97–101). He identifies the 'gifts, immunities and positions' which reflected 'the predominance of the learned professions' (pp. 491–506). Cf. Bowersock (1969, esp. ch. 4).

[93] e.g. in the United States under President Kennedy and in Australia under Prime Minister Whitlam.

educational interests protected. In his discussion of remarriage, Humbert (1972: 295–300) shows that the law took as much care in protecting the education of such children and of *pupilli* as in protecting their property, especially in the case of one parent's remarriage.

SLAVE CHILDREN

The *Digest* of Roman law also gives us glimpses of the education and training of slave children (K. R. Bradley 1991a: 113). Paul reports (*D.* 24. 1. 28. 1) that money might be invested in slave children in various ways, such as for their training (*doctrina*) or maintenance (*alimenta*) or for a wet-nurse to suckle them. If a husband has spent money on children born of women slaves who are part of his wife's dowry, he can later make a claim for some of these expenses but not others. He cannot claim for the expenses of these children's training or maintenance, because he himself makes use of their services; but he can claim for what he has given a *nutrix* for rearing them, because that payment has been to keep them alive. A different situation arose if a slave child born to one of the master's slave women had been abandoned without the owner's knowledge. The owner had therefore been deprived of the services of that child and could claim the child back. If, however, the child had in the meantime been given specialized training ('ad discendum artificium'), a financial invest-ment had been made in him and the original owner must repay the expenses involved.[94]

Literary evidence also attests owners' interest in educating some of their slaves. Educated and highly trained slaves were of considerable value to their owners, either for the contribution which they could make to the owner's household or for their abil-ity to fetch good sale prices. They will have received their educa-tion or training in a variety of ways, for instance informally from other slaves in the household, more formally in *paedagogia* or apprenticeships, or at a school outside the household. Martial (10. 62) refers to slaves going to elementary school (*ludus litterarius*) and to the schools of a *calculator* and a *notarius*. It is more often this vocational training of which we hear, rather than a liberal arts

---

[94] *C.* 8. 51. 1 (a ruling by Severus Alexander in 224).

education, but we know of some who had access to the latter. The slave boy Glaucias, celebrated by Statius (*Siluae* 2. 1) when he died young,[95] was already showing promise beyond his years in literary studies (Menander and Homer: lines 106–24). Some attained the skills for teaching as a *grammaticus* (e.g. Suetonius, *Gramm.* 5–7, 10, 12–13, 15–20, 23) and even, in one known case, as a *rhetor* (Suetonius, *Rhet.* 3). There was some Roman distaste for giving slaves access to higher forms of education, especially philosophy, as seen in Domitian's edict cited above. Seneca (*On Benefits* 3. 21. 2) calls an owner's gift of education to his slave a benefit (*beneficium*) if it involves more than basic training: 'if the master has been indulgent and has given the slave a more liberal education, the studies (*artes*) in which freeborn children are educated'.

Petronius' *Satyricon* illustrates the diversity of education received by slaves. They all valued what they had, recognizing its role in their social and economic betterment. Occasionally a particularly favoured slave received a liberal education, such as Glaucias (above) and Giton (*Satyricon* 58), who had studied geometry, literature, and even rhetoric. But the freedman Hermeros was contemptuous of this, especially as Giton had not acquired good manners or respect for his elders. Hermeros probably shared the more general societal distaste for a slave's receiving an education more appropriate to a freeborn, upper-class boy, but he also valued more highly the more practical education which he himself had received—basic financial calculations and understanding of capital letters and basic ethics, which gave him financial and social credibility. Other slaves' education was of this kind, with an emphasis on arithmetical calculations (especially of money). The old-clothes dealer Echion wants one of his slaves to have a bit more, such as a taste of law, but only for estate management purposes (*Satyricon* 46). He recognizes the value of a trade, such as that of a barber or auctioneer or advocate (*causidicus*). Even one of Trimalchio's favourite boys, who has had some exposure to literature (and can read texts at sight), knows the importance of arithmetic (*Satyricon* 75: he can divide by ten and has worked hard to better himself).

---

[95] Perhaps not more than 7 years old: *Siluae* 2. 1. 124–5.

In the late Republic Crassus, a man of the highest status and of great wealth, had his slaves trained in a wider range of skills and, according to Plutarch (*Crassus* 2), he personally supervised their training. No doubt his grand household could make good use of these readers, clerks, silversmiths, stewards, and table-servants, but he may also have had an eye to their resale value. Atticus reared and trained his own slaves as skilled readers (*anagnostae*: Nepos, *Atticus* 13. 3), for whom he had much personal use but who would also have been in demand for loan, lease, or sale to his friends. A century and a half later, Pliny expressed the high value which he attached to his reader (*lector*) and his concern that a long, dusty journey had damaged Encolpius' voice (*Letters* 8. 1).

By the middle of the first century Seneca was complaining of the excessive specialisms in which slaves were being trained (*On the Happy Life* 17. 2). His use of the word *paedagogium* to refer to the (young) slaves collectively suggests some formal, collective training. They serve in the dining room in costly robes and are specially trained to set and wait on tables. There is even a master-carver ('scindendi obsonii magister') to train them. The law envisaged such a trained staff on a country estate: Ulpian had to consider what 'equipment' should be deemed intrinsic to an estate which was being bequeathed, and the question arose whether domestic staff (slaves) who were normally resident on that estate should be included. Citing Celsus from the early second century, Ulpian declared that they should be. This included the *paedagogia* which an owner kept on the estate: slaves undergoing training but expected to be available for dining-room service when the owner visited (*D.* 33. 7. 12. 32). Pliny seems to have had a *paedagogium* on one of his estates,[96] and other wealthy owners will have had similar organizations. References to dining-room (*triclinium*) service have led some commentators to see these boys as 'ornamental pages', but what we have seen of the cultural context of wealthy mansions and villas should make us realize that dining-room service probably involved more than serving food and wine; it was likely to have included more artistic or intellectual duties

---

[96] *Letters* 7. 27. 13 (although the reference here is more to a dormitory and not explicitly to any training).

as well, such as reading, singing, taking notes, reporting on financial accounts.[97]

The law which bound ex-slaves to provide services (*operae*), even after their manumission, specified some of the services which could be expected of ex-slaves freed before adulthood (*D*. 38. 1. 7. 5, Ulpian): those of a *librarius*, a *nomenclator*, a *calculator*, a *histrio* or other *uoluptatis artifex* (a copyist, a name-announcer, an accountant, an actor or other trained provider of pleasure).

The size and complexity of the imperial household, especially in the capital city of Rome, led to a special training establishment for imperial slave children (boys), the *paedagogium Caesaris*, on the Caelian hill in Rome. It seems to have operated for at least a century from the early second century CE.[98] Inscriptions attest some of the members of this establishment and the bonds that developed within it: there was a term *Caputafricensis* used to describe those attached to this site, 'ad caput Africae'. The ages of boys recorded range from 12 to 18 (*CIL* 6. 8965, 8966). An epitaph from Aquileia, on the northern Adriatic in a strategic highway position, records the death of an imperial slave who had been born and trained in the imperial establishment ('Philagrypnus Aug. uern. ex Kap. Africae') and was presumably travelling in the imperial retinue. His epitaph was dedicated by a

---

[97] Mohler (1940: 275–7) offers very sensible comments on this matter. He points out that it would be very poor management to keep large staffs of young slaves on estates which an owner might visit infrequently, if all they did with their time during the owner's absence was to cultivate their appearance and learn to serve food and drink. Referring to the training of imperial slaves who went on to high positions of public responsibility, he wrote that during their teens these slaves 'had been learning to write perfect Latin and Greek, and had mastered the mathematical knowledge necessary to administer the finances of rich provinces. The skills required for these operations had not been picked up at odd moments while they were seriously concerned with the etiquette of pouring wine or holding cloaks.' As he points out, this understanding of the *paedagogia* makes better sense of Pliny's reference (*Letters* 2. 17. 9) to his guests' use of rooms provided on an estate for the use of his slaves and freedmen. Such rooms were probably 'more than sleeping quarters': they were used for training, but when guests were in residence the training would be suspended and the slaves would be needed in the dining-room. Their freedmen supervisers would oversee this service too.

[98] There may have been other branches, e.g. on the Palatine, where graffiti suggest the existence of a *paedagogium*: Mohler (1940: 273–5).

fellow-member of the training establishment, Heliodorus, who had qualified as a masseur (*unctor*).[99] A Roman inscription (*CIL* 6. 1052) of 198, to Caracalla, the son and virtual co-ruler of the emperor Septimius Seuerus, was dedicated by twenty-four freedmen *paedagogi puerorum*, suggesting a well-organized administrative structure for overseeing the boys (what Mohler calls a 'collegiate organization'). Other specialized posts are recorded (*CIL* 6. 8968–83). The large household of the wealthy and distinguished Volusii family, whose communal burial chambers (*columbarium*) were in use from about 40 to 60 CE, also had a supervisor of slaves, with the title *paedagogus puerorum* which suggests a training role, but he was still a slave when he set up an inscription for his wife.[100]

PROFESSIONS AND TRADES

By the middle of the first century (CE) there was training available in a great variety of technical skills, including those of painters (*pictores*), sculptors (*statuarii*), stone-masons (*marmorarii*), perfumers (*unguentarii*), cooks (*coci*), hairdressers (*ornatrices*), and various kinds of entertainers (wrestlers, dancers, mimes). Columella (*On Agriculture* 1 pr. 3–6) gives a long list of such occupations for which formal training was available, contrasting this with the deplorable lack of training in agriculture.[101] Seneca (*Letters* 88. 18) considers most of these as instruments of luxury and pleasure and therefore not part of the liberal arts. Romans were similarly dismissive of technical training which we would include as part of 'the professions', such as medicine, practised usually by slaves or freedmen, although the great medical scholars of the second century (e.g. Galen, Soranus) were Roman

[99] *CIL* 5. 1039. Philagrypnus was aged 22 when he died, and he had no job-title, so he may have been being trained in a trade more complex than massage. But if these men entered training as boys the bond formed then was a long-lasting one.

[100] This slave, Primigenius, also had the title *ab hospitis*, indicating responsibility for entertainment in the household, consistent with the evidence above for an association between slaves' training and service in the dining-room.

[101] See Petermandl (1997) for discussion of child labour. Joshel (1992: app. 2) has a list of occupational categories. Forbes (1955) provides considerable detail on slaves' jobs and their training.

citizens[102] of much higher status. Professions considered appropriate for Romans included architecture and surveying. Vitruvius wrote a long treatise on architecture and argued for the need of a liberal education for the profession. An architect needed both intellectual and manual skills (*On Architecture* 1. 1. 2). He had to be not only literate but knowledgeable in a wide range of disciplines: draughtsmanship, geometry, history, philosophy, music, medicine, law, and astronomy (1. 1. 3–10). Vitruvius explains at some length the need for all these disciplines and their interrelationship. The architect cannot hope to reach specialist level in all these fields, but this wide education must begin in boyhood. In a later part of his work (6 pr. 4) he expresses gratitude to his parents (the plural must include father and mother) for having him trained in a profession and in one which required a wide knowledge of the liberal arts ('litteraturae encyclioque doctrinarum omnium disciplina'). He also thanks his teachers (*praeceptores*).

Egypt has yielded a number of papyri recording apprenticeship contracts. Although it is always difficult to extrapolate from Egyptian evidence to the rest of the Roman empire, especially to Rome and Italy, K. R. Bradley's study (1991*a*: 103–24) of thirty such documents, covering the first three centuries of the imperial period, presents a picture which is consistent with what we know, from inscriptions and the law, of children in skilled trades and crafts in Italy. Children seem to have begun apprenticeships at the age of 12 or 13. We saw above that children could be expected to do useful work from the age of 5. Ulpian specified several kinds of skilled service which children could perform before the age of 14 (while still *impuberes*): that of *librarius, nomenclator, calculator, histrio*.[103] At least some of these required formal training, so apprenticeships in those trades in Italy could have started well below the age of 14. We have already seen the large staffs kept by Crassus and Atticus, which included *librarii*, and it is clear that Cicero used *librarii* for a variety of purposes, including transcribing details of bills which were proposed for legislation and which were required to be posted in public

---

[102] Roman citizenship not certain for Soranus.

[103] *D.* 38. 1. 7. 5: copyist, name-announcer, book-keeper (low-level accountant), actor. See Béranger (1999) on the *calculator* as teacher and book-keeper, including the 13-year-old *uerna* Melior from Ostia (*CIL* 14. 472).

places.[104] It is possible that we have a scene of such an apprenticeship portrayed on a funerary relief from Pompeii. The picture
of a boy standing before a seated older man, each proffering a
cylindrical container of the kind which held papyri rolls, could
perhaps be a school scene. But similar reliefs involve several
adults and have led De Franciscis (1988) to suggest the possibility of their being scribes. If so, a boy in such a scene would
probably be an apprentice. The jurist Gaius (*D*. 6. 1. 28) gives
examples of slaves who might have been trained in trades, and
these include a *librarius*. *Librarii* were important enough to have
their own guild in Rome, with headquarters in a prominent part
of the Forum.[105] Although none of the eighty-odd *librarii*
attested in inscriptions from Rome has a young age specified
(they are all fully qualified), it is unlikely that so important a craft
did not provide for early training in it, training which the law
reflects.[106]

Juvenal's lament for the sufferings of a *grammaticus*[107] refers in
passing to a weaver teaching his craft in what seem to be dark and
cramped quarters (but the teacher's working area is worse). We
know little of the physical conditions under which apprentices
worked. They probably varied from bad to good as such relationships always have, especially in the periods before industrial
legislation and regulation. Roman law provided some protection,
although when the apprentice was a slave the protection was for

---

[104] In 63 BCE, when the tribune Rullus proposed an agrarian law, Cicero sent
a number of *librarii* to where it was publicly displayed, with instructions to copy
it (presumably each taking a different part, to minimize the copying time) and
bring it to him (*On the Agrarian Law* 2. 13). In 44 BCE Antony was making
capital out of a letter which Cicero had allegedly written to him; but Cicero
responded that authorship of the letter could not be proved by the handwriting
(*chirographum*), because the writing was in the hand of a *librarius* (*Philippics*
2. 8).

[105] The *schola Xanthi*, headquarters of the *collegium* of *librarii*, *scribae*, and
praecones of curule aediles, near the temple of Saturn (Nash (1968) s.v.). A large
inscription (*CIL* 6. 103 = 30692) records members and attests the pair who
rebuilt the headquarters in the time of Tiberius (A. Fabius Xanthus and an
imperial freedman Bebryx Aug. lib. Drusianus) and a certain C. Auillius
Licinius Trosius who restored it in the early 3rd c.

[106] Of the five female *librariae* listed by Treggiari (1976: 78), whom she takes
to be general clerical workers, and who all belong to women, only one has an
age stated, that of 18.

[107] Juvenal 7. 215–43, under 'Schools, Teachers, Curriculum' above.

an owner whose property might be damaged. Ulpian provides this discussion:

If a master wounds or kills a slave while training him, would he be liable under the *lex Aquilia* [108] for criminal injury? Iulianus writes that a master who has blinded a pupil training under him is liable, and so much the more so if he kills him. But this case is put forward: a shoemaker has a pupil who is a freeborn boy, under his father's authority ('ingenuo filio familias'), who is not following instructions satisfactorily, and he strikes at his neck with a shoe-last, knocking out the boy's eye. So Iulianus says that there is no valid action for injury because the shoemaker struck the boy not with the purpose of causing him injury but with the purpose of reminding and teaching him. As to whether there is an action possible on the [apprenticeship] contract, he hesitates, because punishment is allowed to a teacher only if it is moderate (*leuis*). I [Ulpian], however, have no doubt that the shoemaker is liable under the *lex Aquilia*. [109]

Seneca the Elder (*Controuersiae* 10. 4) presents a speaker berating fathers and masters of disabled children for exploiting them as beggars. He hints that the children have been intentionally crippled or otherwise disabled for this purpose. Each child specializes in its own particular kind of disability as if it were a trade (*ars*) by which it earns income. This only works, however, because people's pity (*misericordia publica*) can be stimulated to provide alms.

Boys who were apprenticed were of both slave and free status, but the extant evidence attests girl apprentices of only slave status. Could all girls of free status afford the luxury of an upbringing at home aimed only at domestic skills and preparation for marriage? This seems unlikely: poorer girls surely needed to earn a living or at least contribute to a family's income. But perhaps they obtained their training more informally, from parents working at a trade or from other households in which they had been placed 'in service'. [110] In this respect slave girls who got a formal training at their owner's expense might be considered to have been more advantaged than poor freeborn girls.

[108] A law from the Republican period detailing penalties for damage to property.
[109] *D.* 9. 2. 5. 3. Ulpian repeats this case in *D.* 19. 2. 13. 4.
[110] Some *alumnae* and other foster-children may have been children placed with relatives or friends for this purpose.

CITY AND COUNTRY

All of these opportunities for education and training, for free or slave children, will have been more numerous and of a better quality in larger urban centres than in the country, and especially so at Rome.[111] Pliny's report (*Letters* 4. 13) of the lack of a school at Comum for boys of good family reminds us of the difference between larger and smaller towns: Comum boys had to travel to Mediolanum (Milan) and board there in order to get an education. There are many examples of boys sent to Rome for an education, either because this was not available in their local area or because they sought the superior education available at Rome.[112] Cicero's father, a well-established citizen from Arpinum, brought his sons to Rome to pursue studies and make the necessary contacts (Cicero, *On the Orator* 2. 1. 1). The poet Horace had a similarly perceptive and ambitious father who brought him from Venusia to Rome (Horace, *Satires* 1. 6. 65–78). The father was an ex-slave and quite poor, but he refused to send his son to Flavius' local school, which was attended by centurions' sons. Horace's vivid word-picture portrays these boys as trudging off to school with school-bag and writing tablet slung over their left shoulder. Presumably they could not afford a *capsarius* to carry their equipment, or such luxuries were not available in country towns; whereas Horace's father provided his son with the clothes and attendants appropriate to city life. 'If anyone in the big city crowd had noticed my clothing and attendant slaves, he would think that the expenses came from long-established inherited wealth.' Horace goes on to describe his father's close supervision of his morals in the city environment and his praise and gratitude to his father.

Other poets came to Rome from country towns for a better education. Both Ovid and Persius came from good families, the

[111] W. V. Harris (1989: 233–48) discusses the accessibility of schooling for Romans. At n. 352 he lists towns in Italy where there is some evidence of the availability of formal schooling.

[112] Modestinus (*D.* 50. 1. 36 pr.) tells of a certain Titius who had come to Rome from his *patria* in order to study. He was requested, by his local magistrates, to deliver a decree to the emperor. This might suggest a young man rather than a boy or an adolescent student, but by Modestinus' time (3rd c.) such duties could be entrusted to younger boys.

one from Sulmo and the other from Volaterrae. Vergil came from a humbler background and moved from boyhood in Cremona, first to Mediolanum and then to Rome.[113] They all made the move at an age between 12 and 15, in time for the younger ones to finish their *grammaticus* education and for all of them to enter a rhetorician's school. Although none of the four poets mentioned pursued a public career, a rhetorical education provided an appropriate background of liberal studies for any ambitious and/or talented youth.

Inscriptions, too, attest the allure of the big city for many country boys. The 13-year-old L. Valerius Pudens went to Rome from Histonium (Samnium) for the Capitoline festival in 106 and was the unanimous winner of the Latin poetry prize. His proud home town later dedicated to him a bronze statue and an inscription, from which we learn that he went on to hold senior office under Antoninus Pius in another Samnite town, Asernia (*CIL* 9. 2860). Boys who seem to have remained in their country town but who are recorded as having high educational attainments are Castorius from Volsinii and Petronius Antigenis (aged 10) from Pisaurum (*CIL* 11. 2839, 6435). Castorius, who died young and whose body lies 'sapiens' in the earth, has gone to join the *pii* in heaven. He is addressed as 'docte puer, studiis et iure peritum' ('learned boy, skilled in studies and law'). Part of the large marble slab commemorating Antigenis has been lost, but there remain 17 lines of inscription attesting his learnedness in philosophy, poetry, and Euclid, the care and love invested in his upbringing ('tenere nutritus amatus'), and the role of his father as cheerful guide and *patronus*. From further afield (Africa) came P. Annius Florus to compete in the Capitoline festival in 90. He failed (because of Domitian's prejudice against the educational standards of Africa?) and spent much of his subsequent career as an itinerant teacher before gaining recognition at Rome from Trajan.[114]

---

[113] Ovid, *Tristia* 4. 10. 15–16, where he attributes the move to his father's concern for him ('cura parentis'); Suetonius, *Persius, Vergil* 6. Propertius came from Assisi (Pliny, *Letters* 6. 15), but nothing is known of the circumstances of his move to Rome.

[114] *Vergilius orator an poeta*, pp. 209–14 of *L. Annaei Flori quae exstant*[2], ed. H. Malcovati 1972.

EDUCATION OF GIRLS

Many of the roles in public life for which a rhetorical education prepared young males were not open to females, e.g. a political career, conducting cases in the major courts, or the army. But a broad liberal education was an integral part of upper-class Roman social and cultural life, in which women participated actively, and more than an elementary or 'domestic science' education was necessary for the business and commercial life which was undertaken by men and women. Quintilian (1. 1. 6) had urged that parents (including mothers) should be as well educated as possible. Moreover, women (especially mothers) are often given credit for guiding the educational and career choices of their children, which suggests well-informed judgement and well-developed female personalities. In the second century BCE Cornelia and Laelia were famous mothers who were knowledgeable about oratory, and in the following century Hortensia made a famous speech in public which Quintilian reported was still read in his own day.[115] In circumstances of civil war, exile, other political difficulties, or extended absence of a father on public duty or business, a mother would have to take responsibility and make decisions about the education of her children. Thus the stereotype of the shy, wool-spinning daughter and wife cannot be taken as matching reality, and the conventional epithets attached to women may reflect a traditional ideal but also reflect only a part of women's lived lives. It is likely, then, that girls of good family shared in much of the education available in Roman society of the late Republic and the Empire. Some extant evidence attests

[115] Hortensia was the daughter of Hortensius, the noted orator of Cicero's day. The speech was delivered in the Forum to the triumvirs in 42 BCE, against the imposition of a new tax on women. Appian, *Civil Wars* 4. 32–4, reports the speech. Cicero (*Brutus* 211) pays tribute to the influence of the good speech of Cornelia and Laelia on their children. Laelia was the daughter of a well-known speaker, C. Laelius, whose influence Cicero sees being passed on to three generations of women, all of whom married distinguished senators and one (Laelia's daughter Mucia) married the most famous orator of his day, the Crassus whose conservative influence in oratorial education we have seen above (against Latin rhetoricians). Valerius Maximus (8. 3. 3) adds to Hortensia two other women of the late Republic who pleaded causes publicly: Maesia, from Sentinum, before a praetor, and C. Afrania, the wife of a senator but whom Valerius Maximus accuses of being quite shameless.

this directly and other evidence can lead us to draw similar
conclusions.

Some girls seem to have attended schools from earliest times:
Verginia is an example from the fifth century BCE (see above
under 'Schools, Teachers, Curriculum'). There are explicit references to girls in schools in the imperial period. Martial refers to
boys and girls in the same school, where they share hatred of the
same teacher.[116] Ovid (*Tristia* 2. 369–70), in referring to other
poets who have written about love, specifies that Menander was
often read by boys and girls, 'pueris uirginibus'. Whether this was
at school or at home is not clear but the grouping of boys and
girls suggests a mixed classroom. Boys and girls came together to
rehearse and sing the *carmen saeculare* at the Secular Games.
Horace (*Epistles* 2. 1. 132–4) refers to a chorus of boys and girls
reciting prayers written by a poet.[117] This is probably the Secular
hymn, but there were other religious performances which brought
boys and girls together in this way. In some rituals only girls performed. All of these occasions required training and discipline.[118]

We know of *paedagogi* attached to girls. These were mostly
men. The examples in inscriptions from Rome (*CIL* 6. 2210, 6327,
6330, 33787) refer to girls of good family. Claudia Quinta (2210)
was a freeborn girl whose father had died early and who had
property needing to be administered by a guardian (*tutor*). This
role was filled by her *paedagogus* C. Iulius Hymetus—perhaps surprisingly, as he seems to be a freedman,[119] but her memorial to
him records also his position as a functionary (*aedituus*) of a
shrine of Diana[120] and her appreciation of him as her guide
(καθηγητής) and for his loyal administration of her estate ('ob
redditam sibi ab eo fidelissime tutelam'). He seems to have been
a trusted family retainer. Moreover, his spouse Iulia Sporis was
Claudia's *mamma* (Panciera 1970/71). We know much less of the

---

[116] Martial 9. 68. 1–2. Cf. 8. 3. 15–16: 'et grandis uirgo bonusque puer' will
hate the *magister* if he dictates tragic poetry.

[117] 'castis cum pueris ignara puella mariti disceret unde preces, uatem ni
Musa dedisset?'

[118] Cf. Jaczynowska (1978) and other references in Ch. 7 below.

[119] *Paedagogi* were normally slaves or freedmen, and the nomenclature of all
the dedicatees in the inscription suggests freed status (two brothers and a
mamma all Iulii, with *cognomina* Hymetus, Epitynchanus, and Sporis).

[120] 'Diana Planciana', endowed by the influential Plancii family, probably in
the 1st c. CE (C. P. Jones 1976).

relationship of the two *paedagogi* and the one *paedagoga* who may
have been attached to the one girl, Statilia Messalina (daughter
of (Statilius) Taurus and future wife of Nero), but the slave
Gemellus (6327) and the freed T. Statilius Zabda (6330) and
Statilia T. l. Tyranis (6331) were buried in the family *columbarium*
of the Statilii.[121] The *paedagogus* of (Iulia) Liuia (often known as
Livilla), who married Tiberius' son Drusus, was a freedman of
her grandmother Livia: M. Liuius Augustae lib. Prytanis (33787).
Although such *paedagogi* may have provided tutoring in the
home, the normal role of a *paedagogus* was to chaperone the
school-going child. The daughter of Pontius Aufidianus was
obviously nubile and moving about in public when her father
discovered her sexual activity and had her put to death (to avoid
an enforced marriage) as well as killing her slave *paedagogus* for
failure in his duty of care (Valerius Maximus 6. 1. 3). There are
few references to female *paedagogae*.[122] Verginia, however, is represented as having female carers in attendance when she went to
school in the Forum.

There is evidence for tutors educating girls at home. Pompey's
daughter Pompeia was prompted by her *didaskalos* to read out a
passage from Homer to her father in 62 or 61 BCE after he had
returned from the East.[123] Pompeia was probably no more than
9 years old at that time.[124] Atticus' daughter, Caecilia, had a
grammaticus Q. Caecilius Epirota, but this seems to have been

---

[121] The scholiast on Juvenal 6. 434 says that Juvenal is attacking Statilia
Messalina, who, after Nero's death, flourished in wealth and beauty and intel-
lectual talent—even to the point of studying declamation: 'et opibus et forma et
ingenio plurimum uiguit. consectata est usum eloquentiae usque ad studium
declamandi'. The identification of the two girls named Statilia and the one
Messalina, even within one *columbarium*, is not certain. There is also a
Messalina with a *paedagoga* in another *columbarium* (4459: see above under
'Schools, Teachers, Curriculum').

[122] In Rome, two freedwomen (*CIL* 6. 6331, 9754) and two slaves (4459, 9758).
See above under 'Schools, Teachers, Curriculum'.

[123] It was poorly chosen, from *Iliad* 3. 428, where Helen is ambivalent about
Paris' miraculous rescue from battle with Menelaus: 'You have returned from
the battle; would that you had perished there'.

[124] She was born either by 78 BCE or after 71. The latter now seems to me the
more likely, in view of her being still betrothed (to Faustus Sulla) and not married in 59, and her having pre-adult children (of Faustus) in 46: Appian, *Civil
Wars* 2. 100; (Caesar), *African War* 95.

when she was married to Agrippa.[125] As her teacher was a freedman of her father, Epirota may well have taught her from an earlier age, while she still lived in Atticus' house. Minicia Marcella,
at the age of 12,[126] was a studious girl with an affectionate attachment to her nurses, *paedagogi*, and teachers. The context suggests
the personal, one-to-one relationship of home tutoring.

Upper-class girls grew up in the cultural milieu described
above. Some of the girls mentioned lived in houses with great
private libraries, such as those of Piso, Cicero, and Atticus. They
would have had access to these libraries as well as to the resident
scholars and visiting intellectuals who were guests at dinner, at
readings, and at other functions in the house. This applied in
their city houses and when they were at leisure in their out-of-
town villas. In the late Republic, more than forty leading citizens
can be identified as owning villas on the Campanian coast.
Although these villas were often associated with the pleasures of
the flesh, there were also intellectual and artistic pleasures, with
much philosophical, literary, musical, and political activity.
Clodia and Agrippina the Younger are two examples of women
who enjoyed this lifestyle in townhouse and seaside villa.[127]

The context in which Sulpicia grew up in the Augustan period
is instructive. Several love poems are attributed to Sulpicia in the
collection of elegiac poetry which has come down to us with the
manuscripts of Tibullus' work.[128] Tibullus was one of the poets
in the circle of M. Valerius Messalla Coruinus, a distinguished
man who was a patron of poets and a close relative (probably the
maternal uncle) of Sulpicia. It was not unnatural for an intelli-
gent girl with a good literary education, interacting frequently
with such poets, to try her own hand at composition. Moreover,
Sulpicia's father[129] died when she was young and she became the
pupilla of Messalla. During his long life (64 BCE to 8 CE) Messalla

[125] Suetonius (*Gramm.* 16) refers to her as Agrippa's wife, and the suspicion
of improper relations between Epirota and Caecilia is probably more appropriate to a young adult than to a child. She was betrothed to Agrippa at age 14 and
probably married soon after.

[126] Pliny (*Letters* 5. 16). See Ch. 1 for discrepancy between the age given by
Pliny ('not quite 14') and that of her epitaph.

[127] See D'Arms (1970); Wiseman (1985: ch. 2).

[128] Poems 7–12 of Book 4; or 13–18 of Book 3.

[129] Seruius Sulpicius Rufus, son of Cicero's jurist friend. He probably died
in the proscriptions of 43 BCE.

had a busy and responsible career in politics and the army and was
a prominent orator, so he is unlikely to have had time for close
supervision of his young ward as she grew up. Left to tutors and
the company of poets such as Tibullus and Ovid, she may well
have developed not only her intellect but some sexual maturity.
This makes it more plausible that she wrote the poems attributed
to her, including 4. 7, which claims to attest the consummation
of her affair with 'Cerinthus'. The last two lines (4. 7. 9–10)
proclaim her joy in her 'sin' and her distaste for masking her
expression to protect her reputation. 'Let it be known that I have
been with a man worthy of me as I am of him.'

In one of Tibullus' own poems (4. 6) he presents a well-
educated young woman, a 'docta puella' (Sulpicia), on her
birthday. As she makes her offerings to Juno at the domestic altar,
her mother is anxious to tell her what she should pray for, but the
young woman silently prays for something else, the satisfaction of
her passion. Tibullus asks the goddess to bless this love and he
hopes that the couple can evade the watchful chaperone ('uigilans
custos').[130]

Whether examples such as Sulpicia, Caecilia, and the daughter of Pontius Aufidianus led any parents to decree that education
was dangerous for girls is unknown. There is no evidence of it.
Indeed, the appropriateness of a good education for girls, including philosophy, was argued by the prominent Stoic teacher
Musonius Rufus in the latter half of the first century CE.[131] His
teachings survive in a number of lectures preserved by later writers, one of whom was a student ('Lucius') who wrote soon after
the actual classes. The lectures deserve to be taken seriously as
a reflection of at least one segment of contemporary liberal
educated opinion and not dismissed as theoretical musings of a
recluse, unattached to reality. The concern with practical applications of ethical and philosophical principles is a strong trend in
Roman education and intellectual discussion, and Musonius
specifically enunciates this: 'Whatever precepts enjoined upon

[130] Sulpicia is clearly beyond the age of puberty. She might even be in her
early twenties if her father had died by 43 BCE and this poem was written close
to Tibullus' death in 19 BCE. If so, it is surprising that she is not yet married.
But cf. Statius' stepdaughter below.

[131] Details of Musonius Rufus and translations of his work are based on Lutz
(1947).

[the student] he is persuaded are true, these must he follow out
in his daily life. For only in this way will philosophy be of profit
to anyone, if to sound teaching he adds conduct in harmony with
it' (1. 36. 7–12). Moreover, he was a Roman of equestrian rank
who taught young men of good family whose training was
designed to fit them for public careers, and he himself was active
in public affairs. He was considered dangerous enough to be
exiled by two emperors (Nero and Vespasian), but he became a
friend of the emperor Titus. The titles of some of his lectures can
be taken as reflections of issues currently being debated in Roman
society, e.g. 3 ('Women too should study philosophy'), 4
('Daughters should have the same education as sons'), 13 ('On the
principal aim of marriage'), 14 ('Is marriage an obstacle to philosophy?'), 15 ('Should one obey one's parents?'). He discusses the
human rights and sensitivities of women and slaves: for instance
he argues against men's extramarital sexual activities, even with
their own female slaves (12, 'On sexual indulgence'). His argument is based largely on avoiding a double standard for husbands
and wives, but there is a hint too that slave women have sensitivities and might have a marital-type relationship which deserves
respect.[132]

The arguments in some of these lectures deserve closer inspec-
tion. In 3, Musonius begins with the assertion that females have
been endowed with the same reasoning power as have men. They
are therefore capable of studying philosophy, and this will help
develop virtues such as self-discipline, justice, and courage.
But the application of these virtues will be in the sphere of the
administration of house and family and dedication to a woman's
children. This is, as Cohen and Saller describe it (1994: 53), a
'gendered philosophy'. It recurs in 4, where Musonius argues that
boys and girls should have the same moral education but, because
of their different strengths, there will be some differentiation in
their activities. Nevertheless, he aims at developing an understanding (of right and wrong) in both girls and boys. 'As without
philosophy no man would be properly educated, so no woman
would be.' Although males and females will have different roles,

---

[132] Cf. above, in discussion of curriculum, for the moral, problematic nature
of the declamations which were the basis of rhetorical education in this same
period.

the same virtues should be present in both: φρονεῖν ('having understanding') is necessary for both. Thus what is aimed at for women is a reasoned, autonomous virtue, not a mindless, submissive one. In 13, the principal aims of marriage are procreation and a partnership (emotional and intellectual) between spouses.

These aspects of Musonius' teaching seem to me to make unjustified the view of Cohen and Saller (1994: 50–4) that in early imperial Rome the ideal for wives in elite circles was for a conventional, submissive, non-independent partner. They see husbands as being responsible for the education and socialization of their wives (much younger than them) towards this end, and they claim that there was no real concept of 'shared intellectual pursuits'. But would women have been so uneducated before marriage, like a *tabula rasa* awaiting a husband's imprint? Cohen and Saller recognize that elite culture 'placed great emphasis on philosophical and literary knowledge and on rhetorical polish in the cultivation and presentation of self'. Surely it would have been part of making a girl fit for marriage to give her some exposure to such learning and values at an early age. We have seen some evidence of that, and the picture of adult women in Roman society corroborates that evidence. Roman society was not segregated on a gender basis (although public careers and some theatre seating were). Musonius himself represents women participating actively in philosophical circles (3. 12–15). Some criticized such women for being arrogant and dominating in philosophical argument, but Musonius said that there was nothing intrinsic in philosophy to develop bad habits in men or women.

Juvenal too presented highly educated women. There are the ones who have considerable legal knowledge (6. 242–5): they themselves take the initiative in preparing cases and they brief counsel in some detail ('principium atque locos Celso dictare paratae'). Others have musical expertise (6. 380–92): they sing, play instruments, and, being ineligible themselves to compete in the Capitoline festival, act as patrons, promoting the interests of certain male competitors (e.g. Pollio, a *citharoedus*). And there are literary women (6. 434–56), learned in Vergil and Homer and other poets, who lecture everyone else on such matters and silence various male professionals (*grammatici*, *rhetores*, the *causidicus*, and the *praeco*). He presents the educated woman as aggressively (*audax*) taking her place in various gatherings and conversations in the city, a know-all about everything[133] (6. 398–412). In this last passage his put-down is particularly sexist: the educated woman is shrunken-breasted ('siccis mamillis').

Juvenal is highly critical of such women, but his contemporary Pliny speaks more neutrally of women in his circle who can conduct their own affairs.[134] A more favourable picture of educated women can also be extracted from Martial (e.g. 7. 21, 23; 10. 64) and especially Statius.[135] Statius' tribute to Argentaria Polla, widow of Lucan (*Siluae* 2. 7), presents her as not only a devoted widow but Lucan's intellectual equal: 'doctam atque ingenio tuo decoram'.[136] Martial addresses Polla as a patron in 7. 21, 23 and 10. 64. Although one must allow for flattery in poetry written for patrons, such poetry can be taken as reflecting qualities in patrons which must be plausible and which the patrons will find pleasing. In a more personal poem (3. 5) to his wife Claudia, Statius represents her as a strong-minded woman who shared his professional hopes and experiences. Her daughter by a previous marriage is regrettably not yet married, but has intellectual qualities (*ingenium* and *ars*)—as well as *probitas* and *modestia*.

In all these instances there is a thread of family histories of education and literary activity. Argentaria Polla was the daughter or granddaughter of an epigrammatist and rhetorician

---

[133] The matters on which she pronounces are largely gossip, but there are also weightier matters.

[134] His mother-in-law (mother of his second wife), Pompeia Celerina, was wealthy and would lend him money (*Letters* 1. 4; 3. 19). Furia Prima (10. 58–60) took an active role as accuser of the philosopher Flavius Archippus in Bithynia. Ummidia Quadratilla (7. 24) was an independent lady of means who kept a troupe of mimes but who protected her grandson from her somewhat decadent tastes. Calpurnia Hispulla, the aunt and rearer of Pliny's third wife, emerges as a strong and admirable woman. The literary ability of the wife of Pompeius Saturninus (1. 16) is praised, although Pliny is inclined to give the husband credit for authorship or nurture of his wife's talent.

[135] See White (1975: 284); Hardie (1983 *passim*).

[136] *Siluae* 2. 7. 83. See Hemelrijk (1999, esp. ch. 4). Cf. 2. 2. 147–54 where a Polla, wife of Pollius Felix, is *praedocta* and the intellectual equal of Felix, who has already been praised for his eloquence (*facundia*). Are these two women named Polla the same person? The identification is plausible. Nisbet (1978) thinks that they are the same, and he places the widow of the Stoic Lucan in a new Epicurean context on the Bay of Naples. Cf. Hardie's discussion. Hemelrijk (1999: 129–38) is sceptical.

M. Argentarius. She herself married a poet (Lucan) and became a patron of poets. She probably remarried, to another man of wide cultural interests who also wrote poetry (Pollius Felix). Felix already had a daughter, also named Polla, who married a wealthy Neapolitan aristocrat (Iulius Menecrates) who also wrote poetry (*Siluae* 2. 2. 112 ff.). This younger Polla had three sons for whom the couple had great ambitions, including a senatorial career at Rome (*Siluae* 4. 8). Although Statius focuses on the father, Menecrates, in celebrating these sons, the influence of the mother should not be underestimated, in view of the background of wide culture, education, and patronage noted above. Statius' own wife Claudia had previously been married to a poet (*canorus*). Admittedly, most educated men (and perhaps women) in Roman society wrote poetry at some stage of their lives, or as a continuing hobby, but the families described here have literary activity much more at the core of their lives. They include professionals and patrons, and the women members contribute a continuing family tradition. This is all consistent with their having grown up well educated and with intellectual activities an integral part of their lives.

The examples above of adult educated women can be used to extrapolate backwards, to support the evidence already seen of pre-adult girls receiving a good education and the hypothesis that there were many well-educated women whose education began in childhood and who were raised in a milieu where intellectual expectations of girls were not unusual.[137] In commemorations of girls and women, however, it is conventional, traditional qualities which dominate. Juvenal had given examples of these qualities of the ideal wife (6. 162–9), only to reject such a woman (e.g. Cornelia, mother of the Gracchi) as insufferable: she would be 'formosa, decens, diues, fecunda' ('handsome, proper, wealthy, fertile'), with a long ancestry and notable chastity. We have seen that for even the intellectual women discussed above there are balancing attributes, such as *probitas* and *modestia* for Statius' stepdaughter. Statius (*Siluae* 2. 7. 81–8) has Calliope prophesy for Lucan at his birth a wife (Polla) who will be *casta* (*Siluae* 2. 7. 62), and in addition to her intellectual qualities matching his she will

---

[137] I owe thanks to Emily Hemelrijk for discussion of her book (1999) before publication.

be distinguished by many other qualities (2. 7. 83–6): 'forma, simplicitate, comitate, | censu, sanguine, gratia, decore' ('beauty, artlessness, companionability, property, ancestry, charm, graciousness').

In Fig. 1.10 above we saw the 8-year-old girl Magnilla commemorated as 'learned beyond her years' in a list of other epithets. Another monument with good lettering (*CIL* 6. 33898) tells us that Euphrosyne Pia, a woman of 20, had acquired sufficient education to be characterized as 'learned in the nine Muses' and a philosopher ('docta nouem Musis | philosopha'). Sometimes women are represented visually in the guise of the Muses or with other educational attributes,[138] but young girls are infrequently represented in such scenes, by contrast with monuments of boys which often include scenes of teaching and learning.[139] The occasional scenes of girls (and others) playing musical instruments have been discussed above, with the suggestion that musical skills were associated with hopes of immortality.

Evidence for job training is much more plentiful for males than for females.[140] Yet, as suggested above ('Professions and Trades'), most sub-elite females must have had to earn a living. There is evidence for a range of specialized jobs for female slaves, many associated with care of the female body and attire, others with child care, and others (fewer) with administrative and entertainment skills (Treggiari 1976). A long epitaph (*CIL* 6. 10096) for a 14-year-old mime dancer, Eucharis, recorded the range of skills and training required for her profession ('skilled and learned in all the arts') and the bright future which her profession held for her if she had lived. She had already been freed from slavery by her *patrona* Licinia, whom Wiseman[141] associates with the society and lifestyle of women like Clodia and the sort of *ludi* which noble families put on for the public. Young slave girls would have

---

[138] W. V. Harris (1989: 263 and n. 459) points out the difficulty of interpreting the Pompeian paintings of women holding pens and writing tablets: either these show that the ability to write was an asset in women, and was thus encouraged, or they show that it was exceptional and thus advertised.

[139] I have identified three such scenes for girls in Italy. These are included in Marrou (1938: nos. 1, 8, 13), in a set of sixteen such children on monuments probably originating from Italy. His no. 11 is probably of Asian provenance.

[140] See Joshel (1992), e.g. table 3.1.

[141] Wiseman (1985: 30–5). I thank Tom Hillard, of Macquarie University, for this reference.

received training for such jobs within the household. None of those with professional titles in Treggiari (1976), however, has an age specified less than 16, which suggests a period of training before attaining the professional title. There was legal debate about how much training was necessary for a person to be recognized as professionally qualified. There is the example of girls trained by a *magister* for only two months: there was debate from the time of Celsus (early second century) as to whether they were fully qualified as an *ornatrix*, a 'dresser' (*D*. 32. 65. 3, Marcianus). The law recognized that young girls (slaves or daughters) might be put in charge of shops or small businesses (e.g. as *institor*: *D*. 14. 3. 7. 1, Ulpian). It ruled that they were only agents and that whoever had *potestas* of them had legal liability for the activities. The girls' role, however, suggests a certain level of skill or competence.[142] One career reserved for women was that of the Vestal Virgins, who held considerable religious and public responsibilities in Rome. Girls of upper-class families entered this profession at young ages, between 6 and 10 years. Their training was a form of apprenticeship. Valerius Maximus (1. 1. 7) records one pupil or apprentice (*discipula*) of the chief Vestal Virgin Aemilia.[143]

The evidence for the education and training of girls has had to be largely induced, because of the comparative lack of direct attestation or focus on girls' intellectual and professional skills. This lack of fit between representation and reality shows something of the strength of traditional ideals and conceptualization in Roman society. It is a conflict not unknown in our own contemporary Western society: there is frequent comment on the persistence of female stereotypes or unrealistic ideals in commercial advertising which do not match everyday experience. The extent to which this conflict influences perceptions, expectations, and behaviour of both males and females is a matter of debate. It should remind us that human experience—in this case, that of young girls—is multi-layered and that psychological development is complex.

---

[142] Cf. *D*. 14. 3. 8, Gaius; and K. R. Bradley (1991*a*: 113).
[143] Her inexperience or negligence allowed the fire of Vesta to go out, but the fire miraculously came to life in response to the girl's terrified prayers to Vesta and the sacrifice of her best robe.

Hallett (1984) has argued that there was a special relationship between fathers and daughters in Roman society. Although aspects of her argument have not been accepted by other scholars, it is clear that relationships between males and females were the subject of active discussion by early imperial times. Musonius Rufus focused some of his ethical discussion on treatment of wives and daughters. Lecture 12, 'On the pleasures of love', argued that the only morally permissible sexual relations were those within marriage. Lecture 13, asking what was the principal aim of marriage, answered that it was procreation and a partnership (emotional and intellectual) between spouses. Lecture 14, 'Whether marriage is an impediment to philosophy', argued that the love between husband and wife was the most precious of all love, even above that between parent and child.

The exercises and subject-matter set by rhetorical schools were much concerned with family relationships.[144] A comparison between Cicero and Valerius Maximus illustrates this direction of interest between the late Republic and the early Principate. A study has shown that Valerius Maximus devotes proportionately more attention to *exempla* drawn from familial life. Skidmore (1996) examined eleven categories of examples of familial behaviour and sentiment in Valerius Maximus (such as filial duty, parental love, parental severity). He looked for these in Cicero's philosophical, oratorical, and epistolary writings, taken singly and in total, and found the incidence much lower. Skidmore recognizes the differences in audience and purpose for each author. He identifies Valerius Maximus' aim as 'to provide a property-owning *paterfamilias* with moral guidance on every aspect of his experience, such as the right way to draw up a will or a father's relationship with his children' (1996: 104–5).[145]

Although the present book focuses on children (male and female) rather than spouses, relationships between spouses (a

[144] See above on declamations. Of Calpurnius Flaccus' fifty-three declamations, twelve might be considered to have little or no concern with the family.

[145] There is also difference in genres, which is itself significant: there was now an interest in the sort of 'applied' historical examples presented by Valerius Maximus. What is at first somewhat surprising is that these categories of examples are least frequent in Cicero's philosophical writings and most frequent in his oratorical works. The audience for the oratorical works was wider and more 'popular' than that for the philosophical or even the epistolary writings.

child's parents, step-parents, or other carers) as well as the current attitudes and discussions of the day are an essential backdrop to any child's experience. The discussions will have been more explicit in the well-educated classes, and lower classes will have had little time or capacity to dwell on such matters. But ideals set by upper classes (even more than their behaviour) often set the tone for wider society. The variety of relationships involving children is the subject of the next chapter.

6

Relationships

DEMOGRAPHY dominates, or at least is the ever-present background in any discussion of children's relationships in Roman society. The early death of infants and young children, high mortality rates generally, age gaps between spouses and between siblings, and frequent divorce, remarriage, or other changes in parents' relationships are factors which must always be taken into account, along with conditions of slavery. They made it inevitable that most children would experience changing sets of relationships.[1]

Other aspects of Roman society served also to extend the range of children's relationships beyond those of the immediate nuclear family. Children who went to school were exposed to a variety of extra-familial contacts, not only teachers and fellow-pupils but also passers-by in the streets. We have seen, in the preceding chapter, Quintilian supporting his preference for public schools over private tutoring by reference to the very socializing nature of these interactions and their value as a preparation for public life. 'The city' as such, especially Rome, played an important role complementing the localized activities of 'the neighbourhood'. As we shall see below (Chapter 7), the city provided important services and was the locus of much material splendour and entertainment and grand occasions. Attending these occasions, being in the theatre or amphitheatre, viewing a triumphal procession, walking through splendid arcades, under triumphal arches, past statues of notable citizens, all extended the range of people whom children saw and met, created a sense of being a Roman, and built

---

[1] A great deal of the scholarship on 'the Roman family' in recent decades deals with relationships in one form or another. See the chapters in the three volumes edited by B. Rawson (1986*b*, 1991*b*) or Rawson and Weaver (1997); and Wiedemann (1989); K. R. Bradley (1991*a*); Champlin (1991); Treggiari (1991); Dixon (1992, 2001*a*); Parkin (1992); Saller (1994); Gardner (1998); and Corbier (1999*b*).

up—if only subconsciously—a set of values which conditioned their further development and outlook.

Housing played its part in establishing relationships and values. In the upper classes, especially in families which were politically active, the large house was a status symbol,[2] the setting for many visitors and social and business occasions, and was staffed by a wide range of specialized and general helpers and carers (mostly slaves, many with their own children). Wealthy families moved between different houses at different times of the year, enjoying villas at the coast and in the country as well as a townhouse in Rome or another large urban centre. Poorer families in the city lived in crowded tenement houses, with inescapable interaction between residents and with the street the only playground for children.[3] 'The neighbourhood' played an important role for such a population, whose members were largely pedestrian and had their own local organizations and sense of identity.[4]

As we have already seen, a child's home was the setting for many formative experiences. A birth (in the home) was the occasion for family, friends, and dependants to come together at the house. Here were formed the earliest social networks, and subsequent birthdays were celebrated in the home according to the resources of the family. The Roman house—whether spacious and affluent or cramped and poor—was not the private, protected space of modern Western domestic life. It was the interface between private and public. In the large *atrium* house, in lavish city apartments, and in sprawling country villas of the rich and powerful, a child's parents, singly or together, held receptions which brought into the house visitors of varying status, connected

[2] In the mass of recent scholarship on domestic space, note Wiseman (1987); Wallace-Hadrill (1994); Barton (1996); Laurence and Wallace-Hadrill (1997); Nevett (1997); George (1997); Ellis (2000); Hales (2000); and, for a critique of recent scholarship, Allison (2001).

[3] We know less of rural society, but even there more people probably lived in towns and villages than on isolated farms, with farm workers travelling daily to and from their work. Children who joined the labour force would travel with a group, participate in seasonal festivities, and some of their social activities would be town-centred.

[4] See Ch. 7 below on *uici*. On the reliance on neighbours to confirm one's status and other personal matters, cf. Gardner (1993: 182–7). She aptly calls her ch. 7 'The Face-to-Face Society'. Cf. below (at n. 17) on children's presence in local shops and workrooms.

with the parents in differing degrees of intimacy. Much public business was transacted here, and children were not infrequently present.[5] The adornment and size of the house, along with the statues, inscriptions, family records, and memorabilia—all of which were intended to project the owner's status and achievements to the world—also helped develop in his children a consciousness of self, positioned them in their social world, and provided models for them to emulate. Triumphant generals from at least the second century BCE displayed in their vestibules and on their doorposts some of the spoil which had been part of their triumphal procession.[6] The *imagines* (ancestor masks) which were displayed inside the house—but in the most public area—of high-ranking families had the power to impress visitors and inspire the boys of the family. There was a tradition that famous citizens of the past had been so inspired to match the achievement of their forebears.[7]

A grand house, and its associated family history,[8] had an effect beyond the immediate family. The large slave *familia* resident

---

[5] Claudius' fear of assassination made all morning callers, including women, boys, and girls, subject to bodily security checks (Suetonius, *Claudius* 35). Treggiari (1991: 420) believes that in the late Republic the *salutatio* was an all-male affair.

[6] Especially works of art. In 187 BCE M. Fuluius Nobilior was criticized in the senate by ambassadors from Ambracia for his siege and capture of their city and his removal of statues and other works of art to Rome. One of the consuls defended Fuluius, pointing out that these were not secretive actions: they were the very basis of his claim to a triumph, and he would display such achievements in his procession and then on his doorposts (Livy 38. 43. 10). In the vestibule of Pompey's house in Rome were displayed the beaks (*rostra*) of enemy ships (presumably those of the pirates against whom Pompey waged a successful campaign in 67 BCE): Cicero, *Philippics* 2. 68. See below on Augustus' house. Pliny the Elder (*NH* 35. 6–8) contrasted this practice of former generations, recording public achievement and virtue, with the domestic art and embellishment of his own day. But Juvenal's satire (8) on the *imagines* in unworthy houses indicates that the earlier practice continued. See especially Wiseman (1987) for further discussion.

[7] Sallust, *The Jugurthine War* 4: Q. Fabius Maximus, P. Cornelius Scipio, and other distinguished men were in the habit of saying that they had been spurred on to display qualities (*uirtus*) which would earn reputation and glory (*fama* and *gloria*) equal to that of their forebears whenever they looked on their *imagines*.

[8] Not in the sense of a house passed on and lived in by successive generations of one family, but rather family records—such as *imagines*, statues, and perhaps documents (including contrived genealogies and histories)—and ceremonies such as worship of the *genius* of the head of household and festivals such as the Parentalia.

there (including many children, some—the *uernae*—born in the household) shared to some extent in the aesthetic pleasures of the material environment and, depending on their skills and the favour they found with their owner, they either enjoyed some of the privileges and a comfortable and cultivated life or chafed at the stark contrast between their owner's lifestyle and their own treatment and conditions.

The house was the setting for life-stage ceremonies. We have seen that the birth of a child was an occasion for receiving visitors into the home. This was an opportunity for an older sibling of the new child to greet relatives and be introduced to other visitors, some of whom, with long-standing links to the family, may on a previous occasion have been present to assist at or celebrate the older sibling's own birth. As we shall see below, the age gap between siblings could be considerable. A birth was a time of coming-together, even of reconciliation;[9] of thanks to the gods or fears for the welfare of mother and infant. Not infrequently, it could leave the older child motherless, thus involving him or her in new experiences—death, grief, readjustment to a different family structure. Not only births and birthdays were celebrated in the house, but betrothals, weddings, and deaths, in all of which children had roles.

When Cicero's daughter Tullia was betrothed to Furius Crassipes in April of 56 BCE, Cicero gave an engagement party (*sponsalia*) which seems to have been a male affair—the equivalent of the modern 'stag party'? Cicero refers to it as being in honour of Crassipes (*Q. fr.* 2. 5. 3). He had expected his 10-year-old nephew Quintus to be present, but the boy was ill. On the marriage day there was a banquet at the bride's house, where children had special roles.[10] After the ceremony the bride was escorted to her husband's home, through the streets, by a procession in which specially chosen boys had roles in escorting the bride, one of them (a *camillus*) carrying a basket of symbolic domestic equipment. A chorus of boys and girls sang and lit the way with torches.[11] The songs were in the antiphonal style which

[9] Cf. Ch. 2 for the putting aside of feuds.

[10] See Varro, *On the Latin Language* 7. 34; Servius on *Aeneid* 4. 167; Macrobius, *Saturnalia* 3. 8. 7.

[11] Catullus' poems (61 and 62) are famous literary examples of marriage hymns.

we shall see in other ceremonies, such as the Secular Games, with girls and boys answering each other. The marriage song and other verses were sexually suggestive, indeed ribald, and the proceedings at the banquet and the following day's celebrations (the *repotia*) at the bridegroom's house were often sexually explicit. Children's participation in these activities exposed them early to the realities of sexual life, as did the very nature of domestic space—the openness of the architectural plan, wall-paintings, the comparative lack of privacy, and children's frequent presence in the slave quarters.

Dinner parties, more generally, were a favourite way of entertaining in Roman houses for those who could afford this form of hospitality and display. Children were present at least sometimes on such occasions, observing social interaction and the hierarchy of seating and fare. The effect on children of the lavish spread and loose behaviour at some dinner parties is criticized not only by Juvenal[12] but by the more prosaic Quintilian. In his criticism of ways in which adults spoil or corrupt children, Quintilian claims that 'we train children's sense of taste before we train their ability to speak', and that 'every dinner party resounds with obscene songs; comments to make one blush are noted; and children get used to these things'.[13] Other dinners, of course, were more modest affairs, accompanied by readings and other uplifting entertainment. The literary and moral points of such entertainment could be brought out by parents or slave attendants (cf. Chapter 5 above). Slave attendants, such as *paedagogi*, were responsible for coaching children in polite behaviour which would fit them to eat with adults (Seneca, *Letters* 94. 8). And children could observe for themselves, either from their separate tables or, more informally, running in and out of public rooms and slave quarters. In his boyhood, in the late second century BCE, Lucullus observed the sparing allocation of expensive Greek wine at his father's splendid dinner parties. It was a standard which he delighted in discarding in middle age, when he returned with wealth and exotic produce from his governorship in Asia Minor and was able to provide great quantities of such wine for his pub-

---

[12] *Satire* 14: see below.
[13] Quintilian 1. 2. 6, 8: 'ante palatum eorum quam os instituimus. . . . omne conuiuium obscenis canticis strepit, pudenda dicta spectantur. fit ex his consuetudo.'

lic banquets.[14] Whereas adults reclined on couches,[15] children sat on chairs, usually at tables somewhat removed from adult diners. A scene of boys and girls sitting at such a table is famous because it was where Claudius' son Britannicus ate the meal which killed him (Tacitus, *Annals* 13. 16). Suetonius confirms that Claudius regularly had his children and sons and daughters of other noble families in his company for meals, but claims that the children sat on the arm-rests (*fulcra*) of the adults' couches, in the old-fashioned way (*Claudius* 32). During the period of mourning (*iustitium*) imposed by the emperor Gaius after the death of his sister Drusilla, there was a ban on various forms of entertainment, including 'dining either with parents or with spouse and children' (Suetonius, *Gaius* 24). This suggests that such family dinners were not unusual, but were perhaps more special than everyday occasions.[16]

A glimpse at the range of people often involved in a child's upbringing is provided by Seneca in his letter on anger (*Letters* 94. 8–9). Before a person comes to full knowledge of a good and virtuous life, he has many instructors advising on day-to-day behaviour. 'This is the way to walk. This is the way to eat. This behaviour is appropriate for a man, this for a woman, this for a married man, this for a bachelor. Those who give the most earnest advice cannot themselves put it into effect. These are the instructions of a *paedagogus* to a boy, a grandmother to a grandson; and the schoolteacher who argues that one should not give way to anger is himself the angriest of all.'

Another glimpse, of children frequenting slaves' quarters and neighbourhood workshops, comes from Celsus, who wrote a tract

---

[14] Pliny the Elder, *NH* 14, 96, quoting Varro: the boy never saw a splendid dinner party at his father's place where Greek wine was offered more than once.

[15] Women had sat on chairs in early times, but by at least the 1st c. BCE they normally joined the men on couches (Valerius Maximus 2. 1). See Booth (1991) on reclining as a sign of coming of age.

[16] Sigismund Nielsen (1998: 59) notes 'how widespread common meals in the family were', but suggests that upper-class writers did not attach much importance to such meals. K. R. Bradley (1998a) points out that parents and children did not normally sit together at a common table, as modern families often have. But the advent of television, computer games, and children's independent social lives has already changed that in many homes; and, even when that is still the norm for family meals, pre-adult children seldom join the adult guests at table for a dinner party.

in the late second century attacking Christianity. He claimed that in private homes 'wool-workers, cobblers, laundry-workers, and the most illiterate and bucolic yokels' had an undue influence 'whenever they get hold of children in private and some stupid women with them'. 'They alone, they say, know the right way to live, and if the children would believe them, they would become happy and make their home happy as well. . . . They should leave father and their schoolmasters, and go along with the women and little children who are their playfellows to the wooldresser's shop, or to the cobbler's or the washerwoman's shop, that they may learn perfection. And by saying this they persuade them.'[17] The slave community in a household can be seen as a kind of extended family, with slave children having a variety of relationships (Flory 1978). Freeborn children who had a number of slave carers were also members, in some senses, of the slave community. They spent much time with carers and other slaves, sometimes in slave quarters and sometimes attended by slaves in more general parts of the house. In many societies, ancient and modern, the kitchen has been a favourite meeting place, a place for socializing and socialization. In earlier chapters we have already seen the important roles of carers and attendants (mostly slaves), especially nurses and *paedagogi*. This can lead to a belief in the distancing of a mother from everyday contact with her young children, but Jerome's fourth-century picture of the frazzled housewife shows her balancing babies, toddlers, book-keeping, and supervision of a range of household staff: 'The virgin, who is not married, thinks about God's matters . . . But the woman who is married thinks about worldly matters, how to please her husband . . . Over there, babies are chattering, the household is in uproar, children hang on her mouth for kisses, expenses are being counted up, the outgoings prepared. Here, a team of cooks is girded up to pound the meat, a crowd of weaving-women is buzzing.' Then the husband's arrival home with friends is announced, and the wife is in a flurry to see that all is ready for him. 'The management of the house, the bringing-up of the children, the needs of her husband, the

---

[17] Quoted by Origen (*Against Celsus* 3. 55), a contemporary Christian who quoted Celsus at length in order to rebut his arguments and claims; translation by Henry Chadwick (Cambridge University Press, 1953). I owe this reference to Margaret MacDonald of St Francis University.

training of the slaves—what woman is not distracted by these things from thoughts of God?'[18]

Saller (1984, 1994), K. R. Bradley (1991a), and Dixon (1992), amongst others, have discussed Roman concepts of 'the family' and the absence of a single Latin word denoting the conjugal family (spouses and dependent children). Neither *familia* nor *domus* serves the purpose. Yet there is much evidence that core loyalties and affection were between spouses and between parents and children. The evidence of epitaphs points strongly to the primacy of these relationships in the civilian population, and this is supported by a range of other evidence.[19] These bonds did not exclude other relationships, as this chapter illustrates. Relationships between kin and within the household were fluid enough for a more general term to be needed, and this was often simply 'my own people' (*mei*) or 'his/her own people' (*sui*).

We have seen, and will see again, that many children lost one or both parents early. But none of the measures taken by the state to support children and encourage child-raising took account of children outside the family circle. All such measures provided for children with parents, or children attached to some kind of surrogate parent. There was no concept of children without a personal, individual link to some adult or group of adults. It was only with the development of a Christian state that institutions were established for orphans and foundlings, and even then institutional provision for children was slower in coming than for others in need, such as the ill, the old, and the destitute.[20]

[18] *Against Helvidius* 20 (*PL* 23. 204) 'inde infantes garriunt, familia perstrepit, liberi ab osculis et ab ore dependent, computantur sumptus, impendia praeparantur. hinc cocorum accincta manus carnes terit, hinc textricum turba commurmurat . . . ipsa dispensatio domus, liberorum educatio, necessitates mariti, correctio seruulorum, quam a Dei cogitatione non auocent?' Jerome's arguments against marriage, and in favour of celibacy, were directed at a wide segment of society—not perhaps the upper classes, but many who could afford some slave help.

[19] The fundamental work on this is Saller and Shaw (1984) and subsequent work by Saller and Shaw separately. For my comment on Martin's criticism (1996) of the methodology of Saller and Shaw, see B. Rawson (1997c).

[20] See Pugliese (1984–5: 3184–6) for discussion. Donations to the church for such purposes (*piae causae*) specified *brephotrophia* and *orphanotrophia* less often than other categories (which included *xenodochia*, for the care of foreigners); but institutions may have catered for a variety of charitable functions. Legal provisions to regulate such institutions are known from the eastern part of the empire from the second half of the 5th c., but not from the west until Justinian.

Were the changes in children's familial relationships and perhaps in their places of residence destabilizing? K. R. Bradley (1991a: chapter 6) has written of 'dislocation' in the Roman family and rightly argues that the frequency of remarriage resulted in large numbers of blended families. He usefully raises the question of a child's 'emotional address', and suggests that there are 'negative implications' in the frequency of remarriage in Roman society. He speculates on the impact of such changes on children's emotional development and well-being. There can, of course, be no definitive answer to this question, and not only because of lack of evidence from Roman children themselves. Even today, when the question is more topical than ever, and a wealth of survey material is available, there is no consensus on the implications. There are many arguments, however, that the damaging effects of early trauma and disrupted family relationships can be overestimated.[21] It is at least arguable that the frequent dissolution of the natal nuclear family and the blending of new elements could have made Roman children resilient and adaptive, if there was a network or a structure to provide continuity, support, and affection.

The question of children's possible emotional instability in circumstances of changing relationships arises because of frequent assumptions in our own society that all the functions of parenthood are best fulfilled by the biological parents. Not all other societies, however, make these assumptions. The anthropologist Esther Goody has produced an excellent study (1982) of such matters, with a particular focus on West Africa. Her model of parenthood distinguishes five different roles,[22] which are not always vested in one set of 'parents'. Different allocations and combinations of these roles are culturally determined. She found

[21] Daily newspapers frequently carry arguments on both sides. See Dixon (1999) for discussion and for emphasis on the 'culturally specific ideologies' underlying views and practices relating to children and childhood. An early study (Skolnick 1975) argued that some stress and challenge can be healthy and stimulating, and indeed that a 'smooth and successful' childhood can have negative effects.

[22] Bearing and begetting, nurturance, training, sponsorship, and endowment of civil birth status. Quotations in this paragraph are from Goody (1982: 16–23). Cf. Goody (1999), where she again points out that the 'unitary' view of parenthood in contemporary Western society is so deeply embedded that we do not recognize that it is not also a 'necessary' view of parenthood.

that the splitting-off of these roles to different persons could strengthen personal relationships overall: a supplementary parent–child tie could be created 'without dissolving the remaining links between original parent and child'. Thus our frequent assumption that such role-splitting must weaken the original parent–child relationships is culturally determined and may not apply to Roman family relationships. Goody comments that often 'it is the continued existence of the links between original parent and child which give(s) meaning to the reassignment of other parental roles'. Such role-splitting will affect parent–child relationships and those of 'pro-parent' and child and those of parent and 'pro-parent'. A dense network results. Goody's study envisages situations of necessity ('crisis fostering') and those where the circulation of children is voluntary. Both such situations can be found at Rome.

It is time, then, to analyse the variety of relationships experienced by children, always remembering that children were not passive recipients of adult prescriptions and arrangements but rather that they absorbed, modified, and reconstructed these in their own perceptions. The nature of our evidence provides more detail about upper-class relationships than about others; but funerary inscriptions are overwhelmingly for the sub-elite, the provisions of the law had wide coverage, and iconography[23] yields some insights into many levels of society. Slaves, ex-slaves, and their descendants are well represented in many of these media; but the poorest members of society, whatever their status, are almost invisible. Roman law defined a range of relationships which were especially close and could thus provide 'just cause' for the manumission of a slave as an exception from the age restrictions set down in Augustus' *lex Aelia Sentia*. These included the slave-owner's natural son, daughter, brother, sister, or other blood relation; *collactaneus, educator, paedagogus, nutrix*, and the son or daughter of any of these; *alumnus, capsarius*;[24] and (with certain conditions) a proposed financial agent (*procurator*) or a woman whom the owner intends to marry. Some of these relationships have been discussed in earlier chapters; others will be discussed

---

[23] Cf. Ch. 1, 'Representations'.
[24] 'Fellow-nursling', 'a person who has brought one up', 'schoolchild's attendant', 'nurse', 'foster-child', 'book-carrier'.

below. The jurists are explicit that 'just cause' must be based on real affection (*iustae affectiones*), not mere indulgence (*luxuria, deliciae*).[25]

Many factors militated against close and long-lasting relationships between Roman parents and children. Mortality rates were a major factor, reducing the chances of parents and child developing their relationship together over a period of fourteen or more years. This reduced the impact of *patria potestas* (Saller 1994), once seen as the wide-ranging, inhibiting powers of a stern father over his children. Shaw (2001) has recently shown that the power of life and death allegedly held by fathers (*ius uitae necisque*) was never untrammelled. In addition to demographic factors, there were also divorce, the absence from home of parents (especially fathers) on business or public duty, poverty, slavery, and the roles of wet-nurses and other carers. The historical record, however, is shot through with expressions of affection and close interest and concern between parents and children. Can we speak of 'love'? The word 'love' is so loaded, so culturally dependent, that it is difficult to use it of another society, especially one so remote in time, without fear of misrepresentation. Yet there is a range of expressions in Latin which, to my mind, equate to 'love' as an ideal for parents and children in Roman society, and there is a record of behaviour which indicates frequent translation of ideal into action. Previous chapters have argued for a high degree of sensitivity to childhood and its attributes during the best-documented period, from the first century BCE into the third century CE.

Cicero described the instinctive emotion between parents and offspring as *caritas* (*On Friendship* 27). This emotion exists between many animals and their offspring, he says, and he uses forms of the verb *amare* ('to love') for this mutual emotion. The emotion is much more obvious in humans, and the *caritas* between children and parents is almost indestructible. Cicero goes on to speak of a kind of *caritas* and of *amor* between close

---

[25] Gaius, *Institutes* 1. 18–19; *D.* 40. 2. 11–13, 16, Ulpian. Cf. *D.* 20. 1. 6. 8, Ulpian; Paul, *Sententiae* 5. 6. 16; Gaius, *Institutes* 1. 19; Justinian, *Institutes* 1. 6. 5. The age minima were 20 for a slave owner and 30 for a slave.

friends and men whom we admire for their virtue. Elsewhere Cicero speaks of kinship as society in miniature, and propounds a hierarchy of natural affection within kin: the reproductive instinct is basic, so the primary bond is between spouses; then comes that with their children, and then the communality of the household. Beyond the household are blood relations and marriage relations, and these are bound together by goodwill and affection (*beneuolentia, caritas*), 'for it is a great thing to have the same ancestral monuments, to observe the same worship (*sacra*), and to have burial places in common' (*On Duties* 1. 54). Further on (*On Duties* 1. 58), our greatest duty (*officium*) is due to country and parents (*patria* and *parentes*), because they have given us the greatest benefits. Then come children and the whole household (*domus*), because we are their sole support; then the relatives with whom we are most in harmony (*bene conuenientes propinqui*), whose lot we usually share.

One of the most eloquent statements of the joy of parenthood is, as we saw above (Chapter 1), in Lucretius' lecture to his readers on the finality of death: it will be the end of the joys of family life (but also of sufferings). A century and a half later, Pliny the Younger (*Letters* 8. 23. 7–8) expressed similar regrets when a friend died in the prime of life, leaving behind an elderly mother, a young wife, and an infant daughter. His career had been cut off prematurely, and he left behind 'a bereaved mother, a widowed wife, and an orphan daughter who would never know her father . . . A single day has turned upside down so many hopes, so many joys.'

Literature and epitaphs usually encapsulate ideals about the parent–child relationship. Sometimes they also give evidence of the application of those ideals in everyday life. Occasionally, as in satire, we glimpse the bad influence which parents might have on their children. Both positive and negative comments acknowledge the real influence which parents could have and the interaction between parents and children. Juvenal recognizes that impressionable children will take as their models the behaviour at home of parents, who command respect and emulation. In his *Satire* 14, Juvenal expands on the bad influence. The curse of gambling will pass from father to son while the son is still a boy (*bullatus*); and a father's extravagant taste for elaborate food will be ingrained in a boy by his seventh birthday. The cruel treatment of slaves will not help a boy learn lessons of restraint and the common humanity of slaves. A daughter who has since childhood shared in the secrets of her mother's lovers will have her mother's complicity in her own love-affairs. The listener or reader is urged to avoid holding wild parties at home—or at least to protect children from knowledge of these.[26] Other bad examples are extravagant building schemes (ostentation and impoverishment of finances), the practice of Judaism, and avarice—the last particularly seductive because it has the image of virtue. Modern fathers (in the early second century CE) are represented as pressing their sons[27] too fast with their studies, so that they will 'get on' quickly, either in a lucrative career or in knowing how to amass money in other ways. This is hardly the path to a happy life, to which a proper father should be guiding a child.

A little more soberly, Tacitus has one of his speakers (the conservative Messalla) blame not only nurses (male and female) for bad influence on infants but also parents themselves, who accustom their little children (*paruuli*) to licence and loose talk rather than integrity and modesty. Even in the womb infants are infected by their mothers' passion for actors and gladiators. The home environment ruins children before they even get to school (*Dialogue on Orators* 29). All of this suggests close and frequent interaction between parents and young children.

By early imperial times men going overseas on official duty expected the comfort and pleasure of having with them their wife and, sometimes, their children. Hard-line conservatives still preferred the ban of earlier times against such family 'encumbrances', but they were a small minority.[28] Germanicus made much of being accompanied by his wife Agrippina (the Elder) and several of their children during his various provincial appointments. Sometimes, however, responsibilities towards children could be a

---

[26] Cf. the elderly Ummidia Quadrata, who retained *pantomimi* for her own domestic entertainment but ensured that they performed only when her young grandson was not present (Pliny, *Letters* 7. 24).

[27] In lines 208–9 girls also are urged to learn the value of money even before their alphabet. It is a nurse who dins this lesson into boys and girls in their early years before they learn to walk. Cf. Ch. 5, under 'Early Education'.

[28] Tacitus (*Annals* 3. 33–4) reports a senatorial debate of 21 CE. Tiberius' son Drusus spoke of the unattractiveness of making provincial tours if he were separated from his 'beloved wife, the parent of so many children of their marriage'.

reason to decline such appointments. One senator in 21 CE declined nomination for the plum province of Africa on the grounds of ill health but also because of the age of his children, one of whom was a daughter of marriageable age.[29]

As we saw above (Chapter 5), an important focus of the intellectual discussions of the first century was family relationships. This was reflected in the philosophical lectures of Musonius Rufus; and the topics of the declamation exercises practised by adolescent rhetoric students were particularly concerned with relationships between parents and children. (See further below.)

Roman culture valorized *pietas* amongst the highest of its virtues: it implied loyalty to gods, country, parents, and family.[30] In its family context, it was a reciprocal bond, especially between parents and children. Valerius Maximus included *pietas* in the virtues which he documented in his work, *Memorable Doings and Sayings*, in the early first century CE. His examples of relationships between parents and children are about adult sons and daughters, not young children, but he speaks of two-way commitments and mixes vocabulary of affection with that of *pietas*. The vocabulary for parents' treatment of children is more varied than for children's behaviour to parents. Parents show *amor* and *indulgentia* towards children, as well as severity and moderation. When a daughter suckles her imprisoned mother to keep her alive, the act is not unnatural because the first law of nature is to love and cherish (*diligere*) parents.[31]

The law reinforced the reciprocal relationship. Father and son could not prosecute or give evidence against each other;[32] they were expected to support each other. Children too young to give evidence or to give legal support were used in court to heighten the emotional appeal for a father. In his defence of Publius Sestius in 56 BCE, Cicero used Sestius' son Lucius in this way. He had the son read out, in his boyish voice, a decree favourable to

---

[29] Tacitus (*Annals* 3. 35. 2). The senator also thought that he was unlikely to beat his competitor for this province.

[30] e.g. Cicero, *On the Republic* 6. 16, presents *pietas* as attaching especially to *patria*, and then to *parentes* and *propinqui*. See Saller (1988, 1991).

[31] Valerius Maximus 5. 4, 'On *pietas* towards parents'; 5. 7, 'On parents' love and indulgence to children'; 5. 8, 'On fathers' severity to their children'; 5. 9, 'On parents' moderation towards children under suspicion'.

[32] Gaius, *Institutes* 4. 78; *D.* 22. 5. 4, Paul.

the father. The boyish voice was designed to move the jurors, but also to give notice that he would avenge his family's enemies in the future. It was a son's duty to pursue such enemies in the courts or otherwise, and young men often began a public career by prosecuting a father's accusers. Such expectations had their influence on children's development and outlook: it made them good haters.[33] This affected boys more than girls, and the nature of our evidence specifies fathers and sons more than mothers and daughters as examples of relationships. Females also, however, inherited and maintained family traditions which obliged them to 'do the right thing' by their parents and other relations. Cicero's wife Terentia seems to have nursed resentment against Clodius for ten years for blackening the reputation of her half-sister, the Vestal Virgin Fabia.[34] Little girls listening to family tales could nurse such hostilities much longer. When Iunia Tertulla, a grand old lady closely connected with the late Republican figures Cato, Cassius, and Brutus, died in 22 CE her will recognized many friendly relationships but notably omitted the emperor Tiberius. No doubt she had a say in plans for her funeral procession, which included *imagines* of many distinguished families but drew attention to Brutus and Cassius by their very omission (Tacitus, *Annals* 3. 76).

A story told by Livy (7. 4–5) about a father and son of the fourth century BCE illustrates *pietas* in action and enables us to reconstruct what were the normal expectations of the father–son relationship. The father, L. Manlius Imperiosus, was on trial for his harsh conduct as *dictator*, and the charges were strengthened by allegations of his unjust behaviour towards his son, T. Manlius. The son Titus was slow-witted and inarticulate, so his father sent him to live in the country doing menial work. What a father should have done was keep his son at Rome in his own company, part of the household and its rites and acquiring experience of public life in the Forum, mixing with his contem-

---

[33] Cicero, *In Defence of Sestius* 10. Cf. Valerius Maximus 5. 4. 4 and Dio 36. 40. 4 for another late Republican example, where M. Cotta began a prosecution, on the day of his *toga uirilis* ceremony, against Cn. Carbo in revenge for his prosecution of Cotta's father. Dio says that the prosecution succeeded, so the young Cotta must have had the support of some experienced friends of his father's. See Epstein (1987: 92–4).

[34] Epstein (1987: 109). Epstein has extensive discussion of such enmities.

poraries of equal rank. In other words, the father owed his son
the duty of a proper education: humane personal attention and a
civilized urban environment to bring out the best in him. The son
showed his *pietas* by moving to have these allegations against his
father dismissed.[35]

We saw above (Chapter 5) the care taken by fathers in many
levels of society to ensure a good formal education for their sons.
Fathers themselves were expected to play some role in a son's
moral education, and it was they who sponsored their sons' entry
into the life of an adult citizen. But Claudius, the future emperor,
was another youth held back and kept out of public life because
of his disablement. In this case, he had lost his father in infancy
and thus had a *tutor* to look after his formal interests.[36] He had
a *paedogogus* attached to him well beyond the normal age for
having such an attendant, and claimed later that the man was
boorish and brutal. Claudius did not receive public appointments
of the kind given to other members of the imperial family, and
buried himself in study, especially that of history.[37] Mothers too
played an important part in children's rearing and development
(Dixon 1988) and Claudius' mother Antonia was clearly complicit
in the treatment of Claudius. Indeed, the women of his family
seem to have been harsher than was Augustus himself in ridicul-
ing Claudius and being nervous about the impression which
Claudius might make in public.[38]

The ideal for parents was to rear a number of children who
would survive the parents themselves, attend to their burial and
commemoration, and continue the family line. Sons rather than
daughters could continue the family name, although in the imperial period children sometimes bore both parents' names or even
only the maternal name if that were sufficiently superior in

[35] Cf. Valerius Maximus 5. 4. 3 for this story, where the son is moved only
by natural affection (*naturalis amor*), with no need to be coaxed.

[36] See further below for the frequency of fathers' deaths and the consequent
relationships of children who thus became *pupilli* ('wards').

[37] Suetonius, *Claudius* 2. 2. An exposure in recent times revealed that around
the mid-20th c. (in the reign of King George VI) a member of the British royal
family with a mental disability was sent to an institution and kept out of the
public eye.

[38] For grandmother Livia and sister Livilla, see Suetonius, *Claudius* 3–4, 41.
1–2; and Kokkinos (1992: 28–30 and nn. 83–4).

prestige.[39] A model of good fortune (*felicitas*) was Q. Metellus Macedonicus, so named for his victories in Greece in the mid-second century BCE: in addition to all his political and military honours, he had a long life and was survived by four adult sons who reached the highest magistracies in the state and who officiated at his public funeral. 'This surely is to pass on happily from life rather than to die,' pronounced Velleius Paterculus in the early first century CE.[40]

One of the arguments used by Cicero to persuade the senate in 43 BCE to award an honorific statue to Ser. Sulpicius Rufus, who had died on service to his country, was that this would reward the *pietas* of Sulpicius' son, who had sought this honour for his father. Not that a statue could outdo the son's own character, said Cicero, as a monument to his father. The son was the image (*effigies*) of his father's great qualities, and it was part of his duty to see that his father was properly honoured after death (Cicero, *Philippics* 9. 12). When in Pliny the Younger's day a son predeceased his father and thus could not emulate his career or honour him after his death, the senate awarded statues to both father and son, partly as consolation to the father but also, in Pliny's opinion, as a model to inspire young men to high ideals and to inspire leading citizens to raise children. As a public symbol of the ideal of a close father–son relationship, such a statue helps mould public opinion. It influences youths to aspire to being worthy of their fathers.[41]

Many children were deprived of a close relationship with a parent by a parent's early death. At the age of 5, the probability of having a father alive was perhaps 88 per cent, but by the age of 10 this had reduced to about 75 per cent and by the age of 15 it was about 63 per cent. Corresponding figures for mothers were 91, 81, and 72 per cent.[42] Another way of expressing this is to recognize that 'In any society before the demographic transition the chances

[39] Poppaea Sabina, Nero's wife, used the name of her maternal grandfather, Poppaeus Sabinus, because of his distinguished record as consul, governor, and general, and because of her mother Poppaea, who had distinction and beauty (*gloria* and *forma*) to give her daughter (Tacitus, *Annals* 13. 45. 1).

[40] Velleius Paterculus 1. 11. 6–7: 'hoc est nimirum magis feliciter de uita migrare quam mori'.

[41] Pliny, *Letters* 2. 7. Cf. Ch. 7 below.

[42] Probabilities are for 'ordinary' (non-senatorial) males, as in table 3.1e of Saller (1994). Probabilities for females (table 3.1b) are similar.

of a marriage ending by death before the end of the couple's child-bearing years were high'.[43] Other children lost one parent to divorce. Like Claudius, Cn. Iulius Agricola, a prominent senator of the latter half of the first century CE, lost his father very early—probably soon after his own birth.[44] The infant Agricola was brought up by his mother, Iulia Procilla, who guided his studies and career aspirations, as well as his moral development, well into his adolescence. Many mothers were left with such responsibilities during Rome's history. During the wars and territorial expansion overseas of the last two centuries BCE, men were absent for long periods and many died during those absences.[45] Until it became more frequent for wives to accompany husbands overseas, the rearing of children at home was often left to mothers. Some mothers were famous for their rearing and influence over sons, such as Cornelia, mother of the Gracchi brothers, Julius Caesar's mother Aurelia, and Octavian's mother Atia. The Gracchi and Caesar were no longer children when their fathers died, and their mothers did not remarry.

Many mothers did remarry after the death of a husband or a divorce, which introduced a stepfather into the relationship. Augustus' legislation imposed financial penalties on women who did not remarry, unless they already had earned the privileges due to bearing three or four children.[46] They might then produce children of the new marriage. After a divorce a father had first claim on any children of the dissolved marriage, and there was an assumption that they would reside with him. He had the legal right of custody: a child 'belonged' to its father in every sense. But where the child actually resided and was brought up depended on many factors and was sometimes negotiated by the parents for their own convenience and needs. The child might stay with the mother or it might be raised by another relative. In

---

[43] Saller (1994: 219). Saller continues: 'Amongst first marriages between a twenty-year-old woman and a thirty-year-old man in Rome, one in six would have ended by the death of a spouse within five years, one in three within ten years, nearly one in two within fifteen years, and three in five within twenty years.'

[44] Tacitus, *Agricola* 4. Agricola's birth and education took place in Narbonese Gaul.

[45] Evans (1991) discusses such consequences at length.

[46] The *ius trium/quattuor liberorum*: see 'Introduction' above.

Cicero's day there seems to have been no concern, in legal terms, for the moral fitness of a father to raise his children, although he might lose any claim to use his wife's dowry for their support if he were shown to have behaved badly.[47] By the mid-second century CE, however, it was possible to get a legal ruling that the child should stay with the mother after a divorce, if this seemed best because of the father's bad character. This did not diminish the father's formal *potestas*.[48] There seems to be a real concern for the child's best interests in the jurists' discussion of such cases. In a dispute over where a child should reside, the decision might be deferred and the child stay with father or guardian until the child reached puberty (presumably so that the child's own wishes could be consulted) if it were clear that the father or guardian was of respectable rank and good character; otherwise the decision was to be made forthwith. If both parties (parents) were suspect on any grounds, the child could be put in the care of someone appointed by the court until the child's puberty (*D*. 43. 30. 3. 4, Ulpian, quoting Julian).

Children resided with a stepfather if their mother remarried while she still had them in her care. When Mark Antony was about 10 years old his father died. The father had been on campaign for much of the preceding few years, trying to put down the pirate problem in the Mediterranean. His wife (Iulia) and son saw him only intermittently, and his death in failure left the young Antony with little paternal inspiration or pride. His mother's remarriage brought a stepfather of somewhat higher rank (P. Cornelius Lentulus Sura was consul in 71 BCE) but one whose career brought greater public disgrace. Lentulus was expelled from the senate in 70, and although he regained senatorial office in 63 he used it to abet Catiline's plans to usurp power and was executed when the conspiracy was exposed. The stepfather might thus be seen as a negative influence on Antony's development and adolescence, but who knows what conversations took place within the home in the youth's impressionable teenage

---

[47] Cicero, *Topica* 19. If a divorce was due to the husband's fault, even if it was the wife who took the initiative to divorce, he had no claim to retain any part of the dowry for their support ('pro liberis manere nihil oportet').

[48] A ruling of Antoninus Pius, reinforced by Marcus Aurelius and Septimius Seuerus, in favour of residence of the child with the mother: *D*. 43. 30. 1. 3 and 3. 5, Ulpian.

years? There may have been genuine commitment to radical reform in Lentulus' actions, which could have influenced Antony's future development and political outlook. Cicero's attack on Antony in late 44 BCE assumes a close relationship between Antony and his stepfather. Cicero berates Antony for not making his maternal uncle L. Iulius Caesar his adviser and guide rather than Lentulus: 'You preferred to model yourself on your stepfather rather than on your uncle'.[49]

Octavian (later Augustus) was 4 years old when his father died (Suetonius, *Augustus* 8).[50] Octavian's father had been absent from Rome, as governor of Macedonia, for at least a year before that, so Octavian had had little experience of his father after infancy. He seems to have been brought up by a grandmother until her death, perhaps because of the remarriage of his mother Atia to L. Marcius Philippus. But then he moved to the new household where mother and stepfather saw to his further upbringing and training (Nicolaus of Damascus, *Augustus* 3). There is no information on what happened to his sister Octavia immediately after the death of their father,[51] but brother and sister were near in age and their relationship was close, so it is likely that both moved together to grandmother and then to mother and step-father. The relationship between Octavian and his stepfather seems not to have been close, although Philippus sought a paternal role in trying to dissuade Octavian from becoming Julius Caesar's heir in 44. By then Caesar had assumed a leading role in his grand-nephew's life. Octavian had put on the *toga uirilis* in 47, and Caesar, now pre-eminent in the Roman world, initiated him into public life and supervised his moral and social life. Octavian's mother Atia, who had kept firm discipline over his development, trusted her uncle in this role.[52]

---

[49] Cicero, *Philippics* 2. 14–18: a speech not delivered but whose written version circulated widely.

[50] Details of birth and death dates are not fully documented in this chapter. They can be found in most biographies or standard reference works. Such details are reasonably well established for emperors; for others, estimates may vary by a few months or even years, but not enough to invalidate the discussion here.

[51] There was also a stepsister Octavia, from the father's first marriage.

[52] Suetonius, *Augustus* 8; Velleius Paterculus 2. 59. 3. It was also a maternal uncle whom Cicero proclaimed to Antony in the *Second Philippic* as a more appropriate role model than Antony's stepfather Lentulus.

Octavian became a stepfather himself when he married Livia. Her son Tiberius was very young and she was pregnant with Drusus when she and Octavian married, and for five years after that the boys lived with their father. When, however, the father died in 33 BCE Tiberius and Drusus, aged by then 9 and 5 years, moved to the household of mother and stepfather. There they were brought up with their approximate coeval, Augustus' daughter Julia, who had lived with Octavian and Livia from infancy.[53] Augustus was not only stepfather but *tutor* of Livia's sons.[54] He gave them the education and public positions appropriate to the sons he did not have; but as they moved into their teens he looked beyond them, to youths of his own blood, for prospective heirs and successors (Marcellus, then Gaius and Lucius Caesar). It was only in 4 CE, in the absence of any appropriate males of his own line, that Augustus recognized Tiberius for this role and formally adopted him to make him truly one of his own Julian family.[55]

Octavian had some responsibility for the children of his sister Octavia during the 30s, in the absence of her husband Mark Antony, especially after Antony's liaison with Cleopatra became public and Cleopatra bore a child to Antony in 36 within months of the birth of his daughter by Octavia, Antonia the Younger. In 32 Antony formally divorced Octavia and she left his house in

[53] Octavian had divorced Julia's mother Scribonia immediately on the birth of Julia in 39 BCE (or even during the pregnancy). Scribonia must, however, have maintained contact with Julia over the years, as she chose to go into exile with Julia in 2 BCE and stayed with her until Julia's death in 14 CE (Velleius Paterculus 2. 100. 5; Dio 55. 10–14).

[54] At the request of the boys' father, who perhaps saw this method of sending his sons to their mother's new home as in the boys' best interests (Dio 48. 44. 5).

[55] Octavian-Augustus was himself a Julian only by virtue of his adoption by Julius Caesar (or at least by the provisions of Caesar's will). Augustus did have a surviving grandson Agrippa Postumus, the youngest son of his daughter Julia, and he too was adopted by Augustus in 4 CE (aged 16), but his character put him out of favour. His adoption was an indication of Augustus' lingering wish to have an heir of his own blood, and there were rumours of attempted reconciliations between Augustus and Agrippa Postumus, but from 4 CE Tiberius was clearly the senior heir. Postumus was put to death soon after Tiberius' accession in 14 CE. As far as we know, stepsons were not usually adopted. Sons-in-law were, in dynastic strategies, and Augustus had made Tiberius his son-in-law in 11 BCE by arranging his marriage to Julia. There were no surviving children of that marriage.

Rome and moved to Octavian's household with her five children, three from her first marriage (to C. Marcellus) and the two daughters, Antonia the Elder and Antonia the Younger, by Antony.[56] Here her children joined Julia, Tiberius, and Drusus, all of similar ages (ranging from the 10-year-old Tiberius to the 4-year-old Antonia the Younger). We shall speculate below on the relationships between the children, but here we note the roles of parents and step-parents.

Other examples of arrangements made for fatherless children can be cited from the families which provided emperors over the next two centuries. In 85 CE Hadrian lost his father, so at the age of 9 he was a *pupillus* and came into the formal care of two *tutores* (Trajan and P. Acilius Attianus). It was only in his teens, however, that he seems to have become part of Trajan's household: one can infer that he continued to reside with his mother, in Rome and in Spain, before that.[57] Marcus Aurelius was little more than an infant when his own father died. It was his paternal grandfather who adopted him, but a maternal great-grandfather also contributed to his rearing, as did the emperor Hadrian and a battery of distinguished teachers, and his mother continued to have some role in his upbringing.[58]

The rules of dowry in Roman law took into account the existence and interests of children of a dissolved marriage. Although a woman's dowry returned to her natal family if she predeceased her husband childless, part or all of the dowry remained with the father if there were children to be provided for. Moreover, as the

[56] She also reared Antyllus and Iullus, the sons of Antony by an earlier marriage (to Fulvia). Octavian put the teenage Antyllus to death after the death of Antony in 30 BCE, but the younger Iullus continued as a member of Octavia's household and married one of her daughters. After 30 BCE, Octavia also reared the three children of Cleopatra and Antony (twins aged 10 and a son aged 6): Plutarch, *Antony* 28–9; Dio 48. 24. 3.

[57] Hadrian's mother Domitia Paulina was less successful than the more famous mothers cited above for firm discipline and good guidance of their sons' education. In SHA (*Hadrian* 1–2) criticisms are reported of his Greek studies and his hunting.

[58] SHA, *Marcus* 1–4, where *proauus* probably refers to a step-great-grandfather on his mother's side (Birley 1987: ch. 2 and app. 2). See below on grandfathers. Marcus himself, in his *Meditations* (1. 1–16), records a list of people who influenced his nature and upbringing, beginning with grandfather, father, and mother (admitting that he hardly knew his father).

imperial period developed, individual pacts were made between families to provide even more flexible arrangements than those in the formal law. They tried to anticipate the conflicts which might arise as a result of one or both spouses' remarriage, and the possible disadvantaging of children of the first marriage by a confusion of two patrimonies. Such provisions modified the formal powers of a *paterfamilias*, and were consistent with the gradual limitation of these powers in the second century CE. They are consistent too with the growing recognition, in matters of property, of the bond between mother and child.[59] Humbert (1972) details at length the care often taken with legal arrangements to protect the interests of children (especially in matters of property and inheritance) if a parent remarried. There is a specific example of how one woman (Murdia) balanced her commitments to her surviving husband and the children of two marriages. In an inscription giving details of Murdia's will, the son of her first marriage praised her for her motherly love (*amor maternus*) in making all her children equal heirs but first allocating an extra legacy to the son of the first marriage to acknowledge his claim on the property left to Murdia by her first husband's generosity. Murdia also honoured her second husband by adding a legacy to the dowry which was to go to him.[60]

As we shall see below (Chapter 8), the 'natural' order of things was not infrequently reversed, when children died before their parents. This elicited many expressions of grief, which provide glimpses into ideals, expectations, and experience of relationships. The emotions expressed on epitaphs are usually brief and formulaic, restricted by the size of the funerary stone and perhaps by the social level of the dedicants, who found it easier to rely on the stone-cutter's usual repertoire than on their own creativity. Even the most conventional of these, however, can transmit important information. The dedication for the 9-year-old M. Seruilius Gemellus places his *tria nomina* at the head of the inscription, proclaiming his status, which was superior to that of

[59] See Humbert (1972) for extensive discussion of remarriage, esp. 284–300 for this paragraph. See also Saller (1984, 1994) on dowry; Crook (1967: 105) on pacts; and for *s.c. Orfitianum*, which improved children's access to their mother's property, Crook (1986); Dixon (1988: 51–60); Gardner (1986*b*, 1998).

[60] *CIL* 6. 10230; *FIRA*[2] 3. 70. Motherly love is said to consist in love for one's children (*caritas liberum*) and equal shares in inheritance (*aequalitas partium*).

the parents who set up the epitaph: the names of Stephanus and Fortunata show that they were very likely slaves. The parents had the resources to commission a well-carved marble epitaph to commemorate their *piisimus* son, themselves, and their descendants.[61] Literature could be more expansive, and we shall see examples of this from upper-class fathers, or from other men to console bereaved fathers or mothers. Valerius Maximus' list (5. 10) of parents who bore the death of their children bravely contains only fathers and sons. There are no literary tributes from mothers—as there is almost no literature extant from female authors—but mothers are prominent among the dedicators of epitaphs to young children.[62]

Quintilian's tribute to his two sons, who died at 5 and 9 years of age, includes praise of their intellectual and personal qualities (6 pr. 6–13). Their mother predeceased them, and a grandmother took over the raising of at least the younger, helped by the usual corps of carers. Quintilian retained contact, and took pleasure in the embraces of the younger boy and the child's demonstration that the priority of his affections was for his father. Quintilian had greater responsibilities for the older boy, who was ready to be groomed and trained for an adult life and career. It is clear that Quintilian had emotional bonds with this boy, and, it seems, expected to go on having a role in his education and grooming; but the boy had recently been adopted by a man of consular rank (superior to Quintilian's) and betrothed to a cousin whose father was a praetor. Thus part of a father's care for his son's future could be to surrender him, in some sense, to people who could better advance his public career. Goody's multifaceted model of parenthood is again helpful. The adopting father is a co-parent who offers 'ritual sponsorship' of the boy. Affective ties remain with the original parent, but the co-parent's role, as sponsor, is 'mediation between the child and the external system' (Goody 1982: 27). Quintilian's son would gain a higher rank and entrée to career paths less likely to be available from his original family. There are reciprocities too between parent and co-parent. The adopter gets

[61] *CIL* 6. 26409: ANU Classics Museum 71. 04; late 1st or 2nd c. CE. 'D. M. | M. SERVILIO GEMELLO | VIXIT ANNIS VIIII M. II D. XXVII | FECERVNT PARENTES STEPHANVS | ET FORTVNATA FILIO PIISSIMO | SIBI ET POSTERISQ EORVM'. The son had won freedom, and perhaps Roman citizenship.

[62] See Saller and Shaw (1984) for statistics, and below for examples.

a son and heir, with consequent property and political advantage and personal benefits such as companionship and having a protégé; Quintilian gains worthwhile kinship links and the satisfaction of seeing his son prosper.[63]

If both father and child survived beyond the child's early years, the age gap between them could present difficulties. Tensions are especially observable, in most societies, between father and son as the son grows out of childhood, chafes at restrictions on his personal and public life, and sees himself in some ways as his father's competitor and replacement. Most of the instances known to us, from historical literature, of conflict between fathers and sons involve adult sons. All of the instances in Valerius Maximus' passage (5. 8) 'On the severity of fathers to their children' involve a conflict between fatherly affection and duty to his country: patriotism always has the stronger claim. But a different kind of literature, the rhetorical exercises known as *controuersiae*,[64] gives an insight into more personal family tensions, especially those between father and son. These exercises, set as training for youths in schools of rhetoric, have often been criticized (in antiquity and since) for their artificiality and remoteness from real life. But recent scholarship[65] has shown how they can be used to reveal themes of vital interest to students in those schools—aspects of family life which might be explored in a non-threatening, non-confrontational fictional context that uses a dramatic, highly coloured form to permit the airing of issues with which youths can closely identify. Students in these schools tended to be adolescents in their early to mid-teens, but, as we have seen (Chapter 5 above), younger boys aspired to be part of these schools and some were indeed students at ages which can be defined as those of 'children'. Moreover, mature men attended these schools from time to time as spectators, to observe the progress and skills of the students. They knew that the issues being debated were not irrelevant: they may have recognized them from their own lives, and they had to deal with them in some form in the lawcourts.

[63] Note that in Goody's model the child's 'jurally defined' status is not affected. In Rome the child jurally entered a new family.

[64] Examples of these collected under the title of *The Major Declamations Ascribed to Quintilian* are now usually attributed to the 2nd c. CE. Seneca the Elder's *controuersiae* and *suasoriae* were collected in the first half of the 1st c. CE.

[65] e.g. Beard (1993); L. A. Sussman (1995); Kaster (2001). Cf. Ch. 5 above.

The most active lawcourt, the centumviral court, dealt mainly
with property matters, and in these the protagonists were often
fathers, mothers, stepmothers, and occasionally brothers—the
main characters of the *controuersiae*. Deeper emotional issues
often underlay the conflict which emerged as a property dispute
in the court.[66]

The freedom enjoyed by Romans to use wills to disperse their
property quite widely could cause conflict and resentment within
the family.[67] The law protected children with the action against an
'undutiful will' (*testamentum inofficiosum*), which ensured that children inherited at least a proportion of a parent's property, unless
the parent had strong, defensible grounds for disinheriting. We
cannot know how often a parent held out the threat of disinheri-
tance; perhaps, more often, it was an unspoken threat in the background. Explicit threats appear in the *controuersiae*. The *pietas* due
by fathers and children to each other appears often, but it is not an
uncomplicated concept: there are sometimes conflicts between different forms of *pietas*, for instance that due to a father versus that
due to a mother. These issues sharpened as boys moved into their
teens, but younger boys will have had some consciousness of them,
and, if they had older brothers, they will have observed the impact
on them. Although the rhetorical examples deal with sons' problems rather than daughters' (not surprisingly, as all the students in
these schools were male), some of the conflicts will have involved
daughters, for instance in the choice of a marriage partner.

Widows with pre-adult children were obliged to get a male
tutor (guardian) to take formal responsibility for such children,
especially for their property, if the father had not provided for this
in his will, or arrange for the state to appoint one; but mothers
raising children in their own homes had much responsibility for
the children's everyday lives, as we saw for Procilla and her son
Agricola. Horace referred to this more generally, implying that
the close supervision by mothers grated on growing boys: 'As
the year drags on for orphans[68] kept hard under the thumb of

[66] Cf. Pliny (*Letters* 6. 33) on a daughter's claim against her father and stepmother.

[67] For the wide use of wills, even for modest estates, see Crook (1967);
Champlin (1991); Gardner (1986*b*, 1993, 1998); Saller (1994); Stern (2000).

[68] *Pupilli*, children whose father has died, who were technically orphans in
Roman law.

mothers' (*Epistles* 1. 1. 21–2). Some men provided in their wills for their wives not to remarry while their children were pre-adult. The law would not recognize a husband's general requirement for his wife's continuing widowhood, but it did accept the more limited requirement, 'because it is the care of children which is being imposed rather than widowhood'.[69] As we saw above,[70] the law saw the mother as the appropriate person to administer the funds necessary for her fatherless son's education to age 14.

Mothers could fulfil many parental duties, as Dixon (1988) has shown. Even when a *tutor* was in place, she could continue to have close personal supervision of her children's welfare (Gardner 1998: ch. 3. 5). Pliny's friend Corellia Hispulla was active in making decisions about her son's education, and enlisted Pliny's advice to find a suitable teacher (Pliny the Younger, *Letters* 3. 3). Cicero's choice of words in a letter of 46 BCE (*Fam.* 9. 20) is revealing: his grieving for the fate of his country is deeper and more protracted than that of 'any mother for her only son'. That the symbol of deep grief should be mother rather than father, and for son rather than daughter, reflects the importance of a son (especially if he is the only son) for transmitting his family name and forging a public career, and a mother had a deep interest in this.[71] Seneca wrote a long *Consolation to Marcia* (*Dialogues* 6) on the death of Marcia's son, in which he praised the close bonds between mother and son. The son had been a child when his father died, and as a *pupillus* he was under the care of *tutores* until he turned 14, 'but he was under his mother's care for life' ('sub matris tutela semper').[72] The roles and ideals of mothers and fathers in relation to their children were generally very similar. Our sources often speak of 'parents' without differentiation, and the reciprocal duties and claims of *pietas* between parents and children applied to both mothers and fathers. Mothers, however,

[69] *D.* 35. 1. 62. 2, Terentius Clemens, commenting on Augustus' legislation.

[70] Ch. 5, 'Role of the State': *D.* 33. 1. 21. 5, Scaeuola.

[71] See Dixon (1988: ch. 7 for mothers and adolescent sons, and *passim* for many other aspects of mother–child relationships).

[72] *Consolation to Marcia* 24. 1, using *tutela* in a non-legal sense. Similarly, in the 2nd c., Apuleius represented Aemilia Pudentilla (a Roman citizen of the province of Africa), whom he had subsequently married, as devoting most of fourteen years to the upbringing of her sons, left orphans by the early death of their father and under the *potestas* of their grandfather: *Apology* 68, 'memorabili pietate sedulo aluit'.

were usually closer in age to their children than were fathers, and children at any age were more likely to have a mother surviving than a father.

On epitaphs for children mothers are frequently dedicators, for both sons and daughters. The dedications for sons are a little more frequent than those for daughters,[73] but this reflects the higher probability overall that boys will receive an epitaph, rather than mothers' preference for sons. Some mothers' dedications are very simple, like the small stone inscribed 'To the departed spirits. Siluina lived six years and sixteen days. Her mother Sperata set this up for her sweet daughter.'[74] Others are much more ambitious, such as the large, handsome altar set up by Iunia Venusta for her patron, husband, son, and daughter. Images of these four were sculpted on the altar, above a well-cut epitaph commemorating all their names before her own. She did not have her own image sculpted here, but it is clear that this ex-slave woman had done well and was the driving force in this monument and at the centre of a network of relationships (including a freedman of her own).[75] Jerome's negative account (see above) of the roles of wife and mother also reflects the diverse responsibilities of such women in the domestic environment.

The concept of motherhood was always promoted and highly valued publicly in Roman culture, although there is some evidence that some women resisted it.[76] The birth of a child in the imperial family was much celebrated, and the dynastic reasons for this are obvious. Virtues and duties specifically associated with women of the imperial family often implied fecundity, especially in the second century (even when some emperors' wives did not produce children). (See Chapter 1 above.) Mothers' love for their children is one of the qualities which Musonius Rufus (fragment

[73] See tables 1–6 in Saller and Shaw (1984).

[74] *CIL* 6. 26597: D.M. | SILVINA | V. AN. | VI | D. XVI | SPERATA | MATER | FECIT | FILIAE | DVLCISSI | MAE.

[75] *CIL* 6. 20819. Illustration in B. Rawson (1991a: pl. 5) and Kleiner (1987: pl. XXIX). The inscription reads: DIIS MANIBVS | M. IVNIO PERSO PATRONO | ET M. IVNIO SATYRO | ET M. IVNIO IVSTO | ET IVNIAE PIAE | FECIT | IVNIA VENVSTA CONIVGI SVO | ET FILIS DVLCISSIMIS | VNA CVM PHARNACE LIB.

[76] For promotion, see Dixon (1988, esp. ch. 4). For women's resistance, see B. Rawson (1986c: 11–12, 26–30). Love poetry and Juvenal contain protests at women's attempts at abortion. There is evidence of knowledge and use of contraceptives, however defective.

3) argued was developed by philosophy (and he allowed a role for philosophy in women's lives: cf. Chapter 5 above). A woman trained in philosophy is best situated to protect the interests of husband and children; she loves (ἀγαπᾶν) her children more than life itself. These were ideals continually set in front of wives and daughters. What mothers actually communicated to daughters is unknown, because we have no direct evidence from them.[77]

Stepmothers are frequent in our records, partly because after divorce fathers had first claim on children of the broken marriage and they often remarried, and partly because mothers who died in childbirth or soon afterwards left infants and other children who were seen to need another mother, although wet-nurses and other carers might be available for some of the child's needs. 'The wicked stepmother' is a stereotype in Roman society as in so many others (Dixon 1988: 155–9). Stepfathers did not share this bad reputation.[78] Some tension between stepfathers and step-children was inevitable, both emotionally (competing for the affections of the mother or wife) and in plans for disposition of property; but stepfathers of small children were less involved in day-to-day domestic cohabitation and interaction with the children than were stepmothers. For young children, conflict with stepmothers was more likely to be in the emotional sphere, and in that of domestic discipline, than in matters of property. Property disputes in our sources tend to concern adults,[79] but the

[77] Tibullus (4. 6. 15–16) implies that Sulpicia's mother, anxious (*studiosa*) for her daughter's happiness, wishes for conventional blessings for her, and in the context these would include marriage and children; but Sulpicia silently prays for something different, a much more daring love affair. See on Sulpicia in Ch. 5 above.

[78] Indeed, there seems to have been a special bond between stepfathers and stepsons, at least as adults. In *D.* 22. 5. 4, Paul includes them in the list of those who cannot be forced to testify against each other. Although a stepfather did not have *potestas* over a stepson, he was in a surrogate role for the father who did have, or had had, *potestas*. There was no question of *potestas* or anything similar between stepmothers and stepchildren. Jane Gardner suggests to me that what each coupling has in common in Paul's list is *pietas*. Male and female cousins are included; but, whereas fathers-in-law and sons-in-law are included, mothers-in-law or daughters-in-law are not.

[79] Note the lawcourt success of Pliny the Younger (*Letters* 6. 33), referred to above. The stepdaughter whom he represented was an adult woman of high rank, whose elderly father had remarried and changed his will. A little later, the jurist Gaius said that the main reason for parents' leaving wills which are unjust

stereotype of conflicting interests coloured assumptions about the whole relationship. Good stepmothers are recorded (Dixon 1988: 155); but we know few details, good or bad, about stepmothers' relationships with young stepchildren. Marcus Aurelius is said to have taken a concubine rather than a new wife after the death of his wife Faustina the Younger, 'so as not to impose a stepmother on so many children',[80] but by then all but one of his children were almost certainly adult. Ancient literature does not give us any insight into the reaction of young children to the loss of a mother. Examples below of divorced or prematurely dead mothers enable us to speculate just a little on the experience of motherless children.

OTHER FAMILY RELATIONSHIPS

Other family relatives sometimes stepped in to care for motherless children, but they do not have a large presence in our records (literary, inscriptional, legal, or visual). In Roman law certain categories of women were recognized as having especially close links with a child and a responsibility for its welfare (in this case, financial welfare). From early times, the state had procedures in place to prosecute a *tutor* whose performance of his duties for an orphan was suspect. Women could initiate such prosecutions if they had a close bond (*necessitudo*) with the child and were thus motivated by *pietas*. Such women were mother, nurse, and grandmother; a sister was similarly recognized in the late second century CE.[81]

A child was more likely to have a grandmother living than a grandfather, but the likelihood of having any grandparent alive diminished as the child grew older.[82] Only a minority of children

to their children is the seductive influence of stepmothers (*D.* 5. 2. 4, 'nouercalibus delenimentis instigationibusque corrupti').

[80] SHA, *Marcus* 29. See B. Rawson (1974: 288) for the possibility that the father of Marcus' concubine was a freedman and it was therefore low social status that dictated the choice of *concubina* rather than wife.

[81] *D.* 26. 10. 1. 7, Ulpian, who cites the Twelve Tables as the early source for prosecutions against suspect *tutores* and *curatores*.

[82] Saller (1994: tables pp. 48–65). In Gallivan and Wilkins (1997: tables 10. 9, 10.10), the greater visibility of grandfathers over grandmothers is surely due to the cultural preference of males over females in most categories of inscriptions.

had the opportunity, as they grew up, of forming a close relationship with a grandparent. This in itself would have made the relationship rather special. Part of Pliny the Younger's regret at not having children of his own stemmed from his consequent lack of grandchildren. When he congratulated a friend on acquiring a worthy son-in-law, he offered hopes for the birth of grandchildren as soon as possible, and looked forward to holding these children in his arms 'as if they were my own children or grandchildren, and as if I held them with equal right' (*Letters* 6. 26). Moreover, family circumstances sometimes put grandparents in the role of carers or rearers.[83]

In the imperial family there were sometimes dynastic purposes in rearing a boy in his grandfather's house. When Augustus' grandsons Gaius and Lucius, for example, lost their own father Agrippa in 12 BCE they were 8 and 5 years old and Augustus himself had no son, so emotion and dynastic politics will have given him a fatherly concern for his daughter's orphaned sons. This was formalized in 2 BCE, when he officially adopted them as his sons. By now they were teenagers, but it is clear that for years before that Augustus had been their mentor, taking a close interest in their personal and public training (e.g. Suetonius, *Augustus* 64). In the second century CE, both paternal and maternal grandfathers played a role in the Antonine family, especially in the upbringing of Antoninus (Pius) and Marcus Aurelius when they lost their fathers. By the time that Hadrian drew them both into his dynastic strategy plans, Antoninus was a middle-aged man, but Marcus was only 17 and reluctant to leave the household in which he had been reared.[84]

Some children who later became part of the imperial family were reared early by grandparents because of the death or absence of their own parents, not because of any dynastic plans at that stage. Vespasian was reared by a paternal grandmother in the early first century CE, long before his family counted amongst

---

[83] See Ch. 3 above; and cf. Ch. 5, 'Early Education', above for a role for an older woman relative to supervise children's upbringing.

[84] SHA, *Antoninus Pius* 21, *Marcus* 1–7. Reference to Marcus' mother's house: SHA, *Marcus* 5. In *Marcus* 2, Marcus' mother's continuing influence in his boyhood clearly had a domestic base: she had to persuade him to sleep on a bed in spite of his would-be philosopher's inclination to sleep on the floor.

Rome's most powerful.[85] For the upbringing of his infant daughter Julia, Vespasian's son Titus probably turned to Julia's maternal grandmother when Julia's mother died soon after the child's birth. Titus' family contained a faithful nurse, Phyllis, who had nursed Titus' brother Domitian and now was attached to Julia; but for more general supervision of the child's upbringing a senior matron was required. Titus' own mother was probably already dead.[86] The grandmother and the nurse must have been important anchors in young Julia's life, as her father was away in the East for most of her first seven years or so. One of the quite rare epitaphs involving a grandmother is one for a 2-year-old called Iuuenalis (a slave?), dedicated by grandmother and nurse (*CIL* 6. 20938). Of the other epitaphs recording a grandmother as a dedicator, about half are a joint dedication by grandmother and one or both parents.[87] If grandmothers were alive they could be useful supplementary carers or custodians.

The role of uncle is sometimes said to be rather special in Roman society[88] but it seems to have been more ad hoc than systemic. Julius Caesar was an influential (great) uncle to Octavian, but Antony was closer to his stepfather than to his mother's brother. Once a child lost one or both parents it would be looked after by whatever other relative happened to be available and

---

[85] Suetonius, *Vespasian* 2. Vespasian's father died while on business in Gaul, leaving a wife and two sons, but the date is unknown. Vespasian's mother was still alive, and taking an interest in his career, into at least his young adulthood. If she had been travelling on business with Vespasian's father, that could explain the grandmother's role; and a rural upbringing, on substantial estates, provided a good traditional environment for a boy who at that stage had no political ambitions. He retained fond memories of this place and revisited it frequently.

[86] She was dead by the time that Vespasian became emperor in 69 (Suetonius, *Vespasian* 3), perhaps much earlier. Julia was born in the early 60s, perhaps 64 CE. I accept the argument of B. W. Jones (1992: 38–40) that Julia was the child of Titus' first wife, Arrecina Tertulla. On the death of Arrecina Titus remarried, and another daughter seems to have been born and died, and that wife, Marcia Furnilla, was divorced soon after. Titus was in the East from 66 to 71 CE.

[87] Twelve out of twenty-four epitaphs in *CIL* 6. In one case (20007) an *auonculus* is added; in another, a *tata* (27259); an *auos* (21465); and in 17957 just *auia* and *auos*, grandmother and grandfather, make the dedication, without mention of parents. Dedications by grandfathers are very rare (eight examples).

[88] e.g. Hallett (1984), who stresses the greater influence of mother's brothers (*auunculi*) rather than that of father's brothers (*patrui*).

willing. In the dedications of epitaphs uncles and aunts have a low representation (Saller and Shaw 1984: 136). Some notable examples of these relationships may be noted here. Except for the Cicero brothers, these uncles and aunts seem to have had no children of their own, which may have given them an incentive to raise or promote the interests of a nephew. Julius Caesar was the maternal great-uncle of Octavius; and M. Liuius Drusus (tribune of the plebs in 91 BCE) was the maternal uncle of Cato the Younger, who, as a child, was brought up in Drusus' house.[89] Marcus and Quintus Cicero were paternal uncles to each other's sons and took a close interest in their upbringing (K. R. Bradley 1991a: chapter 8). Messalla Coruinus, maternal uncle of Sulpicia, took her on as ward when her father died, but as argued above (Chapter 5) his circle of friends and contacts probably had more influence on her upbringing than did his own personal presence. In the time of Pliny the Younger, his friend Iunius Mauricus was active in seeking a husband for his paternal niece and a teacher for his nephews.[90] A paternal uncle was the statutory guardian for an orphan, i.e. he was the one to whom the law looked first to take on this duty. There might not, however, have been an uncle surviving who was of an appropriate age (over 25) and who did not have good reason for exemption.[91]

Aunts seem to have been recognized in the festival of the Matralia on 11 June.[92] The exact nature of the festival's connection with women and children is unclear, but evidence of the cult goes back centuries in various parts of Italy, where many votive offerings have been found, including those of swaddled babies and mother-and-child pairs. There was an ancient temple in honour of Mater Matuta in the Forum Boarium in Rome. Prayers seem to have been offered by citizen women for maternal nephews and nieces. The possible role of a maternal aunt at the

---

[89] Valerius Maximus 3. 1. 2a: at the age of about 4, Cato showed precocious *grauitas* and *perseuerantia* during his uncle's tribunship.

[90] Pliny the Younger, *Letters* 1. 14, 2. 18. In 8. 18 Pliny tells the story of the devious uncle of Domitia, who conspired with her father to adopt his niece in order to get her wealth into his own hands but who redeemed himself in the provisions of his will. See below.

[91] Saller (1994: 196–7). Scaeuola envisages just this situation in *D.* 27. 1. 37. pr.

[92] Scullard (1981: 150–1); Beard, North, and Price (1998: 50–1).

lustratio on the naming-day was noted above (Chapter 2). Pliny the Younger's wife Calpurnia had been raised by an aunt, but this was her father's sister and the importance of the paternal name and family tradition is clear from Pliny's letters to the aunt and paternal grandfather.[93] The relationship between Calpurnia and her aunt was close, with the aunt very much a surrogate mother. Pliny and Calpurnia visited the aunt, and when the aunt's father, Calpurnia's grandfather, died Calpurnia immediately made plans to return from Bithynia to Italy to be with her aunt (*Letters* 10. 120). The relatives (*propinquae*) brought up by 'Turia' and her sister and provided with dowries may have been nieces.[94]

Cousins, i.e. sons and daughters of aunts and uncles, are very rare in ancient sources of all kinds (literature, law, inscriptions). The law took account of them to define degrees of relationship: cousins belonged in the fourth degree (*D.* 38. 10. 10. 15, Paul). This set the outer limit of one set of special relationships recognized by the law: within this limit persons could not be forced to testify against one another.[95] What is said below about siblings helps to explain the infrequency of references to cousins. Although there must have been more cousins than indicated by references to them, they were probably not often coevals so did not establish close personal relationships with one another, especially in childhood. They were included in the general categories of cognates or affines, but the cousin relationship as such did not register prominently on the affective map of most Romans.

Siblings might have been expected to provide an important bond for children in a world of lost or distant parents and non-kin carers. They do not figure largely amongst the dedicators of epitaphs, being only marginally more represented than 'the extended family' (Saller and Shaw 1984: 136). A somewhat different picture emerges from the theoretical model of Valerius

---

[93] Calpurnia Hispulla and Calpurnius Fabatus: Pliny the Younger, *Letters* 4. 19, 6. 30, 8. 10.

[94] *CIL* 6. 1527 b (*Laudatio Turiae*) 44–51, a eulogy for a woman once identified as Turia. Her family was disrupted in the upheaval of the civil war period of the late 40s BCE.

[95] *D.* 22. 5. 4, where Paul comments on Augustan legislation. Those protected included father-in-law, son-in-law, stepfather, stepson, cousin or cousin's child. The category of cousins specified female as well as male. Cf. n. 78 above.

Maximus (5. 5). He reasons that siblings are bound together by a range of early shared experiences. In his discussion of family bonds and relationships, he proceeds from children's *pietas* towards parents to the bonds between brothers, citing *caritas* ('affection') and *fraterna beneuolentia* ('fraternal goodwill'). Children owe *pietas* to parents because they owe them life and all sorts of benefits. Siblings receive such benefits together, which helps form the next closest bond. They are born in the same house, they use the same cradle in infancy, they have parents in common, are protected by the same prayers, and derive the same distinction (*gloria*) from their ancestral images.[96] This bond antedates all those who come later—wife, children, friends, relations—and cannot be displaced by these. Later in the first century, Musonius Rufus enunciated the principle of close brotherly bonds. He conceded (fragment 15) that poverty could make it difficult to rear many children and even wealthy parents might neglect (let die) younger children in order to preserve the inheritance of older children. This is a mistake, he says, as brothers are more valuable to children than wealth.[97] Musonius' comments are cast in the context of property and mutual support against the outside world, but he also sets high value more generally on the presence in adversity of a brother. Modern sociologists identify the sibling relationship as an important source of socialization. If there are changes in the number of children in a family, or in the age structure of such children, this will have an effect on the social support and source of education available to any child of that family.

In any Roman family, the number of siblings close enough in age to have close interaction was quite low. Saller's computer simulation of kin relationships at different ages suggests that most

---

[96] Valerius clearly has full siblings in mind here, rather than half- or step-siblings. As with other categories, the examples here are all of adult men in public life, e.g. the emperor Tiberius and his brother Drusus. This may explain why it is brothers rather than sisters who are cited.

[97] It is possible that 'brothers' here is meant to cover male and female siblings. Roman legal texts often use the masculine to include both male and female (Gardner 1995; Saller 1999). But even there the term can be gendered, leaving an impression that it is really only males who are being discussed. Musonius seems to envisage a male and female readership, but in the present context (social support in public life) one has to suspect that he is thinking predominantly of brothers rather than sisters.

children had one or two living siblings. These probabilities, however, can disguise large age gaps. They also include newborn infants who are likely to die before establishing any real relationship with older siblings.[98] Remarriage could add half- and step-siblings, but these could be of very different ages, especially when a father's second or later wife was of a generation younger than himself (K. R. Bradley 1991a: 131–8). Moreover, half- and step-siblings did not share any of the bonds of infancy and early rearing which literary sources identify as the essence of sibling relationships. Even first marriages could have children widely spaced in age. Premature death of some children was one cause; there were also long periods when husbands were absent on business or duty; and there was an unknowable degree of personal choice, for considerations of property, health, or more private reasons. There is no evidence that parents concentrated their child-bearing in the early years of their marriage (Saller 1987: 32). Some well-known mothers bore children over what must have been their whole fertility cycle.[99] The age gap between father and child thus lengthened as the marriage went on, and lengthened further if he remarried (to a considerably younger new wife). The age gap between mother and child was seldom so great.

Few of our sources evoke a picture of a household full of brothers and sisters in the way that some more modern sources do. Studies of households and families of the late eighteenth century in the north-east of the American states (e.g. Demos 1972; Greven 1972) have revealed larger families than in earlier or later periods of English or American history. With better health but few effective methods of family limitation, parents in these states had children at fairly regular intervals, of whom fewer died at young ages. So at some stages of the family life cycle there were many siblings living at home (in comparatively small houses), aged from infancy to young adulthood with few large age gaps. The households in Rome of Octavian and his sister Octavia, which were themselves merged in the late 30s BCE (see above), bear some similarities to this, but some of the siblings in it were half- and step-siblings. The closeness in age of the adults Octavian, his third wife Livia, and his sister Octavia also

---

[98] Saller (1994: table 3.1d). I am grateful to Richard Saller for discussing his tables with me.

[99] e.g. Cornelia, mother of the Gracchi; Faustina the Younger.

contributed to the closeness in age of the children of their various marriages. The children of Antony and Cleopatra, taken in after 30 BCE, were also of a similar age. We know little of the children's interactions. The circumstances of parents' divorces, and Antony's strained relations with Octavian and Octavia, would not seem to our minds to be conducive to harmony and good feeling between the step- and half-siblings; but our perspective might not be appropriate. It was a time of civil war and its aftermath; the harmonizing personality of Octavia should not be underestimated; and the sons of Octavia and Livia may have had a common interest in being trained and prepared for significant roles in public life. Three marriages resulted within this household: Antonia the Younger and Drusus, Marcella and Antonius Iullus, Julia and Tiberius. These were all arranged, political marriages, which say little about mutual affection, but Antonia and Drusus appear to have been very close. Antonia herself, in her adult life, maintained a household which took in boys of other prominent families for political and socializing purposes. One of these, Agrippa (grandson of Herod the Great), was the same age as Antonia's son Claudius and the two had a close personal and political relationship until almost the end of Agrippa's life. In Claudius' own household his only son Britannicus had the company, in residence, of Titus, son of the senator Vespasian and little more than a year older than Britannicus. There may have been other boys of a similar age: we know of Titus because he later became emperor and his earlier relationships were thus of interest. We do not have enough information about other elite Roman families to know whether they too provided such opportunities for quasi-sibling relationships for their children, or whether this was a particular tradition within Julio-Claudian family households. Roman law reflects the possible age gap between siblings when it discusses the guardianship of a child under 14 (*impubes*) by a brother who has reached full legal majority (25).[100]

As with other relationships, the strength of the sibling bond can be paralleled by the strength of hostility when there is a

---

[100] *D.* 27. 1. 28. 1, Papinian; 27. 3. 9. 1, Ulpian. Cf. *D.* 33. 1. 21. 5, Scaeuola, above, for the administration of a younger brother's estate and educational needs.

falling-out.[101] The Romulus-Remus foundation legend of Rome epitomizes this. The only historical examples of such hostility which have been recorded are of adult brothers. Tacitus occasionally refers to the 'well-known' or 'traditional' hatred between brothers.[102] The Domitii brothers, Tullus and Lucanus, were famous for their *pietas*, but the specific aspect of their close bond which is known to us is their joint administration of their family property, sometimes for nefarious purposes.[103] Marcus and Quintus Cicero had a close personal and public association for many years until a breach (not permanent) occurred in the aftermath of the civil war of 49 BCE. They were four years apart in age, but as boys they were thrown together more closely than some siblings through moving from the country to Rome and, as outsiders,[104] having to establish themselves in schooling and, later, in careers. Marcus was always somewhat protective of his younger brother.

Cicero's daughter Tullia was at least eleven years older than his son Marcus—probably fourteen years.[105] When Marcus was born, Tullia had already for some time been engaged to be married,[106] and she married when Marcus was not much more than a toddler.

---

[101] Bannon (1997: 26–43) suggests that inheritance practices could sometimes create conflict between brothers. These issues were unlikely to arise until brothers were of adult age. Similarly, the potential conflict between sisters and brothers over the disposition of dowry and other inheritance (Saller 1994: 219) concerns adult siblings rather than children.

[102] e.g. *Annals* 4. 60 ('solita fratribus odia' of Drusus Caesar and Nero Caesar, two of the sons of Agrippina the Elder and Germanicus) and 13. 17 ('antiquas fratrum discordias' of the stepbrothers Britannicus and Nero).

[103] Pliny, *Letters* 8. 18, re the transfer of Tullus' daughter (Lucilla) between them to exploit her property; Martial 5. 28. 3, referring to them by their natal, pre-adoption names of the Curuii brothers (cf. 1. 36).

[104] The family was quite wealthy but of equestrian status. Cicero broke into the senatorial class in 75 BCE with his entry to the quaestorship. His pride in this achievement, the first time for his family, and then in reaching the consulship, especially at the earliest possible age, reflects the importance of breaking into the senate and then putting his children and further descendants into the charmed circle of ex-consuls, the *nobiles*.

[105] Marcus was born in July of 65 BCE (Cicero, *Att.* 1. 2). Tullia's year of birth is less certain, with various dates proposed between 79 and 75. As Cicero was in the East between 79 and 77, Tullia's birth is unlikely to have been in 78 or 77.

[106] To C. Calpurnius Piso Frugi, in Dec. 67 (*Att.* 1. 3. 3). Cicero was able to refer to his son-in-law (*gener*) in Dec. 63 (*Against Catiline* 4. 3), but the actual marriage might have been a little later (but before Cicero's exile in 58).

She lived in her father's house for only brief periods after that (between marriages), and Marcus can never have known her well. She fulfilled none of the roles of a coeval growing up in the same household—neither playmate nor confidante, with no shared friends or teachers. The deep love between father and daughter and their close communion on many matters—even, it can be inferred, those of politics and public interest—cannot have made Marcus' childhood easy, especially as strains were emerging, or growing, in the marriage of Cicero and Terentia. Marcus did have a paternal cousin, Quintus Cicero, only a year and a half older than himself, and they shared many aspects of their boyhood and adolescence. Cicero was almost a surrogate father for Quintus during the long absences of Quintus senior on overseas appointments, between 61 and 50 BCE (except for the period of Cicero's exile from Italy in 58–57). He took both boys with him when he went to Cilicia as governor in 51, and, at the end of that year, he saw to Quintus' coming-of-age (*Att.* 5. 20. 9).

Cicero's contemporary Pompey married five times, but only one of those marriages produced surviving children. His two sons were born about a decade apart—Gnaeus in the gap between Pompey's return from Africa and departure for Spain (between about 80 and 77) and Sextus between Pompey's return from Spain (in late 71) and his departure for his Mediterranean naval command in early 67. Gnaeus was already moving in a different world as Sextus grew into boyhood. In the late 60s BCE, Gnaeus was ready for the toga of adulthood and for involvement in the political circles so active in Rome at that time. Pompey himself was away until 61, so there must have been some loneliness for Sextus, however many carers he had. When Pompey returned, he divorced the children's mother. Sextus was left in a motherless house at an age somewhere between 6 and 9. In not much more than a year there was a stepmother, Julia, the teenage daughter of Julius Caesar, of an age similar to Sextus' older siblings. And after Julia's death the fifth wife, Cornelia, was only about Sextus' own age. If Pompey's daughter Pompeia was born in the same period as Gnaeus, between 80 and 77, she too was a teenager while her younger brother was still a toddler and, like Tullia, was already having marriage plans made for her.[107]

[107] Pompeia may already have been betrothed to Faustus Sulla in the late 60s, when Faustus was on Pompey's staff in the East. This suggests (but does

Julius Caesar's wife Calpurnia had been married to him for over ten years when her brother Lucius was born in 48 BCE. The age gap between brother and sister was about a quarter of a century, and there could have been no meaningful sibling relationship.[108] A century later, in the Flavian family, the children were widely spaced and the father was absent from Italy for long periods. Vespasian's eldest son, Titus, was born in 39 or 40 CE; the younger son Domitian in 51.[109] Vespasian was absent in military posts from 43 to 47, in 62, and then from 66 to 70. In Titus' early boyhood there was neither father nor brother in the house. In Domitian's early years his brother—already a teenager—was being brought up in the imperial household as a companion and almost surrogate brother for Claudius' son (Nero's stepbrother) Britannicus. Titus then went overseas as a military tribune, returning about 62 (while Domitian was still a child) to marry. From 66 Titus was in the East with his father; so the brothers hardly knew each other.

These examples could be multiplied, but they suffice to show the difficulty, over a long period of Roman history, for children to establish close sibling relationships. The examples come largely from upper-class families, which are better documented, but there is no reason to think that lower-class families had children in larger numbers or more closely spaced. There might, however, have been a class difference in the absences of fathers on military duties. In the Republican period, Roman citizen men were frequently absent on army service.[110] From the beginning of the first

not prove) a date of birth before 77. The date of marriage is uncertain, but their two children were young enough in 46 to be still in their mother's care and not serving in the civil war: (Caesar), *African War* 95, and Appian, *Civil Wars* 2. 100, which suggests that they were still pre-adult and not born before 60, indicating a birth date for Pompeia before 77 rather than after 71. Sextus Pompeius was too young to fight in the civil war in 49–48 BCE: he was sent to Mytilene for safety with Pompey's wife Cornelia (Appian, *Civil Wars* 5. 133).

[108] If the children had the same mother (Rutilia), she had a long—but not impossible—period of fertility. Syme (1986: 330) raises the possibility of a second marriage for the father L. Calpurnius Piso Caesoninus, which would make Calpurnia and Lucius half-siblings.

[109] The date of birth of the daughter Domitilla is unknown. She had been married by the time she died, which was before Vespasian became emperor in 69.

[110] This period is discussed by Evans (1991), whose account does not go beyond the 1st c. BCE.

century BCE the army was professionalized, after which citizens volunteered for long periods of continuous service. During the imperial period, however, the army gradually came to rely on provincials rather than Italians for service in the ranks, reducing the element of absentee fathers in Italian families except for officers, who continued to come from senatorial and equestrian families largely domiciled in Rome.

DISPLACED CHILDREN

The frequent loss of young children, and the frequent lack of siblings of similar ages, help to explain the Roman propensity to raise foster-children and young slaves as surrogate sons and daughters.[111] Adoption from one family into another was one Roman strategy for transferring sons and (less frequently) daughters from one father to another, involving a change of jural identity, but it was not a major element in the new relationships being discussed here. It was a formal, official process, usually transferring young adults rather than children and, as far as we know, practised only in the upper, propertied classes. Quintilian's 9-year-old son is the youngest adoptee recorded, and it is clear that at that age he had not yet left the house of his natural father.[112]

There were many younger children available for some kind of fostering—orphans, poor relations, foundlings, or bright, attractive slaves of an appropriate age in the owner's household. A married couple, or even a single adult, might choose to rear a young child as a surrogate sibling for their own child or as a substitute for a deceased child or for the child they were unable to conceive themselves. In upper-class, propertied families, orphans had a network of support to see to their maintenance and education until adulthood. We have seen something of this above. Fatherless children were technically orphans (*pupilli*), irrespec-

---

[111] See the collection of papers in Corbier (1999*b*), esp. those by Corbier, Gardner, Dixon, Sigismund Nielsen, and Goody.

[112] There is not enough information available to reconstruct the age at which Domitia Lucilla was given in adoption by her father Domitius Lucanus to his brother Domitius Tullus (Pliny, *Letters* 8. 18), or the age at which these two brothers were themselves adopted by Domitius Afer from the Curuius family (cf. n. 103 above).

tive of the presence of a mother. A male guardian (*tutor*) had to be appointed, who sometimes—but not always—came from within the family. This did not prevent orphans' continuing to live with their mothers, nor mothers' continuing to have an interest and influence in their upbringing. Grandparents, uncles, and aunts are all known to have had a role in orphans' upbringing. Female relatives, especially mothers, were seen to be a countervailing influence on guardians, and could call them to account for their administration of an orphan's property.[113] Guardians had a position of trust and responsibility in relation to their wards,[114] and sometimes this was a warm, affective relationship. For Pliny the Younger, for example, his guardian Verginius Rufus exhibited the 'affection of a parent' ('adfectum parentis exhibuit': *Letters* 2. 1. 8). But the relationship was not necessarily of this kind: a guardian was bound by many legal restrictions, he might be only one of several *contutores*, and law and literature have frequent references to fraudulent or negligent guardians. Guardianship was considered something of a burden for Roman men.

In less well-off families, orphans had less access to such networks, and their futures were less well assured. Those taken in by relatives or friends will often have found themselves in an in-service role. Young slaves who were reared by their owners in a quasi-parental role were by definition servants and the property of their owners, but they had better chances of early manumission than most slaves. The most common terms for such children are *alumni/-ae* or *uernae*, and in the inscriptions of Rome these are the most common terms of relationship for children after *filii/-ae* ('sons/daughters').[115] They are still a small percentage compared with sons and daughters, but they are a significant category and it is possible that other children were in these 'fostered' relationships without having the specific term applied to them in the epigraphic record.

Children known as *alumni* or *alumnae* are here referred to as 'foster-children', but this comprises a variety of situations—poor

---

[113] e.g. *D.* 26. 106. 1. 7, Ulpian, cited above for grandmothers.

[114] 'A bond more intense and more sacred . . . than other pervasive forms of social relations such as *amicitia* or *hospitium*': Saller (1994: 203). See all of Saller (1994: 181–203) on guardianship.

[115] Fig. 1 in Sigismund Nielsen (1991), which shows 67.72% for sons and daughters, 8.42% *uernae*, and 5.34% *alumni/-ae*.

orphans, poor relations, foundlings, sometimes apprentices. *Alumni* who are recorded on epitaphs are sometimes of free status, sometimes slave.[116] They are usually young persons (two-thirds of those in Rome whose age is specified are 9 years old or younger; more than three-quarters are not older than 14) in a quasi-familial relationship with an older person. The legal references to *alumni* confirm this picture. The ability to take in extra dependants, like the ability to maintain large numbers of slaves and give many of them their freedom, is a phenomenon of urbanized or prosperous communities. Even in Rome, only about 1 per cent of the surviving inscriptions attest *alumni*. In the rest of Italy, the rate is less than half this, but there are strong regional differences. It is the most populous and prosperous areas which provide most evidence of *alumni*. Often these are the most urbanized areas (those with most towns), but the Aemilia area, which comes closest to Latium-Campania in frequency of *alumni*, had fewer towns than several other areas. It was, however, populous and an area of high agricultural prosperity (as indeed the Emilia-Romagna area is today). Apulia was similarly prosperous and had the third highest percentage of *alumni* attested in Italy. Literary evidence once suggested depopulation of Apulia and the development of large pastoral stations (ranches) in the early imperial period, but more recently landscape archaeology and aerial photography have revealed evidence of widespread, even intensive, cultivation of cereals, olives, and grapes, along with some pastoralism. Young children have often been put to useful work on such properties. The *alimenta* schemes in Roman Italy were designed to raise and keep children in the regions, no doubt to provide agricultural labour in their young years.

Ostia (and its neighbour Portus), Rome's harbour area at the mouth of the Tiber, provide the greatest evidence of *alumni*. Although this may reflect the great archaeological activity in this area, Ostia did provide circumstances conducive to taking in extra children such as *alumni*. The study of Saller and Shaw showed that children under 10 were more heavily represented than any other group in epigraphic dedications in Ostia, and suggested that urbanized centres with high proportions of slaves and freed

---

[116] For a detailed analysis of *alumni* see B. Rawson (1986a), on Rome, and Bellemore and Rawson (1990), on Italy outside Rome, which are the basis for this section.

in the population gave greater attention to the commemoration of younger children (1984: 130). Moreover, many new apartment blocks (*insulae*) were built in the second century CE, and these were generally well planned, solidly built, and comparatively more spacious than earlier housing (Meiggs 1973: 262), affording greater ability to take in an extra child. Ostia was also a close-knit community of many guilds (*collegia*), which provided opportunities for interrelationships within the population. The culture of the neighbourhood (*uicus*) must have been as strong here as in Rome. 'It may have been a source of pride in a community such as this that children, whose parents could not raise them, would be taken in and cared for by relatives, friends, or other concerned adults.'[117]

In the legal texts, *alumni* are minors and dependants. Testators sometimes provided for the support of *alumni* who survived them, and these provisions indicate the ongoing responsibility which fosterers felt for young persons whom they had taken into their care. When a couple, rather than an individual, had been responsible for the rearing of an *alumnus*, a surviving spouse might have to hold some property in trust for the *alumnus*. One husband imposed on his wife the obligation to pass on to their joint *alumnus* whatever she inherited from her husband (*D*. 34. 2. 18. 1, Scaeuola). About 40 per cent of the foster-parents on epitaphs were couples (one male, one female). The law made special recognition of the bonds of affection of a fosterer with an *alumnus*. An *alumnus* would never be used as a pledge in financial affairs, and so could not be seized by a creditor. Although slaves could not normally be freed until they were 30 years of age, *alumni* could be freed below this age because of their close bond with their fosterer, who in this case would become their *patronus/-a*.[118] The law envisaged such young freedmen and freedwomen when it protected testators' provisions for them. For instance, a man left money in his will to his young ex-slave *alumnus*, but until the young person's twenty-fifth birthday this was to be in the hands of a friend, who was to judge the appropriate expenses to be paid to the *alumnus* in the meantime, as the

---

[117] Bellemore and Rawson (1990: 15). See this article for detailed analysis and source references for the study of *alumni* in Italy outside Rome.
[118] Cf. n. 25 above.

affection of a father (*patris affectus*) would dictate (*D.* 33. 1. 21. 4, Scaeuola).

The concept of a parent–child relationship appears too in the legal unease over marriage between a man and his freedwoman-*alumna*. Whereas male slave-owners frequently freed a female slave and married her, the presumption of some kind of filial relationship with an *alumna* raised the fear of incest. It is possible that *alumni* were sometimes the natural children of the fosterer, but there is little evidence for this. As we shall see below, Romans attached little stigma to children born outside formal marriage in the sub-elite classes, and were not reluctant to identify children as *liberi naturales*. Those called *alumni* occasionally have a family relative identified as the fosterer, such as *parens*, *auia*, *uitricus*.[119] But when such children are taken in by someone other than their natural parent it is their fostered status which is identified by *alumnus/-a*. They were not formally adopted,[120] so were not 'full' sons or daughters: they fulfilled some of the roles of such children, but also some of the roles of slaves. It may sometimes have been an uncomfortable middle position, but it gave a chance of survival and rearing to some children whose parents were unavailable, unable, or unwilling to rear them.

In some of the lower-class families attested in inscriptions, there is mention of a fostering figure called a *mamma* (female) or a *tata* (male). These terms were sometimes (and perhaps originally) baby-talk for 'mother' and 'father'.[121] At other times these figures had supplementary or replacement roles, being named either in addition to natural parents or without mention of them. 'Foster-parent' is probably the best single word in English for them, but the term is flexible, capable of referring to parents, grandparents, or other adults, not related, who filled a quasi-parental role. They were sometimes carers (including nurses), but the essence of their relationship with a child was affectionate and familial rather than job-related. In some circles in contemporary Western society, the term 'uncle'—and sometimes 'aunt'—is used similarly for an unre-

---

[119] In *CIL* 6. 16008, the dedicator for the 10-year-old P. Comfuleius Aquilinus is his grandmother Horte(n)sia Tecusa, 'alumno auia suo'.

[120] B. Rawson (1986*a*: 183–4); Bellemore and Rawson (1990: 9–10).

[121] Varro, in Nonius 114 L (81 M): 'cum cibum ac potionem buas ac pappas uocent et matrem mammam, patrem tatam'. See Dixon (1984) and K. R. Bradley (1994: ch. 4) for detailed discussions of *mammae* and *tatae* (mostly from Rome).

lated family friend or carer. To address such a person as 'Uncle John' allows the familiarity of the personal name but tacks on a familial label to apply some structure to the relationship.

More explicitly of slave status were the *uernae*, who shared many of the characteristics of *alumni*. These were usually slave children born in the household of their slave mother's master.[122] The circumstances of their birth gave them a favoured position with master or mistress: they added to their owner's property, they could be a replacement or substitute for the owner's own children, they could be a playmate for an only child (or an only child of young age), and sometimes they may well have been the master's own child by a female slave in his household. Occasionally one or two natural parents are mentioned, but it is usually the relationship with master or mistress which is the dominant or identifying one. The epitaph of a 2-year-old boy (Aricinus) identified him as the *uerna* of Volusia Phoebe, but it was set up by his mother anonymously (*CIL* 6. 12306):

> DIS MANIBVS
> ARICINO VOLVSIAES
> PHOEBES VERNA
> VIX. ANN. II
> MEN. VIII
> FECIT MATER.

The mother was probably also a slave in the same household, that of Volusia (whose family was prominent in Rome in the first half of the first century CE), but she offers no information about herself apart from her motherhood. A century later, the parents of an imperial *uerna* are more forthcoming. The epitaph of the 9-year-old boy Euthymus (also known as Lupus) is headed by his name and his status as one of the emperor's *uernae* ('Caes(aris) n(ostri) uerna'), but his parents take more than half of the epitaph to advertise their own identity and (without names) their dependants and posterity. The father, M. Vlpius Aug. lib. Martialis, is a freedman of the emperor Trajan; the mother Vlpia Prima belongs to the same household; and Trajan

---

[122] The term *uerna* is usually translated as 'home-born slave'. For more detailed analysis, see B. Rawson (1986*a*), on which I draw for this section. See also Sigismund Nielsen (1991); and the large work by Herrmann-Otto (1994).

was most likely the emperor to whom the *uerna* Euthymus belonged.[123]

Whereas the incidence of *uernae* in the general population declined with each increasing age cohort, it increased for imperial slave *uernae*. Adult *uernae* are much more frequent in the imperial household than elsewhere, reflecting their growing importance as their job responsibilities increased. In the service of the emperor, *uerna* is virtually a job description, indicating training roles in the progress towards higher office and, often, manumission.[124] For them, freedom would seldom come before the official age of 30, but, in other households, especially favoured *uernae* were freed earlier. These are not always identifiable, as they would drop the slave designation *uerna* for an indication of manumission or citizenship; but some who died young are still thought of as *uernae*. A simple example from Ostia is the 5-year-old Cornelia Myrsine, whose mistress Cornelia Charis set up the epitaph 'uer(nae) suae'.[125]

One epitaph recording a connection with the imperial family is worth discussion in detail, as it enables us to glimpse several dimensions of relationships involving *uernae*: the prime identification of a child as a favoured slave of its owner, the use of one wet-nurse for slave child and owner's child (thus creating a sibling-type bond between these children of different status), and the circulation of nurses among different but related households.[126] The epitaph reads:

COMMVNIO VERNA
ANTONIAE AVGVSTAE
V. A. II MES. X
COLLACTEVS DRVSI
BLANDI F.

[123] *CIL* 6. 17398. Depending on when the father Martialis was freed, the family might have continued in the imperial household under Hadrian, who could have been the master of the *uerna*.

[124] See Weaver (1972, e.g. 177–8) on imperial *uernae*. Weaver (1972: 207) does have examples of imperial *uernae* who died young, already freed. See below on the *delicium* Moschus (*CIL* 6. 14990). Hermann-Otto (1994, esp. 99–230) draws out distinctions between imperial *uernae* and those in private households.

[125] *CIL* 14. 886. Many of these manumissions, especially if they were death-bed manumissions, were probably informal and the status of the ex-slave would be that of a Junian Latin, not a full Roman citizen.

[126] Cf. above for the use of the same teacher in different households. On *collactanei*, see K. R. Bradley (1991a: 149–55).

Communio, *uerna* of the Augusta Antonia, lived for two years and ten months, the fellow-nursling of Drusus, son of Blandus. (*CIL* 6. 16057)

As fellow-nurslings (*collactei*), Communio and Drusus began life in a sibling-type relationship. Communio was a slave child belonging to Antonia (the Younger), one of the most notable and powerful women of the Julio-Claudian imperial family. Daughter of Antony and Augustus' sister Octavia, she married Drusus (the Elder), brother of Tiberius and son of Livia. The name Drusus for one of the boys on the epitaph should alert us to a possible family connection, although the boy is identified only as the son of Blandus. Blandus and his family were well enough known in Julio-Claudian Rome to have left their mark in the historical record. Rubellius Blandus was a senior senator when he married Iulia, the daughter of Tiberius' son Drusus (the Younger), late in Tiberius' reign. Tacitus (*Annals* 6. 27) presented this as something of a disgrace, not because Blandus was about thirty years older than Iulia (not unusual in Roman marriages) but because Blandus' family background could not match that of Iulia, who was not only imperial by birth but had previously been married to Nero Caesar, son of Germanicus and Agrippina (the Elder). The second marriage did not, however, put Iulia or her children by Blandus beyond the pale of the imperial family. Tacitus later described one son, Rubellius Plautus, as socially equal to Nero in their descendance from Augustus, and it was Plautus' political prominence—and hence perceived dangerousness to Nero— which eventually brought about his exile and murder by Nero.[127]

Tiberius will not have lacked interest in the offspring of his granddaughter Iulia. Either on his behalf or independently Antonia provided a nurse for the son, Rubellius Drusus. Antonia had had a role in the rearing of the future emperor Gaius (and several sons and daughters of Eastern royal houses), and her household was the hub of much of the political and social activity in Rome.[128] At the time of Iulia's marriage to Rubellius Blandus, Antonia had recently protected Tiberius' interests by

---

[127] Tacitus, *Annals* 6. 27; 14. 22, 57–9. Cf. Juvenal 8. 39–47 for satire on the distinguished pedigree of Rubellius Blandus, perhaps a brother or son of Plautus. Syme (1982) discusses details of the marriage of Iulia and Rubellius Blandus.

[128] See Kokkinos (1992: *passim*, e.g. 25, 53, 150–2).

alerting him to Sejanus' plans—and it was Iulia's mother, Iulia Liuia (Livilla), whose relationship with Sejanus brought about her own death in 31 CE. So Antonia had good reason to keep an eye—suspicious or caring, or both—on Iulia's household.[129] The wet-nurse provided must have been a slave in Antonia's household, most probably the mother of Communio, and in order to nurse Iulia's baby she will have moved into that household with her own baby.[130] How long she stayed is unknown, but the use of *collacteus* for Communio when he died two years after his birth suggests that there was some ongoing link between the two households.[131]

The epitaph of one slave child can thus give us an insight into the circulation not only of children but also of carers in Roman society: this illuminates relationships between children of different status, children and adults of different status, and adults within networks which served familial, economic, and (sometimes) political needs.[132] Specific examples of fellow-nurslings are rare in inscriptions and literature in Roman Italy, but they were identified in the *lex Aelia Sentia* as one of the groups so closely linked to their owner that the owner would have just cause to give them their freedom even before the owner reached the normal permissible age of 20 (Gaius, *Institutes* 1. 38–9; *D.* 40. 2. 13, Ulpian), so the practice of simultaneous wet-nursing was probably fairly common and the relationship between quasi-siblings not infrequently continued into young adulthood.[133]

[129] Was the choice of the name 'Drusus' for the son provocative?

[130] Unless Iulia and Rubellius Blandus were living in Antonia's house, which is much less likely, although this is the hypothesis of K. Wachtel in *PIR²* 7. 1 no. 112, an entry which picks up some of the detail set out here.

[131] The time-span of this vignette is quite narrow. The marriage of Iulia and Blandus took place in 33 and Blandus died about 38, after fathering at least three children. The epitaph must have been inscribed early in Gaius' reign, in the two months of 37 between the conferring of the title Augusta on Antonia and her death (March–May). This places the birth of the boys named on the epitaph in 34, about June, which suggests that Drusus was the first-born of Iulia's marriage (which would also fit the choice of the name 'Drusus').

[132] Cf. (above, with reference to grandparents) for the use of the same nurse (Phyllis) for Domitian and then his niece (Flavia) Iulia.

[133] As proposed by K. R. Bradley (1991*a*: 154). Bradley suggests, however, that when fellow-nurslings were of very different social status their early intimacy did not continue into later life. Epithets of affection, which apply to other *collactanei*, are not used in these cases.

Infants were scarcely represented amongst *alumni* or *uernae*, and there is little evidence that the fosterers of these children were wet-nurses. The evidence of names and ages suggests that *alumni* were taken up by foster-parents at some time after infancy. Another reason for the under-representation of infants among *uernae* (apart from the general under-representation of infants in epitaphs) may be the practice of some slave owners of sending pregnant slaves to the countryside for the birth and early rearing of *uernae*. Not all slave owners could afford to dispense with such women's labour in the urban household for an extended period, but wealthier ones could, and they would have expected health advantages from a country environment for pregnant women and infant children. Jurists' comments indicate that there was an expectation that these slaves would return to the urban household, and boy slaves might have returned earlier than girls because of greater job opportunities for boys (especially very young ones) in large households.[134]

Two infant boys are commemorated on an altar dedicated by Publicia Glypte for her son and her *uerna* (Fig. 6.1).[135] The inscription records each boy's details in separate columns, with Glypte's name running along the bottom of both columns:

<table>
<tr><td align="center">D</td><td align="center">M</td><td></td></tr>
<tr><td align="center">NICONI FILIO</td><td align="center">EVTYCHETI</td><td></td></tr>
<tr><td align="center">DVLCISSIMO</td><td align="center">VERNAE</td><td></td></tr>
<tr><td align="center">QVI V MENS XI</td><td align="center">QVI VIX AN I</td><td></td></tr>
<tr><td align="center">DIEBVS VIII</td><td align="center">MENS V DIEB X</td><td></td></tr>
<tr><td align="center">PVBLICIA</td><td align="center">GLYPTE</td><td align="center">FECIT</td></tr>
</table>

To the departed spirits of
[col. 1] Nico, her sweet son, who lived for 11 months and 8 days; and
[col. 2] Eutyches, her home-born slave, who lived for 1 year, 5 months and 10 days;
dedicated by Publicia Glypte

---

[134] In *D.* 32. 99. 3 Paul has to consider the allocation of household effects in accordance with a will. What is the position of a child 'who has been born of a slave woman of the city household and sent to the country estate for rearing (*nutriendus*)'? Did the child belong to the urban or the rural household, or neither? Paul came down on the side of the urban household. Cf. *D.* 50. 16. 210, where Marcianus gives the same opinion. Treggiari (1979: 189–90) makes the suggestion about the health advantages of the countryside and the early recall of boy slaves.

[135] Rome, Villa Albani. *CIL* 6. 22972; Kleiner (1987), pl. XL. 1; DAI EA 4553.

FIG. 6.1   Altar dedicated by Publicia Glypte for infant son and *uerna*.
Rome, early second century CE.

Above the inscription are sculpted two figures of the little boys in togas, each holding a scroll, with a scroll-box between them at their feet. The togas and the appurtenances of schooling are clearly prospective, foreshadowing the boys' futures (now cut off) as well-educated citizens. The representation of Eutyches is especially optimistic, as a slave would not normally look forward to a liberal education or wear a toga; but Glypte advertises what had been her intention—to give Eutyches his freedom and to raise him as a citizen and as a foster-brother to Nico.[136] The sculpture on the pediment of the stone appears to be of Telephus, suckled by a hind, thus alluding to a fostering relationship. Glypte has raised the two boys almost as twins. Eutyches may already have been a surrogate son during Glypte's pregnancy, and she could have looked forward to having him as playmate and companion for her natural son, perhaps also to be suckled by the same nurse.

Pretty little boy or girl slaves were also welcomed in adults' company as pets and adornments. These were *delicia/deliciae* (or associated terms), 'delights' or 'little darlings'. The line between indulgent affection and sexual exploitation must have been blurred. Quintilian refers to their licence of speech, implying the use of obscenities and sexually explicit language.[137] But the term has a wide range of associations and contexts, many involving affection and familial kinds of bonds. Some of the relationships between *delicia* and masters must have amounted to pederasty, and a number of Roman emperors were accused of this in ancient sources (e.g. Augustus, Domitian, Trajan, Hadrian).[138] There is an erotic edge to other references, but we have to remember that

---

[136] Publicia Glypte's *cognomen* suggests that she is more likely to be freed rather than freeborn. The status of Nico is uncertain. If he is a slave, it would be natural for the mother to hope to free him at the earliest opportunity—hence the representation of him in a toga. I prefer this interpretation, retaining the parallelism with Eutyches. But if he has the same *nomen* Publicius (suppressed) as his mother, he could be of freed status (freed either by her after her freedom or by their common owner) or (much less likely in this context) freeborn, born after her freedom.

[137] Quintilian 1. 2. 7, where he is criticizing parents' spoiling of their own children and their tolerance of speech of which not even Alexandrian *deliciae* would be capable (the use of 'Alexandrian' giving a hint of the taste for exotic, imported, young slaves).

[138] As pointed out by Laes (2003), however, sex has always been a favourite kind of political invective. See all of Laes' chapter for a detailed and thoughtful analysis of *delicia*.

attitudes to sexual behaviour are culturally determined, and the physical environment (lack of privacy, erotic art everywhere) was conducive to less inhibited behaviour than in our own society. When it was clear that children were kept purely as pets or adornments, i.e. as luxury items, the law did not recognize the bond between them and their owner as based in the real affection which could justify manumission at an early age.[139] But the distinction was not easy to identify: we know of *delicia* who succeeded in meeting the criteria for early manumission, and the term *delicium* can overlap with that of *alumnus/-a* or *uerna*. Martial's little slave girl Erotion, who died before her sixth birthday, was called by him his *deliciae* and his *uernula* (*Epigrams* 5. 34, 37). The 5-year-old Moschus was not only the *uerna* and *delicium* of an imperial freedman of the mid-first century CE (Ti. Claudius Aug. l. Dalus), but also his *libertus* (*CIL* 6. 14990).

Like the young apprentices whom we saw above (Chapter 5), the 12-year-old jeweller Pagus had obviously been well trained in his art. The pleasure which he gave to master and parents was expressed in the terms 'delicium domini' ('his master's delight') and 'spes grata parentum' ('his parents' gratifying hope') (*CIL* 6. 9437). The child's natural parents were probably themselves favoured slaves in the household, making it more likely that their master would take special notice of their new baby when it was born. Apprentices' relationships with their masters were not always so affectionate and nurturing, as we saw above. The much-loved slave boy Glaucias was his master's *puer delicatus* but had been raised in the house as an *alumnus*, although his own parents were also members of that household.[140] The parents had been favoured with manumission early in Glaucias' life, and Glaucias himself had been freed before his death.

As symbols of luxury and exotic display, *delicia* were most often to be found in urban, wealthy households, and their inscriptions

---

[139] *D.* 40. 2. 16 (Ulpian commenting on the *lex Aelia Sentia*): 'Judges in these cases are to give approval for reasons based not on luxury but on affection (*non ex luxuria sed ex affectu*); for it must be supposed that the law gave justifiable freedom not for self-indulgence but for justifiable affections (*neque enim deliciis sed iustis affectionibus*).'

[140] Statius wrote a long poem of consolation to the master Atedius late in the 1st c. CE when Glaucias died at the age of 12: *Siluae* 2. 1. See also Martial 6. 28, 29, where Glaucias is referred to as a *libertus*.

are heavily concentrated in Roman Italy and Cisalpine Gaul (Laes 2003). More ascetic or less wealthy slave owners sometimes used more rustic, less well-groomed boys on their staffs as symbols of their own standards and ideals. As often, the ritual of dinner provided the setting for such displays. Many of the contemporaries of Seneca the Younger took pride in the very young (pre-pubescent) beauty of their dinner attendants,[141] but he himself claimed not to enjoy dinners prepared and served by retinues of such slaves. He preferred, he said (*On Tranquillity of Mind* 7), a simple meal served by a little home-born slave (*uernula*—still the emphasis on youth) who boasted no elaborate toilette or training. Juvenal adopted the same stance half a century later (11. 146–61): boys were still the expected attendants at dinner, but Juvenal would choose a country boy of few cultural pretensions (*incultus puer*). He preferred an Italian boy, one who spoke Latin but not Greek and one whose hair was short and straight rather than long and curled in the more luxurious fashion. Juvenal's boy is represented as being the son of a shepherd or ploughman and homesick for his mother and his local area. He sounds more like the child of free but poor country parents rather than a slave: there is the element of in-service which we saw for *alumni*.

SLAVE FAMILIES

Many of the foster-relationships discussed above involved slaves in one role or another. Comparatively few of the children had natural parents attested with them. Other slaves, however, managed to stay together, or at least to record themselves, as a biological family group. We cannot always be certain that those attested as father, mother, son, or daughter are really biological relations rather than step- or half-relations, but a sizeable number present themselves as a family group. Although slaves could not formally marry, they often identified themselves as spouses by the same terms (*coniunx*, *maritus*, *uxor*) used for formally married couples. Some of them clearly managed to establish reasonably enduring family relationships.

---

[141] *Letters* 47. 7, 95. 24. Seneca hints that after dinner sexual services might be required in the privacy of the master's quarters.

What emerges strikingly from the inscriptions of these groups is the variety of status to be found in any one group.[142] Although most epitaphs are a snapshot of relationships at one particular moment, they can also reveal something of the life cycle of a family, whose size and structure varied over the years and whose members' status reflects something of the changing fortunes of parents and children. Some groups remained entirely slaves. Some belonged to different households or were dispersed from one household into different households after establishing family relations (but their epitaphs record some kind of unity at the death of a member). Those who remained in one household seem to have had a better chance of gaining manumission for all their members. Three generations are attested as associated with the Cassii household in a detailed epitaph from Rome of the first half of the first century CE (*CIL* 6. 14529). C. Cassius Verecundus erected it for himself and his wife Cassia Damalis, who had been his slave and been manumitted by him ('libertae carissimae et bene mer(enti) idem coniugi'). He included his parents C. Cassius Cotynus and Cassia Moschis who had freed him from slavery and had themselves been slaves of C. Cassius Longinus ('parentibus suis isdem patron(is) libertis C. Cassi Longini'). Verecundus provided also for the inclusion of others of his freedmen and freedwomen (actual or prospective) and their posterity ('et libertis suis libertabusque posterisque eorum').

Slave mothers could be rewarded for bearing a number of children, and might gain freedom ahead of their male partner.[143] Any further children would be freeborn, but until a formal marriage existed these children would be 'illegitimate' (see below on this term) and they bore their mother's *nomen*. Only when both partners were free could their union be formally recognized and their children be freeborn and take the *nomen* of their father. Occasionally an epitaph is elaborate enough to reveal this family

---

[142] See B. Rawson (1966) for a study of approximately 1,500 epitaphs from Rome, each attesting at least one Roman citizen (or at least one bearing a Roman *nomen*), in groups in which there are at least one child and two parents (nearly 5,000 persons in total). This is a picture of the most humble citizens attested for whom there is some record of a 'complete' family.

[143] Freedwomen could earn the privileges of childbirth (*ius liberorum*) by bearing four children, which must have been thought to be a not impossibly high figure.

history. One such example is a handsome marble slab set up by an imperial freedman of Hadrian's reign, P. Aelius Aug. lib. Ianuarius, for two sons and his wife as well as for himself, his own freedmen and his descendants (*CIL* 6. 15317). The name of one of the sons, Ti. Claudius Aug. l. Censorinus, shows that he was born a slave (but won his freedom much earlier than his father),[144] so his mother must have been a slave at the time of his birth. She subsequently won her own freedom (probably from an imperial freedman in Nero's household), and it is very likely that the son whose name heads the epitaph was born after that and was thus freeborn. This son's name, Ti. Claudius Vitalio (which he shares with his mother but not his father), did not identify him as an ex-slave and was placed in larger letters at the top of the epitaph, with his age specified: 11 years, 7 months, 13 days. The father Ianuarius remained a slave for at least fifty years after his (first) son became free, and long after his wife also became free, but the epitaph tells us that he lived with his 'well-deserving and incomparable' wife ('bene merenti et incomparabili') for thirty years. In spite of the different status levels of this group, they seem to have remained together as a family (probably in the imperial household).

This example raises two new topics: the relationships of imperial slaves and freedmen, and the category of 'illegitimate' children.

A special category of slave spouses was attractive, even to free women: imperial slaves (slaves owned by the emperor).[145] Imperial slaves seldom obtained freedom before the age of 30, because they had to fulfil the career grades as slaves in the emperor's service before they could progress to grades held by freedmen. Even as slaves, however, they could be influential, and they had considerable prospects of wealth and influence once freed. They were worth the wait for free women. Although the law normally recognized children born to a free woman as freeborn, some emperors made special rules to retain the services of

[144] Probably from the emperor Nero; Claudius is almost impossible chronologically.

[145] These women were probably of freed status rather than freeborn: there was strong feeling against freeborn–slave unions, especially when the freeborn partner was the woman. But Weaver (1972: ch. 7) argues that some of the female spouses of imperial slaves were freeborn.

the progeny of male slaves for the slaves' owners, especially in the emperor's own service.[146] There may have been good career prospects for such progeny as slaves, but in the second century the basic principle of free birth for children of a free woman was reaffirmed.

When at least one marital partner was a slave, no formal marriage was possible. Any children born in these circumstances belonged to the mother, or, if she was a slave, to her owner. The father had no formal claim—but the blood relationship was recognized for some purposes, including early manumission of a natural son or daughter and avoidance of incest.[147] Such children, not being born of a legitimate marriage, were 'illegitimate'—the Latin term *spurius* is preferable, for reasons outlined below.[148]

Children of a 'proper' Roman marriage were their father's children.[149] Various circumstances besides slavery militated against the formalization of spousal relationships: soldiers (below officer rank) were not allowed to marry during their term of service;[150] only Roman citizens and a few favoured categories of Latins or other non-citizens could form a Roman marriage; senators and their sons could not marry freedwomen or members of certain disreputable professions; and there were minimum age limits and rules against close blood relationship. Poverty did not stand in the way of a legally recognized marriage, as no formal ceremony was required: the law recognized as *matrimonium* a continuing relationship between eligible partners, based on marital intention (*affectio maritalis*).[151] Many of those who were formally ineligible for Roman marriage nevertheless lived in spousal relationships and raised children and were surely regarded by themselves and others as 'a family'. The law, however, did not recognize the nat-

[146] A decree of Claudius' reign (52 CE), the *senatus consultum Claudianum*, specified situations in which children of free women cohabiting with a male slave would be slave-born. See Weaver (1986); Hermann-Otto (1994: 28–33, 115–19).

[147] For the *lex Aelia Sentia* and exceptions to age restrictions for manumission, see n. 25 above.

[148] See B. Rawson (1989) for detailed analysis of *spurii*.

[149] See Treggiari (1991) on *iustum matrimonium* (esp. 15–28, 43–51).

[150] The ban lasted probably from the time of Augustus until the early 3rd c.

[151] 'If you lived together "as" man and wife, man and wife you were' (Crook 1967: 101). This did not preclude ceremonies, which were often held to celebrate a marriage.

ural father of children born of these de facto unions as the *pater-familias* of his children. The children took their family name from their mother if she was free and had a *nomen*; if she was a slave they belonged to her owner. They took their status from that of their mother at the time of their birth.

The father's blood relationship with such children might be recognized, when necessary, but his lack of *patria potestas* prevented him from recognizing them as his legitimate children. The English term 'illegitimate' has so many historical and pejorative overtones that it is best avoided here. *Spurius/-a* is the most common Latin term for such a child.[152] It seldom has the moral stigma of 'illegitimate'—it is simply a function of a child's parents' legal status. In recent modern times the law of a number of countries has grappled with the problem of family terminology to remove 'illegitimate' with its pejorative overtones. In the United Kingdom, the Family Law Reform Act 1987 has substituted the two categories of 'the child of a married couple' and 'the child of an unmarried couple' for the previous 'legitimate' and 'illegitimate', thus focusing on the status of the parents (which was the determining factor in the Roman context) rather than labelling the child.[153]

If *spurii* were freeborn Roman citizens, they came under the same provisions of the law as other citizens. There were some legal disadvantages to illegitimacy, although they scarcely amounted to systematic discrimination. Illegitimate children could not be entered on the birth registers introduced by Augustus, a bar which remained until the time of Marcus Aurelius. They were eligible for public office, but sometimes (for instance, on town councils) they had to yield precedence to legitimately born citizens. As children, they will have grown up in an environment and in relationships similar to those of other children of modest circumstances, and the urban milieu discussed in the next chapter will have shaped them equally.

In this society of many family forms, the conjugal family remained central to Roman ideals and ideology; but it was by no

[152] Other terms are *uulgo quaesiti/concepti* and *liberi naturales* (but the last of these could also refer to all natural children as opposed to adoptive ones).

[153] This is consistent with current international conventions: see Bevan (1989: 60–3). The common term in Australian law is 'ex-nuptial'.

means universally attainable or sustainable, for reasons of demography, divorce, or status. Roman law and custom gave parents a position of respect and influence. A father's formal powers (*patria potestas*) were extensive in concept but restricted by law, custom, and demography. Mothers were perceived as having considerable influence, although technically they were seldom members of the family of their husband and children. This very separateness allowed them independent means, and in the propertied classes they wielded real financial power, which society expected them to use for (amongst other things) the interests of their children. The core Roman virtue of *pietas* influenced familial relationships. It imposed a sense of mutual duty, especially between parents and children.

The parent–child relationship was, then, a core relationship reflected in law, literature, and inscriptions. But it was not an exclusive relationship. Most children lived in a network of other relationships: step- and half-parents and siblings, teachers and fellow-students, neighbours, male or female owners who could be surrogate parents, sometimes (but not frequently) members of the extended family such as grandparents, uncles, aunts, cousins, but more often slave members of the household who were carers or companions. The range of slave members of a household who could provide services, loyalty, and affection for a child was highlighted by the law which, from Augustus' time, allowed grants of freedom before the minimum legal age to a range of carers and companions, as we saw above.

The formative influences of all these personal relationships need now to be set in the wider context of the urban environment, to help us understand their mutual interaction.

7

Public Life

SOME of the relationships discussed in the preceding chapter, and some of the activities discussed in earlier chapters, extended beyond the home into the public sphere. Even the home was a semi-public space—more so than it is for most modern homes. The large upper-class house was designed to accommodate many callers, and poorer housing was necessarily crowded and lacking in privacy. Moreover, climate and culture were conducive to much outdoor activity, or activity in public spaces, so children were often spectators or participants at public festivals, entertainment, and ritual. All of this had a role in a child's development and social-ization. The material context—the very buildings and spaces for public activity, and their adornment—played its part. The city of Rome contained probably three-quarters of a million inhabitants by the mid-first century BCE and over one million in the first and second centuries of this era. This large population had many dif-ferent ethnic, religious, and linguistic components. Public life was crowded, busy, and noisy; much of political, social, and economic life was played out in the public spaces of the centre of the city or the Campus Martius; and people of every rank and degree of wealth or poverty were visible. The visual and aural impact of such activities conditioned all members of the population, not least the young and impressionable. In every aspect of public life which we consider, the physical setting and the accompanying sounds must be borne in mind. Neither monuments nor ceremonies can be considered in isolation: they reinforced each other, and they were perceived differently according to the participant, the viewer, the adornment, the weather, and many other contextual circum-stances.

Religion was the context for many—perhaps most—of the activities which took place in the home and in wider public spaces. Sometimes implicit, sometimes explicit, the religious associations of these activities affected members of the population

in different degrees. All the great festivals were in origin religious
festivals, but the religious dimension was less dominant, in many
people's consciousness, than that of the associated entertainment.
Plays had been associated with early religious ritual, gladiatorial
displays with funerals and dedications to the spirits of the dead,
military triumphs with thanksgivings to the gods; but they all
took on a life of their own, in which religion was often subsumed.
Nevertheless, the presence of priests, the act of sacrifice, the place
of statues of the traditional gods in processions, the ubiquity of
temples and shrines, all provided a religious framework for everyday life. The constant stream of immigrants and foreign visitors
to Rome introduced new cults and exotic images. Within the
household, domestic rites were practised, focusing particularly on
the *Lares* and the *genius*. We cannot assess how deeply people
integrated religion, in any form, into their inner lives; but
children growing up could not escape a consciousness of the role
of the gods in their personal and public lives.

The spatial context of religious observance was significant: in
the household it brought together the resident *familia*, usually in
a communal space such as the *atrium* or, later, in the peristyle; in
public, ritual was usually carried out in the open air, at altars outside temples or at the sites of particular festivals and celebrations.
Except for the 'mystery' religions, ritual was not confined indoors
as in modern churches, mosques, temples, and synagogues.

At the height of the Empire, Rome was a melting-pot for
people from all over the world.[1] Early in the second century CE
Juvenal bewailed this development (in *Satire* 3, for instance), for
the alleged weakening of old Roman culture and marginalizing of
native-born citizens who had no specialized urban skills. A little
later, Aelius Aristides praised it for its enrichment of Rome, making the city a vibrant world capital and trade centre (*Roman
Oration* 61–2). Already in the middle of the first century BCE
Cicero could write that the Latin language and its grammar
needed purging and regularizing because Rome now contained
many who were not native speakers of Latin.[2] Shows given by
both Julius Caesar and Augustus included actors 'in all lan-

---

[1] Noy (2000) discusses many aspects of the lives of people who moved to
Rome.

[2] Words attributed to Atticus in *Brutus* 258.

guages',[3] showing that the immigrant population was significant
enough to be specially catered for.

There was great diversity of dress in the Roman streets, some
of it giving clues as to status, ethnicity, and age as well as personal
taste and wealth (or lack of it). But the white toga, although cum-
bersome and expensive to keep clean, maintained its primacy as
the correct dress code for adult male Roman citizens, especially
in the city.[4] Augustus tried to enforce this code in public places,
and it was still in effect a century later.[5] Vergil (*Aeneid* 1. 282)
characterized the Romans as rulers of the world, 'the toga-ed
race' (*gens togata*).

Ritual, festivals, entertainment, recreation, political and economic life were closely associated with the physical fabric of the
city or town. In any city, each individual resident of a city forms
his or her own image of that city.[6] Each will experience the city
differently according to age, sex, status, and whether they are
native-born or immigrant.[7] In this chapter we shall try to look at
various aspects of urban life through a child's eyes.[8] Bearing in
mind the above differentials, we shall distinguish, where possible,
between the very young and the adolescent, boys and girls, and
slaves, the free poor, and the upper classes. Native-born and
immigrant are more difficult to identify, but we have already seen
(Chapter 5) that some children were brought to Rome by their
parents to benefit from the advantages of the capital city, and
we can draw some conclusions from recent studies of foreign

---

[3] Suetonius, *Iulius* 39. 1, *Augustus* 43. 1.

[4] Cicero (*Philippics* 2. 76) made a distinction between his own correct dress,
which included the toga, and that of Antony.

[5] Suetonius, *Augustus* 40; Juvenal and Martial (see below on entertainment).

[6] The fundamental study of this topic is Lynch (1960). See also Downs and
Stea (1973), in which I found the chapter by Donata Francescato and William
Mebane, 'How Citizens View Two Great Cities: Milan and Rome', particularly
stimulating. Favro (1996) has applied Lynch's approach vividly to Rome of the
period 52 BCE to 14 CE.

[7] Francescato and Mebane found evidence of all these differentials except
sex. Male and female respondents to their survey of Milan and Rome reported
essentially similar images and attitudes to their city.

[8] It would be heavy-handed to make explicit, for every event or monument
below, the likely effect on children. The choice of matters discussed is dictated
by their relevance for children, and the reader is asked to keep the child's perspective in mind throughout.

communities at Rome.[9] The discussion below tends to focus on the positive aspects of the urban environment, and the role of 'the city' in socializing, educating, and stimulating its inhabitants, especially children. The concept of 'the city', however, and especially its civilizing role, are very much under debate at present and are not unproblematical.[10] The less privileged sections of the population, those who are largely silent in our sources, may have identified less with the history, achievements, and opportunities of Rome and the qualities which the city and Roman culture claimed to stand for. But the material improvements, pageantry, and entertainment did offer something to all inhabitants and could not leave them unchanged. The nature of the impact on the most humble can only be hypothesized; but it is arguable that the least sophisticated members of the population (and that includes children) would have accepted the model offered more unquestioningly than would those more educated and more politically astute.

Locality, or neighbourhood, is also a differentiating factor in urban life.[11] Rome had long been organized, for some purposes, on localities (*uici*). Shrines at crossroads had local religious loyalties, and were the focus of local professional, social, or political gatherings. Big occasions like a distribution of food and drink after a sacrifice or a public celebration required local organization. Lucullus' public banquet after his triumph in 63 BCE was organized along these lines (Plutarch, *Lucullus* 37. 4), and Julius Caesar used the *uici* as the basis for his regular distributions of grain (Suetonius, *Iulius* 41). The neighbourhood must also have been part of the organization of public feasts in other Italian towns. Although the smaller size of these towns made such organization less complex, public feasts were frequent and elaborate there. A study of 'euergetic self-representation' in municipal Italy

---

[9] Noy (2000: 64–6) found it difficult to identify children in Rome who were foreign-born. He suggested that 'people tended to come to Rome before they had started to have families'. Children born at Rome to foreign parents are harder to identify, as there will be some degree of assimilation, e.g. in language and name, and less reason to identify geographical provenance.

[10] See, for example, the contributions in Fentress (2000), e.g. the chapters by Woolf and Alcock.

[11] For a stimulating discussion of *uici* and prospects for further study, see Wallace-Hadrill (2001). See also Castrén (2000).

commented on the large number of dining-tables provided (presumably throughout the town), and termed these feasts 'a social
custom that was eagerly incorporated into the civic ideology of
the typical town' (Donahue 1999). Shows given by Julius Caesar
and Augustus were often organized by neighbourhood, using
temporary stands and seating.[12] These local, fairly informal
shows continued for at least two centuries. The legal writer
Ulpian had to define what a stage (*scaena*) was, for the purpose of
classifying as 'of ill-fame' (*infamis*) those who performed on a
scaena. He went back to the definition of Labeo, an authority of
the Augustan age, to define a *scaena* as any structure set up for
giving theatrical performances (*ludi*) anywhere where one can
stand or move to perform, 'in public or private or in the street (*in
uico*), provided that people at large are admitted for the performance (*spectaculum*)' (D. 3. 2. 2. 5).

In the study of the modern cities of Milan and Rome, fewer
Romans than Milanese identified focal points when asked to
sketch a map of how they perceived their city. This was attributed, by the researchers, in part to the lack of a regular street-
pattern in Rome and the fact that the city is cut by the Tiber and
circumscribed by hills—all elements common to ancient and
modern Rome. The Tiber, however, was one of the few focal
points identified by modern Romans; others were two piazzas
and the Vatican. The Vatican is a modern element, associated
with Christianity;[13] but the piazzas serve much the same purpose
as ancient forums. These, and the Campus Martius skirted by the
Tiber, were also focal points for ancient Romans: we shall see
many activities located there. Some modern Romans' maps had
no focal point at all, 'but were sketches of neighbouring streets
around a person's residence, exhibiting a "home orientation" '.[14]
Not surprisingly, middle-class residents could identify more
elements in their perceptions of Rome than could lower-class residents. The lower classes, being less mobile, had a greater home

---

[12] Suetonius, *Iulius* 39. 1, 'regionatim urbe tota'; *Augustus* 43. 1, 'uicatim'. Cf.
Tacitus, *Annals* 15. 37, for Nero's provision of feasts throughout the city ('publi-
cis locis . . . totaque urbe quasi domi uti') to show his attachment to Rome in
64 CE.

[13] But cf. the temple of Jupiter Capitolinus in ancient Rome, which dominated the skyline and was the focus of much public life. See further below.

[14] Francescato and Mebane in Downs and Stea (1973: 135).

orientation. It is easy to picture ancient Rome in this way, even
when one allows for the smaller geographic area occupied then
and the greater readiness of ancient residents to walk considerable distances. Children's mobility, of course, was more limited
than that of adults.

Augustus used this aspect of the city of Rome to advantage. He
divided Rome formally into fourteen regions, subdivided into 265
uici.[15] Julius Caesar had made the *uici* the basis for revising the
census and had recruited the landlords of apartment blocks
('insularum domini') to help with this. No doubt they used their
local agents, who would know the neighbourhood well—who
lived where, and all sorts of personal details such as age, property,
marital status, number of children. Local magistrates (*uicomag-
istri*) took over each neighbourhood from Augustus' time: four
per *uicus*, chosen by the local community. They had added
responsibilities, especially religious, and were usually of freedman
status, so could identify with the lower levels of the population.
Their close association with the cult of the emperor's *Lares* and
genius, and their role of communication between the neighbourhood and more senior administrative officials, gave them considerable power and kudos, and they could be figures to be feared or
cultivated by local children. The geographic area of responsibility
of each *uicomagister* was comparatively small, so the 'neighbourhood boss' was a familiar figure to all local residents. This was the
base from which children's perceptions of public life were formed
and developed. Physical monuments reinforced the religious basis
of the *uici* and the intertwining of the old crossroads cult with
loyalty to the emperor and his family. Several altars are known
which represent the *Lares* of the emperor, sacrificial scenes, and
the participation of boy attendants (*camilli*) in these. The earliest
is from 12 BCE or soon after, and others soon followed, both in
Rome and in many Italian towns. Flowers were ceremonially
placed on the altars twice a year, to mark spring and summer
festivals. The altars and other evidence of neighbourhood life
continue well into the third century.[16] Children's participation in

---

[15] Pliny the Elder attests this number in his own day (*NH* 3. 66).

[16] On *Compitalia* (crossroads festivals) and the altars, including the Belvedere
altar, see Taylor (1931: 186–91); Ryberg (1955: 56–8); Hölscher (1988: 390–3);
Beard, North, and Price (1998: 1. 184–6). On Hadrian's close interest, see
Boatwright (1987: 26–7). Shaw's study of 4th-c. Christian epitaphs from Rome

such life, as performers or general celebrators, provided both socializing and socialization.

A study of the building activities in Rome and other Italian cities and towns gives some insight into what facilities were considered important. Powerful, wealthy individuals (especially the emperor under the Principate) decided on these facilities and funded them, and the aim was often personal glory and aggrandizement, but there was also responsiveness to popular taste. Generals and magistrates of the Republic and emperors and prominent citizens of the Principate all had their reasons for courting popularity and a place in the public memory. There is a remarkably constant set of benefits and monuments bestowed on cities over at least three centuries: temples, games, theatres, triumphal arches, and statues, to which amphitheatres and baths were increasingly added. Romans were unique in ancient societies in advertising monuments and buildings on their coinage: 'buildings were an important part of the Roman cultural outlook'; they were important to 'the notion of civic identity' (Burnett 1999: 154).[17]

Children were constantly exposed to the public spaces of their home towns. If they were already working for a living, their occupation and often their residence were located in and above shops, and there were many errands to be run through the streets. Slave children came and went with their masters or ran errands or did the shopping. And there was much time spent as spectators or participants in public festivals, celebrations, processions, and performances.

Rome had become the point of reference, the model, for city life in Italy by the late Republic. Many public facilities were replicated throughout Italy, albeit on a more modest level than at Rome, but some ceremonies could be experienced only at Rome, notably a military triumph and the elaborate chariot races of the

found that the ecclesiastical offices recorded suggested the parish level rather than more senior levels of Church administration. It seemed to him that 'most of the population was centred on the parish-level of organization' (Shaw 1996: 108).

[17] Further details of monuments and buildings of Rome and other parts of Italy can be found in many reference works, including Nash (1968); Blake (1947, 1968, 1973); Richardson (1992); Coarelli (1974); and *LTUR*.

Circus Maximus.[18] Familiarity with Rome spread as a result of personal visits or stories brought back by those who had visited. The impact made on visitors by the size and splendour of Rome and its activities is well documented over three and a half centuries.[19] It was in the fourth century that Ammianus Marcellinus, who had himself been deeply impressed by Rome when he first visited from his home city of Antioch, reported the emperor Constantius' first sight of Rome in 357:

So then he entered Rome, the home of empire and of every virtue, and when he had come to the Rostra, that most renowned site of ancient power, he stood amazed; and in every direction to which his eyes were drawn he was dazzled by the myriad marvellous sights. . . . Then as he surveyed the various parts of the city circled by the ridges of the seven hills, along the slopes and on level ground, and the nearby environs, he assumed that whatever first met his gaze was the prize amongst all else: the shrine of Tarpeian Jupiter, pre-eminent as heaven is to earth; the baths extending like provinces; the huge bulk of the amphitheatre, strengthened by its bodywork of Travertine stone, whose summit is almost beyond the reach of the human eye; the Pantheon like a rounded city-district, vaulted to its glorious heights; and the lofty columns which rise with platforms to which one may climb, bearing the likenesses of former emperors; the temple of Rome, the forum of Peace, the theatre of Pompey, the Odeum, the Stadium, and amongst these the other adornments of the eternal city. But when he came to the forum of Trajan, a construction unique under any sky, as we believe, and wonderful even in the unanimous opinion of the gods, he stood fast in astonishment, turning his gaze around the gigantic complex which no words could describe and which would never again be attempted by mortal men.[20]

---

[18] Humphrey (1986: ch. 10) discusses the circus buildings known in Italy outside Rome. They were few and small, and closely associated with the home towns or estates of a few emperors (Augustus, Nero, Antoninus Pius).

[19] e.g., at the beginning of the 1st c. CE, Strabo 5. 3. 8; in 143 Aelius Aristides in his speech of praise to Rome, *Roman Oration* 6–9; and in the 4th c. as quoted below. In the mid-1st c. Pliny the Elder (*NH* 36. 24. 102–23) reviewed the architectural wonders of Rome, noting particularly the Circus Maximus, the Basilica Aemilia, the forum of Augustus, the Temple of Peace, sewers and aqueducts, as well as the increasing magnificence of houses and the temporary theatres of Scaurus and Curio (58 and 52 BCE respectively).

[20] *Res Gestae* 16. 10. 13–15. Some phrases here have been borrowed from the Loeb Classical Library translation by John C. Rolfe.

In spite of the flowery language of a courtier, this gives some sense of the excitement which Rome could arouse. If adults were so impressed, one can gauge the greater susceptibility of children's minds to the lessons of the capital city.

Children living in lesser urban centres and country towns experienced public life which was in some ways less intense and less elaborate than at Rome. Regional variation, which has remained significant in Italy to the present day, made every town different. But throughout Italy, from the late second century BCE, there was a strong element of the same Roman culture.[21] Honorific statues of distinguished citizens were erected in public places, reminding viewers of these citizens' personalities and the kind of contributions to public life which were so honoured. These could be civic and intellectual as well as military. Cicero's high estimation of his own services to the state as consul in 63 BCE might seem excessive, but there was tangible evidence of some similar view in municipal towns: there was, for instance, a gilded bronze statue set up in Capua for him as the town's patron because of the security measures which he took to protect the town in 63 BCE during the 'Catilinarian conspiracy' (Cicero, *Against Piso* 25). A man of lower social standing, the freedman M. Verrius Flaccus, was recognized by Praeneste (probably his home town) for his scholarly achievements. He was a distinguished teacher, engaged by Augustus to teach his own grandsons, and he organized a

---

[21] Many of the types of public buildings in use at Rome can be identified in Italian towns of the late Republic. See J. M. Carter in Barton (1989: 33–6) on Cosa, Alba Fucens, Pompeii, and Aletrium for forum and basilica, a Capitolium and other temples, and sometimes baths and a theatre. Amphitheatres became more numerous from the second half of the 1st c. CE, but the circus was rare outside Rome. After the destruction of Cremona in the civil wars of 69 CE, the citizens who returned made their first priority the rebuilding of the town squares and temples ('fora templaque': Tacitus, *Histories* 3. 34). Crawford (1996: 428–33) discusses aspects of local culture 'in which traditional local practices were abandoned during the late Republic and the early Empire', leading to a more homogeneous Italy than before or since: he cites funerary practice, building styles, artefacts, population movements (a 'mixing process'). Vitruvius (5. 1. 1), writing in the late 1st c. BCE, envisages his rules for forums and basilicas applying to 'the cities of Italy'. For aspects of Romanization earlier than the 1st c. BCE, see Torelli (1999). Guy Bradley warns that cultural change need not mean 'one identity *replacing* another', but he recognizes that by the 1st c. BCE there was considerable 'monumentalization of Umbrian settlement centres according to well-established Graeco-Roman principles of urbanism' (2000: 267, 225).

version of the Roman official calendar which was inscribed on a
marble wall in the forum at Praeneste. In this part of the forum
a statue was set up for him. Over a century later, Suetonius saw
this monument.[22] As seen above (Chapter 5), some boys were
publicly commemorated in Italian towns for their intellectual
achievements. And although a Roman triumph could be celebrated only at Rome, the triumphing general's home town might
share the glory by recording the achievement there, as Arretium
did for L. Aemilius Paullus' triumphs of 181 and 167 BCE.[23]
Country towns, moreover, were treated to impressive processions
when notable citizens were returning to Italy on significant occasions. As Brundisium was the main port for re-entry from the
East, the southern part of Italy, along the Appian Way, benefited
most from this traffic. In 62 BCE, on his return from the
Mithridatic War, Pompey disbanded his army at Brundisium but
gathered an admiring retinue as he proceeded to Rome through
Italian towns (Plutarch, *Pompey* 43). Germanicus' widow,
Agrippina the Elder, made the most of her route from
Brundisium to Rome in 19 CE when she travelled with her husband's ashes, accompanied by two of her children (one of them
the infant Livilla) (Tacitus, *Annals* 3. 1).

Houses were a significant part of the public landscape. They
were, as stated in the previous chapter, the interface between private and public. From the first century BCE, increasing personal
wealth was expended on ambitious building schemes—elaborate
houses and their decoration, and associated statuary and gardens.
Lucullus was famous for his gardens, art, baths, libraries, and
elaborate facilities for pleasure and comfort in Rome and on other
estates (Plutarch, *Lucullus* 39–42). Catiline used examples of such
men to stir up resentment and revolutionary zeal in his accom-
plices. Sallust represents him speaking in this way to fellow-
senators and other men of standing from Rome and Italian
towns, who might be expected to have ambitions for a similar
lifestyle (*Catilinarian Conspiracy* 20):

Who in the world, who has the spirit of a man, can tolerate that they
should have an excess of wealth to pour out on filling up the sea with

---

[22] Suetonius, *Gramm.* 17. Fragments of this calendar, the *Fasti Praenestini*,
still survive, e.g. *CIL* I². XV.
[23] *CIL* I². p. 194, an inscription recording Aemilius' magistracies, triumph,
and successful war over Perseus.

buildings and levelling mountains, while we lack means even for necessities? They join together two or more houses, when we have not a home to call our own. They buy pictures, statues, and embossed metal, they destroy new-built houses and erect others, in short they squander and dissipate their funds in every way and yet they cannot exhaust their wealth with all their wanton spending.

The taste for elaborate houses, gardens, and art collections, and for properties in different parts of Italy, continued in Roman life. The letters of Pliny the Younger—a man of generally sober lifestyle—are witness to this for the late first century CE and the first part of the second. There were, of course, exceptions. The wealthy Atticus scorned this form of display (Nepos, *Atticus* 13–14), and Augustus cultivated the image of living simply.[24] Agrippa criticized the accumulation of art (much of it the fruits of foreign conquest) in private houses and proposed that it should be reclaimed for the public sphere (Pliny the Elder, *NH* 35. 26). But Vitruvius, writing on architecture in the Augustan period, made explicit the importance to high-ranking citizens (*nobiles*) of expensive and extensive houses with gardens, libraries, picture-galleries, and basilicas (6. 5. 2). The owners needed these, said Vitruvius, in order to perform their public duties.

A grand house was part of a person's public persona. Visitors who made the morning call (the *salutatio*) saw the *atrium* as a sign of the owner's power and prestige. Even those who never set foot inside such a house often passed close by, in the street. In the Republic, politically active men lived near the action, never far from the Forum. Even if their houses were on high slopes such as the Palatine they were very visible, and others were closer to busy thoroughfares. In the imperial period, leading citizens still found it convenient to be close to the senate-house, the courts, and the other activities of the various forums. The *salutatio* ceremony continued.[25] Over a period the residences of the imperial

---

[24] Suetonius, *Augustus* 72. A contemporary account, that of Ovid in his *Tristia* 3. 1, makes much of how Augustus' house on the Palatine stood out as something special; but this is in the context of Ovid's hopes for a pardon from Augustus and permission to return from exile. The special features of Augustus' house noted by Ovid are those which could be said to make Augustus god-like: doorposts distinguished by captured weapons, the oak wreath for saving citizens' lives, and the laurel insignia of military triumph.

[25] Saller (1982: 128–9) gives evidence for the continuation of the *salutatio* into the 3rd c.

family came to dominate the Palatine and thus to allow its members to withdraw more from public view when they chose. But visibility was vital to their power, and they not only were out in public frequently but received large numbers of callers, guests, and officials in their own residences.

In the cramped quarters of ramshackle tenements inhabited by the poor, by recent immigrants and many ex-slaves, there was enforced intermingling and sharing of space with others of diverse cultures and backgrounds. At this level of society the need to use public space was particularly strong; but from all levels the population poured out to enjoy festivals, entertainment, and the public facilities provided by leading citizens and, increasingly, by the emperor.

PUBLIC SPACE

Public facilities were expanded and improved at an accelerated rate from early in the second century BCE, as Roman power in the Mediterranean increased and Rome itself was becoming an international capital city. At first, the benefits were mainly entertainment and embellishment of existing public space; then new buildings (especially temples) were vowed and erected; and from the first century BCE a greater variety of monuments appeared. All these benefits, but especially the monuments, statues, and inscriptions, redounded to the reputation and glory of individual citizens and then emperors. Those who used the streets of Rome could not be unaware, in varying degrees, of the achievements of Rome and a long line of leading (male) citizens.

Already in the third century BCE Rome was being embellished with imported art. It was in Sicily that the Romans first came into close contact with Greek material culture and began to transfer much of it back to Rome. During the Second Carthaginian War, in 211 BCE, M. Claudius Marcellus celebrated two 'ovations' for victories over Syracuse and displayed in his procession much royal treasure, such as silverware, bronzeware, other furniture, precious clothing, and notable statues, as well as other spoils and distinguished captives (Livy 26. 21. 6–10). Statues and paintings which he had confiscated were used to embellish the temples to Honos and Virtus which he had vowed, and they attracted many foreign visitors; but they had largely disappeared by the end of the first century BCE (Livy 25. 40. 2–3). Livy attributes to Marcellus the beginning of the Roman enthusiasm for Greek art and hence the growth in the practice of plunder of anything sacred or profane.

From the second century BCE there was increasing momentum in the embellishment of Rome to reflect the city's greatly increased power and prosperity.[26] Romans were becoming more familiar with the art and trappings of the Hellenistic monarchies of the East as a result of increasing two-way traffic: Roman businessmen, governors, generals and their staffs travelled to the East and sometimes spent long periods there; Eastern businessmen, embassies, professionals, and intellectuals visited Rome. Of all these, victorious Roman generals brought back the largest quantities of Greek art for the embellishment of Rome. Much of this was displayed in their triumphal procession, and although some of it later went into private homes much of it was placed permanently on public view. Thus, added to the increasing number of monuments honouring and commemorating Roman magistrates and their families, there was a growing accumulation of statues, paintings, friezes, and arches; buildings too were being erected which had been vowed for military success. Rome was becoming a sort of museum—but a living one, with real connections to collective memory and new achievements. In Republican times there were occasionally statues of women erected in public places, attesting to viewers that women too could make a valuable public contribution and provide models of worthy public behaviour (see Chapter 1 above). Cloelia of the late sixth century BCE personified bravery and patriotism; Cornelia, mother of the Gracchi and daughter of Scipio Africanus, was used by Augustus to portray the ideal mother. Certainly in the imperial period there were many statues of women, especially (but not only) those of the imperial family, in public places. They were sometimes in familial scenes, but they often represented particular virtues or attributes.

---

[26] Scipio Africanus the Elder celebrated a notable triumph over Carthage in 201 BCE. Livy (30. 45), however, did not give it the colourful detail which he gave to later triumphs. Scipio brought into the treasury a large amount of silver, but there is no record of works of art or commemorative monuments. He funded games to celebrate his triumph (Polybius 16. 23. 5).

There were occasional declutterings of commemorative monuments,[27] and in the early Principate Augustus did a more systematic clearance of such clutter, magnificent and historically significant though much of it was. He transferred many statues of famous men from the Capitoline to the Campus Martius (Suetonius, *Gaius* 34) and gradually developed his own new forum as the place for such records of distinguished military service.[28] Statues continued to accumulate in temples and other public spaces. Claudius had to confront this problem when he became emperor.[29] At the end of the first century Pliny the Younger was gratified that a senatorial friend of his (Vestricius Spurinna) had been voted a 'triumphal' statue, i.e. one showing him wearing triumphal insignia for victories in Germany. Moreover, Spurinna's young son, who had predeceased him, had also been granted a statue, partly in honour of a career begun successfully but mainly as a consolation to his bereaved father. Pliny elaborated on the wider functions of such statues (*Letters* 2. 7): they provide an object lesson (*exemplum*), aiming to win young men to a life of service ('ad bonas artes') and to persuade leading citizens to take on the responsibility of raising children. Pliny envisaged contemplating the young man's statue in the street, and summed up: 'If we get consolation from the busts of our dead set up in our homes, how much more do we get from statues in public places, which recall not only men's forms and faces but also their distinction and reputation.'

Accounts of Roman triumphs give a taste of the spectacle available to those who used the streets and public spaces of Rome, and its potential impact on young eyes and minds. The triumph-

[27] e.g. 179 BCE (see below on censor M. Aemilius Lepidus); and by the censors of 158 BCE: Pliny the Elder, *NH* 34. 30.

[28] For a detailed study of honorific statues in Rome from the early Republic to the Augustan period, see Sehlmeyer (1999).

[29] Dio 60. 5. 4–5. Claudius asserted that he would have to consider what to do with all the statues in temples and other public buildings; but there is no evidence that he stemmed the tide. In the imperial period, however, the emperor was the one who initiated the honour of a statue in a public place, and could overrule other suggestions. Bergemann (1990) provides detailed evidence for the award of even equestrian statues (a special honour) to many men beyond the imperial family in the imperial period: those of senatorial and equestrian rank and decurions of Italian town councils, but not freedmen. Hadrian honoured a number of men with statues in the Forum (Dio 69. 7. 4).

ing general wore special garb and make-up which presented him as superhuman, almost divine. The triumphal procession assembled in the Circus Flaminius, a well-demarcated space in the south of the Campus Martius (but not formally structured as later circuses were to be). This was one of the significant areas of Rome: it and the Roman Forum were the sites of most of the monuments and dedications of the Republican period, and it was a hotly contested space. It was a natural place for people to flock to, for a range of activities and to see the beginning of a triumph. There were many reminders of Roman history and exemplary individuals for those waiting around for the procession to set off. Anyone who has watched children at a procession will have seen them run to catch the procession at a number of points along the route, and we can picture Roman children doing something of the same. The precise route of the triumph is not certain, but it probably proceeded from the Circus Flaminius through the Forum Holitorium, skirting the southern slopes of the Capitoline and the Palatine hills, through the Circus Maximus, to enter the Sacred Way at its eastern end and thence through the Forum to ascend the Capitoline and finish in the temple of Jupiter Capitolinus (Fig. 7.1).[30] This route took it past temples such as those of Hercules Musarum and Pietas, built in the Circus Flaminius in the first half of the second century BCE to commemorate military victories and to house associated spoils and works of art; later there were porticoes and the theatre of Marcellus in this area; and in the Forum[31] the route went past shops, houses, and ancient temples such as those of Vesta and of Castor and Pollux. The setting enhanced the aura of success of the current *triumphator* and provided a history lesson of Rome's past achievements and notable individuals.

Triumphs came thick and fast in the first fifty years or so of the second century. They continued to be characterized by large quantities of gold and silver and bronze as bullion, coinage and manufactured goods, as well as armour and high-ranking captives. The lessons for Roman spectators were that other countries could be fabulously wealthy, that this wealth was now becoming available for the public good at Rome, that the elaborate arms of

[30] Favro (1996: 90 fig. 45) reproduces a drawing of Richard H. Abramson showing part of this suggested route. See Fig. 7.1.
[31] For development of the Forum see Purcell (1995).

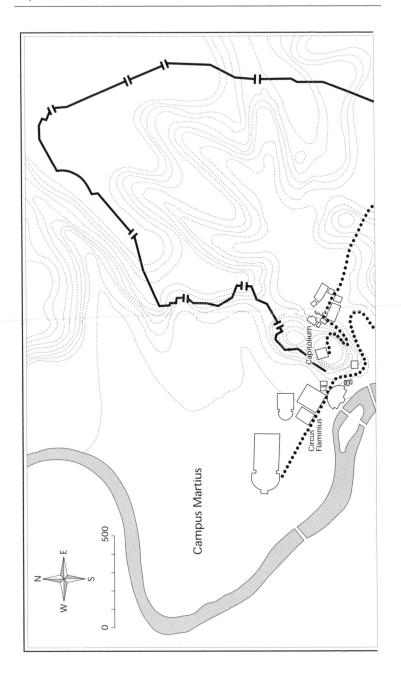

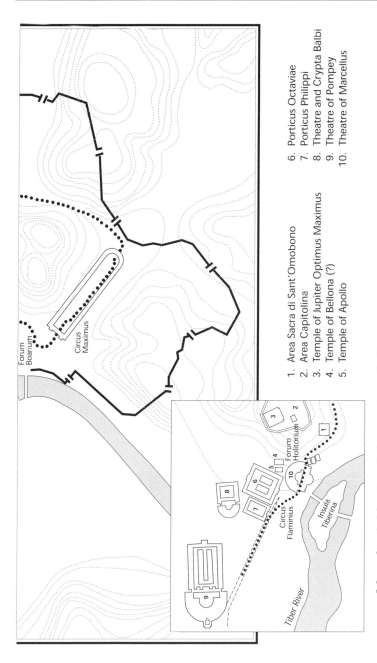

1. Area Sacra di Sant'Omobono
2. Area Capitolina
3. Temple of Jupiter Optimus Maximus
4. Temple of Bellona (?)
5. Temple of Apollo

6. Porticus Octaviae
7. Porticus Philippi
8. Theatre and Crypta Balbi
9. Theatre of Pompey
10. Theatre of Marcellus

FIG. 7.1 Map of probable triumphal route, through the south-western Campus Martius, Rome.

other powerful countries were now succumbing to Roman prowess, and that Rome was taking over leadership from the famous kings and rulers of the rest of the Mediterranean. Livy (45. 39. 4–13) referred to *tanta nomina*, 'such great names', i.e. names that resonated with history and power, when King Perseus and his sons were led as captives in 167 BCE.

These lessons were underlined in many ways by the various uses made, over time, of the spoils of triumphs. Apart from those items taken for embellishment of the generals' own homes, or deposited in the public treasury, a sizeable amount of the wealth displayed in the triumphal procession was dedicated by *triumphatores* for public entertainment and the enhancement or building of particular monuments. Inside private homes, visitors (who could be numerous, as we have seen) saw statues, inscriptions, and artworks associated with victories; in the street outside private homes, passers-by saw the decorated doorposts and trophies; and in wider public spaces inscriptions, statues, and artwork recorded the achievement of past and present *triumphatores*. All of this enhanced the standing of these families in Roman estimation, hence their power and influence. It is hardly surprising that the award of triumphs was often contested and caught up in the vigorously competitive internal politics of Rome. Examples of the interrelationship between individual and public pride are the monuments set up by a son on behalf of M. Acilius Glabrio, who triumphed over Antiochus (III) and the Aetolian League in 190 BCE. The son dedicated the temple—fittingly, to Pietas—which his father had vowed. He also erected a gilded equestrian statue of his father in the Forum Holitorium, the first gilded statue to be seen at Rome.[32]

The celebrations for victories broadened the perspective of Romans in other ways. Great games were organized, offering theatrical performances, animal shows, athletes (a new element in 187 BCE). Banquets became a popular element in these celebrations. In 167 L. Aemilius Paullus' great display of entertainment and banquets at Amphipolis (Livy 45. 32) was represented as beating the Greeks at their own game: he was a man who could not only conquer in war but could also arrange a banquet and organize games. Rome now was more than a military machine: she

[32] Livy 40. 34. 4–6; Valerius Maximus 2. 5. 1.

had acquired Greek culture. But Greek culture was also put to the service of Roman history. Artists and intellectuals came to work at Rome. M. Fuluius Nobilior took on campaign with him to Greece the poet Ennius, who then wrote a play (*Ambracia*) on the campaign and other verse compositions on Roman historical topics, as well as plays on the model of Greek tragedies.

It was in the office of censor that some Roman men took responsibility for major public works. In 179 the censors Fuluius Nobilior and M. Aemilius Lepidus had considerable funds allocated to them by the senate for a range of works (Livy 40. 51–2). These included harbour works, embellishment of temples, bridge works, a market, a basilica, porticoes, an aqueduct, and arches (*fornices*). Aemilius decluttered the surroundings of the temple of Jupiter on the Capitoline by removing statues, shields, and military standards attached to or near the surrounding columns. The aim may have been aesthetic, but all of those things would have been memorials of previous magistrates' achievements (largely in war), so Aemilius was, intentionally or otherwise, reshaping Roman history, leaving cleaner outlines for the reception of contemporary and future inhabitants of Rome.

The temples to Diana and Juno Regina which Aemilius dedicated in his censorship were in the Circus Flaminius, and the dedications were celebrated with theatrical and horse-racing games. The most remarkable building initiated by Aemilius was the Basilica Aemilia, a colonnade on the northern side of the Forum which became a virtual family monument as later generations of the Aemilii restored and expanded it (see below). The basilica was a welcome architectural development in Rome and Italian towns to cater for business and leisure, especially the spectacles and entertainment traditionally held in the Forum.[33] Our present Aemilius was also commemorated by a notable equestrian

---

[33] Vitruvius 5. 1. 1–4. The earliest basilica in Rome had been the Basilica Porcia, built by Cato the Elder as censor in 184 BCE (Livy 39. 44; Plutarch, *Cato the Elder* 19. 2). This was adjacent to the then senate-house on the western side. It was destroyed in riots over the death of Clodius in 52 BCE (Asconius on *Pro Milone*, Stangl 32). Cato attracted much criticism for the severity of his censorship. Plutarch notes particularly the criticism of the basilica: although it was rather plain compared to later basilicas, perhaps this new public facility was seen as a bid for public favour. During one of Pliny the Younger's big court cases, not only was the court area itself full but people were crammed into the upper levels of the basilica, leaning over, trying to see and hear (*Letters* 6. 33. 4).

statue in honour of his heroism as a boy. He was represented
explicitly as a boy rather than an adult (see Chapter 1 above and
Fig. 1.3). As one examines the public life of Rome, its ceremonies
and its visual context, one is struck by the frequency with which
children were before the eyes of the public, although, as we saw
above, visual representations of them in these roles were rare until
the imperial period.

Another Macedonian war, this time against King Perseus, provided another triumph, celebrated by L. Aemilius Paullus in 167.
Paullus had destroyed many of the weapons captured in the war,
but gathered together the bronze shields for shipment to Rome.
Also amassed at Amphipolis for transport was a large variety of
artistic booty, which attracted great attention from the international crowd assembled there (Livy 45. 33. 1–7). There were
statues, paintings, textiles, vessels of gold, silver, bronze, and
ivory of high craftsmanship. Some of these spoils—arms and
textiles—decorated Paullus' ship, a huge royal ship, as he sailed
up the Tiber to return to Rome. The banks of the Tiber were
lined with welcoming crowds to admire this new phenomenon. A
few days later, the other two generals involved in the war against
Perseus (Anicius and Octauius) also sailed up the Tiber, and all
three were awarded triumphs by the senate.

Paullus' triumph was challenged by appeal to the people, a
challenge fuelled by his soldiers' discontent at the size of their
share of the booty. The speech attributed to the magistrate who
defended Paullus' claim to a triumph (Livy 45. 39. 4–13) outlined
what would be missed if Paullus and his troops did not celebrate
a triumph: the sight of rich booty, enemy arms, golden statues,
marble sculpture, ivories, paintings, textiles, embossed silver,
gold, royal coinage (all destined for the treasury); the spectacle of
a distinguished and immensely wealthy king and his sons ('tanta
nomina') as captives; the sight of Paullus—twice consul and con-
queror of Greece—entering the city in his chariot; honour to the
gods, sacrificial animals, and a banquet for the senators on the
Capitoline.

Paullus did celebrate his triumph, over three days.[34] In addition to the booty already mentioned, there were the king's ships,

[34] Livy 45. 40–2; Diodorus Siculus 31. 8. 10–12; Plutarch, *Aemilius Paullus*
32–4.

of a size never before seen, beached on the shores of the Campus
Martius. Rome was not a naval power, so the impact of these
ships was all the greater. For most Roman children this was their
first sight of such ships, opening a whole new world of transma-
rine nations, wealth, and adventure. A special dock seems to have
been built for the ships, and they remained in the Tiber for many
years, as a kind of naval museum or holding-station for
hostages.[35] L. Aemilius Paullus imported talent as well as booty
to Rome. He brought back with him from Athens the artist and
philosopher Metrodorus to do the artwork for his triumph and to
be tutor to his children (Pliny the Elder, *NH* 35. 135). And he was
responsible for the transfer of Perseus' library to Rome, allowing
the two sons with him ('lovers of learning') to take it for themselves (Plutarch, *Aemilius Paullus* 28. 6).[36]

Perhaps the peak of importation of Greek art into Italy was in
146–145 BCE, when Q. Caecilius Metellus (Macedonicus) and L.
Mummius celebrated triumphs over Macedonia. In 146 Metellus
returned to Rome and celebrated a triumph for his victories in
Greece in the previous two years (Valerius Maximus 7. 5. 4). One
of the prizes which he brought back was a famous set of bronze
statues of horsemen, sculpted by Lysippus, which has become
known as the 'Granikos Monument'. Alexander the Great had set
up these statues at Dium (Dion) in Macedonia, commemorating
those of his officers (the 'Companions') who had fallen at the
Granikos battle against the Persians in 334. Metellus set them up
in Rome in his new portico complex, the Porticus Metelli, in the
Circus Flaminius,[37] which was, as we have seen, a much-
frequented space and often the assembly point for triumphs.

Stories of Alexander were widespread in the Mediterranean
world and beyond, and would have been well known to children,

[35] Polybius (36. 5. 9) reports that the 300 Carthaginian hostages brought to
Rome in 149 were held 'in the dock of the large warship with 16 banks of oars'.
(I thank Tom Hillard, of Macquarie University, for this reference.) Walbank
(1979), in his commentary on this passage, suggests that both the ship and the
dock installations were used as 'a prison for hostages'.

[36] These two sons rode in his triumphal procession. See below, under
'Festivals', for the two sets of sons in 167 BCE.

[37] Velleius Paterculus 1. 11. 3–7, 2. 1. 2; Valerius Maximus 7. 1. 1, 7. 5. 4; Pliny
the Elder, *NH* 7. 145, 34. 65. Metellus built a temple to Jupiter Stator and had
an ivory statue made of Jupiter. The Granikos statues were opposite the temples of Juno and Jupiter in the Circus Flaminius (Pliny the Elder, *NH* 36. 40).

even those who did not learn about them at school. However garbled or vague their knowledge, there was the central fact that Alexander was a heroic and glamorous king and probably the greatest general ever. Now a Roman general had taken over one of Alexander's notable monuments and it was part of the fabric of Rome: there would be a stirring of imagination, pride, and patriotism. This monument was still a notable embellishment of its site in the first century CE (Velleius Paterculus 1. 11; Pliny the Elder, *NH* 36. 40). None of the set is now extant.[38] But one can probably get some idea of what they were like by looking at an extant, nearly contemporary representation of Alexander on a marble sarcophagus (Fig. 7.2).[39] It is in a scene usually taken to depict the battle of the Issos (Syria, 333).[40] There is a similar representation in a mosaic from the House of the Faun in Pompeii, which is probably based on an original painting of *c.*330 which was also copied on South Italian vases.[41]

Lysippus sculpted many portraits of Alexander, and some of these found their way to Rome. Nero had one of Alexander as a boy (Pliny the Elder, *NH* 34. 63) and had it gilded (an 'improvement' later reversed). Pliny the Elder (*NH* 34. 64) comments on the highly lifelike quality of the Granikos portraits and the great attention to even the smallest details. The detail of the individual equestrian figures would be appreciated in Rome, where horse-riding skills were a desired accomplishment and equestrian games were popular. The heroic boy Aemilius Lepidus (see above) had been honoured with an equestrian statue, and this form of commemoration continued to be a prized honour.[42]

---

[38] But a statuette in Naples has sometimes been identified as one: *OCD³*, A. F. Stewart, *s.v.* 'Lysippus'.

[39] The 'Alexander sarcophagus' from Sidon, for King Abdalonymos, probably sculpted 320–310 BCE (Stewart 1990: 194 fig. 594).

[40] But Badian (1999) argues for Gaugamela.

[41] Stewart (1990). Here, it is not Alexander but Darius who is the main focus. Darius exemplifies a critical turning point in the fates of men: he is about to see success turn to defeat.

[42] e.g. Sulla, Pompey, Caesar, Octavian. Cicero will have had the Aemilius statue in mind, as well as these adult precedents, when he moved a vote in the senate in 43 BCE for a gilded equestrian statue to M. Aemilius Lepidus (the soon-to-be triumvir). When Metellus Scipio (consul 52 BCE) set up a 'squadron of gilded horsemen' on the Capitoline to commemorate his ancestors, Cicero criticized Scipio's incorrect use of an earlier statue to represent one of his own

FIG. 7.2 Relief of Alexander on horseback. Sarcophagus, Sidon, late fourth century BCE.

Purcell (1995: 330) has applied an apt phrase, 'cavalry culture', to late archaic Rome. This was a continuing feature of Roman culture. Games in the circus gave pride of place to horse events of various kinds. In the imperial period equestrian figures of

ancestors (*Att.* 6. 1. 17, 50 BCE). After the 1st c. BCE, equestrian statues continued to be frequent for at least a century; but they were largely monopolized by emperors and their families. See Burnett (1999: 157, 160) for an estimate of frequencies.

emperors were popular, and that of Augustus in his new forum had associations with Alexander.[43] The new festivals established by Augustus, Nero, and Domitian all included equestrian competitions.[44] Equestrian displays were also popular, and, although horse riding and manoeuvres were an elite activity, they were clearly a favourite spectator sport and surely popular with boys irrespective of whether they themselves were likely to be able to participate. Various festivals and ceremonies provided such spectacle: see below on the Troy Game. And Juvenal's picture (1. 59–62) of a youth galloping along the Via Flaminia to impress his girlfriend indicates that horse riding was also a favourite form of private recreation. Festivals and art reinforced the ideals, ambitions, and historical perspective of young boys.

Plunder from the Greek world (including Sicily) continued to be brought to Rome and displayed in public spaces well into the first century BCE, as generals used the splendour of their triumphs and their public generosity to enhance their reputations and power. But supplies were dwindling, so copies were made more frequently and new works commissioned. Captured wealth continued to be an important element in Roman triumphs, but Rome had become clearly wealthier than most other nations in the world, and much of her wealth now derived from regular taxes from the provinces. So generals and magistrates looked to make their mark with enduring physical monuments. Temples continued to be important, but Pompey's theatre, the new Basilica Aemilia, and Caesar's forum took Rome into a new phase of public facilities and urban splendour.

Triumphs continued to be important in the Principate. The fact that from Augustus' time full triumphs came to be restricted to the emperor or members of his family did not diminish the public's interest in them. In spite of the widespread Roman Peace, many emperors found it important to present themselves as

---

[43] A statue of Augustus in a four-horse chariot was voted to him by the senate (*RG* 35), and in the new forum there were two pictures, by Apelles, featuring Alexander: one of War and a triumphant Alexander, and one of Alexander riding triumphantly in a chariot in a scene paralleled by the statue group of Augustus (Pliny the Elder, *NH* 35. 27. 93–4).

[44] The *Sebaste*, *Neronia*, and *Capitolia* festivals.

triumphatores.[45] Wealth and exotic spoil continued to be an important element,[46] but symbolic elements were also emphasized, such as the expansion of empire under Claudius and Trajan and the captured Jewish *sacra* under Vespasian and Titus. The ever-increasing public works were no longer associated so closely with military victories. A triumph was for entertainment, for the stirring of national pride, and for strengthening loyalty to the imperial family. The emperor provided banquets throughout the city (again using the neighbourhoods, the *uici*, as bases), as well as graphic displays of Roman valour and the geographical extent of Rome's victories. Josephus, who was present at the triumph of Vespasian and Titus in 71 CE, reported that the whole population turned out for the parade: 'When the day had been announced on which the triumphal procession would take place, no one of that countless population in the city was left at home. All streamed forth and took up every position where they could get a foothold, leaving free only the space necessary for passage of those on whom they were to gaze' (*Jewish War* 7. 122). One must allow for exaggeration and flattery, and no doubt there were some in Rome too indifferent or overworked to attend; but Josephus gives a credible account of the general atmosphere of enthusiasm and pride.

Claudius might seem to us one of the most un-martial of the Roman emperors, but his triumph in 44 CE was important to him for his reputation and was celebrated with great elaborateness ('magno apparatu': Suetonius, *Claudius* 17). He had made a successful expedition to Britain in 43 and expanded the Roman Empire by making Britain a new province. Provincial governors and exiles were invited to come to Rome for the triumph. The procession included those men who had won 'triumphal decorations' (*triumphalia ornamenta*) in the British expedition, and one

---

[45] In the first two centuries: Claudius, Vespasian, Titus, Domitian, Trajan, Marcus Aurelius, Commodus, out of thirteen emperors after Augustus (not counting the short-term emperors of the year 68); and Antoninus Pius accepted acclamation as *imperator* for extending the Roman frontier in Britain north of Hadrian's Wall.

[46] e.g. in the triumph of Vespasian and Titus, after the Jewish War, there were Eastern art and tapestries and the invaluable fittings of the Temple at Jerusalem (Josephus, *Jewish War* 7. 132–50). Trajan brought back much bullion from his victories in two Dacian wars.

of those (M. Crassus Frugi) was allowed the special privilege of wearing the palm-embroidered garment of a victor and riding a decorated horse ('equo phalerato et in ueste palmata') because this was the second time he had received the honour. Claudius' coinage of 46–7, gold and silver,[47] records the triumphal arch planned to commemorate his triumph: the single span supported an equestrian statue of the emperor between trophies, which included the naval crown with ships' beaks to represent his conquest of Ocean, and the inscription proclaimed the victory over the British, 'DE BRITANN(is)'. This was the first military triumph celebrated in Rome for many years and the first by a reigning emperor since 29 BCE. Thus for most Romans, and for all children, it was a unique spectacle. Claudius' 2-year-old son was associated with the victory by being given the title 'Britannicus'. Claudius also catered to the taste for visual representation by presenting a pageant on the Campus Martius showing the storming and sacking of a fortified town and the surrender of the British kings. Claudius presided over this in the cloak of a general (*paludamentum*).[48]

In 66 Nero welcomed Tiridates to Rome to crown him king of Armenia. It was a diplomatic triumph rather than a military one, but the event was staged with all the pomp and pride of the formal Roman triumph.[49] Tiridates' splendid procession had attracted crowds throughout his long journey from the East, and in many towns in Italy young and old witnessed this as he made his way down from the north to Naples and then to Rome. This kind of display helped Italy share in the emotion of the occasion—great spectacle, and symbols of great wealth and power making their way to subject themselves to the emperor at Rome—and contributed to the favourable reputation which Nero enjoyed outside Rome. At Rome itself, large crowds gathered in

---

[47] *RIC*[2] I. p. 123 nos. 30, 33–4.

[48] Suetonius, *Claudius* 21. Claudius also added spoils (*hostilia spolia*) and the naval crown to the civic crown on the gable of his house on the Palatine. On Britannicus, see below under 'Festivals'.

[49] Suetonius, *Nero* 13; Dio 63. 2–7. From the year 66 Nero's coins have 'IMP(erator)' before his name, to indicate his victory in the Parthian question; and coin types celebrate the closing of the gates of the temple of Janus, the award of a triumphal arch, Securitas, and Victory (*BMCRE* I, pp. clxvi–clxxiv and 230–47).

the Forum to watch the coronation ceremony, which included
Tiridates' handing over to Nero, as hostages, the young sons of
the royal house which ruled Parthia, Media, and Armenia. The
visual impact was great, especially as a new generation was viewing triumphal proceedings for the first time. At the games in
Pompey's theatre later, the setting was lavishly decorated, providing evidence of Rome's wealth and cultural achievement. In the
Forum, the emperor sat on the Rostra in full triumphal garb,
military standards positioned around him; the senate was in
attendance; the Praetorian Guard was drawn up in full armour
round the Forum; and the king in his own ceremonial robes made
obeisance before the emperor. The king was raised to his feet and
crowned, and subsequently returned to rebuild his capital city
Artaxata with Roman help; but the young foreign princes
remained at Rome, providing a visual and mental lesson for all of
how Rome incorporated the power of the rest of the world.

Vespasian and Titus presented another staging of the high
points in a war, even grander than Claudius', as part of their
triumph in the Jewish War (Josephus, *Jewish War* 7. 139–47).
Vespasian had been associated with Claudius' successes in Britain
and, decorated with triumphal insignia (Suetonius, *Vespasian* 4),
will have been part of Claudius' triumphal procession in 44. His
son Titus, 4 years old at the time, had particular reason to
remember with pride and admiration Claudius' triumph and displays. In the displays of 71, elaborate machinery, richly decked,
was the base for representations of battles, storming of cities, and
general devastation. Children love any spectacular display, and
these graphic and extravagant pageants of Roman victories not
only excited their senses but carried clear messages of Roman valour, wealth, and supremacy. Did they also excite pity? Josephus
himself, a captured Jew who had come to live at Rome as an honoured intellectual, hinted at the pathos of the Jewish scenes (and
the element of Jewish responsibility in the war): hands raised in
helpless supplication, temples aflame, homes demolished, rivers
no longer sustaining agriculture, men, or animals but flowing
across a country which was in flames on all sides, 'sufferings the
Jews brought on themselves when they committed themselves to
war' (*Jewish War* 7. 145). We can only guess at children's reaction
to such a pageant, but Jewish children must have been, at best,
ambivalent. If children took the lead from their parents' reaction,

Jewish children's parents who were recent immigrants may well have grieved at the destruction of their homeland. We do not know to what extent their children identified with the ethnic and religious character of Jews. If they had been in Rome long enough, perhaps born there, they might have been so well conditioned that even they accepted the message that Rome was invincible and that any attacks on the Roman Peace were counterproductive.[50]

The more lasting memorials of the Jewish War, however, provided a more positive, more generally acceptable image of Roman victory, focusing less on bloody scenes of battle than on the concepts of peace and victory. Vespasian's Temple of Peace, internally, celebrated the victory in the Jewish War by being the depository of much of the spoil from that war, but internally and externally it also glorified the consequent peace and the cultural benefits which that brought. Its elegant, peaceful setting included gardens and porticoes, and it housed notable collections of art and books. It was described by Pliny the Elder as 'one of the three most beautiful buildings the world has ever seen' (*NH* 36. 102). Titus' arch, commemorating success in the Jewish War, chose to record in its sculpture the Jewish *sacra* and Titus in his triumphal chariot rather than bloody scenes of battle. The arch, with inscription and sculpture, remained the preferred form of military commemoration. Most emperors had such arches erected, although only a few remain, notably those of Septimius Seuerus and Constantine. The columns which some emperors chose for the record of their military successes provided greater scope than did arches for narrative and graphic detail. The two extant columns, of Trajan and Marcus Aurelius,[51] portray Roman victories on the northern frontiers. There are ferocious scenes of battle, but also scenes of captive women and children which are, to a modern eye, full of pathos (see Chapter 1 and Fig. 1.13); but the effect on the population of ancient Rome, including children, is more difficult to assess.

---

[50] There were local concentrations of Jewish communities in parts of Rome, especially across the Tiber, which could strengthen a sense of solidarity. See MacMullen (1974: 180 n. 92); Leon (1995); Noy (2000: 157–284).

[51] See Becatti (1957, 1982); and Kleiner (1992: 214–20, 295–301) with further references.

The temple of Jupiter on the Capitoline, the focus of triumphal processions, was the largest and most sacred monument in Republican Rome. Frequent fires over a long period, in the Republic and in the Principate, provided an opportunity for more splendid restorations (but always within traditional guidelines). The civil war battles of 83 BCE severely damaged the temple, including the ancient terracotta image by Volca of Veii. A new image of gold and ivory was made, based on that of Zeus at Olympia.[52] The prestige attached to rebuilding and rededicating the temple after 83 caused much political infighting. Catulus had made significant progress by 69 BCE, but not enough to prevent a move by Caesar in 62 to transfer the responsibility to Pompey (fresh from his victory over King Mithridates in the East).[53] Again, in the first century CE, the rebuilding of this temple after civil war occasioned much public ritual. There was great ceremony involved in clearing and rededicating the site in 70–1 CE. Tacitus (who would have been present) later described part of the ceremony of 70 in graphic detail,[54] and Vespasian insisted on being personally involved when he returned from the East, removing the first load of debris by his own hand (Suetonius, *Vespasian* 8). In little more than ten years (in the year 80) the temple was again damaged by fire, and finishing its rebuilding was one of the first duties undertaken by Domitian when he became emperor (Dio 66. 24. 2). The Flavians repeatedly displayed this temple on their coinage: Vespasian almost every year until 76, when the restoration was probably complete, and then Titus and Domitian.[55] Their image was closely associated with this monument: they aimed to be identified in the public consciousness with its triumphal, religious, and architectural glories, and it was visible to all from most parts of Rome.

Most of the city's building activities provided scope for the many artists now resident in Italy, especially in Rome. Temples, of course, housed statues of gods and goddesses, which continued to be an important part of the artistic output (*NH* 36. 34–5). Some

---

[52] Stewart (1990: 230); cf. figs. 859/372–5.

[53] Suetonius, *Iulius* 15. The move failed, and Catulus seems to have finalized the project by the time he died in 60 BCE.

[54] *Histories* 4. 53: see below, under 'Festivals'.

[55] Vespasian: *BMCRE* 2, pp. 133, 144, 155, 158, 160, 168; Titus in 80–1: p. 261; Domitian (perhaps) 94–6: p. 346 and Statius, *Siluae* 1. 6. 100.

of the art being used to embellish other public spaces may have been purely decorative. Even purely decorative art carried a message of prosperity and power, and mythological scenes will have lent themselves to readings not fully accessible to modern commentators. Other art, however, had more explicit historical or moral messages, some from Rome's own history. The historical reliefs which developed from the first century BCE reflect a growing interest in using art of this kind for didactic purpose.

One of the earliest examples of a Roman historical relief is that on one side of the 'Ahenobarbus altar', found in the Circus Flaminius and dating perhaps to about 70 BCE (Wiseman 1974) but possibly the early 90s.[56] On three sides it has mythological scenes (of the marriage of Neptune and Amphitrite). On the fourth side are scenes of a Roman census and a sacrifice.[57] This combination of mythology and history is puzzling and slightly jarring, but Wiseman has proposed an attractive explanation and identification. He attributes it to L. Gellius, censor in 70 BCE, whose genealogy claimed a link with Neptune and the world of the sea and whose career laid some claim to naval achievement. Thus the altar 'shows us how a Roman statesman, and one thoroughly imbued with his ancestral traditions, wished to project himself to the citizens of Rome—half as a censor, half as the descendant of Greek sea-nymphs'. 'The men of the late Republic lived simultaneously in two worlds, and took seriously the idioms of each.'[58]

The Basilica Aemilia, whose origin in 179 BCE we have noted, was used to enhance the role of the Aemilii family in Roman history over many generations. In 78 BCE, the consul M. Aemilius Lepidus (father of the later triumvir) was involved in an ambitious reconstruction of the Basilica, adding an extra colonnade and an upper storey. Shields were attached to the horizontal

[56] A date in the early 90s would attribute the altar to M. Antonius, censor in 97, who had won naval victories in 101. Torelli (1982: 5–16) argues for the traditional attribution to Cn. Domitius Ahenobarbus, censor in 115 BCE.

[57] See Stewart (1990: 228–9 and figs. 843–6) for illustration and discussion.

[58] This is an attractive and persuasive hypothesis for the mind-set of the elite. Wallace-Hadrill (1998) applies a similar approach, using the concept of code-switching. There has been other discussion recently of how mythological representations worked in Rome, but the impact of mythological scenes in public spaces on the sub-elite, and especially on children, needs to be further explored.

courses between the upper and the lower colonnades.[59] Similar shields were also attached to his house (Pliny the Elder, *NH* 35. 12). These shields provided their own visual history lesson. They purported to bear the images of those who had owned and used them.[60] The monument combined family and national history; and the long-standing statue of the boy Aemilius, on the Capitoline hill above, enabled children to identify more closely with the events and values represented. From the late 50s BCE the Basilica was lavishly rebuilt, receiving columns of imported variegated marble, circular arches to make it a real arcade, gaining an extra aisle, and having the New Shops incorporated into it (Dio 49. 42). This was a stunning monument, in one of the busiest and most cosmopolitan parts of the Forum: here money-changers operated, and the magistrate in charge of foreigners' law cases (the *praetor peregrinus*) had his tribunal nearby. The wooden ceiling of the building made it fire-prone, like many other buildings in Rome. A fire in 14 BCE provided the opportunity for a sumptuous restoration. Augustus took an interest in this, and had a portico built into it in honour of his grandsons and now adopted sons Gaius and Lucius Caesar. This busy thoroughfare was an ideal place to advertise the new young male members of Augustus' house: Augustus virtually took over another family's monument for his own family—indeed dynasty.[61] In the mid-first century CE Pliny the Elder described the Basilica as one

[59] His son advertised this on his coinage (*denarii*) of 61 BCE, e.g. *BMCRR* I, no. 3650; *RRC* 419/3b.

[60] Pliny the Elder calls this a martial practice, a special mark of *uirtus*. He identifies Appius Claudius, the consul of 495 BCE, as the initiator of this practice. Claudius included representations in miniature of children of his family: such inclusion of children, says Pliny, particularly attracts popular favour. Cf. Ch. 1 above.

[61] The Basilica continued to be associated with the Aemilian name, which was recognized by Tiberius in 22 CE when another Lepidus sought permission to refurbish it from his own (comparatively modest) means (Tacitus, *Annals* 3. 72, using the name for the new Basilica, 'basilica Pauli', but describing it as *Aemilia monumenta*). Tiberius associated himself with new work on the Basilica and with the portico to Gaius and Lucius Caesar, perhaps to strengthen the legitimacy of his succession as a Julian. The inscription which is partially extant, recording Lucius as *princeps iuuentutis* and as consul-elect at age 14, is usually attributed to Augustus; but C. B. Rose (1997: 31) has recently revived the argument of Panciera (1969) that it was due to Tiberius (*CIL* 6. 36908; cf. Suetonius, *Augustus* 29. 4).

of the three most beautiful buildings in the world (*NH* 36. 102; along with Vespasian's Temple of Peace (see above) and the Forum of Augustus (*NH* 36. 102)). It had continued to reflect glory on the descendants of the Aemilii Lepidi, but this may have done the family more harm than good. They could be seen as real competitors to the reigning Julio-Claudians, and suffered many disasters. The name and other descendants had died out by 65 CE (Syme 1986: 192, 283).

Agrippa's large programme of public works under Augustus provided many functional and instructive monuments. One of the most remarkable was his map of the world, and Augustus took responsibility for seeing this through to completion after Agrippa died (*NH* 3. 17). Agrippa's map reinforced, in a more enduring way, the impact of maps and geographical sketches displayed previously in Roman triumphs: Rome ruled most of the known world; the world was Roman.[62] In Pompey's triumph of 61 BCE he had displayed inscriptions listing the fourteen nations and the pirates conquered, and much was made of his conquests on three continents (Plutarch, *Pompey* 45); he summed up his trophies as representing the conquest of the whole world, the *oikoumene* (Dio 37. 21. 2). In 46 a statue was erected on the Capitoline to Julius Caesar with a globe at his feet.[63]

Agrippa's map was a much more ambitious and permanent visual representation than its predecessors of the world being conquered by the Romans. Agrippa saw it as the presentation of the world for the view of the people of Rome,[64] and he planned it in great detail. If his aim was for the Roman public to view this and learn from it, it had to be in a well-frequented area. It was

[62] For several generations of modern children in many parts of the world, maps of the British Empire used to have the same effect: the 'red bits' dominated the picture of much of the known world. For a reconstruction of Agrippa's map, see Moynihan (1985). Models (*simulacra*) of captured cities had been displayed in Roman triumphs from early on, e.g. in M. Marcellus' ovation over Syracuse in 211 BCE (Livy 26. 21. 7). It continued beyond Agrippa's time, e.g. in Germanicus' triumph of 17 CE (Tacitus, *Annals* 2. 41) and in the pageants of Claudius and of Vespasian and Titus (see above). Agrippa's map provided a point of reference for later displays.

[63] See Weinstock (1971: 35–59) for representations of the world associated with Pompey and Caesar; specifically pp. 42–5 on the globe. For Caesar's plans for a world map, see Wiseman (1992: 22–42).

[64] 'orbem terrarum urbi spectandum': Pliny the Elder, *NH* 3. 17.

designed to be part of a portico in an area below the Quirinal, bordering what was known as the 'Campus Agrippae'. This area has not been well excavated, but we know that after Agrippa's death (12 BCE) his sister Vipsania developed his plan in the Porticus Vipsania and that Augustus took responsibility for the completion.[65] This may have been associated with the dedication of Augustus' new forum in 2 BCE.[66] Augustus had already provided the means for estimating the size of the Roman empire with his 'Golden Milestone', showing the distances to various parts of the empire. Agrippa's map was part of an elegant new portico, set in parklands, to attract Romans to visit—families at leisure or on their way to festivals and processions. Nicolet (1991: 114) sees the map as an essential ingredient in the projection of Augustus as leader and pacifier of the world (*orbis terrarum*). Augustus may have tried to persuade a poet to apply his talent to projecting this image. 'It is a subject worthy of an epic poem. But it would be fulfilled not in poetry, but by means of the *Res Gestae*, the *Forum Augustum*—and the map of Agrippa.' Nicolet draws attention to the role of such a map in the education of the young—in expanding their mental horizons and in inspiring pride in Rome's glorious past and the present emperor's exploits—by quoting from a speech made by a rhetorician (Eumenius) in the late third century CE for the restoration of school buildings at Augustodunum (modern Autun) in Gaul. Eumenius stresses the importance of the porticoes near these buildings, in which are representations of places and their names from all over the Roman world. He recognizes that the young 'learn more clearly with their eyes what they comprehend less readily by their ears', and he summarizes the impact of such geographical displays thus: 'For now, now at last it is a delight to see a picture of the world, since we see nothing in it which is not ours'.[67]

The interest in the wider world was reflected in the growing taste for shows of exotic animals, and this interest was matched

---

[65] Dio 55. 8. 3–4, where Augustus is given credit for making the Campus Agrippae public property. Cf. 54. 29. 4 for Agrippa's provision for this in his will.

[66] See Nicolet (1991: 110–14) on the political role of Agrippa's map.

[67] *Panegyric* IX (20. 2–21. 3) of *XII Panegyrici Latini*, ed. R. A. B. Mynors, Oxford 1964. Translation by Nixon (1994), with useful commentary.

in art. A south Italian artist of the late Republic, Pasitiles,[68] visited the docks on the Tiber to observe the wild animals being imported and to make sketches for his metal engravings. On one visit to lions and panthers from Africa, he was attacked by one of the animals, which had got loose.[69]

Rome's passion for sculptural decoration of almost every public space meant not only that there were friezes, paintings, and statues incorporated in all new buildings but that valuable collections of art were on view in temples, forums, theatres, baths, basilicas, and in the increasing number of public libraries. When Asinius Pollio built the first public library in Rome after his military triumph in 39 BCE, he brought together in it a fine collection of marble statues and other art to which he was keen to attract public viewers. Works of Praxitiles and his son and of Scopas were there. There were representations of Jupiter, and the themes seem to have been largely mythological.[70] But in libraries from Pollio's time there were also busts (*imagines*) of famous intellectuals, echoing the literary works collected in the library (*NH* 35. 9–10). Only older and privileged children were likely to visit public libraries, but for them the busts reinforced the respect due to intellectual figures of the past. In Pollio's library the only contemporary man honoured with such a bust (*imago*) was Varro (Pliny the Elder, *NH* 7. 115).

The plethora of new buildings and monuments in the imperial period provided opportunities for sculptural decoration, often in a great variety of expensive materials, particularly marbles. Many friezes contained moral or historical lessons. In the first part of the second century CE, friezes in Trajan's forum[71] were of huge proportions: Kleiner (1992: 220–3) speaks of 'a one-hundred-foot-long monumental frieze with figures ten feet tall'. They probably celebrated victories in the Dacian wars, but parts

[68] Pliny the Elder, *NH* 36. 40. Pasitiles was one of those who obtained Roman citizenship in the widespread grants to regions of Italy after the 'Social War' of 89–88 BCE.

[69] See below on animal shows as entertainment.

[70] Pliny the Elder, *NH* 36. 33–34, 23–5. Similarly, the art in the Portico of Octavia, which was dedicated in 11 BCE, was largely of gods and goddesses; but there were also figures of legend and two associations with Alexander (Pliny the Elder, *NH* 35. 114, 139; 36. 15, 22–5, 33–5).

[71] On the basilica or temple at the northern end; probably commissioned or finished by Hadrian.

were incorporated into the arch of Constantine in the fourth
century. The figure of Trajan on horseback in battle is reminiscent of representations of Alexander. Other arches carried friezes
focusing on emperors' civic or military achievements.

Living so much, as they did, in the public areas of their towns
and cities, the people of Italy will have become very familiar with
the monuments around them and taken note of new ones as they
were added. The extent to which they extracted the full symbolic
value of monuments and ceremonies depended on their education, status, and age or experience. Older members of the
population remembered the origin and associations of older monuments, although tradition could not but be modified or distorted
as older residents passed on their memories and comments to the
young. The more educated members of the population, young or
old, were in the best position to appreciate the mythological or
historical nuances of friezes, dedications, ceremonies, and monuments. Writers, especially historians, drew on this familiarity to
add resonances to their stories and arguments. Cicero was a master at exploiting this in his speeches, and he adapted his allusions
to his audience.[72]

The religious and superstitious associations of the city were
always strong and could be awakened in members of all classes.
During the 'Catilinarian affair' which extended over 65–62 BCE,
portents were eagerly seized upon. In 64, lightning struck several
monuments on the Capitoline hill, alarming residents of Rome.
The destruction of a statue of Jupiter was a particularly visible
sign of divine anger, which required sacrifices to be offered to
expiate such wrath, and a new, larger statue of Jupiter had to be
erected. The potency of such a statue is clear in the decision to
place it in a position looking east down the Forum, towards the
rising sun, 'so that those plans which had been formed secretly
against the safety of the city and empire would be revealed for the
understanding of the Roman senate and people'.[73] Addressing
the public in the Forum, Cicero repeatedly gestured to the new
statue which they could see above them and which, fortuitously,
had been set in place only that very December morning in 63 BCE

---

[72] See Vasaly (1993) for many examples. She is concerned (p. 7) with the
effect on an audience of 'the ambiance in which a speech takes place'. She asks,
'What role might the representation of places and things play in oratory?'

[73] Cicero, *Against Catiline* 3. 20; Dio 37. 9.

when the conspiracy had been exposed. Cicero attributed Rome's salvation to Jupiter himself. Thanksgivings had been decreed and Cicero urged his audience to celebrate them, with wives and children.[74] Children who lived through that episode were young adults in the turmoil of the 40s BCE and took with them a strong sense of the evil of sacrilege and the importance of respecting and propitiating the gods. The maintenance and exploitation of the city's physical fabric and rituals reinforced this outlook.

Public alarm at the continuing disruptions and violence of the 50s BCE was fuelled by further damage to public monuments. Once civil war had broken out in 49 such portents increased, and again damage to religious and civic monuments on the Capitoline was seen as particularly sinister (Dio 41. 14). When Caesar emerged from the civil war as victor, his assumption of potentially divine trappings may have offended some members of the upper classes, but for much of the population his role as a bringer of peace and healing was enhanced by the erection of fine new statues of him and their association with Rome's traditional gods (Dio 43. 45).

The recognizability and importance of statues of distinguished mortals are obvious from the anger vented on some of them at times of crisis, when these individuals were in disfavour. In 49, gilded equestrian statues on the Rostra of Pompey and Sulla—both perceived as enemies of Caesar in past or present times—were destroyed by angry mobs. But Caesar had these statues re-erected;[75] they had a role to play in restoring the continuity of Roman history and establishing Caesar's place in a long historical tradition. Augustus was to make similar but much more extensive use of visual reminders of previous Roman history, especially in his new forum. These uses of human and divine representations helped mould children's attitudes to the good and the bad in public life. They learned of the power of religion, and their perception of history was affected by the erection or destruction of monuments of individual men.

---

[74] Cicero, *Against Catiline* 3. 21. Cicero's references to the setting: 'illud signum' twice in 3. 20; 'ille Iuppiter', 'haec templa' 3. 22; 'Iouem illum' 29. Cf. his *On the Command of Cn. Pompeius* 70 (66 BCE), also delivered from the Rostra in the Forum: 'I call all the gods to witness—especially those who watch over this place, this hallowed spot, and who especially see into the minds of all those who enter on public life'.

[75] Suetonius, *Iulius* 75. 4; Dio 42. 18. 2, 43. 49. 1.

Julius Caesar went on to appropriate the symbolism of public space on a broad front, and in this he was followed by the whole series of Roman emperors. His new arcade, the Basilica Iulia, was to provide enlarged space for civic activities, but especially for the lawcourts.[76] This visible sign of the restoration and strengthening of law and order sent an important message to the population of Rome and beyond. It offered promise of a secure and honoured career ahead to the youths training to be orators. (Cicero in his late teens had despaired of a public career while the courts were shut in a period of turmoil and civil war.) Caesar's new basilica was to match the long-established Basilica Aemilia across the Forum, rivalling the achievements of a long line of distinguished members of the Aemilian family. Augustus completed the Basilica Iulia as Caesar's heir and the continuer of the Julian family name.

The enormous building programme of Augustus, over his long life, is well known. Temples (new or restored) were a constant element. They had been a constant element in buildings undertaken by generals and magistrates during most of the Republic, but Augustus established a monopoly over temple-building during his regime (Beard, North, and Price 1998: 196). His temples ranged from that of Mars Ultor vowed in 43 BCE (and dedicated in 2 BCE), to the eighty-two restored and others built in 28 BCE, to the new shrine to Vesta on the Palatine when Augustus became *pontifex maximus* in 12 BCE, and various restorations still in train at his death and continued by Tiberius. The temple to the deified Julius Caesar was the precedent for those to many deified emperors, often in the Forum.[77] Other notable additions to the cityscape under Octavian-Augustus included the voting-enclosure (the Saepta) planned by Caesar for the Campus Martius, the refurbished senate-house (the Curia Iulia),

---

[76] Quintilian (12. 5. 6) refers to the centumviral court in action here in the second half of the 1st c. CE. It was an acoustical challenge to speakers when several courts were in action at the same time: Quintilian praises an ex-consul who made his voice heard above all the ambient noise.

[77] From Claudius on, some imperial women were also deified. Livia was associated with the temple of Diuus Augustus. Hadrian's mother-in-law Matidia and Antoninus Pius' wife Faustina the Elder had their own temples dedicated to them (although the name of Faustina's husband was later added to the inscription).

numerous porticoes (often including impressive art galleries),[78] several public libraries, two new theatres, an amphitheatre, aqueducts and bridges and refurbishment of major highways, with the Golden Milestone erected at the western end of the Forum in 20 BCE to mark Rome's position at the centre of a web of communications.[79] The impact of these buildings and monuments, and especially the temples, on the Roman skyline might be better appreciated by comparison with another city less high-rise than those of the twenty-first century, such as early eighteenth-century London. Rebuilding after the Great Fire of 1666 was undertaken with great energy, overseen by the king (Charles II) and Christopher Wren. Of the eighty-seven churches destroyed, fifty-two were rebuilt; Augustus had rebuilt all eighty-two requiring restoration in 28 BCE (*RG* 20). Canaletto's paintings of the Thames embankment in 1750–1 show the sky bristling with the spires of newly restored churches (Fig. 7.3). Rome offered many perspectives for Augustus' new and restored temples to make similar impact on the inhabitants of Rome.

The city was embellished with many statues. These were increasingly of Augustus in various roles and guises, but many remained of other distinguished citizens. A definitive set of statues commemorating Rome's history and legends was erected in the new forum of Augustus. Triumphal arches and a column appeared (Appian, *Civil Wars* 5. 54), most (but not all) honouring Augustus or members of his family. To complement the image of military victory, the bringing of peace was celebrated by the closing of the gates of the Temple of Janus in the Forum[80] and the dedication of the richly sculptured Altar of Peace. Notable amongst public inscriptions were the consular and triumphal lists (*fasti*) inscribed on Augustus' triple Parthian arch of 19 BCE in the Forum: these were records of a long series of civic and military achievements.

[78] e.g. the porticus of Octavia in the Circus Flaminius, which contained a bilingual library and a large collection of works of art. Pliny the Elder (*NH* 35. 114, 139; 36. 15, 22) cites paintings and statues and adds other works of art in nearby temples (*NH* 36. 214, 34–5).

[79] The *Milliarium Aureum* was a gilded bronze pillar inscribed with the names of cities of the empire and distances: Dio 54. 8. Cf. above on Agrippa's map.

[80] Three times: 30 BCE, 25, and another (unknown) date.

FIG. 7.3   London and the Thames river, mid-eighteenth century. Painting by Canaletto.

Agrippa played a leading role in the public works programme, and his new baths on the Campus Martius (which contained notable artwork[81]) were an impressive addition to the recreational and aesthetic life of Rome. Other citizens had contributed monuments early in Augustus' reign, but increasingly Augustus established his monopoly of such works in Rome. Some citizens diverted their wealth and ambitions for display to the building of massive tombs on the edge of the city, such as the pyramid-shaped tomb of Cestius, the drum tomb of Caecilia Metella, the idiosyncratic sculpted one of the baker-contractor Eurysaces (for himself and his wife), and the *columbaria* of dependants, mostly freedmen and freedwomen, of leading citizens.[82] Augustus himself understood the impact of such sepulchres and began his own mausoleum very early (28 BCE). Country towns benefited from the generosity and ambition of individual citizens who could no longer indulge in public buildings at Rome.[83] Private homes, in Rome and elsewhere, continued to be embellished with fine art, which enhanced their owners' power and prestige.[84]

City buildings thus continued to testify to the importance of religious, political, and military activities in Roman life, and they provided new opportunities for cultural interests, recreation, and entertainment. Roads, bridges, and the Golden Milestone promoted the perception in the Augustan period that Rome was the centre of a large world, and the increasing beauty of the city strengthened this perception for residents and visitors alike. A strong sense of history, and Rome's important place in it, was fostered by the commemorative monuments of individual Romans and the organization and embellishment of public spaces such as the forums and the Campus Martius. Numerous inscriptions—honorific, funerary, religious, and civic—reinforced this impact, their very form impressing even those who could not read them. When Caesar moved and rededicated the Rostra in the Forum in 44 BCE he included the bronze inscription of Rome's foundation law code, the Twelve Tables. This was believed to date from the fifth century, but must have been reinscribed after the fourth-

---

[81] Pliny the Elder, *NH* 34. 62, 35. 26, 36. 189.

[82] e.g. of Drusus the Elder, L. Arruntius, Marcella, T. Statilius Taurus, Livia.

[83] See Eck (1997) for some examples from the 1st and 2nd centuries.

[84] Cf. pp. 278–9.

century Gallic sack of Rome and numerous disasters. Children knew of the Twelve Tables from an early age and many had once learnt them by heart at school.[85] The public display of this set of laws, on the same platform as statues of distinguished military and civic leaders, proclaimed the law as one of the basic elements of Roman society.[86] Early in the first year of the Flavian government (70 CE), a senatorial commission set about re-establishing 'the laws' and reinstating them in their public places on bronze tablets. Once Vespasian had arrived back in Rome he took in hand the reinscribing and replacement on the Capitoline of 3,000 bronze tablets containing important historical records: 'decrees of the senate and decisions of the people on alliances, treaties, and individual privileges' (Suetonius, *Vespasian* 8).[87] After the damage and destruction of civil war these were signs of a return to normality and a visible token of restoration of a foundation of Roman public life. Simpler but similar messages were conveyed by the pictorial language and the lettering on Roman coins. The curiosity and interest of children had much to stimulate them, and those of impressionable ages had their perceptions of themselves and their society shaped by their material context.

Fires, floods, and lightning were amongst the natural disasters which continually damaged the city fabric and provided the need for restorations, rebuilding, and improved administration.[88] These were the main concerns of the Julio-Claudian emperors, until in the 60s Nero took advantage of a devastating fire in Rome to go well beyond normal restoration work. He had already given attention to places of recreation and entertainment. His new baths (the first since Agrippa) incorporated a gymnasium for athletic exercises, still a comparative novelty in Rome, and were

[85] Cicero, *On the Laws* 2. 59, says that no one learns them 'now', i.e. at the end of the Republic in the 40s BCE. Diodorus Siculus (12. 26) reports seeing the Twelve Tables on Caesar's Rostra.

[86] The Forum was also the setting for lawcourt cases, many of which continued to be held in this public place well into the imperial period.

[87] Tacitus (*Histories* 4. 40) attributes the damage to the passage of time: a senatorial commission was established 'qui aera legum uetustate delapsa noscerent figerentque'. Suetonius attributes the destruction of the bronze tablets in the temple of Jupiter on the Capitoline to the civil war.

[88] e.g. a serious flood in 15 CE; fires in 27, 36, 64, 80 and 192 CE; an earthquake in Campania in 62, followed by the eruption of Mt. Vesuvius in 79.

of unprecedented splendour.[89] His amphitheatre and circus provided new public facilities for entertainment and display.

The years from the Flavians to the Antonines were a high peak of building activity in Rome and Italy.[90] There was great emphasis on entertainment, for instance in baths and amphitheatres. It is notable that the town of Pompeii, after the earthquake of 62 CE, gave priority to rebuilding the amphitheatre and baths rather than theatres and other public buildings.[91] In Rome, the Flavians exploited the populist symbolism of building the biggest amphitheatre of all (the Flavian Amphitheatre, later known as the Colosseum) on the site of the ornamental lake of Nero's Golden House. Domitian continued to balance military reputation and cultural development in his reign, in processions and festivals, in new buildings such as the Odeum (for musical and oratorical performances), and the library collection in the Portico of Octavia. His new stadium catered for athletics. Temples, however, were maintained—especially that of Jupiter Capitolinus—and some new ones were built, notably Venus and Rome under Hadrian and his rebuilding and expansion of the Pantheon, and the temple of the Deified Faustina under Antoninus Pius.

Trajan's new forum was a stupendous new space for commerce, culture, and leisure,[92] but it was dominated by the symbolism of military victory: the six-horse chariot over the triumphal gateway at the entrance on the south side, the equestrian statue of Trajan in the centre of the forum, reliefs in the basilica, and the column towards the rear proclaiming details of military victories against Dacia. Hadrian completed the forum works and embarked on his

[89] Philostratus (*Apollonius* 4. 42), reporting a Cynic philosopher's attack on the decadence and extravagance of the baths. Tacitus (*Annals* 14. 47. 3) refers to them in association with a 'Greek' distribution of oil, even to senators and equestrians. Suetonius (*Nero* 12) associates the new baths and gymnasium with the Neronian festival of musical, gymnastic, and athletic competition, 'on the Greek model'. Dio (61. 21. 1) also refers to a musical performance (of Nero) in the gymnasium, which would hark back to the Greek association of athletics and music in the training of the young.

[90] Other peaks were under Augustus and Septimius Seuerus: see Burnett (1999: 155–61).

[91] Zanker (1998: 129–33). Even a new bath building had been begun by the time of the eruption of 79.

[92] Shops, libraries, porticoes, and basilicas. See Anderson (1984) and Boatwright (1987: 74–98).

own active building programme from almost the beginning of his reign (117). During the next thirty years he 'permanently changed the urban landscape' (Boatwright 1987: 236). There were no new monuments to military achievements, but the peace and prosperity of the empire were celebrated in various ways.[93] An Athenaeum was built in the Forum to accommodate public readings and lectures and to contribute to education in the liberal arts. Both Greeks and Romans performed here, but it enhanced the place of Greek language and literature in the city. Intellectual talent from the whole of the Roman world could now be appreciated in the centre of the city.[94] It was probably Hadrian who finished the twin libraries in Trajan's forum, on either side of Trajan's column. The population of Rome, including children, enjoyed greater social amenities in the city, and Hadrian took a close interest in the administration of the neighbourhoods (*uici*).[95] The restorations of older buildings and monuments, especially in the Campus Martius, enhanced a sense of continuity and tradition, laying a firm base for Antoninus Pius' celebration of Rome's 900th anniversary in the year 148. Hadrian's Mausoleum, the grandest imperial tomb since Augustus' and built on the model of that tomb, dominated the view across the river at the north-western end of the city.[96]

FESTIVALS

The embellishment of Rome was, as we have seen, closely associated with celebratory festivals. The dedication of a new or

[93] The large series of 'province' coinage is one record of this.

[94] Aurelius Victor 14. 3, 'ludus ingenuarum artium'; Boatwright (1987: 207–8).

[95] Pedestrian access and movement were helped by a ban on heavy wheeled traffic (SHA, *Hadrian* 22); new porticoes were built; and the Forum, the traditional heart of the city, was renovated and expanded, with extensive new shops and the development of the eastern end below the towering heights of the new temple of Venus and Rome. Hadrian and the *uici*: Boatwright (1987: 26–7). Women received greater public prominence than at any time since the Julio-Claudians, being honoured on coins, in porticoes, and with the temple of the deified Matidia (mother-in-law of Hadrian): Boatwright (1987: 61, 96–7).

[96] Of the monuments erected in Rome from the latter part of the 2nd c. CE into the 4th, military memorials and places of entertainment or socializing are the most striking, e.g. the column of Marcus Aurelius, the arches of Septimius Seuerus and Constantine, the baths of Caracalla, of Diocletian, and of Constantine, and the basilica of Maxentius.

restored building, especially a temple, was accompanied by
games, some of which became a fixed festival in the Roman
calendar. There was an extraordinary range of festivals in the
calendar, and many other occasions too presented spectacle and
ritual. Anthropologists have learned to 'read' such occasions and
performances for what they reveal of a culture,[97] such as common
ideals and values, the locus and nature of power, and the deeper
structures of society. Festivals and ritual play a role in forming
civic identity and civic solidarity, sometimes at a national level,
sometimes at a local level. Kertzer (1988: 180) illustrates this well
in his discussion of celebrations of May Day and the October
Revolution in the (then) Soviet Union. Even though these ceremonies had become routine by the 1980s they still attracted huge
crowds, and observers found them impressive. 'The rites continued to have an important political effect, with their dramatic display of military might, the prominent place occupied by the
national leadership, the sea of red flags and banners, and the ven-
erated portraits of the founding fathers.'

   This effect can be seen in many Roman rituals. In the
Republic, city building and entertainment were often associated
with a military triumph, and the triumphal procession itself was
a major entertainment. Even when the triumph became the
prerogative of the emperor and close members of his family, and
when the emperor himself had not always taken the prime role in
achieving the military victory, the impact was strong. The entertainment value remained, and it was still capable of inspiring
strong emotions, reinforcing ideology, and setting a model for
those present, especially the impressionable young. A few
privileged children took part in the triumph as prime participants, riding in or alongside their father's victory chariot or being
engaged in religious ritual. Some foreign children participated
abjectly in the procession as captives, and are so represented on
certain monuments.[98] Many more children were observers. So it

---

[97] Clifford Geertz has been a leading authority in this approach.

[98] Pompey, cheated of his main enemy in his triumph of 61 BCE by
Mithridates' death, displayed other family members as captives, including five
children of Mithridates (Plutarch, *Pompey* 45). Currie (1996) discusses the representation of children on Trajan's column as 'captives and wretched refugees'
or as 'happily Romanised'. Cf. above on Titus and on imperial columns; and see
below on children in religious ritual in the Republic and the Principate.

was for other festivals and processions: many children attended, some participated, each taking away from this experience a lesson and impression appropriate to his or her status, age, and education.

In the triumphal procession of L. Aemilius Paullus in 167, Paullus' party came last, himself resplendent in gold and purple followed on horseback by his two adult sons who had been adopted into other families, Q. Fabius Maximus and P. Cornelius Scipio, and then cavalry and infantry. These two sons (from his first marriage) had served with him in Greece. His two younger sons (from his second marriage), aged 12 and 14 (*praetextati*), were expected to ride with their father in his triumphal chariot. But both the younger sons fell ill and died within days of the triumph, one funeral being held just before the triumph and the other just after. The poignancy of this, and Paullus' loss of sons to continue his name, added to the impact of his procession. Aemilius' loss, after so much success, was taken to be an *exemplum* of the sudden reversal of fortune in men's lives. Livy (45. 40. 6) describes the fates of both Perseus and Aemilius similarly as 'documentum humanorum casuum'.

There had been a long tradition of generals' young children having this role in the triumphal procession,[99] and some later generals had it commemorated on coinage. Roman coins of 101 and 71 BCE showed sons of Marius and Pompey, respectively, riding alongside their father's triumphal chariot.[100] Comparatively few generals would have such young sons available by the time they earned a triumph. At the end of 71 two other generals besides Pompey celebrated triumphs, but they were much older than the 35-year-old Pompey (whose accelerated career was highly irregular) and there is no evidence of sons in their parades. Pompey was consul-elect by the time of the triumph and

---

[99] Cicero (*For Murena* 11) referred to this in 63 BCE: 'cum sedere in equis triumphantium praetextati potissimum filii soleant', i.e. pre-adult sons ride on triumphing generals' horses. These would be the side (or trace) horses helping to draw the chariot. Sons not yet skilled at such riding would ride in the chariot itself.

[100] Silver in 101 BCE: *RRC* 326/1, where Crawford admits the possible identification of the small accompanying figure as Marius' 8-year-old son; gold in 71: *RRC* 402, where Pompey's elder son, Gnaeus (aged between 5 and 9 years), can be identified.

upstaged his colleagues several times in 71–70 (B. Rawson 1978: 39–44). The presence of a young son for his triumph was a happy bonus for his public-relations superiority, endearing him all the more to the populace.[101]

Octavian considered it important to follow this tradition in his multiple triumph of 29 BCE in Rome, although he had no son of his own. Accompanying his chariot on horseback were a nephew and a stepson, both of whom were to be prospective heirs at different times. Marcellus was aged 14 and Tiberius 13 (Suetonius, *Tiberius* 6), and neither had yet attained the status of adulthood (the *toga uirilis*). In 17 CE Germanicus, the epitome of the family man,[102] celebrated a triumph for victories against the Germans, and was accompanied in his chariot by all five of his then children. They were aged from 11 to just 1 year old, and two of them were girls.[103] A daughter had ridden in her father's procession in 143 BCE, but Ap. Claudius Pulcher's triumph had not been officially awarded, and Claudia, a Vestal Virgin, rode with him to give the procession sacrosanctity and to prevent interference.[104] Germanicus' display of family pride was complemented in the decoration of the arch erected in his honour in the Circus Flaminius in 19, after his death. Above the arch an unprecedented number of statues commemorated three generations of the family of Germanicus, who was himself represented in a triumphal chariot.[105] Flory (1998) sees the presence of Germanicus' children in the victory parade as 'the advertisement of dynastic continuity'. She discusses the increasing presence of emperors' wives and

---

[101] Cf. the presence of President John F. Kennedy's son, the infant 'John-John', in the White House in the early 1960s. The efforts of Tony Blair, Prime Minister of the United Kingdom, to protect his newly born son from media attention in 2000 also reflect the great popular interest in young children of famous citizens in our own times.

[102] He was to have six surviving children, most of them born or reared in provinces where he was serving between 6 and 18 CE.

[103] Tacitus, *Annals* 2. 41. Probable dates of birth for the children of Germanicus and Agrippina the Elder are 6 (Nero Caesar), 7 (Drusus), 12 (Gaius), 15 (Drusilla), 16 (Agrippina), and 18 (Livilla). Barrett (1996: app. 1) reverses Drusilla and Agrippina in this list.

[104] Cicero, *For Caelius* 34; Valerius Maximus 5. 4. 6.

[105] For further details, see Ch. 1 above. The arch is no longer extant, but many details have been revealed by the fragments of a large bronze inscription discovered in Spain in 1982 (the Tabula Siarensis: see C. B. Rose 1997, Catalog 37).

children in triumphal processions and concludes that by the mid-second century 'the female children of the emperor, if he had them, had become regular participants in the triumphal procession'. When Claudius celebrated his triumph, it is unlikely that he did not follow his brother Germanicus' example and take his 2-year-old son in his chariot for the parade. Suetonius (*Claudius* 27) records other instances of Claudius' display of his son at public functions, for instance at the games and military parades, and a triumph was the opportunity to extend this appeal and Claudius' dynastic hopes. Over a century later, Marcus Aurelius, the first emperor since Vespasian to have a natural son available as heir and the first since Claudius to have very young children at the time of a triumph, was accompanied by male and female children in his triumph in 166.[106]

Children were associated with the religious ritual of triumphal celebrations. The procession culminated in the sacrifice of special animals, often white oxen, on the Capitol. The priests responsible for this were accompanied by boys (*camilli*) who carried libation dishes of precious metal.[107] Children had long been used in religious and propitiatory ceremonies, because of the quality of purity often associated with children. Sometimes the children had to be particularly qualified, such as by having both parents alive and still married to each other. Thus death and divorce were implicitly factors which derogated from a child's wholeness and ability to mediate between state and the gods.

During the Second Punic War children were frequently involved in such ceremonies. In the dark days of 217 BCE, when Hannibal was entrenched deep in Italy, public prayers and vows were offered to seek the gods' help for the Romans. Members of the whole population, city and country, were involved: specifically men, women, and children.[108] Children took a more prominent role in later years, processing to temples and singing hymns. This was an honourable but arduous duty, requiring disciplined preparation and physical stamina. Roman ritual depended to a

---

[106] SHA, *Marcus* 12. 10. Two sons, Commodus and Verus, were aged 5 and 3; at least two daughters were aged 7 and younger.

[107] e.g. gold and silver dishes at the triumph of Aemilius Paullus in 167 BCE: Plutarch, *Aemilius* 32.

[108] Livy 22. 10. 8. Cf. Macrobius, *Saturnalia* 1. 6. 12–14: boys and girls, including—for the first time—children of ex-slaves.

large extent on memorization and an oral tradition: neither priests nor children had written scores available for most of the ceremonial (Scheid 1990: 673–6). In 207 BCE Rome's pontiffs ruled that sinister portents must be expiated by a procession of twenty-seven singing girls (*uirgines*). The girls had to practise and learn a hymn composed by the poet Livius Andronicus.[109] Their procession began in the Campus Martius, made its way into the city and Forum, then out through the Forum Boarium to Juno's temple on the Aventine—a considerable distance. The girls led the procession, behind sacrificial animals (two white cows) and two new wooden statues to be dedicated to Juno. Behind them came the ten magistrates responsible for sacrifices and religious ritual (the *decemuiri*), in full regalia. At the culmination of the procession the two cows were ritually sacrificed. There was no room for sentimentality about such animals when Rome's national interests were at stake. Children and other members of the population witnessed such bloody (and potentially messy) rituals at many ceremonies of entreaty and celebration.

Two centuries and more later, children were still playing a similar role.[110] In 70 CE they were an important part of the ceremony to begin restoration of the temple of Jupiter on the Capitoline, when Vespasian initiated the rebuilding of the temple after the civil wars which resulted in his becoming emperor. Vespasian himself had not yet returned to Rome from the East, but he instigated the process from a distance, being in no doubt that this act of restoration was of prime importance for present reconciliation and future hope. The presence of children helped to legitimate this and it offered all the parents and children who attended the prospect of a better life ahead. Tacitus, who almost certainly witnessed these events as a young teenager in 70 CE, provided the following account (*Histories* 4. 53):

[109] Livy 27. 37. 5–15. Another portent intervened before the public performance, and the girls' hymn was to take account of that too. Livy comments that the hymn would sound primitive and unpleasing to his own contemporaries, more than two centuries later. Livy records similar ceremonies for 200 and 190 BCE (31. 12. 9–10, 37. 3. 1–6), the latter involving twenty children (ten freeborn boys and ten girls) both of whose parents were still alive.

[110] See below for their prominent role in the Secular Games of 17 BCE. In Gaius' reign the temple to the deified Augustus was completed, and at its dedication in the Forum choruses of boys and girls of distinguished families sang a hymn and the Troy Game was performed (Dio 59. 7. 1).

On 21 June, under a tranquil sky, the whole area which was being dedicated for the temple was marked off with chaplets and garlands.
Soldiers with auspicious names entered, bearing boughs of good omen
Then came the Vestal Virgins accompanied by boys and girls who had
both parents alive, and they sprinkled the site with water drawn from
springs and rivers. Then the praetor Helvidius Priscus, guided by the
pontifex Plautius Aelianus, purified the area with the ritual sacrifice of
pig, sheep, and bull, and placed the entrails upon a turf altar. He prayed
to Jupiter, Juno, and Minerva, and the protecting gods of the empire,
that they would prosper this enterprise and with their divine assistance
raise up their seat of worship which had been begun by the devotion
(*pietas*) of men. Then the praetor touched the chaplets which were tied
around the foundation stone, and to which ropes were attached. At the
same moment, the other magistrates, the priests, senators, knights, and
a large proportion of the people, putting forth a great effort, eagerly and
joyfully dragged the huge stone into place. From all sides they cast into
the foundations nuggets of gold and silver, offerings of unsmelted metal
in the natural state: the diviners warned against polluting the work by
the use of stone or gold intended for any other purpose.

A traditional festival which came to feature children prominently was that of the Secular Games. It celebrated the turn of a
century (approximately) in Roman history, and had been held at
least twice in the Republican period.[111] Augustus' renewal of
these Games in 17 BCE gave them a higher profile, which proved
so attractive that several subsequent emperors juggled the chronological calculations to ensure that the celebrations fell in their
own reigns. The centrality of children in Augustus' celebration is
consistent with his other family-oriented policies, especially from
18 BCE, but children maintained a significant role in the celebrations of Claudius (47 CE) and Domitian (88 CE), and probably the
later ones of Septimius Seuerus (204).[112] The participation of
children helped to emphasize optimism for the future, adding to

---

[111] Celebrations in 249 and 146 BCE are attested (Valerius Maximus 2. 4. 5).
The 3rd-c. (CE) writer Censorinus listed earlier ones (*On Anniversaries, De die
natali* 17). For details of the festival, see Zanker (1988: 167–72) and Beard, North,
and Price (1998: 1. 201–6). The basic document is the inscription *CIL* 6. 32323–6,
available (most of it) in translation in Beard, North, and Price (1998: 2. 140–4),
containing details of 'formal sacrifices, theatrical performances, banqueting,
choral singing and circus games'.

[112] Antoninus Pius celebrated the 900th anniversary of Rome's foundation
in 148, and Philip ('the Arab') the next centenary in 248, but these celebrations
were not included in the official list of Secular Games.

the ceremonies giving thanks for the past. The whole ceremony had a role of binding the community together. Any community celebration—sporting, musical, political, commemorative—can play such a role, but a religious dimension gives an added strength in many societies. In Roman religion, and especially the Secular Games, religious ritual was co-extensive with national. For children involved in these Games, whether as direct participants or as observers, there was a subliminal commitment to Rome's gods, the emperor,[113] and Rome's values.

The timing of the Games in 17 BCE, in the first three days and nights of June, as late spring passed into early summer, emphasized fertility and rebirth. Mothers and children had prominent roles. There was a family element in the traditional story of the origin of the festival. A man whose three children were ill found a cure for them by following certain rites on the bank of the Tiber in the Campus Martius. To give thanks to the gods a festival of three days and three nights was established (Valerius Maximus 2. 4. 5). Augustus not only revived ancient ceremonial but also added new details. He introduced the goddess who assisted childbirth, under her various names of Ilythia or Lucina or Genitalis.[114] Specially selected married women (110 of them) offered banquets for Juno and Diana. This was a national festival, not 'just' a female rite, and women were an integral part of the festival. Young girls saw women playing this integral part, in no sense marginalized. Girls themselves played an equal part with boys in the performance of the hymn (the *carmen saeculare*) written specially for the occasion by the poet Horace.

It was on the third day of the festival that choruses totalling twenty-seven boys and twenty-seven girls sang the hymn, first at the temple of Apollo on the Palatine and then on the Capitoline hill. The logistics of organizing these performances were formidable, as anyone would attest who has helped organize a large inter-

[113] The prominence of Apollo reflected the emperor's close association with that god.

[114] Ilythia in the inscription; the three names in Horace, *Secular Hymn* (*Carmen saeculare*) 13–16. Putnam (2000: 61–9) discusses 'the connection of Diana with birth and the continued importance of generation, and regeneration, at the initiation of Horace's poem'. There are allusions to Augustus' marital legislation; and, says Putnam, the poetic means by which Horace highlights the theme of birth, rebirth, and fecundity are 'lexical fruitfulness' and 'poetry's generative capability that mimics the fertility for which the verses pray'.

school performance today. A number of rehearsals were necessary. The choir probably had three groups of boys and three of girls, each having its own part to 'sing' in response to other parts and then joining in unison. Considerable interaction between boys and girls was inevitable. Moving them from the Palatine to the Capitoline provided further opportunity for such interaction. Children of good family were, no doubt, closely chaperoned during these activities. But games and theatrical performances associated with the festival were held day and night and no chaperoning system is foolproof. Augustus gave instructions that no young people, male or female, were to attend night-time entertainment unless accompanied by an adult relative (Suetonius, *Augustus* 31. 4); but this could hardly have been systematically policed. Clearly many children were out and about during these celebrations. For all of them, the importance of children in the symbolism and performance of the festival was clear to see. For those who actually performed, it was an occasion which would be remembered and retold throughout their lives. Horace envisaged the girl performers thus: 'When you are married you will say, "When the centennial festival came round, I performed the hymn celebrating the gods, trained in the measures of the poet Horace"' (*Odes* 4. 6).[115]

The Secular Games were supposed to occur only once in anyone's lifetime, but sixty-four years later Romans were treated to the same spectacle under Claudius, and again forty-one years later under Domitian. Domitian's coins (gold, silver and bronze) portray a sequence of ceremonial acts.[116] On one type a procession of children holding branches is followed by Domitian and another adult male (as in Fig. 1.7). On another, the citizen receiving purificatory material is accompanied by a child. This unprecedented representation of ritual detail and of children's participation reflects aspects of Domitian's interests and his

[115] Young participants in modern festivals have had similar experiences. Most recently in Australia, thousands of children (not the competing athletes) who performed songs and dances in the opening and closing ceremonies of the 2000 Olympic Games in Sydney had hours of rehearsal, the excitement and pride of the ceremonies themselves, and much talk of how long they would remember it all.

[116] *RIC* 2. 167 nos. 115–19; 201–2 nos. 375–83, 385–7: a herald's announcement, the distribution of purificatory material to citizens, the offering of crops by citizens, the emperor's leading of Roman matrons in ritual prayer to Juno, various scenes of making sacrifice, and processions of children.

period which are attested in other ways. He was deeply interested in religious ritual and tradition; he fostered education and developed cultural competitions in which children could participate; and the inclusion of a child in a distribution scene foreshadows the frequent presence of children in similar scenes, such as *congiaria* and *alimenta*, in the early second century.[117] Children were to be much more prominent visually in second-century public representations, and this is consistent with increased attention to children's interests and their role in public life.[118]

In the part of Claudius' Secular Games celebrated in the Circus, prominence was given to the Troy Game, providing a display of high-ranking (*nobilis*) boys and youths in equestrian manoeuvres. Claudius' own son Britannicus performed on horseback, although aged only 6. His stepson—Agrippina the Younger's son L. Domitius, to be known as Nero after his adoption by Claudius in 50—also performed, and at the age of 10 he was able to show superior horsemanship which won applause from the crowd (Tacitus, *Annals* 11. 11; Suetonius, *Nero* 7. 1). The Troy Game was part of Roman tradition.[119] The most detailed and famous account of it is given by Vergil, in the part of the *Aeneid* (5. 545–600) describing the anniversary games given by Aeneas in Sicily at the grave of his father Anchises. After a series of contests of physical skill amongst the adult men, Aeneas brought on a cavalry display of the Trojan boys in his expedition, led by his son Ascanius (Iulus). 'Now the boys ride in, before the eyes of their fathers, | In perfect dressing, a brilliant sight on their bridled horses.' The leaders of the three squadrons and their horses are described as they parade past their family members and the other adult men: the boys are nervous (*pauidi*) under this scrutiny, but then elated by the applause which they receive. At the signal of a shout and a whip-crack, they re-form into two opposing sides.

---

[117] The only precedent of which I am aware is the coinage celebrating Nero's first *congiarium* in 57 CE (*BMCRE* 1. 224–5 nos. 136–8), which has on the reverse a child standing behind an adult male receiving a handout from an attendant who sits on a platform in front of Nero. The child is not on the types of the coins for the second *congiarium*.

[118] Cf. B. Rawson (1997a and 2001) for distribution scenes.

[119] Revived by Sulla. Cato the Younger was one of the two boy leaders in a performance in Sulla's time: Plutarch, *Cato the Younger* 3.

[They] wheeled apart and then, at the word of command, again
Came galloping back and charged one another with lances levelled.
Next, they staged a new set of manoeuvres and counter-manoeuvres,
Keeping their relative positions, each group, while performing their
    maze of
Evolutions—a mimic engagement of mounted troops:
Now they turn their backs in flight, now wheel and charge
With lance in rest, and now ride peacefully, file by file.[120]

This helps us visualize the Troy Game performances of Vergil's
own day. In his youth there was a performance, by boys of high
rank, 'according to ancient tradition' (Dio 43. 23. 6; cf. Suetonius,
Iulius 39. 2), at Caesar's triumphal celebrations of 46 BCE. In 29
BCE there was another performance, to honour the deified Caesar
at the dedication of his temple in the Forum. Tiberius, aged 13,
led the older boys.[121] Vergil did not live to see the later performances of Augustus' reign, which Augustus used to give his
grandsons (now adopted as his sons) a prominent role in public
life.[122] In 13 BCE, at the dedication of the theatre of Marcellus,
the 7-year-old Gaius Caesar participated, and in 2 BCE he and
Lucius Caesar, now aged 18 and 15,[123] had general supervision of
the horse races associated with the dedication of the temple of
Mars Ultor in Augustus' new forum. Augustus' youngest grandson (Agrippa Postumus), at 10 years of age, was still young
enough then to participate in the Troy Game. On all these occasions there were extravagant shows of exotic animals, usually ending in their slaughter, providing an outlet for the excitement and
for the hunting and militaristic zeal stirred in boys at large who
had come to watch the pageant and the competitive manœuvres
of the Troy Game. Augustus himself suspended performances of
the Troy Game in the latter part of his reign because families
became concerned at accidents suffered by the boys.[124] But, as we
saw above, they were later resumed.[125] Representations of young

---

[120] Translated by C. Day Lewis, The World's Classics, Oxford University
Press, 1986.

[121] Suetonius, *Tiberius* 6: 'ductor turmae puerorum maiorum', implying that
younger boys also performed.

[122] Dio 54. 26. 1, 55. 10. 6; cf. Suetonius, *Augustus* 43. 2.

[123] Both had now reached adult status through the *toga uirilis* ceremony.

[124] Suetonius, *Augustus* 43. 2, for two instances of a broken leg.

[125] See also Suetonius, *Gaius* 18. 3, and Dio 60. 5. 3 for Gaius; and Suetonius,
Claudius 21. 3, for Claudius.

boys on horseback are known from later periods. One on a marble altar from the Trajanic period comes closest to what a boy in the Troy Game might have looked like (Fig. 7.4). The 10-year-old freeborn boy C. Petronius Virianus Postumus sits astride his

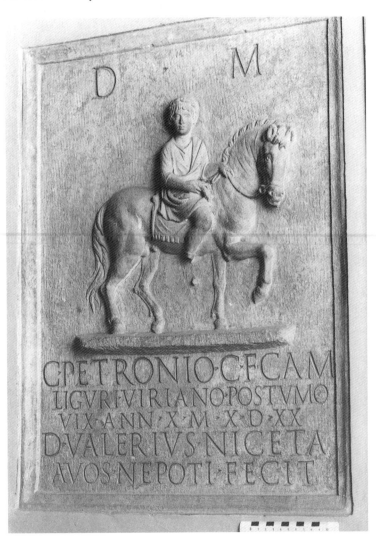

FIG. 7.4 C. Petronius Virianus Postumus, aged 10, on horseback. Rome, early second century CE.

horse on a fringed saddle-cloth, wearing the ceremonial dress of the equestrian order (the *trabea*), his head crowned with olive leaves.[126]

Other cavalry parades had their place in the Roman calendar. The annual parade of able-bodied men of equestrian rank, the *transuectio equitum*, was held on 15 July. It had a long tradition of processing from outside the walls of Rome through the Forum to the temple of Castor and Pollux. Dionysius of Halicarnassus (6. 13. 4) described the splendour of the spectacle in Augustus' time, claiming that up to 5,000 participants were involved. The emphasis was on younger men of equestrian rank, in the full flower of physical fitness.[127]

The temple of Mars Ultor, dedicated in Augustus' new forum in 2 BCE, became the site for many ceremonies associated with boys, young men, and Rome's military reputation,[128] including the coming-of-age ceremony when boys took on the *toga uirilis*, and an annual cavalry parade on 1 August before the steps of the temple. The architecture of the complex reinforced the symbolism of the ceremonial. The two facing porticoes commemorated the civic and military achievements of a long line of distinguished Roman citizens, a historical pageant of statues and inscriptions

---

[126] The olive wreath was awarded for victories in the Olympic festival; but it was also associated with funerals. Both associations may hold here. The boy's epitaph (*CIL* 6. 24011) was dedicated by his grandfather, D. Valerius Niceta. The grandfather's different family name, his lack of status indication, and the possible slave associations of his *cognomen* Niceta suggest that he might have been an ex-slave: he would have reason to take pride in the success of the third generation of his family in attaining equestrian status. For illustration and discussion, see Kleiner (1987: 187–8, no. 61, and pl. XXXVII. 1); and Gabelmann (1977: 336–7). Cf. the later (3rd-c.?) statue of marble and alabaster, where the raised right hand of the boy Eutychos held perhaps a whip or a lance (Aurigemma 1958: 174 no. 502 and pl. CIII) or represents a gesture of farewell (Seston 1949): discussed further below in Ch. 8 (Fig. 8.2).

[127] Cf. Valerius Maximus (2. 2. 9), who refers to a twice-yearly parade of the *iuuentus* of the equestrian order, at the Lupercalia in February and at the *transuectio* of 15 July. After Germanicus' death in 19 CE, his *imago* had a special place in the parade which he had himself led during his lifetime. The equestrian order also dedicated a section of its own seating in the theatre to its younger members in honour of Germanicus: Tacitus, *Annals* 2. 83.

[128] Suetonius, *Augustus* 29. 2; *Gaius* 44. 2; Dio 55. 10: boys' coming-of-age ceremony, departure of generals for overseas commands, senatorial decrees on triumphs, dedications of triumphing generals, location of recovered military standards, annual cavalry parade, marking of end of censors' term of office.

led by Aeneas and Romulus: an ideal setting for inculcating civic and military ideals, for anchoring the present to the past, and for embedding a sense of historical continuity. For a youth who was being formally recognized as an adult, it provided identity, helped him place himself, and gave a sense of belonging. Gaius Caesar had taken on the toga of manhood in 5 BCE and had been given the title of *princeps iuuentutis*, 'leader of youth'. For the dedication of the temple he was designated one of the six *seuiri equitum*, the officials in charge of the games associated with the dedication of the temple.[129] A century and a half later, Antoninus Pius gave his intended heir, Marcus Aurelius, the same role and titles.[130]

Other towns in Italy had youth organizations, whose purposes—at least at an early stage—included the training and display of physical prowess. They went well back in Italic tradition, but were reinvigorated by Augustus' encouragement of a more formal role for the young in public life. These organizations became more widespread in the West and more highly developed in the second century CE, becoming more like a *collegium* with their own meeting-places, officials, and patrons.[131] Their activities became more religious and funerary than sporting or martial. Often they were associated with religious festivals of their home towns. The general term used, *iuuenes*, suggests a membership of young adult males, but the evidence also includes children and females. Females were attested in much the same language as males, and they could hold office in the group. The cult of Diana at Tusculum seems to have been in the hands of only females, but the language in other inscriptions suggests that some of the organizations were mixed, consisting of both males and females. The fact that one of the females who was the priestess who led the sacred dances was a girl who died at the age of just under 7 years[132] reflects the growing practice of admitting children to a formal role in political and structured municipal life. This was

    [129] Taylor (1924) discusses the probable early origin of these officials, their role in public ceremonial as leaders of the equestrian youth, and the evidence of Italian towns.

    [130] SHA, *Marcus* 6; Dio 71. 35.

    [131] Taylor (1924); Mohler (1937); Jaczynowska (1978); Ginestet (1991).

    [132] *CIL* 6. 2177: Flauia Vera, *praesul sacerdos Tusculanorum*. Females as *sodales iuuenum* are attested in Tusculum (*CIL* 14. 2531, 2635), Reate (*CIL* 9. 4696), and Mediolanum (*CIL* 5. 5907).

largely a compliment to a parent for past or promised services to
a town, but it also foreshadowed hereditary office which developed in the later Empire.[133] In addition, it also gave children a
corporate life of their own. They were not normally part of the
public banquets provided in Italian towns.[134]

For dynastic purposes, Augustus gave his adopted sons Gaius
and Lucius Caesar public prominence at early ages. When each
took the *toga uirilis* at the age of 14 he was designated consul for
the future (*RG* 14), but Augustus was firm that they should not
take up that office before they were 20 years old (Dio 55. 9. 2).
When Gaius Caesar, at the age of only 13, was allowed to lead the
celebrations for Augustus' return to Rome from Germany in 7
BCE, he needed the help of one of the consuls for that year (Piso)
(Dio 55. 8). Although the minimum age for magistracies became
lower than that of Republican times, men were normally out of
their teens when they first took public office at Rome, until late
in the imperial period.[135] Augustus did give senators' sons opportunities for accelerated familiarity with public life.[136] These boys
were allowed to attend meetings of the senate as soon as they had
put on the *toga uirilis*. There was a tradition that this privilege
dated back to the early Republic.[137] Senate meetings were held
in the senate-house (the *curia*) or in a temple, and the main

---

[133] Garnsey (1974) discusses the twenty-five *praetextati* on the list of decurions at Canusium in 223 CE. He sees these boys as future decurions, from established families, who were present at council debates but could not vote. He
identifies real competition for places on the council at this date, although the
hereditary principle is in evidence: it would not be imposed compulsorily for
some considerable time yet. Kleijwegt (1991) argues for the hereditary principle,
and favouritism for the young sons of the elite, in Italian towns from late
Republican times.

[134] See above, with reference to 'neighbourhood'.

[135] Wiedemann (1989) has a useful chapter on 'Citizenship and Office
Holding'; but recent research and my own further work have led me to a somewhat different viewpoint.

[136] Suetonius, *Augustus* 38: 'quo celerius rei publicae assuescerent', 'so that
they could acquire familiarity with public affairs sooner'.

[137] Pliny the Younger, *Letters* 8. 14. 5–8. Pliny's experience of this in his own
day was at an age when he was considering candidacy for office. He was probably about 17 years old when he was adopted as patron by the town of Tifernum,
where he had recently inherited land from his uncle Pliny the Elder. Pliny says
that he was scarcely more than a boy ('me paene adhuc puerum') and that the
town showed more enthusiasm than good judgement.

entrance door was normally open during debates. The deep porch of these buildings would accommodate many sons of senators, standing and crowding round the door during crucial debates.[138]

In Italian towns there are records of boys admitted to the town council (the *decuriones*) at very young ages. However precocious such boys were, they could not have been properly functioning members of the council. Their role can be seen as similar to that of senators' sons at Rome: admitted as observers (probably within the council chamber itself), when schooling and recreation permitted. Their rank was clearly intended as an honour to their families. The evidence suggests that sometimes the honour was for a father who was himself ineligible for office (especially ex-slaves) but who had wealth to bestow on the town. The date of most of the known examples is uncertain, but probably from the second century (CE) onwards.[139] An example from Pompeii, however, must pre-date the eruption of 79 CE. There, the 6-year-old N. Popidius N. f. Celsinus (a freeborn boy) was admitted as a member of the *decuriones*, free of entry fee, because of his generosity in restoring the temple of Isis which had collapsed in the earthquake of 62 CE. The language of the honorific inscription suggests that this honour was in spite of the boy's young age: 'cum esset annorum sexs'.[140] Other evidence from Pompeii gives us the child's parents' names and indicates that the Popidii were influential in Pompeii over a long period. There may have been two branches of the family, one of some social standing and the other freedmen.[141]

Festivals celebrated by Domitian provided opportunities for children to compete and distinguish themselves. His celebration of the Secular Games in 88 took Augustus as its model for chronological calculation and for details of the traditional ritual.

---

[138] Taylor and Scott (1969: 557) paint a vivid picture of this. Pliny implies that debates were not so spontaneous and free in his own time. The porch and environs of temples often housed art of various kinds, providing subliminal history lessons for those who spent time there (see above).

[139] e.g. *CIL* 14. 306, 341, 2170; 9. 3573, for boys aged 4 and 12, at least two of whom seem to have freeborn fathers.

[140] *CIL* 10. 846, subjunctive mood. This temple was one of the first buildings to be restored, and one of the few fully restored before the eruption of 79.

[141] Parents: *CIL* 10. 847, 848. Our boy's father was a freedman (he had been *minister Augusti*) and thus ineligible himself to become a decurion. See further in Castrén (1975).

There were new festivals, too, notably the four-yearly Capitoline Games in honour of Jupiter. The first celebration was in 86, at the dedication of the new temple of Jupiter on the Capitoline (after the fire of 80). The new temple was extravagantly embellished with gold and fine marble, which could not fail to make an impression on the young competitors and observers. These games included contests of a 'musical, equestrian and gymnastic' nature (Suetonius, *Domitian* 4). They were more varied than previous games, including Nero's *Neronia* of 60 CE, which had also had these three divisions (Suetonius, *Nero* 12. 3). In addition to competitions in Greek and Latin poetry, Greek and Latin oratory was added;[142] the standard individual lyre-playing-and-singing had variations added; and in the stadium there were foot-races for girls as well as for boys.[143] Domitian's annual celebration of the Quinquatria, a festival held at his Alban villa in March in honour of Minerva, also included competitions in both oratory and poetry. Competition was intense at these festivals, especially at the Capitoline Games, which attracted to the capital city contestants from all over the empire. We have seen P. Annius Florus' visit from Africa while still a boy; Martial (9. 40) tells us of a competitor from Egypt. The 11-year-old Q. Sulpicius Maximus competed in the Greek poetry section, but his memorial commemorating this presents him in the pose of an orator (cf. Chapter 1 above). Composition and delivery of Greek and Latin prose and verse were appropriate preparations for future orators, and those boys who had ambitions for future public life looked to prizes in these competitions to spur them on their way. Wiseman's cameo sketch (1984) of two small boys of the year 105 CE illustrates both the role of young children in public life and 'the relevance of literature in public life'. A record (*CIL* 6. 2075) of several meetings of the priesthood of the Arval brethren in 105 includes the names of four boy attendants: they were of senatorial family, with both fathers and mothers alive. Their role in religious ritual is consistent with other examples noted above. They were carefully chosen, and Wiseman's analysis of their ancestry suggests that they came from families with long

---

[142] See Ch. 5 above.

[143] Dio (67. 8) refers to the girls' foot-race in Domitian's 'costly spectacle'. The girls' race did not survive beyond Domitian's reign, but the Capitoline festival continued for centuries.

political traditions and literary accomplishments ('*summi uiri* and *magna ingenia*'). Upper-class citizens took literary culture very seriously. They were in the audience—or competing—when boys performed at literary festivals, and when boys were chosen for roles of honour in public life their political and cultural traditions might be taken into account.

Festivals such as Domitian's served Roman interests well in encouraging literary and rhetorical studies. The lack of age-categories is consistent with what we have seen of the push to develop precocious talents quickly and to enable youths to enter public life as early as possible.[144]

At the spectator sports and entertainments which were increasingly catered for in the imperial period by permanent structures—theatres, amphitheatres, circuses—children were present, but often segregated from adults. The horse and chariot spectacles in the circus were considered appropriate family entertainment. Augustus set the tone by attending with his wife and grandsons, and seating in general was fairly informal.[145] When games were held in general public areas, such as the Forum, family groups and indiscriminate seating or standing must have been the norm; but at the permanent theatres and amphitheatres a hierarchy of seating developed. Senators and then equestrians had received special seating in the Republic, and Augustus confirmed that they and distinguished visitors should sit in the front rows, other male citizens further back, with women and then slaves further back again. Vestal Virgins, as females with special religious and political status in Roman society, had their own places of honour at the front. The hierarchical impact was increased by the dress of all those sitting in the lower section of the theatre: Augustus required Roman citizens to wear the toga on formal occasions, including at the theatre, and the block of sparkling white reinforced in children's minds the privileges and pride of male Roman citizenship.[146]

[144] Both Nero and Domitian had Greek models in mind when they established their festivals, but there were differences from their models (e.g. there were no age categories for the poetry and oratory contests, although Augustus had had such categories, on the Greek model, in his *Augustalia* at Naples).

[145] Suetonius, *Augustus* 45; Juvenal (11. 202) envisages men and women sitting next to each other at the circus.

[146] Suetonius, *Augustus* 40. 5, 44. 2, 'media cauea'. Special seating was provided for soldiers and veterans, which confirmed the value placed on military

Under Augustus children could also observe the priority accorded to married men, reinforcing the ideal of marriage which Augustus promoted in legislation. There may have been relaxation of some of the rules from time to time, but the essential hierarchical criteria continued. In the late first century the poet Martial satirized an effeminate but wealthy man who preened himself on the privileges of equestrian status—including special seats in the theatre and distinctive dress—and who pointed scornfully at the poor; but, said Martial (5. 41), he could not hope to sit in the married men's seats. The legislated privileges for marriage and parenthood remained, and later emperors maintained and even extended hierarchical seating principles to the circus.[147] They also reinforced the dress rules from time to time, when slackness had crept in.[148] One of the attractions of country towns for some people was the greater informality of dress and seating at the theatre.[149] In Rome boys had their own section, but this was probably intended only for boys from families of a certain standing and wealth. There was a section for their *paedagogi* nearby, no doubt to keep an eye on their behaviour. Augustus' concern here is similar to his instructions for the chaperoning of children at night-time entertainment (see above). But many children did not have *paedagogi* and must have fitted into the theatre where they could, with family or other companions.

Athletic contests, where competitors performed naked, were deemed unsuitable for women and girls, who were denied access while such contests were in progress.[150] Indeed, there was a body of opinion at Rome that athletics and gymnasium sports had a corrupting effect on participants. They were associated with excessive leisure for young men, and nakedness and close bodily

prowess in Roman society. On the whole question of seating, see E. Rawson (1987).

[147] Claudius allocated special seats in the circus for senators only, and Nero then separated out the equestrians (Suetonius, *Claudius* 21, *Nero* 11; Tacitus, *Annals* 15. 32). Cf. the section of the equestrian seating set apart for younger members (*iuuentus*) after 19 CE (see above).

[148] e.g. Domitian: Suetonius, *Domitian* 8. 3.

[149] Juvenal 3. 172–8, 11. 204. Cf. Martial (10. 47. 5), on the burden of wearing the toga: an element of the happy, carefree life is freedom from the toga ('toga rara').

[150] Suetonius, *Augustus* 44. 3. See Suetonius, *Augustus* 43. 1, for temporary seating set up by Augustus in the Campus Martius for athletics.

contact were thought to lead to improper relationships (i.e. homosexuality).[151]

Public shows of various kinds had a long history in Roman culture. Religious festivals (*ludi*) always included an element of entertainment, originally in the theatre. Powerful, ambitious individuals had long offered shows (*munera*) to the people to celebrate their successes (especially military victories) and to win political and social favour. Exotic animals were a prime attraction over a long period. Gladiatorial contests were originally associated with funerals, as a tribute to the valour of the deceased and as a means of assisting the family or community through the rite of passage of death: from separation, through ordeal, to reintegration. The Circus Maximus was the major site in Rome, but otherwise venues were temporary ones, in the Forum or on the Campus Martius. Such venues continued to be used even after stone theatres and amphitheatres were built. The temporary structures and associated machinery became very elaborate in the late Republic and presentations were increasingly extravagant and costly. Towns of south and central Italy had permanent theatres and amphitheatres well before Rome, where there was political resistance to such buildings. When, however, Rome began to build such structures, they were not only grander than any others but their vaulted design lent itself superbly to the hierarchical and efficient distribution of crowds.[152]

The attraction of public shows is obvious in many modern societies: there is admiration for physical and performing skill (including often a well-informed analysis by lesser practitioners or 'armchair' fans), a bond of solidarity between diverse elements of the population, but also the thrill of competitiveness between supporters of opposing sides; and relief from everyday routine, especially in a pleasant outdoor setting or in elaborate venues of a standard not available in one's own home or local community. Much of this applied in Rome and other Italian towns where, for

---

[151] Tacitus, *Annals* 14. 20–1, with reference to the *Neronia*; Pliny the Younger, *Letters* 4. 22, for approval of a friend's suppression of *gymnicus agon* at Vienne in Gaul but despair of the disappearance of athletic competitions at Rome.

[152] Zanker (2000a: 37). The earliest amphitheatre in Italy was probably that built at Pompeii about 80 BCE. In Rome, the first theatre was built in 55 BCE and the first amphitheatre in 29 BCE.

the majority, everyday life and housing were drab and uncomfortable and for the elite there was need of display of wealth,
status, and power. Children were easily caught up in all this. In
the late first century CE, a conservative speaker criticizing modern society was represented by Tacitus as blaming the passion for
'actors, gladiators, and horses' for children's lack of interest in
serious studies.[153] The home is full of such talk, and young men
can talk of nothing else in their lecture-rooms.

Sporting entertainment provided opportunities for the betting
and gambling for which Romans seem to have had a great taste.
In the theatre, loyalties to particular actors (especially the *pantomimi* of the imperial period) could stir rowdy and even riotous
behaviour.[154] The violent nature of much of the public entertainment itself has often been commented on, especially the bloodi-
ness of animal hunts, gladiatorial fights, and the fates of humans
condemned to the amphitheatre. Assessments of the effects on
audiences vary, from pronouncements of brutalization to theories
about catharsis, the salutary release of tensions. Kyle has summa-
rized the amphitheatre as a 'highly symbolic, ritualized realm
where Roman society used "deep play" to confront threats and
terrors, fears and fetishes, order and disorder'.[155] It is difficult to
know what emotions and behavioural models children transferred
from the amphitheatre to the rest of their lives. Cicero, who
expressed distaste for these sorts of games,[156] could nevertheless
present them also as a lesson for the young in bravery and even
honour. At its best, all their training gave the performers the

---

[153] *Dialogue on Orators* 29. Messalla is the speaker: 'histrionalis fauor et glad-
iatorum equorumque studia' leave no room for *bonae artes*. Messalla says that
these vices seem to be conceived almost in the mother's womb—which confirms
other evidence that women attended and had a passion for such shows.

[154] Examples: under Tiberius (Tacitus, *Annals* 1. 77, 4. 14; Suetonius, *Tiberius*
37. 2, including reference to a north Italian town); under Nero (Tacitus, *Annals*
13. 24–5).

[155] Kyle (1997: 97) follows the Geertz school here, in a review of one of three
recent books on the amphitheatre. He has elaborated his views in his recent
book (1998). Another good synthesis of recent scholarship, with bibliography, is
provided by Potter and Mattingly (1999).

[156] e.g. letters of 55 and 54 BCE: *Fam.* 7. 1, *Q. fr.* 3. 4. 6. A decade later, in his
work *On Duties* (2. 55), in contrasting prodigality with true generosity, he used
as examples of prodigality ephemeral benefactions such as public feasts, distributions of meat, gladiatorial shows, elaborate games, and animal hunts. True
generosity consisted of help to one's friends and those in distress.

power to provide a model in how to face pain and death, even though they might be criminals or barbarians.[157] Those condemned to die in the amphitheatre could be perceived as non-persons—condemned criminals, slaves, traitors, foreigners—whose fate had little to do with a child's own friends and acquaintances. Deaths in the arena might be a form of ritualized execution, but Roman Italy did not normally display executions in public thoroughfares in the way that some later European societies have done. The effect of public executions on eighteenth-century France has been vividly discussed by McManners (1981).[158] On the rare occasions when this was done in Roman Italy, it was for maximum shock value, such as in the aftermath of Spartacus' slave rebellion.[159] When individual slaves had been crucified, their bodies were required to be taken down and buried promptly, by contrast with other ancient (and modern) societies which exposed such bodies.[160]

Higher emotions came into play with the deaths of some citizens, whose funerals provided a parade of national ideals and virtues and a whole panoply of Roman history. When distinguished citizens died, usually members of senior senatorial families, their funerals were public occasions of great ceremonial: they were indeed great theatre. Sometimes the funeral was at public expense, a kind of state funeral; other funerals were provided by the deceased's family but in full public view. Various Italian towns awarded 'state' funerals,[161] and although citizens of the highest rank had their funerals in Rome some of the ceremonial was reflected in Italian towns. When Augustus' adopted sons Lucius

---

[157] Cicero, *Tusculan Discussions* 2. 41: the performer might be a *perditus homo* or a *barbarus*.

[158] He writes (383–5) of the women and children of all social classes who attended, including 'the women of quality who had hired strategic windows' along the route to the execution. He speculates on whether the same people attended regularly or not, citing some evidence that children were among the *habitués*. An execution was 'a real-life theatre production' in which 'the crowd knew the cast and speculated keenly how well each would perform his role' (387).

[159] Appian, *Civil Wars* 1. 120: most of Spartacus' followers died in the field, but 6,000 survivors were captured and crucified along the road from Capua to Rome.

[160] Bove (1966: 40); Bodel (1994).

[161] *Funus publicum*. In Brixia (*CIL* 5. 4192) and in Pompeii (*CIL* 10. 1024) the deceased was also awarded the honour of an equestrian statue.

and Gaius Caesar died in 2 and 4 CE respectively, all public business was suspended in Rome for a considerable period, and a similar suspension (a *iustitium*) and other marks of respect were observed in Italian towns with which they had been especially associated.[162]

Expenditure on funerals was restricted by Roman law (Cicero, *On the Laws* 2. 59–66), but the magnificence and impact of high-ranking funerals derived largely from the display of family tradition and history and the praise of the deceased's own achievements. The procession from the deceased's home comprised not only family members and friends, and ex-slaves of the family who had been given their freedom in the deceased's will, but also various professional attendants: musicians (especially flute-players), dancers, paid mourners, and actors wearing the family's ancestor masks (the *imagines*).[163] It was important to maximize the visual impact and to achieve a large audience.[164] Heralds invited the population to attend, and a public holiday was often declared, to encourage a large attendance.[165] The children in the procession served a double purpose. They advertised to the world the continuity of the family line, and they themselves imbibed Roman history and their family's place in it. Perhaps it was fear of the impact that Germanicus' children might make which motivated Tiberius not to grant an official funeral for him in 20 CE. Germanicus' widow Agrippina the Elder had already been accompanied by two of her six children on the long sea voyage back from Antioch to Brundisium: the infant Julia Livilla and the 7-year-old Gaius. The reception of this threesome at Brundisium, and at towns along the overland route to Rome, is vividly described by Tacitus (*Annals* 3. 1–2). The four other children, aged from 2 to 13 years, joined the procession at Tarracina, about 100 kilometres south of Rome.[166]

---

[162] *CIL* 9. 5290 and 11. 1421 for Gaius; 11. 1420 for Lucius.

[163] Polybius (6. 53–4) is the chief ancient source. See Flower (1996) for good detailed discussion.

[164] Cf. the importance of having the funerary monument and its epitaph near a public thoroughfare, to be visible to many.

[165] This is made explicit in an inscription from Capua (*CIL* 10. 3903): legal business is to be suspended for one day to allow the populace to turn out in force for the public funeral of a notable citizen.

[166] One might compare the impact of the role of the two young sons of Diana, Princess of Wales, in her funeral procession in London in 1997.

The *imagines* of ancestors who had held high public office were worn by actors (chosen for appropriate physique where possible) dressed with the insignia of that office. This created a vivid procession of Roman history and one family's role in it. It moved through the Forum, past many of the historic buildings noted above, to the official platform (the Rostra) used by magistrates and decorated with many memorials of Roman history. Thus the family procession merged with the history of all of Rome. The funeral speech (the *laudatio*) highlighted these connections: the individual's own achievements, the family's contribution over a long period, and the values and traditions for which this history stood. The speech was usually given by a son or the closest male relative. Demographic reality meant that this was sometimes quite a young person, and it might be the first public responsibility for a young boy. We have seen above (Chapter 5) how a boy's education could help train him for these responsibilities.

Octavian gave the *laudatio* for his maternal grandmother Julia (Julius Caesar's sister) in 51 BCE, when he was only 11.[167] There had been several precedents for public funerals for women in the previous fifty years. Caesar himself had used the funerals of his aunt Julia and his wife Cornelia to exploit their political (Marian) associations. In 51 Caesar could not return from his military command in Gaul, and was no doubt glad that Octavian, his sister's only male relative, be given early exposure to the public as a speaker. When Caesar's daughter Julia had died in 54, she had the honour of a state funeral and burial in the Campus Martius, but the *laudatio* was surely given by her husband Pompey, who was not motivated to dwell excessively on Julian family history. Octavian, at the age of just on 9, will have been present at that funeral, probably walking with other relatives in the procession. That experience, and what he had imbibed of Julian traditions from Caesar and other relatives, helped prepare him for his role in 51. But standing, at that age, on the magistrates' platform (the Rostra), to address a very large and diverse audience, required poise and training and was an experience not soon to be forgotten. By 43 BCE he was a seasoned politician and was in a position to make the most of his *laudatio* for his mother Atia (daughter of the Julia for whom Octavian spoke in 51).

---

[167] Suetonius, *Augustus* 8. 1: 'in his twelfth year'.

Tiberius was only 9 when his father died, and as the elder son he gave the *laudatio*. Being a Claudian on both sides of his family and having a Livian connection, he had a rich store of ancestral history to draw on. Speaking in front of so many distinguished *imagines* helped him affirm his own identity. But when, over sixty years later, in 29 CE, his own mother, Livia, died he remained on Capri and left it to Livia's 17-year-old great-grandson Gaius (the future emperor) to deliver the *laudatio*.

The ceremonial of public funerals, and the use of *imagines* in them, continued until at least the end of the second century. From the early third century, these seem to have been restricted to the emperors; but there is evidence of the *imagines* within the home at Rome until the sixth century.[168]

---

[168] Flower (1996: 263–9), who discusses the continuing importance of the *imagines* under Christianity and their protection as part of a child's inheritance.

8

Death, Burial, and Commemoration

THE ritual of large funerals was bound to have a formative effect on children, as observers or participants, for reasons outlined above.[1] More generally, children had frequent experience of death in a society of high mortality, disease, recurrent epidemics, and the hazards of everyday urban life.[2] When Horace wrote of the dangers and obstructions in negotiating the streets of Rome, he mentioned building operations and funerals in the same breath.[3] The law required burials and cremations to take place beyond the city walls (for reasons of hygiene, public safety, and religious pollution), so funeral processions along the roads leading out of town were a frequent sight, although some of them took place at night. Children were inured to such sights from an early age. There was no escape from a constant consciousness of death. We saw, in the preceding chapter, the important role of funerals in Roman public life. Funerary memorials and other monuments associated with prominent citizens helped mould the values and identity of those who observed them. Public places were full of statues, honorific inscriptions (often listing the public offices held by the dedicatee), lists of consulships and triumphs in official *fasti*, and philanthropic dedications; and for privileged individuals there were grand tombs in the Campus Martius.

In some modern Western societies children have normally been kept away from funerals and associated rites, to protect

---

[1] This chapter incorporates some material from two earlier papers: B. Rawson (2002; 2003). McWilliam (2001) covers some of the same material, adding statistical detail.

[2] Rural life must have been equally dangerous and unpredictable. We have little evidence of everyday life on farms; but much of the rural population lived in towns—small or large—which were subject to many of the same conditions as discussed here.

[3] *Epistles* 2. 2. 74, 'tristia robustis luctantur funera plaustris' ('melancholy funerals contend with heavy wagons'). Infants might be buried within the city walls: see below.

them from pain and perhaps (subconsciously) the pollution of death. There is no indication of such an attitude amongst the Romans. Admittedly, death required purification, and immediately after a death only close family members (apart from the undertaker) would normally be near the corpse. There is no suggestion that child members of the family were excluded. What we know of the funeral procession indicates a place for children. When Agrippina the Elder returned to Rome from the East in 20 CE with the ashes of her husband Germanicus, her children Gaius and Julia (Livilla) accompanied her not only on the long sea voyage from Syria to Brundisium but overland to Rome and undoubtedly in the procession on the day of burial. This was, of course, a branch of the imperial family and Agrippina was advertising her children as potential successors to the emperor and consorts of emperors; but there was obviously no religious or social custom which made their participation taboo or inappropriate. At the ceremonial funeral of the emperor Pertinax in 193 CE, some time after his actual death, his effigy lay in state in the Forum, and the procession to honour him included choruses of boys and men (Dio 75. 4–5). Bodel's study (1999) of an Italian funerary relief of *c*.50 BCE identifies in the funeral cortège a mother and two daughters, the daughters still being children. An anthropological study of a poor community in Brazil has argued that the presence of children in the funeral procession for infants socializes the children to accept infants' deaths as natural and thus to be prepared for the loss of their own children later (Scheper-Hughes 1987*b*: 146).

The ethos which encouraged prominent Romans to bring out busts and masks of ancestors to be worn by younger members of their family in the funeral procession surely encouraged children in such a family to take interest and pride in the funeral. The *laudatio* could, as we have seen, be given by a quite young person. There was ritual associated with the burial site on the day of burial, and on the ninth day following (when a meal marked the end of the first period of mourning), and on later anniversaries.[4] These later occasions seem to have been celebratory, rather than bleak, occasions: they were the part of the rite of passage which

---

[4] See Cicero, *On the Laws* 2. 55. I use 'burial' here to cover both inhumation and cremation.

marked the reintegration of the deceased into the survivors' world.[5] They were so much part of the family calendar that it is inconceivable that children did not participate.

It was the responsibility of parents to see to a Roman's funeral;[6] otherwise the heir was responsible. Sometimes the heir must have been very young, and even if an older person were acting on his or her behalf to make the necessary arrangements the heir would be prominently visible at the funeral. The probabilities of various relatives dying as the child grew older have been calculated by Saller (1994). Nearly a quarter of 10-year-olds would already have lost a father (about 15 per cent a mother), and by the age of 15 that proportion would have risen to a third (or a quarter for mothers), leaving many young orphans (fatherless children, *pupilli*).

Commemoration and remembrance of the dead were important to a wide range of the population, even if carried out at a more modest level than in the funerals and monuments discussed above. At the poorest level, there was little prospect for anything beyond anonymous mass graves or communal cremations. But many others managed to leave some marker.[7] Roman culture set considerable store not only on proper disposal of the dead but also on the sacrosanctity of the burial place, leaving something of one's self for posterity, and having a place where family and friends could come together to remember the deceased individual. The tomb was a symbol of a family's continuity, which meant (among other things) continuity of the family name (the *nomen*). If natural or adopted children were lacking, ex-slaves could fulfil this role. The sacrosanctity of tombs was taken seriously by Roman society and misuse punished. Provision was frequently made for access to a family tomb even after a property changed hands. Tomb inscriptions often stipulated 'hoc monumentum

---

[5] See Harmon (1978: 1601–2). Modern anthropological studies of death have been influenced by the structure proposed by Van Gennep (*Rites de passage*, originally in 1909, translated into English 1960) of three stages: separation (*séparation*), transition or liminality (*marge*), incorporation or reintegration (*aggrégation*). More recent discussion in Huntington and Metcalf (1979).

[6] Paulus in Festus 68 L *s.v.* '*euerriator*'; Cicero, *On the Laws* 2. 48.

[7] See Bodel (1986/1994, and 2000) on graveyards and disposal of the dead. On the affordability of tombs and epitaphs, there has been much debate; but I am persuaded by the evidence of costs versus available resources and by the discernible Roman wish for some material and durable sign of one's existence. See discussion in Saller and Shaw (1984: 127–8).

heredem non sequetur' ('this monument will not go to the heir') and specified fines to be paid for alienation or violation of a tomb. There was a public responsibility (often vested in a town council) for overseeing such protection.[8] Burial clubs (*collegia*) could see to appropriate burial and commemoration if family or *familia* were not available. The fixed place on the calendar allocated for remembrance of the dead and visiting graves was the Parentalia in February, although, obviously, visits and domestic remembrances could also take place at any other time. Children surely participated in such visits and festivals. In the Italian town of Mediolanum (modern Milan) the parents of Ursilla Ingenua set up a fund, when she died at the age of 8, for the celebration of her memory at the Parentalia. The celebration was to include a scattering of roses by a girls' youth organization.[9]

The fixed place on the calendar gave the dead an integral place in Roman public and private life, and perhaps induced social solidarity in this context. In our own society, the only widely observed public remembrance day for the dead is for the war dead, which does encourage some social togetherness and sense of history. Our lack of an occasion for the general dead, and lack of formal rules or conventions for mourning, may contribute to many people's confusion and uncertainty about appropriate behaviour in bereavement. Children especially grow up without such experience in integrating death into their ongoing lives.

Cremation was the dominant form of disposal of the dead in the Roman world in the first two centuries CE, so epitaphs were usually placed on niches for cinerary urns, often in the communal buildings called *columbaria* ('dove-cots'). Epitaphs were thus often brief, but the kind of detail recorded is strikingly constant: it is detail about personal relationships, and overwhelmingly about close family relationships. Though succinct, these epitaphs have permitted illuminating reconstructions of family structure and sentiment.[10] Upper-class men might give prominence, in their memorials, to magistracies and other features of public life;

---

[8] De Visscher (1963: 112–23), who believes that the penalties became heavier and more frequently expressed from the 2nd c. CE, when tombs had become more 'individualistic' and less likely to be protected by family solidarity.

[9] The *iuuenae Corogennates*: *CIL* 5. 5907, probably 3rd c.

[10] See Saller and Shaw (1984) and subsequent work by Saller and Shaw separately. Cf. Ch. 6 above.

some artisans (male and female) recorded their trade; but many had little to record beyond their name and the names of those closest to them. The form of Roman nomenclature allows deductions about status and relationships.[11] The primary bonds evidenced for the sub-elite population are between husband and wife and between parents and children (Saller and Shaw 1984: 137). These relationships were not, of course, the only relationships of people in this society: some did not have family to commemorate them, and even those who did will have interacted in various ways with a wider range of people. But what most of them chose as their only record for posterity was close family relationships.[12]

The fact that children were memorialized in art and on tombstones indicates recognition of them as individuals and of childhood as a distinctive phase of human development. The often-alleged under-representation of the very young (and especially of young females) has been used to generalize about the lack of importance of children and the frequency of abandonment and infanticide of female infants. Many categories of pre-modern populations have had lower rates of memorialization than their actual proportion in the population would warrant.[13] The pro-

---

[11] For a detailed survey of the evolution of Roman nomenclature, see Salway (1994). For some brief remarks on the implications of nomenclature see B. Rawson (1986c: 13).

[12] Most of the memorials to children and women do not come from upper-class families. Even when we take into account the comparatively small numbers of senatorial and equestrian families, this is a puzzle. The literary and legal evidence reflects considerable concern with the welfare of children and grief for their premature deaths. How then did the upper classes memorialize non-career members of their families? The career inscriptions memorialize only adult males and by no means all of them. Did children and women have a place in the *tablinum*? Were their memorials on private country estates (as Cicero planned for Tullia)? But the actual funerals of Roman residents must have taken place at Rome, and we know of a few grand memorials set up in the vicinity, presumably where the cremation took place (see Ch. 7 above). Eck (1997) argues that in the imperial period funerary monuments for the upper classes, outside the imperial family, were increasingly located outside Rome, often on private estates.

[13] Henry (1959) compared the epitaphs in a French cemetery (in Lyons) dating from about 1812 to 1834 with official death figures for part of the same period. He found that the proportion of epitaphs for under-fifteens (male and female) was much lower than their actual mortality rate. This was true also for young men, aged 15 to 34, but not for young women of that age range. Men were over-represented in epitaphs in the age range 35 to 54. Henry concluded that in that

portion of children in the total number of Roman commemorations is lower than their probable mortality rate. In the age group 0–5 years the mortality rate was probably nearly 50 per cent but in the inscriptions a lower percentage (20 per cent) is recorded. Nevertheless, age group by age group, children are the most heavily represented group commemorated.[14] Children of all ages are commemorated, although there are comparatively few infants and there is an emphasis on children under 10 years of age.

In the absence of official death registers from antiquity, it is impossible to compare the rates of dedications for any age group with actual death rates. Model life tables have been our best means of comparing the dedications with the probable mortality rates. The excavation of cemeteries in Italy has until recently not provided useful or accessible supplementary material. The practice of cremation and the lack of systematic collecting of bones by modern archaeologists have contributed to this. Some years ago, Russell commented (1985: 49) on the apparent under-representation of children in Italian cemeteries, leading him to comment, 'The indifference to infanticide morally is paralleled by an indifference to burying children, especially infants, carefully.' But newer excavations and newer understandings of burial practices and patterns are giving us more and better evidence to work on.[15] Mays (1998), reporting on his archaeological work in Britain on Roman and medieval sites, discussed factors influencing the evidence for infant burials. Many factors can lead to the under-representation of infants in cemeteries. The thinner, more fragile bones of infants may survive less well in the soil, especially

place at that time females were most valued (their deaths were most regretted) in the full flower of their youth; but males had that status in a range two decades older, during or after material success.

[14] See, for examples, Shaw (1984), especially tables C–G, showing high representation of under-tens, especially in Rome and Roman Italy.

[15] Ery (1969) claimed that in two small cemeteries excavated in the Central Danubian Basin, one from the 3rd–4th c. and the other from the 10th–12th, the age-group distributions of the skeletal remains agreed in their general trend with UN model life-tables for underdeveloped countries (1969: 53). Cf. Lassère (1987). Recent work on skeletal remains in the Herculaneum area may provide new material for such analyses in Italy. An African cemetery in an area (Sitifis) settled by Roman veterans has yielded a large number of skeletons of young children, all carefully buried (Février and Guery 1980): 35% of the burials were aged 0–5 years; 14% were prenatal or perinatal births.

'hostile' soil (Mays 1998: 21–2). Moreover, there may have been different burial practices for infants; small infant bones might be missed by archaeologists and so figure less among the bones recovered; and human activities such as ploughing can interfere with interred bones, especially the shallower burials of infants. When Mays compared ages at death of perinatal burials from Roman and medieval sites, he found differences in age distribution which led him to conclude that 'substantial numbers' of the Roman burials were full-term babies buried immediately after birth, i.e. that they were evidence of infanticide. But 'the fact that the same perinatal age at death pattern holds for Roman cemetery as well as non-cemetery sites . . . indicates that victims of infanticide in Roman times in Britain were not always denied regular burial' (Mays 1998: 66).

In Roman Italy, Capitanio (1974) published a lengthy account of his careful excavation of a cemetery in the Picenum region, yielding nineteen infants or young children amongst fifty-three inhumations of the first and second centuries CE. More recently, Soren and Soren (1999) have published a large work on their excavations at a site (Lugnano) in southern Umbria, about 70 kilometres north of Rome, which have revealed a fifth-century (CE) cemetery of forty-seven children, all carefully buried.[16] All but one of these were infants or premature foetuses, all buried at about the same time. The demographic implications of this have not yet been fully discussed, but explanations already suggested have been an epidemic (malaria?) or some disastrous natural event (a collapse of the harvest?) such as to lead to high levels of infant death or abandonment. Abandonment or infanticide need not be the only explanations for perinatal deaths: this is one of the most dangerous periods in the existence of a foetus or infant, even in normal circumstances. A 'catastrophic mortality' pattern, due to natural disasters and disease epidemics, has been proposed by Storey and Paine (1999) to explain some funerary evidence. Epidemics probably broke out every year, according to seasonal variation.[17] Some were associated with the heat of mid-summer

[16] Soren and Soren (1999). I have not yet personally seen this large and expensive report. I rely here on the announcement for it and, especially, on the review by W. V. Harris (2000).

[17] See Duncan-Jones (1996) on many aspects of epidemics, esp. pp. 109–11 for frequency of serious epidemic; also Shaw (1996) and Scobie (1986). Shaw

(August), others with autumn (September). Particularly virulent epidemics or plagues are known for the years 65, 79, 165–80, and 189 CE. Although such outbreaks struck all age groups and status levels, children were especially vulnerable to some illnesses, such as diarrhoea and dysentery,[18] and had built up less resistance to other diseases than older members of the population. At Lugnano the infants might have been buried separately from other age groups. We know of other special arrangements for the burial of the very young. Babies aged less than forty days could be buried within the city walls (under the walls of houses): they were not sufficiently developed individuals to cause religious pollution. And they were usually interred rather than cremated.[19]

Special arrangements have always applied to young deaths in European history. It is only in very recent times in Western societies that there has been any recognition of infants or perinatal deaths in public cemeteries. Even today, miscarriages, stillbirths, and the deceased newborn are usually dealt with by the hospital where they occur, and some hospitals have special areas set aside for the scattering of ashes or arrange for communal burials in a special part of a cemetery. Not so very long ago, such remains were disposed of as merely hospital waste. Nowadays it is not unknown (but probably not the general practice) for infants to

(1996: 118–19) uses pre-modern Italian death records to suggest that infants' deaths might have peaked in mid-winter. Robert Sallares has given notice of a forthcoming book on malaria in ancient Italy.

[18] Celsus (*On Medicine* 2. 8. 30) specifies that children up to age 10 were most affected by this condition (*deiectio*). Marcus Aurelius wrote to Fronto, in the mid-2nd c. CE, of the emaciating effects of diarrhoea on his infant daughter: 'Our little Faustina is slightly better and may recover. The diarrhoea and fever have stopped, but she is extremely emaciated, and there is still a bit of a cough' (Fronto, *Letters* 4. 11 = H 1. 202). This daughter died in infancy (see below).

[19] Juvenal 15. 140, 'et minor igne rogi' ('too young for the cremation couch'). Pliny the Elder (*NH* 7. 72) defines this as before their teeth had grown (i.e. before seven months): these infants could not provide the ritual remnants to be gathered up after cremation. The late 5th-c. commentator Fulgentius explained the rare word *suggrundaria* as the burial place of infants aged less than forty days, whose bones and tiny bodies would not provide enough mass for a proper cremation (*Sermones antiqui* 7). See Néraudau (1987: 196) on archaeological evidence for the burial of infants under the eaves of houses in the early period of Rome. He surmises that this practice did not survive the period of the Twelve Tables (5th c. BCE).

have an identifiable, individual burial place in a public cemetery, sometimes with a tombstone and personal items associated with the infant. Even these burial places are likely to be in 'liminal areas', separate from the main part of the cemetery.[20]

Even if infants were often buried more carefully than was once thought, they were memorialized less frequently than were other children. Epitaphs for those under 1 year, or even under 2 years, are a small proportion of all extant epitaphs. My rough calculation is that in the almost 40,000 inscriptions in *CIL* 6 only about 170 are for children under 1 year of age, i.e. about 0.4 per cent.[21] *Alumni* in Rome fare a little better for commemoration: about 1.4 per cent of those attested have an age of less than 1 year recorded. In the rest of Italy, however, there are no *alumni* recorded with so young an age.[22] Some reasons for this are clear. In most, perhaps all, societies, a child is not considered a 'real' person until it has developed certain functions, for instance the ability to walk or speak. The very first few days after birth are especially a time of limbo, when chances of survival are at their lowest.[23] There is another danger period at four to six months. Until recently, public notices in newspapers of deaths and funerals have not included stillborn or scarcely surviving babies, but occasional instances can now be found. The Romans did not give an infant a name until

[20] I owe much of the modern material and insights here to the excellent discussion by Scott (1999), especially her ch. 3. Further development away from anonymous burials of infants is reflected in a new 'Butterfly Garden' in Perth (Australia), dedicated in January 2001. It was welcomed by families not only for its identifiable location for each infant's memorial (e.g. an inscribed pebble in a stream, or a specific plant with a small plaque) but also for its attractive and peaceful ambience, encouraging visits by parents and other children, thus integrating the deceased infant into the whole family. (Although infant mortality is now low in Western societies, SIDS (Sudden Infant Death Syndrome, or 'cot death') remains a danger and a particular source of angst and guilt for many parents.) Older women spoke of the way in which the experience of infant death had been suppressed in their youth.

[21] Based on the inscriptions containing 'VIXIT' or some version of that word. This probably does not capture all relevant cases. Garnsey's estimate (1991: 52), based on a sample of 16,000 epitaphs from Rome 'and elsewhere in Italy', is 1.3%.

[22] For Rome, see B. Rawson (1986a: 182); for Italy, Bellemore and Rawson (1990: 5).

[23] Neo-natal mortality rates are still comparatively high, especially in poorer countries. See Parkin (1992: 93–4) for figures and discussion.

the eighth day (for females) or ninth (for males).[24] The first birthday was a significant date for some official purposes, such as for upgrading a Junian Latin parent to full Roman citizenship, and for calculating eligibility for the *ius trium liberorum* under Augustus' legislation.

Literary sources are vague about the number of children ever-born. Natality was not important to the writers; what was important was the survival of children, especially into adulthood and beyond the death of their own parents, thus ensuring transmission of property and name and, it was hoped, proper attention to the burial and commemoration of parents. Deaths of infants are therefore less likely to have been recorded in literary and other sources.[25] Large pre-industrial societies are characterized by high death rates and high birth rates (Hopkins 1987: 115). In the Gracchi family twelve children were born to Ti. Sempronius Gracchus and Cornelia, but only three survived (the brothers Tiberius and Gaius, famous for their radical politics in the latter part of the second century BCE, and Sempronia, wife of Scipio Aemilianus) (Plutarch, *Ti. Gracchus* 1. 7). We know the figure twelve because of the fame of this family, but we know nothing of the nine who did not survive. We know of the death of the younger sons of L. Aemilius Paullus (aged 12 and 14) in 167 BCE because of the timing of the deaths and the use of this example as a model of the sudden reversal of human fortunes.[26] Even in the prolific imperial family of Marcus Aurelius and Faustina the Younger, where births of children were especially important, it is not possible to recover names or other details for all of the at least fourteen children who are thought to have been born to those parents. More information can be derived from coin evidence

[24] There were problems in the early Christian Church about early baptism of an infant who was likely to die. G. W. Clarke (1986: 303–5) discusses this in his commentary on Letter 64 of the 3rd-c. Church writer Cyprian. He believes that by this time infant baptism was well established, but that there was hesitation about baptizing babies under eight or nine days of age. He explains this in terms of 'the essential uncleanness of the very young infant' and a ritual taboo in Jewish thought against circumcision before the eighth day; and possible influence from the Roman naming-day.

[25] But Suetonius (*Gaius* 7–8) consulted official records (the *acta*) for Gaius' birth date and place, and found the number and order of all nine children born to Agrippina the Elder and Germanicus.

[26] Cf. Ch. 7 above.

than from literature, and we can make some deductions from names. For instance, when we find a second daughter being named Faustina (Annia Galeria Aurelia Faustina, the future wife of the co-emperor Lucius Verus), we can deduce that the first Faustina, born about three years earlier, had died.[27]

Under-representation in commemoration and vagueness about natality must in some ways reflect an undervaluing of infants, an outlook which did not see the infant as yet a full individual, and which is confirmed by rules for mourning. After the eighth or ninth day, however, Roman infants had a name. They were thus not so anonymous as the young children of early nineteenth-century America discussed by Ariès.[28] In formal terms, mourning for infants was expected to be briefer than that for older persons: there was no formal mourning for an infant less than a year old; for ages up to 3 years there was only marginal mourning (*sublugetur* is the term used); then mourning increased progressively up to the full period of ten months according to age; at the age of 10 years mourning was as for adults. A fragment from the third-century jurist Ulpian preserves these rules:

Parents are to be mourned for a year, as are children older than 10 years. Pomponius [a jurist of the mid-second century] says that in this context a year is ten months—a plausible argument, since younger children are mourned for as many months as they have lived down to the age of three; a child younger than three years does not receive formal mourning but a marginal form (*non lugetur, sed sublugetur*); a child less than a year old receives neither formal mourning nor a marginal form (*neque lugetur neque sublugetur*).[29]

But this does not tell us whether or not parents and other members of the family were saddened and distressed by such deaths. Studies of other societies have shown that the frequency of child

---

[27] Birley (1987). See below on Marcus' own references to the illnesses and deaths of children.

[28] Ariès (1981: 447): in lists of families, children under 1 year are usually unnamed. Scheper-Hughes (1987*b*: 147) found that in a disadvantaged community in Brazil, with high infant mortality, the nurturance of infants was 'less individualized and personalized' than in better-off areas. Many infants 'remain unchristened and unnamed until they begin to walk and talk' or until impending death brings on an emergency baptism.

[29] *Frag. Vat.* 321 = *FIRA*[2] 2. 536. Plutarch attributed this legislation to the early period of King Numa (*Numa* 12 = *FIRA*[2] 1. 12).

deaths and therefore the expectation of losing some, at least, of one's children early does not inure parents to such loss. Golden (1990: 82–90) discusses this for classical Athens and cites comparative evidence from other societies, commenting: 'It seems, then, that more than demography governs the reaction to a child's death in high-mortality populations in general' (p. 85).[30] Even in Victorian England infant mortality was high and there is evidence (at least from the upper classes) of considerable grief and mourning at such deaths.[31]

The rules for formal mourning, however, are intended to help people structure their public lives (such as what public activities they might attend, what clothing they should wear[32]), and are more relevant to people with public responsibilities and a public image to uphold than to people of lower strata. Similarly, the literature of the educated upper classes contains ideals of comportment—self-restraint, dignity, philosophical consolation. None of this tells us much about inner emotions or behaviour, especially in the mass of the population.

The upper, educated classes were able to externalize their grief in funerary ritual and philosophical, consolatory literature. It has been argued (Gunnella 1995) that the lower classes, for whom these avenues were less accessible, thus expressed grief more frankly and uninhibitedly. In a study of consolatory literature and epigrams, Strubbe (1998) discusses the development of consolatory speeches in schools of rhetoric and argues that it is rhetoric, rather than philosophy, that reflects the idea that grief is difficult to console. There are thus more extreme expressions of grief and its uncontrollability in rhetorical speeches than in philosophical

[30] He also points out that in societies which tolerate infanticide parents may grieve deeply for the death of children who have been reared. Cf. Golden (1988), drawing on the work of anthropologists; he makes a strong case for real grief and grieving for the death of the very young even in societies of high infant mortality. Cf. Scheper-Hughes (1987b: 140): 'both severe selective neglect *and* strong sentiments of maternal attachment coexist'.

[31] Jalland (1996: 180–5). Scheper-Hughes (1987a: 5) finds, in a wide range of evidence from different societies and periods, 'a sometimes exquisite and doting love lavished on infants and children by parents representing all social classes' and 'the pain and anguish they experienced at their children's illnesses or death'.

[32] e.g. Paulus (*Sententiae* 1. 21. 14) reports that a person in mourning must abstain from banquets, ornamentation, and the wearing of purple and white ('qui luget abstinere debet a conuiuiis ornamentis purpura et alba ueste').

writing. (We have already seen that some upper-class writers dismissed rhetorical school exercises as artificial and exaggerated.) Roman sarcophagi whose scenes of mourning include parents and slave attendants do present the parents of a deceased child with a more 'subdued demeanour' than that of the slaves, who exhibit a more emotional 'distraught response': the parents seated by the funeral couch have a fixed stare or downcast eyes, whereas the slaves 'are shown gesticulating expressively, leaning towards the child's body, and reaching out to touch his face'.[33] This art represented Romans of some standing, in attitudes of ideal composure. But ideals and training did not prevent some notable Roman men from making emotional displays of grief for infant deaths. Seneca wrote a long letter, for the edification of Lucilius, on the futility and ungratefulness of grieving at death (*Letters* 99). In it he takes his friend Marullus as an example of a mature man, who should know better, grieving extravagantly at the death of a young son ('filium paruulum'): Seneca criticizes Marullus' emotional reaction ('molliter ferre': 99. 1). Seneca's arguments are that the boy had lived for so short a period that no hopes could have been invested in him; he might have turned out badly, as sons often did. Seneca grants (99. 15–16) that it is natural to show emotion at the time of death, but one should not overdo it so as to make a display. He grants also (99. 23) that one should not suppress memory of a lost one; it is less than human not to remember one's own dead, to bury memory with the body. It is good to speak often of the lost one, to remember his talk and jokes (even that of a very young one: 'quamuis paruoli'). But those who mourn and miss those who died young ('in aetate prima raptum') should put the death in perspective by realizing how short any life is in comparison with eternity (99. 31). It is clear that Marullus was deeply moved by the death of the infant, and even Seneca, playing the rational philosopher, admits the human and individual qualities of the lost son. Pliny the Younger sympathized with his friend Minicius Fundanus, for whom no philosophical training was adequate to console him for the death of his 12-year-old daughter.[34]

---

[33] George (2000), focusing on three sarcophagi in detail in a wide-ranging discussion of 'biographical' sarcophagi.

[34] *Letters* 5. 16. Cf. Ch. 1 for discrepancy between Pliny and epitaph.

The poet Statius wrote a long (sympathetic) poem (*Siluae* 2. 1) describing the grief exhibited by Atedius Melior at the death of his little foster-child (*alumnus*) Glaucias.[35] Juvenal concluded *Satire* 15, a deeply hostile attack on the inhumanity of Egyptians, with a moving passage on Nature's gift of compassion to the human race, evinced by the gift of tears (lines 131–40):

Nature, who gave us tears, thus proclaims her gift to the human race of tender hearts; this emotion is the best part of us . . . It is nature's impulse which makes us groan when the funeral of a girl ripe for marriage crosses our path, or when the earth closes over an infant, one too young for the funeral pyre.

His expression for compassion, or tenderness, is 'mollissima corda', using the same word which Seneca used to describe Marullus' reaction to the death of his infant son. Such compassion is part of human nature, and a virtue. Herodes Atticus, that pragmatic, often ruthless citizen of Athens and Rome in the mid-second century, powerful in political and cultural circles, could weep at the death of his newborn son. His pupil, the young Marcus Aurelius, asked another of his teachers and literary figure Fronto to write a letter of consolation to Herodes, who was not bearing the death calmly ('non aequo animo'). Fronto's consolation focused on the role of a child as hope for the future: any such loss is painful, but, Fronto continues, Herodes is young enough to replace the loss and thus to have new hope.[36] Marcus himself set out in his *Meditations* principles of calmness and resignation for facing the death of a child.[37] We have seen above (Chapter 1),

---

[35] See discussion by Laes (2003).

[36] Herodes was probably less than 40 at this time. Fronto, *Letters* 1. 6. 7 (Marcus to Fronto); 1. 8, in Greek, Fronto to Herodes.

[37] The following examples are from the *Meditations*. There is further information in Fronto's correspondence and in the *Historia Augusta* life of Marcus. One of the lessons which Marcus had learnt from one of his teachers was to be unflinching in bearing the pain caused by the loss of a child (1. 8). One should aim for freedom from fear; so do not pray, 'Let me not lose my child', but 'Let me not fear to lose my child' (9. 40). Marcus uses Homeric quotations to explain the transitoriness of everything, and thus to train himself not to give way to grief and fear: children are like the leaves which the wind scatters to the ground; but everything shoots again in the spring, and the forest puts forth new leaves to replace those blown to the ground (10. 34). He quotes Epictetus to say that just as 'only a madman looks for figs in winter, it is mad for a man to look for a child when he may no longer have one. A man tenderly

however, that in his letters there is frequent personal concern for his young children and those of Fronto, especially in their ill health.

Within some fairly general attitudes to the very young, there can be significant cultural differences. An example of this is the contrast, within Rome itself, between Latin-language and Greek-language memorials to children. The two communities lived in the one city at the one time, but Latin-language epitaphs favour the young while the Greek ones reveal an almost opposite pattern. MacMullen, in his classic work on 'the epigraphic habit' in the Roman world, illustrated this graphically, showing that Latin epitaphs for ages 0–9 accounted for over 30 per cent of all the ages specified, but the Greek ones for these ages accounted for only 10 per cent of Greek epitaphs specifying ages. Corresponding figures at the other end of the age scale show an increase in Greek epitaphs after the age of 30 and again after the age of 70, whereas the proportion of Latin epitaphs decreased steadily with age, especially after age 30.[38] Within the western Mediterranean, it was in large urban areas and amongst large slave populations that young children received the highest percentage of epitaphs. Northern Italy provides more evidence than southern Italy, and each provides more than Africa or Spain (Shaw 1984 and 1996). The rate of commemoration for deceased children must indicate something of the valuation of children in any society, but we do need to be conscious of the operation of regional and cultural factors. Boys had a better chance than girls

---

kissing his child should whisper to himself, 'Perhaps tomorrow he will die', and this is not ill-omened: it recognizes a natural process, like the reaping of ears of grain.

[38] MacMullen (1982: fig. III). Ery (1969) originally produced this graph, which represents data from the first two centuries CE. He also showed a striking chronological change: in the 3rd and 4th cs. the Greek and Latin patterns became much more similar, with the Latin emphasis on young children weakening a little and the Greek emphasis increasing considerably. Ery comments (p. 62), 'This change can probably be attributed to the interaction of the two coexisting and locally adjacent groups, further substantiated by the fact that no such alteration can be observed in any one of the other Italian examples.' Another factor was probably the Christianization of more of the lower classes, which would be reflected in the Greek-speaking population at Rome. Shaw (1991: 80) discusses the emphasis on children in commemorations by Christians in Roman Italy. Clauss (1973) confirms the Latin–Greek contrast.

of being commemorated at young ages, but from about the age of 10 girls tended to equalize the proportions: they were becoming more useful as workers by then and were coming to the age when they could be considered for marriage.[39]

Where sculpture embellishes funerary monuments, children are often represented graphically and realistically.[40] Italian iconography reveals a lively interest in babies and young children from an early period. Although Attic monuments from the late fifth century developed more realistic representations of children, the infrequency of associated inscriptions makes it difficult to establish individuality or to identify relationships.[41] In Italian funerary sculpture, especially of the first two centuries CE, inscriptions combined with sculpture to represent children as individuals and help contextualize them in their relationships. Funerary monuments which have biographical scenes often include infancy as part of the life cycle. There is particular pathos in the commemoration in Fig. 6.1, one of the comparatively few inscriptions with associated sculpture dedicated to infants. Publicia Glypte dedicated this altar for two infant boys, her son and her *uerna*. We have discussed above (Chapter 6) the hopes for the future invested in these children, and the use of the Telephus symbolism to represent the fostering of an infant. A use of the Roman wolverine, the *lupa Romana*, suckling Romulus and Remus would have made more explicit the close association of the two boys and their probable co-fostering; but the Telephus myth is nevertheless relevant enough to suggest that it was consciously chosen for this occasion.[42]

---

[39] B. Rawson (1986a: 179–80). Cf. Scheidel (1996: table 1), where maximum prices for female slaves reach those for males only in the 8–16 age group; and McWilliam (2001: 79) on the higher female to male sex ratio in ages 13–14 in her selection of children's epitaphs from several parts of Italy.

[40] For more discussion of funerary representations of children, see Ch. 1 above.

[41] Clairmont (1993) has a detailed catalogue. He admits (27–9) how easy it is to misinterpret relationships when there are no inscriptions. Cf. Hirsch-Dyczek (1983: 12).

[42] Tombstones must often have been bought 'off the shelf', and their appropriateness is sometimes not obvious. But it would be very rare to find a ready-carved tombstone with a twin-like pair of boys on it. For the use of the *lupus Romana*, see B. Rawson (2003), where I thank Monica Truemper and Carolyn Osiek for their contributions to these comments.

Children who survived infancy had a better chance of being commemorated. They had begun to be taken seriously as continuers of the line, and often a child's epitaph gave evidence of a status superior to that of its parents, as in Fig. 1.5: there were freeborn children of freed parents, freed children of slave parents (B. Rawson 1966 and 1986*b*: 23–4). The hope of a better life which had thus been sparked must have sharpened the sense of loss when such a child died young. Sometimes 'substitute' children had been brought into the family—foster-children, stepchildren, specially favoured slave children born and raised in the household (*alumni, filiastri, uernae*)—and when they died they too disappointed the hopes of a 'parent'.[43]

Sarcophagi were gradually coming into use at Rome from the early second century CE.[44] The earliest sarcophagus in the Vatican cemetery under St Peter's (probably Hadrianic) was made for a six-month-old infant (Toynbee and Ward-Perkins 1956: 88). Inside there are rounded corners and a tiny head-rest, and on each of the short sides is the figure of a grieving parent. The broader surfaces of sarcophagi provided greater scope for ornamentation and for details of children's (and others') lives, which must have been a stimulus to their increasing use. As the natural container for inhumation, sarcophagi were preferred by Christians if they could afford them,[45] but Christians gave little attention to the details of everyday life or to the representation of children as individuals. For them, death was the occasion to look ahead to a blessed new life, and all Christians were children of God, irrespective of age. Biblical scenes were thus used fairly indiscriminately for children and adults alike.[46]

There is little Christian evidence before the fourth century. Sculpture on earlier children's sarcophagi often depicted scenes,

---

[43] For relationships attested on funerary monuments, see Ch. 6 above.

[44] Inhumation had been practised at an earlier period in Rome, but cremation was the norm from the 1st c. BCE into the 2nd c. CE. Some of the early sarcophagi were receptacles for urns of ashes.

[45] Sarcophagi were comparatively expensive, but their use went beyond the upper classes. Other members of Rome's population, e.g. ambitious freedmen, adopted this form of commemoration readily, as they had adopted other forms from the 1st c. CE onwards.

[46] See B. Rawson (2003). Huskinson (1996: 119) points out that by the later 3rd c. compositions on sarcophagi in general were already becoming formulaic, and that figured elements had a subordinate role in decorative scenes.

retrospectively, from their past lives or (in prospect) the lives which they would have lived in adulthood. The funeral eulogy for an adult man often traced the life chronologically (*contextus*), starting with 'the natural character (*indoles*) shown in the earliest years', then his education (*disciplinae*), followed by the pattern of his adult achievements, in word and deed (Quintilian 3. 7. 15). Thus there was an interest in biographical progression, and the first two elements specified by Quintilian could be represented and commemorated even for children, although they had no achievements to be praised in a formal *laudatio* at the funeral. The biographical sequences on children's sarcophagi date particularly from the late second and early third centuries. They usually refer to boys' activities, and depict boys in scenes of schooling or recreation. Children are often represented with pets (animals and birds). The goat is a favourite, and boys' games often include driving a goat-cart.[47] As we saw above (Chapter 3), Quintilian articulated the role of play and games in a child's education. Education, or some form of schooling or training, was highly valued in a wide range of Roman society: it was the key to a better future.[48] The future was more circumscribed for girls, without serious career opportunities. Laments for girls' early deaths usually referred to the sadness of parents or to the girls' failure to attain motherhood. There was less scope for sculptural narration in this than in boys' circumstances.

A well-known sarcophagus showing the life stages of a boy who died young is that of M. Cornelius Statius: a finely sculpted piece of the mid-second century CE, 1.49 m long and 0.475 m high, originally from Ostia but now in the Louvre in Paris (Fig. 2.2). The four stages portrayed are: the mother nursing the newborn baby, watched by the father; the father, standing, dandling his infant son; the boy driving a goat-cart; the boy reading from a scroll to a seated man (probably a teacher, perhaps the father). The inscription beneath the sculpture is broken, but reveals that the boy was freeborn and that the dedicators were probably his

---

[47] See K. R. Bradley (1998b) on pets and representations of them with children. Kleiner (1987: 115) suggests that the goat has symbolic significance, promising reincarnation.

[48] Cf. Ch. 5 above.

parents.[49] Another sarcophagus, slightly later and somewhat smaller, but also from Ostia (now in the British Museum), has lively scenes on the side of boys playing games with nuts. On the lid is the mother's dedication to her 4-year-old freeborn son.[50]

The scene of 'the first bath' reflected the interest in infancy. As we saw above (Chapter 1), the 'first bath' had often been associated with the infant god Dionysus, but that association was probably less important now than the general interest in stages of a child's life cycle. At the other end of the cycle, the death scene portrayed the child on its funerary couch, often flanked by grieving parents.[51] One popular theme on children's sarcophagi was the race of a charioteer. Whitehead (1984: 42) sees this motif as symbolizing the dangers and pitfalls of life. Where the charioteer is a child, who falls from the chariot during the race, the symbolism may be that of the tragedy of those who die young, before their course has been completed.

The early death of children evoked a variety of expressions of grief and regret. Sometimes the regret is for the loss of benefits to parents in later life: there will be no one to carry on the family name, no one to bury the parents and tend their tomb. Sometimes the grief is more for the loss of a loved individual, valued for what it has already contributed to one or more adults' life. Seneca expressed the unpreparedness of parents for their children's deaths, in spite of their observation of frequent other 'untimely' deaths. 'We nevertheless look on our infants and visualise them putting on the toga, doing military service, and succeeding to their father's property. . . . There is nothing to forbid their performing the last rites for you and the delivery of your funeral speech by your children; but prepare yourself for placing your son on the pyre, whatever his age. . . . No death is not untimely (*acerbum*) when the parent follows the bier.'[52]

---

[49] *CIL* 14. 4875: M. CORNELIO M. F. PAL. | STATIO P. . . | . . . FECER. Illustrations of the sarcophagus are in many publications, e.g. Huskinson (1996: pl. II.1); Amedick (1991: pls. 52.1–12, 53.4–5); B. Rawson (1999: fig. 1).

[50] *CIL* 14. 532: D. M. | L. AEMILIO DAPHNO POMP | TINA VIXIT ANN. IIII D. VI | LIVIA DAPHNE FIL. DVLCISSIMO. Illustrations in Huskinson (1996: pl. IV.4); Amedick (1991: pls. 93.1, 2, 5); B. Rawson (1991*a*: pl. 4 (b)).

[51] See B. Rawson (1991*a*: pl. 4a) for one example. Cf. George (2000).

[52] Seneca, *Consolation to Marcia* 9. 2, 17. 7. Cf. Néraudau (1984).

Quintilian's account (6 pr. 10–11) of the deaths of his two young sons is one of the most moving literary accounts which survive from Rome. The praise of their charms and achievements is extravagant, but it serves to point up the great loss suffered—the boys' loss of brilliant futures and the father's loss of sons who inspired in him such love and pride. Quintilian's wife predeceased the boys, only a few months before the death of the younger child, who died when just 5. The child's grandmother took over his rearing, but Quintilian claims that his son devoted his greatest affection to his father, Quintilian ('mihi blandissimus'), which increased Quintilian's suffering at this death. The surviving son became Quintilian's one hope, pleasure, and support.

His life was not just in bud, like that of my other son, but he had passed his ninth birthday and had demonstrated sure, well-formed fruit. I swear by my own sufferings, by my own unhappy consciousness, by his departed spirit, the godhead of my grief, that I saw in him qualities of the mind, not only for grasping the subjects of his studies (I have wide experience in this, and have seen no more outstanding example) and for self-motivated learning (as his teachers well know), but also qualities of integrity, loyalty, humanity, generosity, which certainly might have aroused fear of this great blow, since it has commonly been noted that premature ripeness brings on too early a death and that there is some force of envy which cuts short such great hopes, obviously to prevent our human affairs advancing beyond what has been allocated for man. . . . With what courage he bore his illness of eight months, to the wonder of his doctors! How he comforted me in his last hours! . . . O, the embodiment of my unfulfilled hopes, was it *you* whose fading eyes, *you* whose fleeing spirit I looked on? It was your cold, bloodless body which I embraced: could I receive your last breath and go on breathing the common air? I deserve the torment which I suffer, I deserve these thoughts.[53]

Quintilian's differentiation between the somewhat nebulous promise of very young children and the more solid qualities of slightly older children is reflected in the behaviour of other Romans and reinforces the comparative lack of identity which we observed in infants. Suetonius' account of the death of three of the nine children born to Agrippina the Elder and Germanicus

---

[53] The italics are intended to bring out something of the linguistic contrast in the Latin between actuality and expectation: it is the father who is dealing with the death of a son, rather than the son doing his filial duty for the father.

implies that the two who died in infancy made little impact of
personality, but the boy who was just coming out of infancy
(*puerascens*) established himself in others' affections through a
lovable and lively disposition.[54] Augustus kept a likeness of this
great-grandson in his bedroom, and Livia dedicated another, in
the guise of a Cupid, in Venus' temple on the Capitol.[55]

Regulus, a senator of the late first century CE, grieved extravagantly for his one son, who died in the autumn, in one of the
unhealthiest times of the year. The boy's pet animals and birds
were slaughtered at his funeral pyre, and Regulus retired to his
suburban villa to grieve. The depth of grief and sense of loss come
through Pliny the Younger's account (*Letters* 4. 2) in spite of
Pliny's hostility to Regulus. Quintilian and Regulus were contemporaries of the emperor Domitian, who was a man of his own
time in his commemoration of the son who had died in childhood. Domitian's son was about 9 years of age when he died, the
same age as Quintilian's elder son and a likely age for the death
of Regulus' son.[56] When Domitian became emperor, he issued
gold and silver coinage celebrating the son's apotheosis.[57] His
bronze coinage also celebrated his wife Domitia as the mother of
the deified child.[58] We have no record of Domitia's own grief.[59]
We do know, however, that the marriage went through periods of
tension, and the likely date of Domitia's (temporary) exile is 83
CE, close to the likely date of the death of their son.[60] In modern
times, the loss of a young child may have the effect of drawing
the parents closer together for comfort, but is also known to lead
to recriminations, alienation, and even divorce.

Epitaphs echo this grief of parents for the loss of a young
child, and the phrase often used for such a death is *funus*

---

[54] *Gaius* 7–8; 'insigni festiuitate', 'amabili pueritia'.

[55] See *LTUR* IV: 114, 119–20 for shrines of Venus on the Capitol.

[56] On Domitian's son, see Desnier (1979). He explains the image of the boy
as a naked infant on the gold and silver apotheosis coins as an image of 'heroic
nudity', and points out that on the bronze coins with his mother the boy is more
like his real age (born 73 CE, died 82 or 83). Cf. Ch. 1.

[57] *RIC* 2. 179–80 nos. 209a, 213: 81–4 CE.

[58] *RIC* 2. 209 nos. 440–1.

[59] For Regulus and Quintilian, the wives had already predeceased the young
sons.

[60] See B. W. Jones (1992: 33–8).

acerbum/aceruum, 'a bitter/unripe death'. The analogy with the ripeness of fruit had been alluded to by Quintilian in his phrase 'premature ripeness brings on too early a death',[61] and was made explicit in a dedication by another father, this time in an epitaph for his daughter: 'Our bodies are like apples hanging on a tree: they either fall when they are mature or come tumbling down too soon when they are unripe.'[62] In another (*CIL* 6. 10097) a boy speaks from the grave, hoping that the passer-by will never experience grief, as his parents are now suffering, for a premature death: 'sic numquam doleas pro funere aceruo'. It was a common complaint that a parent had to see to the burial of a child, when the normal expectation should have been that the child would perform that duty for a parent. On an altar of the latter part of the first century CE, the death is recorded of a 9-year-old boy, Successus, and then of his mother Caesia Gemella. The boy's father (also Successus) makes this complaint: 'Premature death has made a parent perform the duty which it was proper for a son to do for his father.'[63] The death of a child of this age could be more troubling than that of an infant. H. J. Rose (1923) argued that children beyond infancy were already launched on their life career, but they had not achieved maturity: they had not married or produced posterity, so they were in 'a troublesome intermediate stage of ghosthood'. Infants, however, had hardly lived, so they were virtually non-persons; they might even reappear in the guise of another newborn infant; so their death could not pollute. Vergil (*Georgics* 4. 476–7) lists among the shadows in the underworld those deprived of light and trapped by the Styx, 'boys and unmarried girls, and young men placed on the funeral pyre before the eyes of their parents'.

There were many statements of the nothingness or grimness beyond death, as in the epitaph for the 8-year-old boy L. Paquedius L. f. Ser. Ampliatus, whose last line reads 'infelix iaceo nunc cinis et lacrimae' ('unfortunate one, I lie here now as ashes and tears') (*CIL* 6. 23818). In the town of Pisaurum an epitaph

---

[61] 'celerius occidere festinatam maturitatem' (6 pr. 10, above).

[62] *CIL* 6. 7574: '. . . quo modo | mala in arbore pendunt | sic corpora nostra | aut matura cadunt aut | cito acerua ruunt | Domatius Tiras | filiae dulcissimae'.

[63] *CIL* 6. 26901: 'quod fas parenti | facere debuit filius | mors immatura fecit | ut faceret parens . . .'.

(*CIL* ii. 6435) for the 5-year-old Petronius Antigenes identifies his *domus aeterna* as the abominable sphere of Tartarus ('taetra Tartarei sidera'), where he must abandon all hope and fortune. The unfairness of his fate is highlighted by the record of how hard he had studied and the opportunities given him by his father Hilarus. From the expression 'pater ipse patronus', these opportunities would seem to have included freedom from slavery: the father is also ex-owner.

The premature death of a child could be seen as an unnatural break with the normal order of things and thus necessitating special rites to placate angry spirits. The spirits of the prematurely dead (the *lemures*) were thought to wander until the effluxion of the time allotted by Fate.[64] Vergil described these spirits as amongst the unhappy dead in the underworld, caught in the mire across the Styx and far from the blessed fields of Elysium (*Aeneid* 6. 427–9). They include infants, 'snatched from the breast, on the threshold of life and robbed of the sweetnesses of life, carried off by a black day and drowned in the bitterness of death':

> infantumque animae flentes, in limine primo
> quos dulcis uitae exsortis et ab ubere raptos
> abstulit atra dies et funere mersit acerbo.

The festival of Lemuria in May recognized the presence of such wandering spirits amongst the living and propitiated them to hasten their return to the underworld. This unease, and fear of pollution, were probably the reason for giving priority of burial to the prematurely dead in Italian towns. The evidence for this regulation comes from Puteoli, in an inscription of the first half of the first century BCE, but it probably applied more generally to other Italian towns.[65] Such concerns eased as a more benign popular belief grew up around the end of the second century or early in the third. This was that children who died very young had

---

[64] Archaeological evidence which seems to reflect this has been found in the area of Roman Dacia: statuettes have been found in children's graves (Hampartumian 1978). These belong to the period of the High Empire (2nd to 4th c.), but until comparable material is found elsewhere we do not know how much to attribute to local belief and practice and how much to more generalized cultural factors or Romanization. Similar figurines have been found in north-west Pannonia and in Greece, where there was widespread influence of Hecate and Dionysus.

[65] See further discussion in B. Rawson (2002) and below.

been untouched by the world and thus they returned to the heavens whence they had come. The belief is not found in literary sources but in inscriptions. It is reflected, for example, in an inscription set up by an imperial freedman, Eutiches, to his 2-year-old son Eutychos: twelve lines of Greek elegaics followed by the dedication in Latin, surmounted by a relief depicting the child's apotheosis (Fig. 8.1). This and other inscriptions rejoice that the child has been saved the long wait in Hades which the prematurely dead might expect. It is purity, innocence, rather than virtue and learning which the child can thank for such release (Seston 1949; Boyancé 1952).[66] Eutychos is characterized as having known neither the bad nor the good of life: οὐ κακὸν οὐδὲ ἀγαθὸν γνούς βίος ὅττι φέρει.

FIG. 8.1   Relief and epitaph for Eutychos, aged 2. Apotheosis. Rome, late second to early third century CE.

[66] Learning continued to be highly prized, well into the Christian period. But there is nothing quite like the 1st-c. altar commemorating the extraordinary learning of Q. Sulpicius Maximus (Kleiner 1987: 45). The Eutychos memorial belongs to the late 2nd or early 3rd c. CE.

There had been a long tradition of associating the soul with the aether and the stars, as in Neo-Pythagoreanism. In the Roman period the divine implications of this were sometimes exploited for political purposes, as in the observation of a star after the death of Julius Caesar, exploited by Octavian-Augustus, and of one after the death of Antinous, welcomed by Hadrian. Funerary monuments with astral symbolism are not common in Roman Italy, being more frequent in Roman Africa and in Gaul.[67] Such symbolism and its application to children were not, however, unknown at Rome. As we saw above, Domitian represented his dead son on coinage as an infant reaching up to seven stars above him. The mythological associations were of a son translated to the heavens as the star Arcturus to join his spiritual mother, the constellation The Great Bear, and summoned by his father Jupiter (B. Rawson 1997*b*: 78). One tombstone found in Rome which contains symbolism of this kind commemorates a 10-year-old girl, Iulia Victorina. Her epitaph (*CIL* 6. 20727), probably from the first century CE, was dedicated to her as 'filiae dulcissimae' by her parents C. Iulius Saturninus and Lucilia Procula. Her bust, on the front of the altar above the epitaph, is surmounted by a crescent moon. On the back of the stone is the bust of an adult woman whose head is backed by the rays of the sun. These two portraits may be taken to represent two phases of the deceased girl's passage to eternal life in the heavens: her initial abode in the moon and her later ascent to the sun (Prieur 1986: 136; Kleiner 1987: catalogue 15, pl. X.3–4).

Jupiter's eagle had been associated in myth with the translation of the young Ganymede to the heavens, to serve Jupiter (e.g. *Aeneid* 5. 252–5). An epitaph to a young son reflects this myth (*CIL* 6. 35769): the parents of L. Malius Epagathus refer to him as 'nostrum Ganymeden' and want to follow soon after their prematurely dead son (*immaturum*). Seston points out (1949: 317) that Eutychos' direct translation to the skies has saved him from the long period in Limbo traditionally assigned to the prematurely dead. He sees a revulsion in the imperial period against the traditional view, because of parents' affection for their children. He sees this change in another epitaph from Rome, in which the

---

[67] See Prieur (1986: 132–8) for these associations. Prieur attributes the astral symbolism in Gaul, Spain, Britain, and the Danube provinces to Celtic influences.

little girl (*paruola*) Anullina proclaims her escape from the underworld and her translation to the stars, distinguishing between her
earthly remains and her soul thus:

> . . . SED MEA
> DIVINA NON EST ITVRA SVB
> VMBRAS   CAELESTIS
> ANIMA. MVNDVS ME SVMP-
> SIT ET ASTRA. CORPVS HABET
> TELLVS ET SAXVM NOMEN
> NANAE.[68]

A much grander statement of this new hope for an existence
beyond the grave is on a large, finely inscribed marble slab dedicated by a grandfather (Sex. Ossianius Sex. f. Com.) for his
grandson M. Lucceius M. f.[69] No age is given for the grandson,
but on demographic probability and the reference to his 'youth
damned by a melancholy fate' ('tristi damnatam sorte iuuentam')
he can be taken to have died young. The epitaph expounds the
joy of the new life after death, but also gives details of the hor-
rors of the more normal fate in the underworld. In the first of
three columns the grandfather tells of his grief that his grandson
had been snatched away by a premature death ('praematura
morte'), but then of his vision of Lucceius, larger than life, shin-
ing brightly in the sky and reassuring his grandfather that there
is no need to weep for him, now that he has been translated to
the stars of heaven and has become a god (*deus*). In the other two
columns Lucceius tells of the dark and threatening places of the
underworld which he has escaped and the opportunities for him
now to choose whatever form of divinity he likes and a future
which will be everlasting (not terminated by devouring time,
'tempus edax').

There was a problem for Christians in any attempt to represent the dead as gods or heavenly beings. Tertullian gave strong
expression to this at the end of the second century, in his criticism of pagans' attitudes to their own gods:

[68] *CIL* 6. 12087. 'But my divine spirit will not go down below, beneath the
Shades; it is destined for the skies. The heavens and the stars have taken me up.
The earth contains my body, and my stone the name of a ghost.'

[69] *CIL* 6. 21521 (= 34137). The stone is broken at the end of the grandfather's
name, so it is not certain whether or not he had a *cognomen*, but the grandson
did not. Dates of early and late 1st c. CE have been suggested (see *CIL*).

What honour do you pay to your gods which you do not equally offer to your dead? You erect temples to the gods—equally to the dead; you erect altars to the gods—equally to the dead; you inscribe the same letters in their inscriptions, you give the same form to their statues, according to each person's profession or business or age. An old man's representation is taken from Saturn, a youth's from Apollo, a girl's from Diana . . .[70]

Thus there are no parallels in Christian art for the heroization of mortals.

Néraudau (1987), discussing mostly literary usage of *funus acerbum*, argues for a development from the early Republic[71] to imperial times, when he identifies the emergence of sentimental values attached to children and childhood. Earlier, the unnaturalness of children's deaths involved pollution and thus their funerals were brief and nocturnal. Later, the unnaturalness caused demonstrative grieving and lamentation because display of feeling was now acceptable in the new climate of sentiment about children. But excessive display was still frowned on, as the child's legal status remained defective: it could claim no autonomy or civic achievement (and thus no *laudatio* could be offered). Néraudau does not, however, confront the question of whether an abbreviated funeral was considered appropriate for the young in the changed, imperial climate. There are examples to suggest that by imperial times even children could have a splendid funeral and in daylight. The epitaph of the early second century for the 6-year-old Marcianus (Fig. 5.1) claims that the whole neighbourhood poured out to watch his funeral procession and grieve for the loss of the young intellectual prodigy (*CIL* 6. 7578).

There is evidence, in various media, for a changing attitude to children and childhood—or at least a changing manifestation of feeling, and greater visibility of children in these media—in the imperial period.[72] In the first century BCE, undertakers were required to bury most people in the order in which corpses were reported to them; but premature deaths (*funus acerbum*) had to

---

[70] *To the Nations* 1. 10. 25–36; cf. *Apology* 13. 7.

[71] The earliest examples of the phrase in literature are from Plautus, referring to the death of young soldiers (*Amphitruo* 190) and to the potential death of a young woman prostitute in her role as daughter to mother (*Asinaria* 595).

[72] See e.g. B. Rawson (1997*a*) on iconography and (1997*b*) on other art, inscriptions, papyri, law, and literature. Cf. 'Introduction' above.

be given priority and dealt with quickly.[73] Were undertakers bound by the same rules in later periods? This depends somewhat on whether the idea of pollution remained strong, and the belief that the prematurely dead had restless spirits. The evidence suggests that such ideas did persist, in spite of some examples of the development of an alternative view of the fate of those who died young. But in the context of new parental sensibilities suggested above, and changed views on the appropriateness of funerary display for the young, funerals for children might not have been so abbreviated and speedy. There is an ambivalence here which need not cause surprise in a matter of religion and family emotion. The earlier injunction to undertakers may have been less relevant in a later period, but the high rate of child mortality would still have been an incentive to deal quickly with many such deaths. In those circumstances many children failed to receive material, public commemoration of their lives and deaths. They were, however, commemorated more frequently than older age groups (as noted above), reflecting a particularly Roman *pietas* and affection felt by parents and others for the young. Within the general category of children, some age groups were memorialized more frequently than others, providing an insight into Roman concepts of children's roles and value and the degree of loss felt at their deaths. That children should have been commemorated in such numbers, and sometimes in such elaborate style, is a remarkable feature of Roman culture. There is no parallel for it in earlier or later societies before the twentieth century.[74]

---

[73] Puteoli inscription (*AE* 1971 no. 88): see B. Rawson (2002). The other categories for priority also involve pollution and unease—suicides by hanging, criminal slaves, decurions (town councillors).

[74] Ariès (1981: 231) writes of the 'remarkable development' in France and Italy in the 16th c. in which 'even children and adolescents now became entitled' to an epitaph, with expressions of praise and grief for the young ones. But examples of children aged below 14 years are rare. Cf. p. 528, where children are said to be frequent in some Parisian cemeteries of the mid-19th c.

CHRONOLOGICAL GUIDE

Some of the dates below are approximate; but this Guide is intended to encourage readers constantly to place sources in chronological context and to distinguish primary from secondary sources.

509–27 BCE: the period of the Republic.

From 27 BCE: the Principate (rule by the *princeps*, 'leading citizen') or imperial period.

EMPERORS' REIGNS

27 BCE–14 CE	Augustus

Julio-Claudians

14–37	Tiberius
37–41	Gaius (Caligula)
41–54	Claudius
54–68	Nero
68–69	(Year of the Four Emperors) Galba, Otho, Vitellius, Vespasian

Flavians

69–79	Vespasian
79–81	Titus
81–96	Domitian
96–98	Nerva
98–117	Trajan
117–138	Hadrian

Antonines

138–161	Antoninus Pius
161–180	Marcus Aurelius
161–169	Lucius Verus co-emperor
180–192	Commodus
193, Civil War	Pertinax, Didius Iulianus, Septimius Seuerus

Severans

193–211	Septimius Seuerus
211–217	Caracalla

JURISTS

Late Republic, died 43 BCE	Seruius (Sulpicius Rufus)
Augustan period	Labeo
Augustan period	Capito
Julio–Claudian period	Proculus
Flavian period	Pegasus
Trajan–Hadrian period	Celsus
(to be distinguished from the writer Celsus)	
Hadrian–Antonine period	Saluius Iulianus
Hadrian–Antonine period	Pomponius
Mid-second century	Caecilius
Second half of second century	Gaius
Marcus Aurelius period	Scaeuola
*c.*200	Papinian
Late second, early third centuries	Paulus (Paul)
(*Sententiae* attributed to him may be later)	
Late second, early third centuries	Ulpian
(*Regulae* attributed to him may be later)	
Early third century	Marcianus
First half of third century	Modestinus
First half of third century	Callistratus
Sixth century	Tribonianus

(oversaw compilation and editing of earlier law, including jurists'
interpretations and emperors' judgments, as *Institutes*, *Digest*, and
Codex
under emperor Justinian)

First half of fourth century	*Fragmenta Vaticana*: excerpts from a collection of texts

LITERARY AUTHORS

BCE

Late third, early second centuries	Plautus
116–27	Varro
106–43	Cicero
100–44	Julius Caesar

90–55	Lucretius
84–54	Catullus
86–35	Sallust
100–25	Cornelius Nepos
70–19	Vergil
65–8	Horace
60–19	Tibullus
50–16	Propertius

BCE–CE

59 BCE–17 CE	Livy
43 BCE–18 CE	Ovid
Augustan period	Vitruvius
Augustus–Tiberius period	Valerius Maximus
Augustus–Tiberius period	Velleius Paterculus
55 BCE–37 CE	Seneca the Elder
4 BCE–65 CE	Seneca the Younger

CE

Nero period	Petronius
23–79	Pliny the Elder
35–95	Quintilian
40–96	Statius
40–104	Martial
61–112	Pliny the Younger
55–117	Tacitus
46–120	Plutarch (wrote in Greek)
First half of second century	Juvenal
70–140	Suetonius
98–138	Soranus (wrote in Greek)
Antonine period	Fronto
Late second century (not the jurist)	Celsus
150–235	Cassius Dio (wrote in Greek)
Third to fourth centuries	Scriptores Historiae Augustae (SHA) various writers whose biographies form the *Historia Augusta* ('the Augustan History')
200–258	Cyprian
340–420	Jerome

GLOSSARY

A simplified explanation, for the non-expert reader, of Latin and technical terms used in the text.

atrium   The hall at the front of the traditional Roman house.

bulla   Locket worn by freeborn boys until puberty or assumption of toga of adulthood.

Campus Martius   'The Field of Mars'. The plain bordering the Tiber river on the north-west of Rome.

collactaneus **and variants**   Someone nursed by the same wet-nurse; foster-brother.

columbarium   Tiered niches for cinerary urns; a depository for ashes of groups of dependants of leading citizens, especially in the Julio–Claudian period.

curator   Caretaker, protector of property of young males between puberty and age 25.

decurions   Town councillors, members of municipal governing body (the size of which varied from a handful to over 100).

educator   'Bringer-up', supervisor of young children.

filiation   Part of Roman name (e.g. 'M. f.') indicating 'son or daughter of . . .'; sign of freeborn Roman citizen.

Forum   Original Forum, 'Roman Forum', as opposed to later forums built by emperors.

genius   The divine spark, essence of a man.

Hellenistic   Describes the period from Alexander the Great's spread of Hellenic civilization, usually from his death in 323 BCE, as opposed to Classical Greece (sixth to mid-fourth centuries BCE).

ius trium liberorum   'The rights from having three children' (*ius quattuor liberorum* for four children).

Junian Latin   A slave freed informally, who thus had freedom but not full Roman citizenship.

Lares **(plural of** *Lar***)**   Protective spirits of a place, especially of a household or crossroads.

Ludi Saeculares, 'Secular Games'   Festival intended to be held at approximate intervals of 110 years, to mark the end of one *saeculum* (century or age) and the beginning of another.

manumission   The freeing of a slave.

matrimonium iustum or *nuptiae iustae*   A valid Roman marriage.

nomen   The family name of a Roman citizen; followed first name, *praenomen*; followed by *cognomen* if citizen bore one. Many females bore only a *nomen*.

Octavian-Augustus   Born C. Octauius 63 BCE; became C. Iulius Caesar Octauianus through adoption by Julius Caesar 44 BCE, hence 'Octavian'; given title 'Augustus' 27 BCE.

ordo   Order, rank (senatorial, equestrian).

ouatio   'Ovation'—an inferior form of a triumph.

paedagogus   A child's attendant, usually associated with going to school.

paterfamilias   Male head of household, who had *potestas* (real or potential) over members of the household (including slaves, usually not wives) and all direct descendants (e.g. son, daughter, grandchildren).

potestas, patria potestas   Set of legal powers held by a male Roman citizen over property and persons of his household and their descendants.

praetextatus   Roman citizen boy before adulthood, who wore the *toga praetexta*, a toga with a purple border.

salutatio   Morning reception ceremony.

spurius   A person not born of a valid marriage; technically 'illegitimate', but see text for context of status rather than morality.

sui iuris   'In his or her own power'; legally independent (but women and children might still have a male guardian, *tutor*).

senatus consultum (s.c.)   Decree of the senate; it had force of law in the imperial period.

triumph   Ceremonial parade awarded to a general (*triumphator*) after significant military success.

tutor   Guardian, one who had legal *tutela*; administered orphan children's estates, provided authority for some property dealings by some women.

tribe (*tribus*)   A division of the Roman people; one of the thirty-five tribes used for voting purposes in the Republic.

REFERENCES

Alcock, S. (2000). 'Heroic Myths, but Not for Our Times', in E. Fentress (ed.), *Romanization and the City: Creation, Transformations, and Failures.* Portsmouth, RI: *Journal of Roman Archaeology,* 221–6.

Allison, P. M. (2001). 'Using the Material and Written Sources: Turn of the Millenium Approaches to Roman Domestic Space'. *American Journal of Archaeology,* 105: 181–208.

Amedick, R. (1991). *Die Sarkophage mit Darstellungen aus dem Menschenleben: T.4, Vita privata.* Berlin: Mann.

Anderson, J. C. (1984). *The Historical Topography of the Imperial Fora.* Brussels: Latomus (Collection Latomus, v. 182).

Andreae, B. (1977). *The Art of Rome.* Trans. R. Wolf. New York: H. M. Abrams.

Arangio-Ruiz, V. (1974). 'Lo status di L. Venidio Ennico ercolanese', in L. Bove (ed.), *Studi epigrafici e papirologici.* Naples: Giannini, 535–51. Originally pub. in *Mélanges Henry Lévy-Bruhl* (Paris, 1959), pp. 9–24.

Argetsinger, K. (1992). 'Birthday Rituals: Friends and Patrons in Roman Poetry and Cult'. *Classical Antiquity,* 11: 175–93.

Ariès, P. (1960). '*L'Enfant et la vie familiale sous l'Ancien Régime.* Paris: Librairie Plon.

—— (1962). *Centuries of Childhood.* Harmondsworth, Eng.: Penguin Books. Rev. edn. 1973.

—— (1981). *The Hour of Our Death.* Translated from the French original, 1977. New York: Knopf.

Astolfi, R. (1970). *La lex Iulia et Papia.* Padua: CEDAM.

Aurigemma, S. (1958). *The Baths of Diocletian and the Museo Nazionale Romano.* 4th edn. Rome: Istituto Poligrafico dello Stato.

Avery, G., and Reynolds, K. (2000). *Representations of Childhood Death.* London: Macmillan.

Badian, E. (1999). 'A Note on the "Alexander Mosaic"', in F. B. Titchener and R. F. Moorton Jr. (eds.), *The Eye Expanded: Life and the Arts in Greco-Roman Antiquity.* Berkeley: University of California Press, 75–92.

Balsdon, J. P. V. D. (1969). *Life and Leisure in Ancient Rome.* London: Bodley Head.

—— (1979). *Romans and Aliens.* London: Duckworth.

Bannon, C. (1997). *The Brothers of Romulus: Fraternal* Pietas *in Roman Law, Literature and Society*. Princeton: Princeton University Press.

Barrett, A. (1996). *Agrippina: Sex, Power, and Politics in the Early Empire*. New Haven: Yale University Press.

Barton, I. M. (ed.) (1989). *Roman Public Buildings*. Exeter: University of Exeter.

—— (1996). *Roman Domestic Buildings*. Exeter: University of Exeter.

Beard, M. (1993). 'Looking (Harder) for Roman Myth: Dumézil, Declamation and the Problems of Definition', in F. Graf (ed.), *Mythos in mythenloser Gesellschaft: das Paradigma Roms*. Stuttgart und Leipzig: Teubner, 44–64 (Colloquium Rauricum, Bd.3).

—— (2000). 'The Spectator and the Column: Reading and Writing the Language of Gesture', in J. Scheid and V. Huet (eds.), *Autour de la colonne Aurélienne. Geste et image sur la colonne de Marc Aurèle à Rome*. Turnout: Brepols, 265–79.

Beard, M., North, J., and Price, S. (1998). *Religions of Rome, i. A History; ii. A Sourcebook*. Cambridge: Cambridge University Press.

Beard, M. *et al.* (1991) (eds.). *Literacy in the Roman World*. Ann Arbor: *Journal of Roman Archaeology* (Supplementary series no. 3).

Beaumont, L. (forthcoming). 'The Changing Face of Childhood: The Representation of Children in Greek Art from the Archaic to the Hellenistic Periods'.

Beazley, J. (1947). *Etruscan Vase Painting*. Cambridge: Oxford University Press. Repr. 1976, New York: Hacker.

Becatti, G. (1957). *Colonna di Marco Aurelio*. Milan: Editoriale Domus (Album d'Italia, n. 9).

—— (1982). 'La Colonna Traiana, espressione somma del rilievo storico romano'. *Aufstieg und Niedergang der römischen Welt*, II, 12, 1: 536–78.

Bell, H. I. (1937). 'A Latin Registration of Birth'. *Journal of Roman Studies*, 27: 30–6.

Bellemore, J., and Rawson, B. (1990). '*Alumni:* The Italian Evidence'. *Zeitschrift für Papyrologie und Epigraphik*, 83: 1–19.

Béranger, A. (1999). 'Les "calculatores" '. *XI Congresso Internazionale di Epigrafia Greca e Latina. Atti*. Rome: Quasar, 639–47.

Berczelly, L. (1978). 'A Sepulchral Monument from Via Portuense and the Origin of the Roman Biographical Cycle'. *Acta ad Archaeologiam et Artium Historiam Pertinentia*, 8: 49–74 and plates I–XI.

Bergemann, J. (1990). *Römische Reiterstatuen: Ehrendenkmaler im öffentlichen Bereich*. Mainz: Von Zabern.

Bertier, J. (1996). 'La Médecine des enfants dans l'époque impériale'. *Aufstieg und Niedergang der römischen Welt*, II, 37, 3, 2147–227.

Bestor, J. F. (1991). 'Ideas about Procreation and Their Influence on Ancient and Medieval Views of Kinship', in D. I. Kertzer and R. P.

Saller (eds.), *The Family in Italy from Antiquity to the Present*. New Haven and London: Yale University Press, 150–67.

Bevan, H. K. (1989). *Child Law*. London: Butterworth.

Bieber, M. (1973). 'The Development of Portraiture on Roman Republican Coins'. *Aufstieg und Niedergang der römischen Welt*, I, 4, 871–98 and 38 plates in separate volume.

Bildkatalog Vatican (1995). *Bildkatalog des Skulpturen des Vatikanischen Museums*. Bd. 1, *Museo Chiaromonti*. 3 vols. Bd. 2, *Museo Pio Capitolino*. 2 vols. Deutsches Archaeologisches Institut. Berlin: de Gruyter, 1995–8.

Birley, A. (1987). *Marcus Aurelius: A Biography*. London: Batsford. Rev. edn. First edn. pub. 1966.

Blackstone, Sir Wm. (1765–9). *Commentaries on the Laws of England*. Oxford: Clarendon Press.

Blake, M. E. (1947). *Roman Construction in Italy from Tiberius through the Flavians*. New York: Kraus Reprint. Reprint 1959.

—— (1968). *Ancient Roman Construction in Italy from the Prehistoric Period to Augustus: Chronological Study Based in Part upon the Material Accumulated by E. B. Van Deman*. New York: Kraus Reprint.

—— (1973). *Roman Construction in Italy from Nerva through the Antonines;* ed. and completed by D. T. Bishop. Philadelphia: American Philosophical Society (Memoirs, v. 96).

Blayney, J. (1986). 'Theories of Conception in the Ancient Roman World', in B. Rawson (ed.), *The Family in Ancient Rome: New Perspectives*. London and Sydney: Croom Helm, 230–9.

Bloomer, W. Martin (1997). 'Schooling in Persona: Imagination and Subordination in Roman Education'. *Classical Antiquity*, 16: 57–78.

Blumenfeld-Kosinski, R. (1990). *Not of Woman Born: Representations of Caesarian Birth in Medieval and Renaissance Culture*. Ithaca, NY, and London: Cornell University Press.

Boatwright, M. T. (1987). *Hadrian and the City of Rome*. Princeton: Princeton University Press.

Bodel, J. (1986/1994). 'Graveyards and Groves: A Study of the *Lex Lucerina*'. Special issue of the *American Journal of Ancient History*, 11: 1–133.

—— (1999). 'Death on Display: Looking on Roman Funerals', in B. Bergmann and C. Kondoleon (eds.), *The Art of Ancient Spectacle*. Washington: National Gallery of Art, 259–81.

—— (2000). 'Dealing with the Dead: Undertakers, Executioners and Potter's Fields in Ancient Rome', in V. M. Hope and E. Marshall (eds.), *Death and Disease in the Ancient City*. London and New York: Routledge, 128–51.

Bonfante, L. (1984). 'Dedicated Mothers'. *Visible Religion*, 3: 1–17.

Bonfante, L. (1985). 'Votive Terracotta Figures of Mothers and Children'. *Italian Iron Age Artefacts in the British Museum: Papers of the Sixth British Museum Classical Colloquium.* London: British Museum Publications, 195–203.

—— (1997). 'Nursing Mothers in Classical Art', in A. O. Koloski-Ostrow and C. L. Lyons (eds.), *Naked Truths: Women, Sexuality and Gender in Classical Art and Archaeology.* London and New York: Routledge, 174–96.

Bonner, S. F. (1977). *Education in Ancient Rome: From the Elder Cato to the Younger Pliny.* London: Methuen.

Booth, A. (1979). 'Elementary and Secondary Education in the Roman Empire'. *Florilegium*, 1: 1–14.

—— (1991). 'The Age for Reclining and its Attendant Perils', in W. J. Slater (ed.), *Dining in a Classical Context.* Ann Arbor: Michigan University Press, 105–20.

Boschung, D. (1987). *Antike Grabaltäre aus den Nekropolen Roms.* Bern: Stämpfli.

Bove, L. (1966). 'Due nuove iscrizioni di Pozzuoli e Cuma'. *Rendiconti dell'Accademia di Archeologia, Lettere e Belle Arti di Napoli*, 41: 207–39.

—— (1971). 'Trois fragments d'une grande inscription sur marbre . . .'. *Année Epigraphique*, no. 88, 37–41.

Bowersock, G. W. (1969). *Greek Sophists in the Roman Empire.* Oxford: Clarendon Press.

Bowman, A. K., and Woolf, G. (1994) (eds.). *Literacy and Power in the Ancient World.* Cambridge and New York: Cambridge University Press.

Boyancé, P. (1952). '*Funus acerbum*'. *Revue des Études Anciennes*, 54: 275–89.

Bradley, G. (2000). *Ancient Umbria: State, Culture and Identity in Central Italy from the Iron Age to the Augustan Era.* Oxford: Oxford University Press.

Bradley, K. R. (1986). 'Wet-Nursing at Rome: A Study in Social Relations', in B. Rawson (ed.), *The Family in Ancient Rome: New Perspectives.* London and Sydney: Croom Helm, 201–29.

—— (1991a). *Discovering the Roman Family: Studies in Roman Social History.* New York and Oxford: Oxford University Press.

—— (1991b). 'The Imperial Ideal in Suetonius' *Caesares*', in H. Temporini and W. Haase (eds.), *Aufstieg und Niedergang der römischen Welt.* Berlin: de Gruyter. 2. 33. 5, 3701–32.

—— (1994). 'The Nurse and the Child at Rome. Duty, Affect and Socialisation'. *Thamyris*, 1. 2: 137–56.

—— (1998a). 'The Roman Family at Dinner', in I. Nielsen and H. Sigismund Nielsen (eds.), *Meals in a Social Context.* Aarhus: Aarhus University Press, 36–55.

—— (1998*b*). 'The Sentimental Education of the Roman Child: The Role of Pet-Keeping'. *Latomus*, 57: 523–57.

—— (1999), 'Images of Childhood. The Evidence of Plutarch', in S. Pomeroy (ed.), *Plutarch's Advice to the Bride and Groom and A Consolation to his Wife*. New York and Oxford: Oxford University Press, 183–96.

—— (2000). 'Fictive Families: Family and Household in the *Metamorphoses* of Apuleius'. *Phoenix*, 54: 282–308.

Brind'Amour, L. and P. (1971). 'La Deuxième Satire de Perse et le *dies lustricus*'. *Latomus*, 30: 999–1024.

Broughton, T. R. S. (1951–2; 1960). *The Magistrates of the Roman Republic*, T. R. S. Broughton with M. L. Patterson. 2 vols. New York: American Philological Association (Philological Monographs, no. 5).

Brunt, P. A. (1971). *Italian Manpower, 225 BC–AD 14*. Oxford: Clarendon Press.

Buckland, W. W. (1963). *A Text-book of Roman Law from Augustus to Justinian*. 3rd edn. rev. by P. Stein. Cambridge: Cambridge University Press.

Burnett, A. (1999). 'Buildings and Monuments on Roman Coins', in G. M. Paul (ed.), *Roman Coins and Public Life under the Early Empire: E. Togo Salmon Papers II*. Ann Arbor: University of Michigan Press, 137–64.

Cannon, A. (1989). 'The Historical Dimension in Mortuary Expressions of Status and Sentiment'. *Current Anthropology*, 30: 437–58.

Capitanio, M. (1974). 'La necropoli romana di Portorecanati'. *Atti della Accademia Nazionale dei Lincei. Notizie degli Scavi di Antichità*, ser. 8, 28: 142–445.

Carp, T. (1980). '*Puer senex* in Roman and Medieval Thought'. *Latomus*, 39: 736–9.

Carter, J. (1989). 'Civic and Other Buildings', in I. M. Barton (ed.), *Roman Public Buildings*. Exeter: University of Exeter, 31–65.

Castrén, P. (1975). Ordo populusque pompeianus: *Polity and Society in Roman Pompeii*. Rome: Bardi.

—— (2000). '*Vici* and *insulae*: The Homes and Addresses of the Romans'. *Arctos*, 34: 7–21.

Champlin, E. (1978). 'Pegasus'. *Zeitschrift für Papyrologie und Epigraphik*, 32: 269–78.

—— (1991). *Final Judgments: Duty and Emotion in Roman Wills, 200 B.C.–A.D. 250*. Berkeley: University of California Press.

Christes, J. (1979). *Sklaven und Freigelassen als Grammatiker und Philologen im antiken Rom*. Wiesbaden: Steiner (Forschungen zur antiken Sklaverei, Bd. 10).

Clairmont, C. (1970). *Gravestone and Epigram. Greek Memorials from the Archaic and Classical Period*. Mainz on Rhine: Verlag Phillip von Zabern.

——. (1993). *Classical Attic Tombstones*. 9 vols. Kilchberg, Switzerland: Acanthus.

Clark, M. E. (1983). '*Spes* in the Early Imperial Cult: "the hope of Augustus"'. *Numen*, 30: 80–105.

Clarke, G. W. (1986). *The Letters of St. Cyprian of Carthage*. Translated and annotated by G. W. Clarke. New York and Ramsey, NJ: Newman Press. Vol. iii (Ancient Christian Writers: the Works of the Fathers in Translation, v. 46).

Clauss, M. (1973). 'Probleme der Lebensaltersstatistiken aufgrund römischer Grabinschriften'. *Chiron*, 3: 395–417.

Coarelli, F. (1974). *Guida archeologica di Roma*. Verona: Mondadori.

—— (1978). 'La Statue de Cornélie, mère des Gracques, et la crise politique à Rome au temps du Saturninus'. *Le Dernier Siècle de la république romaine et l'époque augustéenne*. Strasbourg: AECR, 13–28.

Cohen, D., and Saller, R. P. (1994). 'Foucault on Sexuality in Greco-Roman Antiquity', in J. Goldstein (ed.), *Foucault and the Writing of History*. Oxford: Blackwell, 35–59, 262–7.

Corbier, M. (1999*a*). 'Adoptés et nourris'. *Adoption et fosterage*; sous la direction de M. Corbier. Paris: De Boccard, 5–40.

—— (1999*b*). *Adoption et fosterage*; sous la direction de M. Corbier. Paris: De Boccard (De l'archéologie à l'histoire).

—— (1999*c*). 'La Petite Enfance à Rome: lois, normes, pratiques individuelles et collectives'. *Annales. Histoire, Sciences Sociales*, 6: 1257–90.

—— (2001). 'Child Exposure and Abandonment', in S. Dixon (ed.), *Childhood, Class and Kin in the Roman World*. London: Routledge, 52–73.

Crawford, M. H. (1974). *Roman Republican Coinage*. London: Cambridge University Press. 2 vols.

—— (1996). 'Italy and Rome from Sulla to Augustus'. *Cambridge Ancient History*, vol. 10. 2nd edn. Cambridge: Cambridge University Press, 414–33.

Crook, J. (1967). *Law and Life of Rome*. London: Thames and Hudson.

—— (1986). 'Women in Roman Succession', in B. Rawson (ed.), *The Family in Ancient Rome: New Perspectives*. London and Sydney: Croom Helm, 58–82.

Currie, S. (1996). 'The Empire of Adults: The Representation of Children on Trajan's Arch at Beneventum', in J. Elsner (ed.), *Art and Text in Roman Culture*. Cambridge: Cambridge University Press, 153–81.

D'Arms, J. H. (1970). *Romans on the Bay of Naples: A Social and Cultural Study of the Villas and their Owners from 150 B.C. to A.D. 400*. Cambridge, Mass.: Harvard University Press.

De Franciscis, A. (1988). 'Un rilievo funerario da Pompei', in R. I. Curtis (ed.), *Studia Pompeiana & Classica in honor of Wilhelmina F. Jashemski*. New Rochelle, NY: Caratzas. Vol. 1, Pompeiana, 97–104.

Demand, N. (1994). *Birth, Death and Motherhood in Classical Greece*. Baltimore and London: Johns Hopkins University Press.

De Mause, L. (1974). 'The Evolution of Childhood', in L. De Mause (ed.), *The History of Childhood: The Evolution of Parent–Child Relationships as a Factor in History*. New York: Psychohistory Press, 1–73.

Demos, J. (1972). 'Demography and Psychology in the Historical Study of Family-Life: A Personal Report', in P. Laslett (ed.), *Household and Family in Past Time*. Cambridge: Cambridge University Press, 561–9.

Desnier, J.-L. (1979). 'Diuus Caesar Imp. Domitiani f'. *Revue des Études Anciennes*, 81: 54–65.

D'Espèrey, S. F. (1986). 'Vespasien, Titus et la littérature'. *Aufstieg und Niedergang der römischen Welt*, II, 32, 5, 3048–86.

De Visscher, F. (1963). *Le Droit des tombeaux romains*. Milan: Giuffrè.

Dixon, S. (1984). 'Roman Nurses and Foster-Mothers: Some Problems of Terminology'. *AULLA. Australasian Universities Language and Literature Association Proceedings*. Canberra: ANU Press, 9–24.

—— (1988). *The Roman Mother*. London: Croom Helm.

—— (1992). *The Roman Family*. Baltimore: Johns Hopkins University Press.

—— (1999). 'The Circulation of Children in Roman Society'. *Adoption et fosterage*; sous la direction de M. Corbier. Paris: De Boccard, 217–30.

—— (2001*a*) (ed.). *Childhood, Class and Kin in the Roman World*. London and New York: Routledge.

—— (2001*b*). *Reading Roman Women*. London: Duckworth.

Dolansky, F. (1999). 'Coming of Age in Rome. The History and Social Significance of Assuming the *toga virilis*'. Victoria, BC: University of Victoria. MA thesis.

Donahue, J. F. (1999). 'Euergetic Self-Representation and the Inscriptions at *Satyricon* 71.10'. *Classical Philology*, 94: 69–74.

Downs, R. M., and Stea, D. (1973) (eds.). *Image and Environment: Cognitive Mapping and Social Behavior*. Chicago: Aldine Publishing Company.

Dubuisson, M. (1992). 'Le Grec à Rome à l'époque de Cicéron: extension et qualité du bilinguisme'. *Annales: économies, sociétés, civilisations*, 47: 187–206.

Duncan-Jones, R. (1996). 'The Impact of the Antonine Plague'. *Journal of Roman Archaeology*, 9: 108–36.

Dury-Moyaers, G., and Renard, M. (1981). 'Aperçu critique de travaux relatifs au culte de Junon'. *Aufstieg und Niedergang der römischen Welt*, II, 17, 1, 142–202.

Dyson, S. L. (1992). *Community and Society in Roman Italy*. Baltimore and London: Johns Hopkins University Press (Ancient Society & History).

Eberle, A. F. (1990). 'Un sarcophage d'enfant au J. Paul Getty Museum'. *Roman Funerary Monuments in the J. Paul Getty Museum*, vol. 1. Malibu, Calif.: *The Museum*, 47–58.

—— (1997). 'Rome and the Outside World: Senatorial Families and the World They Lived In', in B. Rawson and P. Weaver (eds.), *The Roman Family in Italy: Status, Sentiment, Space*. Oxford: Clarendon Press, 73–99.

Eckert, M. (1988). *Capuanische Grabsteine: Untersuchungen zu den Grabsteinen römischer Freigelassener aus Capua*. Oxford: BAR.

Ellis, S. P. (2000). *Roman Housing*. London: Duckworth.

Epstein, D. (1987). *Personal Enmity in Roman Politics, 218–43*. London: Croom Helm.

Ery, K. K. (1969). 'Investigations on the Demographic Source Value of Tombstones Originating from the Roman Period'. *Alba Regia*, 10: 51–67.

Evans, J. K. (1991). *War, Women and Children in Ancient Rome*. London and New York: Routledge.

Evans Grubbs, J. (1995). *Law and Family in Late Antiquity: The Emperor Constantine's Marriage Legislation*. Oxford: Clarendon Press.

Eyben, E. (1973). 'Die Einteilung des menschlichen Lebens im römischen Altertum'. *Rheinisches Museum*, 116: 150–90.

—— (1993). *Restless Youth in Ancient Rome*. London and New York: Routledge.

Favro, D. (1996). *The Urban Image of Augustan Rome*. Cambridge: Cambridge University Press.

Felletti Maj, B. M. (1953). 'Le pitture di una tomba della Via Portuense'. *Rivista dell'Istituto Nazionale d'Archeologia e Storia dell'Arte*, n.s. 2: 40–76.

Fentress, E. (ed.) (2000). *Romanization and the City: Creation, Transformations, and Failures. Proceedings of a conference held at the American Academy in Rome to celebrate the 50th anniversary of the excavations at Cosa, 14–16 May 1998*. Portsmouth, RI: *Journal of Roman Archaeology* (Supplementary series, no. 38).

Février, P.-A. and Guery, R. (1980). 'Les Rites funéraires de la nécropole orientale de Sétif'. *Antiquités Africaines*, 15: 91–124.

Fildes, V. (1986). *Breasts, Bottles and Babies: A History of Infant Feeding*. Edinburgh: Edinburgh University Press.

—— (1999). *Prinzenbildnisse Antoninischer Zeit*. Mainz: Von Zabern.

Flemming, R. (2000). *Medicine and the Making of Roman Women: Gender, Nature, and Authority from Celsus to Galen*. Oxford: Oxford University Press.

Flory, M. B. (1978). 'Family in *familia*: Kinship and Community in Slavery'. *American Journal of Ancient History*, 3: 78–95.

—— (1998). 'The Integration of Women into the Roman Triumph'. *Historia*, 48: 489–94.

Flower, H. (1996). *Ancestor Masks and Aristocratic Power in Roman Culture*. Oxford: Clarendon Press.

Francescato, D., and Mebane, W. (1973). 'How Citizens View Two Great Cities: Milan and Rome', in R. M. Downs and D. Stea (eds.), *Image and Environment: Cognitive Mapping and Social Behavior*. Chicago: Aldine Publishing Co., 131–47.

French, V. (1986). 'Midwives and Maternity Care in the Roman World'. 'Rescuing Creusa: New Methodological Approaches to Women in Antiquity'. Special issue of *Helios*, 13: 69–84.

—— (1988). 'Birth Control, Childbirth and Early Childhood', in M. Grant and R. Kitzinger (eds.), *Civilization of the Ancient Mediterranean: Greece and Rome*. New York: Scribner. vol. 3, 1355–62.

Gabelmann, H. (1977). 'Römische Grabbauten in Italien und den Nordprovinzen', in U. Hoeckmann and A. Krug (eds.), *Festschrift für Frank Brommer*. Mainz: Von Zabern, 101–17.

—— (1985). 'Römische Kinder in *toga praetexta*'. *Jahrbuch des Deutschen Archäologischen Instituts*, 100: 497–541.

Gallivan, P., and Wilkins, P. (1997). 'Familial Structures in Roman Italy: A Regional Approach', in B. Rawson and P. Weaver (eds.), *The Roman Family in Italy: Status, Sentiment, Space*. Oxford: Clarendon Press, 239–79.

Gardner, J. F. (1986a). 'Proofs of Status in the Roman World'. *Bulletin of the Institute of Classical Studies of the University of London*, 33: 1–14.

—— (1986b). *Women in Roman Law and Society*. London and Sydney: Croom Helm.

—— (1993). *Being a Roman Citizen*. London: Routledge.

—— (1995). 'Gender-Role Assumptions in Roman Law'. *Echos du Monde Classique/Classical Views*, 39: 377–400.

—— (1996). 'Hadrian and the Social Legacy of Augustus'. *Labeo*, 42: 83–100.

—— (1998). *Family and familia in Roman Law and Life*. Oxford: Clarendon Press.

—— (1999). 'Status, Sentiment and Strategy in Roman Adoption'. *Adoption et fosterage*; sous la direction de M. Corbier. Paris: De Boccard, 63–80.

Garnsey, P. (1974). 'Aspects of the Decline of the Urban Aristocracy in the Empire'. *Aufstieg und Niedergang der römischen Welt*, II, 1, 229–50.

Garnsey, P. (1991). 'Child Rearing in Ancient Italy', in D. I. Kertzer and R. P. Saller (eds.), *The Family in Ancient Italy from Antiquity to the Present*. New Haven and London: Yale University Press, 48–65.

Garnsey, P., and Saller, R. P. (1987). *The Roman Empire: Economy, Society and Culture*. London: Duckworth.

Gazda, E., and Haeckl, A. (1993). 'Roman Portraiture: Reflections on the Question of Context'. *Journal of Roman Archaeology*, 6: 289–302.

Gennep, A. van (1960). *The Rites of Passage*. Trans. (from the French) by M. B. Vizedom and G. L. Caffee. London: Routledge & Kegan Paul. First pub. in French, 1909.

George, M. (1997). 'Repopulating the Roman House', in B. Rawson and P. Weaver (eds.), *The Roman Family in Italy: Status, Sentiment, Space*. Oxford: Clarendon Press, 299–319.

—— (2000). 'Family and *familia* on Roman Biographical Sarcophagi'. *Mitteilungen des Deutschen Archäologischen Instituts. Römische Abteilung*, 107: 191–207.

—— (2001). 'A Roman Funerary Monument with a Mother and Daughter', in S. Dixon (ed.), *Childhood, Class and Kin in the Roman World*. London and New York: Routledge, 178–89.

Gercke, W. B. (1968). *Untersuchungen zum römischen Kinderporträt, von den Anfangen bis in Hadrianische Zeit*. Ph.D. thesis. Hamburg.

Ginestet, P. (1991). *Les Organisations de la jeunesse dans l'Occident romain*. Brussels: Latomus (Collection Latomus, v. 213).

Goette, H. R. (1989). 'Beobachtungen zu römischen Kinderportraits'. *Archäologisches Anzeiger des Deutschen Archäologischen Instituts*, 453–71.

Golden, M. (1988). 'Did the Ancients Care when their Children Died?' *Greece and Rome*, 35: 152–63.

—— (1990). *Children and Childhood in Classical Athens*. Baltimore and London: Johns Hopkins University Press.

—— (1997). 'Change or Continuity? Children and Childhood in Hellenistic Historiography', in M. Golden and P. Toohey (eds.), *Inventing Ancient Culture: Historicism, Periodization and the Ancient World*. London and New York: Routledge, 176–91.

Goody, E. (1982). *Parenthood and Social Reproduction: Fostering and Occupational Roles in West Africa*. Cambridge and New York: Cambridge University Press.

—— (1999). 'Sharing and Transferring Components of Parenthood: The West African Case'. *Adoption et fosterage*; sous la direction de M. Corbier. Paris: De Boccard, 369–88.

Gordon, A. E. (1983). *Illustrated Introduction to Latin Epigraphy*. Berkeley: University of California Press.

Greven, P. J. (1972). 'The Average Size of Families and Households in the Province of Massachusetts in 1764 and in the United States in

1790: An Overview', in P. Laslett (ed.), *Household and Family in Past Time.* Cambridge: Cambridge University Press, 545–60.

Gruen, E. S. (1968). *Roman Politics and the Criminal Courts, 149–78 B.C.* Cambridge, Mass.: Harvard University Press.

Gunnella, A. (1995). 'Morte improvvise e violente nelle iscrizioni latine', in F. Hinard (ed.), *La Mort au quotidien dans le monde romain: actes du colloque organisé par l'Université de Paris IV.* Paris: de Boccard, 9–22.

Haines-Eitzen, K. (2000). *Guardians of Letters; Literacy, Power, and the Transmitters of Early Christian Literature.* Oxford: Oxford University Press.

Hales, S. (2000). 'At Home with Cicero'. *Greece & Rome,* 47: 44–55.

Halfmann, H. (1986). Itinera principum: *Geschichte und Typologie der Kaiserreisen im römischen Reich.* Stuttgart: Steiner (Heidelberger althistorische Beitrage und epigraphische Studien, Bd. 2).

Hallett, J. P. (1984). *Fathers and Daughters in Roman Society: Women and the Elite Family.* Princeton: Princeton University Press.

Hampartumian, N. (1978). 'Child-Burials and Superstition in the Roman Cemetery of Sucidava (Dacia)'. *Hommages à Maarten J. Vermaaseren . . .* Leiden: Brill. Vol. 1, 473–7 and plates XC–XCI.

Hanson, A. E. (1994). 'A Division of Labor: Roles for Men in Greek and Roman Births'. *Thamyris,* 1: 157–202.

Hardie, A. (1983). *Statius and the* Silvae: *Poets, Patrons and Epideixis in the Graeco-Roman World.* Liverpool: Cairns.

Harmon, D. P. (1978). 'The Family Festivals of Rome'. *Aufstieg und Niedergang der römischen Welt,* II, 16, 2: 1592–1603.

Harris, M. H. (1995). *History of Libraries in the Western World.* 4th edn. Metuchen, NJ: Scarecrow Press.

Harris, W. V. (1989). *Ancient Literacy.* Cambridge, Mass.: Harvard University Press.

——— (1994). 'Child-Exposure in the Roman Empire'. *Journal of Roman Studies,* 84: 1–22.

——— (2000). Review of David and Noelle Soren (eds.), *A Roman Villa and a Late-Roman Infant Cemetery: Excavation at Poggio Gramignano, Lugnano in Teverina.* Rome: 'L'Erma' di Bretschneider, 1999. *Bryn Mawr Classical Review,* 27 Oct. 2000, four-page printout.

Helbig, W. (1895–6). *Guide to the Public Collections of Classical Antiquities in Rome.* 2 vols. Leipzig: Baedeker.

——— (1963–72). *Führer durch die öffentlichen Sammlungen klassischer Altertümer in Rom.* 4 vols. 4th edn. Tübingen: Wasmuth.

Hellerman, J. (2001). *The Ancient Church as Family.* Minneapolis: Fortress Press.

Hemelrijk, E. (1999). Matrona docta: *Educated Women in the Roman Elite from Cornelia to Julia Domna.* London and New York: Routledge.

Henry, L. (1959). 'L'Âge du décès d'après les inscriptions funéraires'. *Population*, 14: 327–9.

Herrmann-Otto, E. (1994). Ex ancilla natus: *Untersuchungen zu den 'hausgeborenen' Sklaven und Sklavinnen im Westen des römischen Kaiserreiches*. Stuttgart: Steiner (Forschungen zur antiken Sklaverei, Bd. 24).

Hillard, T. (1973). 'The Sisters of Clodius Again'. *Latomus*, 32: 505–14.

—— (2001). 'Popilia and *Laudationes Funebres* for Women'. *Antichthon*, 35: 45–63.

Hirsch-Dyczek, O. (1983). *Les Représentations des enfants sur les stèles funéraires attiques*. Krakow: Jagiellonian University.

—— (1988). 'Historische Reliefs'. *Kaiser Augustus und die verlorene Republik: eine Ausstellung im Martin-Gropius-Bau, Berlin . . .* [M. Hofter, head of editing team]. Mainz: Von Zabern, 351–400.

Hopkins, K. (1965). 'Contraception in the Roman Empire'. *Comparative Studies in Society and History*, 8: 124–51.

—— (1983). *Sociological Studies in Roman History*, ii. *Death and Renewal*. Cambridge: Cambridge University Press.

—— (1987). 'Graveyards for Historians'. *La Mort, les morts et l'au-delà dans le monde romain . . .* publié sous la direction de F. Hinard. Caen: Université de Caen, 113–26.

Humbert, M. (1972). *Le Remariage à Rome: étude d'histoire juridique et sociale*. Milan: Giuffrè.

Humphrey, J. H. (1986). *Roman Circuses: Arenas for Chariot Racing*. London: Batsford.

Huntington, R., and Metcalf, P. (1979). *Celebrations of Death*. Cambridge: Cambridge University Press.

Huskinson, J. (1996). *Roman Children's Sarcophagi: Their Decoration and its Social Significance*. Oxford: Clarendon Press.

Jackson, R. (1988). *Doctors and Diseases in the Roman Empire*. London: British Museum.

Jaczynowska, M. (1978). *Les Associations de la jeunesse romaine sous le haut-empire*. Wroclaw, etc., Zaklad Narodowy Imienia Ossolinskich Wydawnictwo Polskiej Akademii Nauk (Archiwum Filologiczne, 36).

Jalland, P. (1996). *Death in the Victorian Family*. New York: Oxford University Press.

Jones, B. W. (1992). *The Emperor Domitian*. London and New York: Routledge.

Jones, C. P. (1976). 'The Plancii of Perge and Diana Planciana'. *Harvard Studies in Classical Philology*, 80: 231–7.

Joshel, S. R. (1986). 'Nurturing the Master's Child: Slavery and the Roman Child Nurse'. *Signs*, 12: 3–22.

—— (1992). *Work, Identity and Legal Status at Rome: A Study of the Occupational Inscriptions.* Norman, Okla.: University of Oklahoma Press.

Jouer dans l'antiquité: Musée d'Archéologie Méditérranéenne, Centre de la Veille Charité, novembre 1991–février 1992. Marseille: the Museum, 1991.

Kampen, N. B. (1981a). 'Biographical Narration in Roman Funerary Art'. *American Journal of Archaeology*, 85: 47–58 and plates 7–12.

—— (1981b). *Image and Status: Roman Working Women in Ostia.* Berlin: Mann.

—— (1988). 'Before Florence Nightingale: A Prehistory of Nursing in Painting and Sculpture', in A. H. Jones (ed.), *Images of Nurses: Perspectives from History, Art and Literature.* Philadelphia: University of Pennsylvania Press, 6–39.

Kaster, R. (2001). 'Controlling Reason: Declamation in Rhetorical Education at Rome', in Yun Lee Too (ed.), *Education in Greek and Roman Antiquity.* Leiden: Brill, 317–37.

Kennedy, G. A. (1972). *The Art of Rhetoric in the Roman World, 300 B.C.–A.D. 300.* Princeton: Princeton University Press (A History of Rhetoric, vol. 2).

Kepartová, J. (1984). 'Kinder in Pompeji: eine epigraphische Untersuchung'. *Klio*, 66: 192–209.

Kertzer, D. I. (1988). *Ritual, Politics and Power.* New Haven: Yale University Press.

Kiss, Z. (1966). 'Un portrait de fillette romain au Musée de Varsovie'. *Mélanges offerts à Kazimierz Michalowski.* Warsaw: Panstwowe Wydawnictwo Naukowe, 505–8.

Kleijwegt, M. (1991). *Ancient Youth: The Ambiguity of Youth and the Absence of Adolescence in Greco-Roman Society.* Amsterdam: Gieben (Dutch Monographs on Ancient History and Archaeology).

Kleiner, D. E. E. (1977). *Roman Group Portraiture: The Funerary Reliefs of the Late Republic and Early Empire.* New York: Garland.

—— (1978). 'The Great Friezes of the Ara Pacis Augustae: Greek Sources, Roman Derivatives and Augustan Social Policy'. *Mélanges de l'École Française de Rome: Antiquité*, 90: 753–84.

—— (1985). 'Private Portraiture in the Age of Augustus', in R. Winkes (ed.), *The Age of Augustus: Interdisciplinary Conference held at Brown University, 1982.* Providence, RI: Brown University, 107–35.

—— (1987). *Roman Imperial Funerary Altars with Portraits.* Rome: G. Bretschneider.

—— (1988). 'Roman Funerary Art and Architecture: Observations on the Significance of Recent Studies'. *Journal of Roman Archaeology*, 1: 115–19.

References

Kleiner, D. E. E. (1992). *Roman Sculpture*. New Haven and London: Yale University Press.

Knothe, H.-G. (1982). 'Zur 7-Jahresgrenze der "Infantia" im antiken romischen Recht'. *Studia e Documenti Historiae et Iuris*, 48: 239–56.

Kockel, V. (1993). *Porträtreliefs stadtrömischer Grabbauten: ein Beitrag zur Geschichte und zum Verständnis des spätrepublikanisch-frühkaiserlichen Privatporträts*. Mainz: Von Zabern.

Kokkinos, N. (1992). *Antonia Augusta: Portrait of a Great Roman Lady*. London and New York: Routledge.

Köves-Zulauf, T. (1990). *Römische Geburtsriten*. Munich: Beck.

Kyle, D. G. (1997). 'Rethinking the Roman Arena: Gladiators, Sorrows and Games'. *Ancient History Bulletin*, 11: 94–7.

——— (1998). *Spectacles of Death in Ancient Rome*. London and New York: Routledge.

Laes, C. (2003). 'Desperately Different? The Use of *delicia*-children in the Roman Household', in D. Balch and C. Osiek (eds.), *Early Christian Families in Context: A Cross-Disciplinary Dialogue*. Chicago: Eerdmans.

Lane Fox, R. (1994). 'Literacy and Power in Early Christianity', in A. K. Bowman and G. Woolf (eds.), *Literacy and Power in the Ancient World*. Cambridge: Cambridge University Press, 126–48.

Lassère, J.-M. (1987). 'Difficultés de l'estimation de la longevité: questions de méthode'. *La Mort, les morts et l'au-delà dans le monde romain* . . . publié sous la direction de F. Hinard. Caen: Université de Caen, 91–7.

Laurence, R., and Wallace-Hadrill, A. (eds.) (1997). *Domestic Space in the Roman World: Pompeii and Beyond*. Portsmouth, RI: *Journal of Roman Archaeology* (Supplementary series, no. 22).

Leach, E. (1990). 'The Politics of Self-Presentation: Pliny's Letters and Roman Portrait Sculpture'. *Classical Antiquity*, 9: 14–39.

Lefkowitz, M., and Fant, M. (1992). *Women's Life in Greece and Rome. A Source-Book*. 2nd edn. Baltimore: Johns Hopkins Press.

Leiwo, M. (1995). 'The Mixed Languages in Roman Inscriptions', in H. Solin, O. Salomies and U.-M. Liertz (eds.), *Acta colloquii epigraphici Latini*. Helsinki: Societas Scientiarum Fennica, 293–301.

LeMoine, F. (1991). 'Parental Gifts: Father–Son Dedications and Dialogues in Roman Didactic Literature'. *Illinois Classical Studies*, 16: 337–66.

Leon, H. (1995). *The Jews of Ancient Rome*. Peabody, Mass.: Hendrickson.

Lévy, J.-Ph. (1952). 'Les Actes d'état civil romains'. *Revue Historique de Droit Français et Etranger*, 30: 449–86.

Loeb, E. H. (1979). *Die Geburt die Gotter in der griechischen Kunst der klassischen Zeit*. Ph.D. diss. Jerusalem: Shikmona.

Lutz, C. E. (1947). 'Musonius Rufus: The Roman Socrates'. *Yale Classical Studies*, 10: 3–147.

Lynch, K. (1960). *The Image of the City*. Cambridge, Mass.: Technology Press.

McDaniel, W. B. (1948). *Conception, Birth and Infancy in Ancient Rome and Modern Italy*. Coconut Grove, Fla: Business Press.

McManners, J. (1981). *Death and the Enlightenment: Changing Attitudes to Death among Christians and Unbelievers in Eighteenth-Century France*. Oxford: Clarendon Press.

MacMullen, R. (1974). *Roman Social Relations 50 BC–AD 284*. New Haven: Yale University Press.

—— (1982). 'The Epigraphic Habit in the Roman Empire'. *American Journal of Philology*, 103: 233–46.

McWilliam, J. C. (1990). 'Children in Rome and Italy in the Early Empire'. Honours thesis. Canberra: Australian National University.

—— (2001). 'Children among the Dead: The Influence of Urban Life on the Commemoration of Children on Tombstone Inscriptions', in S. Dixon (ed.), *Childhood, Class and Kin in the Roman World*. London: Routledge, 74–98.

Manson, M. (1978). '*Puer bimulus* (Catulle, 17, 12–13) et l'image du petit enfant chez Catulle et ses prédécesseurs'. *Mélanges de l'École française de Rome, Antiquité*, 90: 247–91.

—— (1983). 'The Emergence of the Small Child at Rome'. *History of Education*, 12: 149–59.

Marchi, A. de (1896–1903). *Il culto privato di Roma antica*. 1975 reprint. 2 vols. New York: Arno Press.

Marrou, H.-I. (1938). Mousikos aner: *étude sur les scènes de la vie intellectuelle figurant sur les monuments funéraires romains*. 1964 reprint. Rome: 'L'Erma' di Bretschneider.

—— (1956). *A History of Education in Antiquity*. Translated from the 3rd French edn. 1977 reprint. London: Sheed & Ward.

Marshall, A. J. (1976). 'Library Resources and Creative Writing at Rome'. *Phoenix*, 30: 252–64.

Martin, D. (1996). 'The Construction of the Ancient Family: Methodological Considerations'. *Journal of Roman Studies*, 86: 40–60.

Mays, S. (1998). *The Archaeology of Human Bones*. London and New York: Routledge.

Meiggs, R. (1973). *Roman Ostia*. 2nd edn. Oxford: Clarendon Press.

Meillet, A. (1920). *Dictionnaire étymologique de la langue latine*. Paris: C. Klincksieck.

Mildenberg, L. (1984). *The Coinage of the Bar Kokhbar War*. Aarau: Sauerländer.

Millar, F. (1977). *The Emperor in the Roman World, 31 B.C.–A.D. 337.* London: Duckworth.

—— (1988). 'Cornelius Nepos, "Atticus" and the Roman Revolution'. *Greece and Rome,* 35: 40–55.

Mohler, S. L. (1937). 'The *Juvenes* and Roman Education'. *Transactions of the American Philological Association,* 68: 442–79.

Mohler, S. L. (1940). 'Slave Education in the Roman Empire'. *Transactions of the American Philological Association,* 71: 262–80.

Moynihan, R. (1985). 'Geographical Mythology and Roman Imperial Ideology', in R. Winkes (ed.), *The Age of Augustus: Interdisciplinary Conference held at Brown University 1982.* Providence, RI: Brown University, 149–62.

Murray, J. S. (1991). 'The Alleged Prohibition of Abortion in the Hippocratic Oath'. *Echos du Monde Classique/Classical Views,* 35, n.s. 10: 293–311.

Nash, E. (1968). *Pictorial Dictionary of Ancient Rome.* Rev. edn. 2 vols. Rome: Deutsches Archäologisches Institut.

Néraudau, J. (1984). *Être enfant à Rome.* Paris: Collection Realia, Les Belles Lettres.

—— (1987). 'La Loi, la coutume et le chagrin: réflexions sur la mort des enfants'. *La Mort, les morts et l'au-delà dans le monde romain . . .* publié sous la direction de F. Hinard. Caen: Université de Caen, 195–208.

Nevett, L. (1997). 'Perceptions of Domestic Space in Roman Italy', in B. Rawson and P. Weaver (eds.), *The Roman Family in Italy: Status, Sentiment, Space.* Oxford: Clarendon Press, 281–98.

Nicolet, C. (1991). *Space, Geography and Politics in the Early Roman Empire.* Ann Arbor: University of Michigan Press.

Nielsen, Hanne Sigismund *see* Sigismund Nielsen, H.

Nisbet, R. G. M. (1978). '*Felicitas* at Surrentum (Statius, *Silvae* II.2)'. *Journal of Roman Studies,* 68: 1–11.

Noy, D. (2000). *Foreigners at Rome: Citizens and Strangers.* London: Duckworth.

Orme, N. (2001). *Medieval Children.* New Haven and London: Yale University Press.

Paige, K. E., and J. M. (1981). *The Politics of Reproductive Ritual.* Berkeley: University of California Press.

Panciera, S. (1969). 'Miscellanea epigrafica, IV'. *Epigraphica,* 31: 104–20.

—— (1970/1). 'Nuovi documenti epigrafici per la topografia di Roma antica', *Rendiconti della pontificia accademia romana di archeologia,* 43: 109–34.

Parkin, T. G. (1992). *Demography and Roman Society.* Baltimore and London: Johns Hopkins University Press.

Pelling, C. (1990). 'Childhood and Personality in Greek Biography', in C. Pelling (ed.), *Characterization and Individuality in Greek Literature*. Oxford: Oxford University Press, 213–44.

Petermandl, W. (1997). 'Kinderarbeit im Italien der Prinzipatszeit. Ein beitrag zur Sozialgeschichte des Kindes'. *Laverna*, 8: 113–36.

Pfuhl, E., and Mobius, H. (1977–9). *Die ostgriechischen Grabreliefs*. Mainz: von Zabern.

Pirson, F. (1996). 'Style and Message on the Column of Marcus Aurelius'. *Papers of the British School at Rome*, 64: 139–79.

Pollini, J. (1987). *The Portraiture of Gaius and Lucius Caesar*. New York: Fordham University Press.

Pollitt, J. J. (1986). *Art in the Hellenistic Age*. Cambridge and New York: Cambridge University Press.

Pollock, L. (1983). *Forgotten Children: Parent–Child Relations from 1500 to 1900*. Cambridge: Cambridge University Press.

Pomeroy, S. B. (1997). *Families in Classical and Hellenistic Greece: Representations and Realities*. London: Clarendon Press.

Potter, D. S., and Mattingly, D. J. (1999) (eds.). *Life, Death and Entertainment in the Roman Empire*. Ann Arbor: University of Michigan Press.

Prieur, J. (1986). *La Mort dans l'antiquité romaine*. Rennes: Ouest-France (Collection 'De mémoire de l'homme').

Prosopographia Imperii Romani (1897–8). Ed. H. Dessau. 1st edn. Berlin: Reimer. Later edns. pub. by de Gruyter, 1933– .

Pugliese, G. (1984–5). 'Assistenza all'infanzia nel principato e "piae causae" del diritto romano cristiano'. *Sodalitas: scritti in onore di Antonio Guarino*. 10 vols. (Biblioteca di Labeo, vol. 8). Naples: Jovene, vol. 7, 3175–89.

Purcell, N. (1995). 'Forum Romanum (the Republican Period)', in E. Steinby (ed.), *Lexicon Topographicum Urbis Romae*. Rome: Quasar, vol. 2, 325–42.

Rawson, B. (1966). 'Family Life among the Lower Classes at Rome in the First Two Centuries of the Empire'. *Classical Philology*, 61: 71–83.

—— (1974). 'Roman Concubinage and Other *de facto* Marriages'. *Transactions of the American Philological Association*, 104: 279–305.

—— (1978). *The Politics of Friendship: Pompey and Cicero*. Sydney: Sydney University Press.

—— (1986a). 'Children in the Roman *familia*', in B. Rawson (ed.), *The Family in Ancient Rome: New Perspectives*. London and Sydney: Croom Helm, 170–200.

—— (1986b) (ed.). *The Family in Ancient Rome: New Perspectives*. London and Sydney: Croom Helm.

Rawson, B. (1986c). 'The Roman Family', in B. Rawson (ed.), *The Family in Ancient Rome: New Perspectives*. London and Sydney: Croom Helm, 1–57.

—— (1989). '*Spurii* and the Roman View of Illegitimacy'. *Antichthon*, 23: 10–41.

—— (1991a). 'Adult–Child Relationships in Roman Society', in B. Rawson (ed.), *Marriage, Divorce and Children in Ancient Rome*. Oxford: Clarendon Press, 7–30.

—— (1991b) (ed.). *Marriage, Divorce and Children in Ancient Rome*. Oxford: Clarendon Press.

—— (1995). 'From "Daily Life" to Demography', in R. Hawley and B. Levick (eds.), *Women in Antiquity: New Assessments*. London: Routledge, 1–20.

—— (1997a). 'The Iconography of Roman Childhood', in B. Rawson and P. Weaver (eds.), *The Roman Family in Italy: Status, Sentiment, Space*. Oxford: Clarendon Press, 205–32.

—— (1997b). 'Representations of Roman Children and Childhood'. *Antichthon*, 31: 74–95.

—— (1997c). ' "The Family" in the Ancient Mediterranean: Past, Present, Future'. *Zeitschrift für Papyrologie und Epigraphik*, 117: 294–6.

—— (1999). 'Education, the Romans and Us'. *Antichthon*, 33: 81–98.

—— (2001). 'Children as Cultural Symbols: Imperial Ideology in the Second Century', in S. Dixon (ed.), *Childhood, Class and Kin in the Roman World*. London and New York: Routledge, 21–42.

—— (2002). 'The Express Route to Hades', in P. Mckechnie (ed.), *Thinking Like a Lawyer*. Leiden: Brill, 271–88.

—— (2003). 'Death, Burial and Commemoration of Children in Roman Italy', in D. Balch and C. Osiek (eds.), *Early Christian Families in Context: A Cross-Disciplinary Dialogue*. Chicago: Eerdmans.

Rawson, B., and Weaver, P. (1997) (eds.). *The Roman Family in Italy: Status, Sentiment, Space*. Oxford: Clarendon Press.

Rawson, E. (1987). '*Discrimina ordinum:* The *Lex Julia Theatralis*'. *Papers of the British School at Rome*, 55: 83–114.

Reinach, S. (1912). *Répertoire des reliefs, grecs et romains*, t.3, *Italie-Suisse*. Paris: Leroux.

Richardson, L. (1992). *A New Topographical Dictionary of Ancient Rome*. Baltimore and London: Johns Hopkins University Press.

Riddle, J. M. (1992). *Contraception and Abortion from the Ancient World to the Renaissance*. Cambridge, Mass.: Harvard University Press.

Ridgway, B. (2000). *Hellenistic Sculpture*, ii. *The Styles of ca. 200–100 B.C.* Madison: University of Wisconsin Press.

Robert, R. (2000). 'Ambiguité de la gestuelle "pathétique" sur la colonne Aurélienne', in J. Scheid and V. Huet (eds.), *Autour de la colonne Aurélienne: geste et image sur la colonne de Marc Aurèle à Rome.* Turnout: Brepols, 175–97.

Rogoff, B., Sellers, M., Pirrotta, S., Fox, N., and White, S. (1975). 'Age of Assignment of Roles and Responsibilities to Children: A Cross-Cultural Survey'. *Human Development*, 18: 353–69.

Roller, M. B. (1997). '*Color*-blindness: Cicero's Death, Declamation and the Production of History'. *Classical Philology*, 92: 109–30.

Rose, C. B. (1990). ' "Princes" and Barbarians on the Ara Pacis'. *American Journal of Archaeology*, 94: 453–67.

—— (1997). *Dynastic Commemoration and Imperial Portraiture in the Julio-Claudian Period.* Cambridge: Cambridge University Press (Cambridge Studies in Classical Art and Iconography).

Rose, H. J. (1923). 'Nocturnal Funerals in Rome'. *Classical Quarterly*, 17: 191–4.

Rowland, R. J. (1972). 'Cicero and the Greek World'. *Transactions of the American Philological Association*, 103: 451–61.

Russell, J. C. (1985). *The Control of Late Ancient and Medieval Population.* Philadelphia, Pa.: the Society (Memoirs of the American Philosophical Society, 160).

Ryberg, I. S. (1955). *Rites of the State Religion in Roman Art.* Rome: American Academy in Rome (*Memoirs*, v. 22).

Saller, R. P. (1982). *Personal Patronage in the Early Empire.* Cambridge: Cambridge University Press.

—— (1984). '*Familia, domus* and the Roman Concept of the Family'. *Phoenix*, 38: 336–55.

—— (1987). 'Men's Age at Marriage and its Consequences in the Roman Family'. *Classical Philology*, 82: 21–34.

—— (1988). '*Pietas*, Obligation and Authority in the Roman Family', in P. Kniess and V. Lasemann (eds.), *Alte Geschichte und Wissenschaftsgeschichte: Festschrift für Karl Christ.* Darmstadt: Wiss. Buchges., 393–410.

—— (1991). 'Corporal Punishment, Authority and Obedience in the Roman Household', in B. Rawson (ed.), *Marriage, Divorce and Children in Ancient Rome.* Oxford: Clarendon Press, 144–65.

—— (1994). *Patriarchy, Property and Death in the Roman Family.* Cambridge: Cambridge University Press.

—— (1999). '*Pater familias, mater familias,* and the Gendered Semantics of the Roman Household'. *Classical Philology*, 94: 182–97.

—— (1990/2000). 'Domitian and his Successors: Methodological Traps in Assessing Emperors'. *American Journal of Ancient History*, 15: 4–18.

Saller, R. P., and Shaw, B. D. (1984). 'Tombstones and Roman Family Relations in the Principate: Civilians, Soldiers and Slaves'. *Journal of Roman Studies*, 74: 124–56.

Salway, B. (1994). 'What's in a Name? A Survey of Roman Onomastic Practice from c. 700 B.C. to A.D. 700'. *Journal of Roman Studies*, 84: 124–45.

Scarpellini, D. (1987). *Stele romane con* imagines clipeatae *in Italia*. Rome: 'L'Erma' di Bretschneider.

Scheid, J. (1990). *Romulus et ses frères: le collège des frères arvales, modèle du culte public dans la Rome des empereurs*. Rome: École Française de Rome.

Scheid, J., and Huet, V. (2000) (eds.). *Autour de la colonne Aurélienne: geste et image sur la colonne de Marc Aurèle à Rome*. Turnout: Brepols.

Scheidel, W. (1996). 'Reflections on the Differential Valuation of Slaves in Diocletian's Price Edict and in the United States'. *Münstersche Beiträge zur antiken Handelsgeschichte*, 15: 67–79.

Scheper-Hughes, N. (1987a). ' "Basic strangeness": Maternal Estrangement and Infant-Death Critique of Bonding Theory', in C. M. Super (ed.), *The Role of Culture in Developmental Disorder*. Orlando: Academic Press, 131–51.

—— (1987b). *Child Survival: Anthropological Perspectives on the Treatment and Maltreatment of Children*. Dordrecht and Boston: Reidel

Schofield, R. (1986). 'Did Mothers Really Die? Three Centuries of Maternal Mortality', in L. Bonfield, R. Smith, and K. Wrightson (eds.), *The World We Have Gained: Histories of Population and Social Structure*. New York: Blackwell, 231–60.

Scobie, A. (1986). 'Slums, Sanitation and Mortality in the Roman World'. *Klio*, 68: 399–433.

Scott, E. (1999). *The Archaeology of Infancy and Infant Death*. Oxford: Archaeopress (BAR International Series 819).

—— (2000). 'Unpicking a Myth: The Infanticide of Female and Disabled Infants in Antiquity', *TRAC 2000* (Proceedings of the Tenth Annual Theoretical Roman Archaeology Conference London 2000), ed. G. Davies, A. Gardner, and K. Lockyear. Oxford: Oxbow Books, 143–51.

Scullard, H. H. (1981). *Festivals and Ceremonies of the Roman Republic*. London: Thames and Hudson (Aspects of Greek and Roman Life).

Sehlmeyer, M. (1999). *Stadtrömische Ehrenstatuen der republikanischen Zeit: Historizität und Kontext von Symbolen nobilitären Standesbewusstseins*. Stuttgart: Steiner.

Sered, S. S. (1994). 'Husbands, Wives and Childbirth Rituals'. *Ethos*, 22: 187–208.

Seston, W. (1949). 'L'Épitaphe de Eutychos et l'héroïsation par la pureté'. *Hommages à Joseph Bidez et à Franz Cumont*. Brussels: Latomus, 313–22 and plate 24 (Collection Latomus, v. 2).

Shaw, B. D. (1984). 'Latin Funerary Epigraphy and Family Life in the Later Roman Empire'. *Historia*, 33: 457–97.

—— (1987). 'The Age of Roman Girls at Marriage: Some Reconsiderations'. *Journal of Roman Studies*, 77: 30–46.

—— (1991). 'The Cultural Meaning of Death: Age and Gender in the Roman Family', in D. I. Kertzer and R. P. Saller (eds.), *The Family in Italy from Antiquity to the Present*. New Haven and London: Yale University Press, 66–90.

—— (1996). 'Seasons of Death: Aspects of Mortality in Imperial Rome'. *Journal of Roman Studies*, 86: 100–38.

—— (2001). 'Raising and Killing Children: Two Roman Myths'. *Mnemosyne*, 54: 33–77.

Shorter, E. (1976). *The Making of the Modern Family*. London: Collins.

Shumka, L. (1997). 'Children and toys'. MA thesis. Victoria, BC: University of Victoria.

Sigismund Nielsen, H. (1987). '*Alumnus:* A Term of Relation Denoting Quasi-adoption'. *Classica et Mediaevalia*, 38: 141–88.

—— (1991). '*Ditis examen domus*'. *Classica et Mediaevalia*, 42: 221–40.

—— (1997). 'Interpreting Epithets in Roman Epitaphs', in B. Rawson and P. Weaver (eds.), *The Roman Family in Italy: Status, Sentiment, Space*. Oxford: Clarendon Press, 169–204.

—— (1998). 'Roman Children at Mealtimes', in I. Nielsen and H. Sigismund Nielsen (eds.), *Meals in a Social Context: Aspects of the Communal Meal in the Hellenistic and Roman World*. Aarhus: Aarhus University Press.

—— (2001). 'The Value of Epithets in Pagan and Christian Epitaphs from Rome', in S. Dixon (ed.), *Childhood, Class and Kin in the Roman World*. London: Routledge, 165–77.

Skidmore, C. (1996). *Practical Ethics for Roman Gentlemen: The Work of Valerius Maximus*. Exeter: Exeter University Press.

Skolnick, A. (1975). 'The Family Revisited: Themes in Recent Social Science Research'. *Journal of Interdisciplinary History*, 4: 703–19.

Smith, R. R. R. (1991). *Hellenistic Sculpture: A Handbook*. London: Thames and Hudson.

Solin, H., Salomies, O., and Liertz, U.-M. (1995) (eds.). *Acta colloquii epigraphici Latini, Helsingiae, 3.–6. Sept. 1991 habiti*. Helsinki: Societas Scientiarum Fennica.

Soren, D. and N. (1999). *A Roman Villa and a Late-Roman Infant Cemetery: Excavation at Poggio Gramignano, Lugnano in Teverina*. Rome: 'L'Erma' di Bretschneider.

Stanton, G. (1969). 'Marcus Aurelius, Emperor and Philosopher'. *Historia*, 18: 570–87.

Stern, Y. (2000). 'The Testamentary Phenomenon in Ancient Rome'. *Historia*, 99: 413–28.

Stewart, A. F. (1990). *Greek Sculpture: An Exploration.* 2 vols. New Haven: Yale University Press.

Stone, L. (1969). 'Literacy and Education in England, 1640–1900'. *Past and Present*, 42: 69–139.

Stone, L. (1977). *The Family, Sex and Marriage in England, 1500–1800.* London: Weidenfeld and Nicolson. Also 1979 abridged and revised edn.

Storey, G. R., and Paine, R. R. (1999). 'Latin Funerary Inscriptions: Another Attempt at Demographic Analysis'. *XI Congresso Internazionale di Epigrafia Greca e Latina, Roma, 18–24 settembre, 1997: atti.* 2 vols. Rome: Quasar, v. 1, 847–62.

Strubbe, J. H. M. (1998). 'Epigrams and Consolation Decrees for Deceased Youths'. *L'Antiquité Classique*, 67: 45–95.

Stuart Jones, H. (1968). *A Catalogue of the Ancient Sculptures as Preserved in the Municipal Collections of Rome. The Sculptures of the Palazzo dei Conservatori.* 2 vols. Reprint of 1926 edn. Rome: Bretschneider.

—— (1969). *A Catalogue of the Ancient Sculptures as Preserved in the Municipal Collections of Rome. The Sculptures of the Museo Capitolino.* 2 vols. Reprint of 1912 edn. Rome: Bretschneider.

Sussman, G. (1980). 'The End of the Wet-Nursing Business in France, 1874–1914', in R. Wheaton and T. Hareven (eds.), *Family and Sexuality in French History.* Philadelphia: University of Pennsylvania Press, 224–52.

Sussman, L. A. (1995). 'Sons and Fathers in the *Major Declamations* Ascribed to Quintilian'. *Rhetorica*, 13: 179–92.

Syme, R. (1958). *Tacitus.* 2 vols. Oxford: Clarendon Press.

—— (1982). 'The Marriage of Rubellius Blandus'. *American Journal of Philology*, 103: 62–85.

—— (1986). *The Augustan Aristocracy.* Oxford: Clarendon Press. New York: Oxford University Press.

Taylor, L. R. (1924). '*Seviri equitum Romanorum* and Municipal *seviri*: A Study in Pre-military Training among the Romans'. *Journal of Roman Studies*, 14: 158–71.

—— (1931). *The Divinity of the Roman Emperor.* Middletown, Conn.: American Philological Association (Philological Monographs, no. 1).

Taylor, L. R., and Scott, R. (1969). 'Seating Space in the Roman Senate and the *senatores pedarii*'. *Transactions of the American Philological Association*, 100: 529–82.

Temkin, O. (1956) (ed. and trans.). *Soranus' Gynaecology.* Baltimore: Johns Hopkins Press.

Thomas, J. A. C. (1975). 'Delictal and Criminal Liability of the Young in Roman Law'. *Société Jean Bodin. Recueils*, 38: 9–31.

Thylander, H. (1952). *Étude sur l'épigraphie latine: date des inscriptions, noms et dénomination latine, noms et origine des personnes*. Lund: Gleerup.

Too, Y. L. (2001). *Education in Greek and Roman Antiquity*. Leiden: Brill.

Torelli, M. (1982). *Typology and Structure of Roman Historical Reliefs*. Ann Arbor: University of Michigan Press.

—— (1999). *Tota Italia: Essays in the Cultural Formation of Roman Italy*. Oxford: Clarendon Press.

Toynbee, J., and Ward Perkins, J. B. (1956). *The Shrine of St. Peter and the Vatican Excavations*. London: Longmans, Green.

Treggiari, S. (1969). *Roman Freedmen during the Late Republic*. Oxford: Clarendon Press.

—— (1976). 'Jobs for Women'. *American Journal of Ancient History*, 1: 76–104.

—— (1979). 'Questions on Women Domestics in the Roman West'. *Schiavitù, manomissione e classi dipendenti nel mondo antico*. Rome: Università degli Studi di Padova, 185–201 (Pubblicazioni del Istituto di Storia Antica, 13).

—— (1991). *Roman Marriage: iusti coniuges from the Time of Cicero to the Time of Ulpian*. Oxford: Clarendon Press.

Turcan, R. (1966). *Les Sarcophages romains à représentations dionysiaques: essai de chronologie et d'histoire religieuse*. Paris: Boccard.

Turfa, J. M. (1994). 'Anatomical Votives and Italian Medical Tradition', in R. D. de Puma and J. P. Small (eds.), *Murlo and the Etruscans: Art and Society in Ancient Etruria*. Madison: Wisconsin University Press, 224–40.

Vasaly, A. (1993). *Representations: Images of the World in Ciceronian Oratory*. Berkeley: University of California Press.

Vermeule, C. (1977). *Greek Sculpture and Roman Taste*. Ann Arbor: University of Michigan Press.

Veyne, P. (1978). 'La Famille et l'amour sous le haut-empire romain'. *Annales: économies, sociétés, civilisations*, 33: 35–63.

Walbank, F. W. (1979). *A Historical Commentary on Polybius*, iii. *Commentary on Books XIX–XL*. Oxford: Clarendon Press.

Walker, S. (1995). *Greek and Roman Portraits*. London: British Museum Press.

Wallace-Hadrill, A. (1994). *Houses and Society in Pompeii and Herculaneum*. Princeton: Princeton University Press.

—— (1998). 'To be Roman, Go Greek: Thoughts on Hellenization at Rome', in M. Austin, J. Harries, and C. Smith (eds.), Modus Operandi: *Essays in Honour of Geoffrey Rickman*. London: Institute of Classical Studies, 79–91.

Wallace-Hadrill, A. (2001). 'Emperors and Houses in Rome', in S. Dixon (ed.), *Childhood, Class and Kin in the Roman World*. London and New York: Routledge, 128–43.

Weaver, P. R. C. (1972). *Familia Caesaris: A Social Study of the Emperor's Freedmen and Slaves*. Cambridge: Cambridge University Press.

Weaver, P. R. C. (1986). 'The Status of Children in Mixed Marriages', in B. Rawson (ed.), *The Family in Ancient Rome: New Perspectives*. London and Sydney: Croom Helm, 145–69.

—— (1990). 'Where Have All the Junian Latins Gone? Nomenclature and Status in the Roman Empire'. *Chiron*, 20: 275–305.

—— (1997). 'Children of Junian Latins', in B. Rawson and P. Weaver (eds.), *The Roman Family in Italy: Status, Sentiment, Space*. Oxford: Clarendon Press, 55–72.

Weinstock, S. (1971). *Divus Julius*. Oxford: Clarendon Press.

White, P. (1975). 'The Friends of Martial, Statius, and Pliny, and the Dispersal of Patronage'. *Harvard Studies in Classical Philology*, 79: 265–300.

Whitehead, J. K. (1984). *Biography and Formula in Roman Sarcophagi*. Ph.D. thesis, Yale University. Ann Arbor: University Microfilms International.

Whitmarsh, T. (2001). *Greek Literature and the Roman Empire: The Politics of Imitation*. Oxford: Oxford University Press.

Wiedemann, T. (1989). *Adults and Children in the Roman Empire*. London: Routledge.

Wilkinson, B. (1964). 'A Wider Concept of the Term *parens*'. *Classical Journal*, 59: 358–61. (For other works by this author see under Rawson, B.)

Williams, W. (1976). 'Individuality in the Imperial Constitutions: Hadrian and the Antonines'. *Journal of Roman Studies*, 66: 67–83.

Williamson, L. (1978). 'Infanticide: An Anthropological Analysis', in M. Kohl (ed.), *Infanticide and the Value of Life*. Buffalo, NY: Prometheus Books, 61–75.

Wiseman, T. (1974). 'Legendary Genealogies in Late Republican Rome'. *Greece and Rome*, 21: 153–64.

—— (1984). 'Two Small Boys with Famous Names: A Study in Social History'. *Opus*, 3: 93–7.

—— (1985). *Catullus and his World: A Reappraisal*. Cambridge and New York: Cambridge University Press.

—— (1987). '*Conspicui postes tectaque digna deo:* The Public Image of Aristocratic and Imperial Houses in the Late Republic and Early Empire'. *L'urbs: espace urbain et histoire*. Rome: École Française de Rome, 393–413.

—— (1992). *Talking to Virgil: A Miscellany*. Exeter: Exeter University Press.

Woolf, G. (1994). 'Power and the Spread of Writing in the West', in A. K. Bowman and G. Woolf (eds.), *Literacy and Power in the Ancient World*. Cambridge: Cambridge University Press, 84–98.

—— (1998). *Becoming Roman. The Origins of Provincial Civilization in Gaul*. Cambridge: Cambridge University Press.

—— (2000). 'Urbanization and its Discontents in Early Roman Gaul', in E. Fentress (ed.), *Romanization and the City: Creation, Transformations, and Failures*. Portsmouth, RI: *Journal of Roman Archaeology*, 115–31.

Wrightson, K. (1982). 'Infanticide in European History'. *Criminal Justice History*, 3: 1–20.

Zanker, P. (1975). 'Grabreliefs römische Freigelassener'. *Jahrbuch des Deutschen Archäologischen Instituts*, 90: 267–315.

—— (1988). *The Power of Images in the Age of Augustus*. Ann Arbor: University of Michigan Press. Originally pub. in German.

—— (1995). *The Mask of Socrates: The Image of the Intellectual in Antiquity*. Berkeley: University of California Press (Sather Classical Lectures, v. 59).

—— (1998). *Pompeii: Public and Private Life*. Trans. [from the German] by D. L. Schneider. Cambridge, Mass.: Harvard University Press.

—— (2000*a*). 'The City as Symbol: Rome and the Creation of an Urban Image', in E. Fentress (ed.), *Romanization and the City: Creation, Transformations, and Failures*. Portsmouth, RI: *Journal of Roman Archaeology*, 25–41.

—— (2000*b*). 'Die Frauen und Kinder der Barbaren auf der Markussäule', in J. Scheid and V. Huet (eds.), *Autour de la colonne Aurélienne: geste et image sur la colonne de Marc Aurèle à Rome*. Turnout: Brepols, 163–74.

INDEX OF SOURCES

GENERAL INDEX

abandonment, *see* exposure
abortion 114–16
acculturation 162, 168, n.48
Acilius Glabrio, M. 286
acting, *see* entertainment
adoption 233–4, 250
adultery 114, 115, 119
Aelia Capitolina 55
Aelia Procula 48
Aemilii family 287–8, 298–300, 305
Aemilius Lepidus, M. 26–7, 28, 287–8, 290, 299
Aemilius Lepidus, M., consul 78 BCE 298
Aemilius Lepidus, M., triumvir 26, 290 n. 42
Aemilius Paullus, L. 278, 286, 288–9, 313, 345
Aeneas 29, 32–3, 34 n. 25, 320, 324
affectio maritalis, see *maritalis affectio*
affection 95, 220, 221, 223, 233, 234, 244, 246, 251, 253, 262, 268, 363
Afrania, C. 197 n.115
age classifications 127, 135, 136–7, 328, 363
ages Ch. 4 *passim*, 244–5, 246
Agricola, Cn. Iulius 227, 235
agriculture 61, 191, 252
Agrippa, Herod, *see* Herod Agrippa
Agrippa, M. Vipsanius 31, 35, 103, 156, 200, 240, 279, 308, 309
Agrippa, M. Vipsanius, map 300–1
Agrippa Postumus 230 n. 55, 321
Agrippina the Elder 35–6, 97, 222, 247 n. 102, 257, 278, 333, 337, 345 n. 25, 355
Agrippina the Younger 38, 103, 143, 200
Albius P. f. Memor, P. 51–2
Alexander the Great 289–91
alimenta 41, 59–64, 187, 252, 320
alumni/-ae, see foster-children
amphitheatres, *see* theatres
ancestor masks, *see imagines*
Anchises 32–3, 34 n. 25, 320
animals:
  cart-driving 129, 353

see also pets 50, 78, 91 n. 130, 129–30, 137, 288, 301–2, 315, 316, 321, 330, 331
Annius Florus, P. 196, 327
Antiochus of Ascalon 153
Antonia the Elder 231
Antonia the Younger 53 n. 58, 64 n. 81, 80, 225, 230–1, 246, 257–8
Antoninus Pius 63–4, 196, 228 n. 48, 240, 310, 311, 324
Antonius Gnipho, M. 118–19, 180
Antonius Iullus 231 n. 56, 246
Antony, Mark 35, 193 n. 104, 228–9, 230–1, 241, 257
Antyllus 231 n. 56
Anullina 361
Apollo 23, 26, 109, 318, 362
Apollonius 154–5
apotheosis 76, 77, 82, 356, 359–61, 465, 469–71
Appius Claudius 164
apprenticeships 146, 182, 187, 192–4, 207, 252, 262
Apuleius 158
Ara Pacis Augustae 31, 34–5, 42, 306
architecture 172, 192, 279
Argentaria Polla, *see* Polla, Argentaria
Argentius, M. 204–5
Aricinus 255
Aristodemus of Nysa 158–9
arithmetic 151, 178, 188
Arkteia festival 145
Arpinum 143, 195
Arretium 278
art collections 278–81, 286, 288, 292, 302
art work 59, 60, 298, 302, 303, 308
Ascanius (Iulus) 32–3, 34 n. 25, 320
Asclepiades of Prusa 120
Atedius Melior 349
athletic contests, *see* games
Atia 157, 227, 229, 334
atrium 84, 211, 270, 279
Attica, *see* Caecilia Attica
Atticus, Q. Caecilius Pomponius 83, 155, 156, 158, 180, 192, 199–200, 279